Her Gold and Her Body

Her Gold and Her Body

JAMILA VERGHESE

VIKAS PUBLISHING HOUSE PVT. LTD.

VIKAS PUBLISHING HOUSE PVT LTD

576, Masjid Road, Jangpura, New Delhi-110 014 Ph. 4615313, 4615570
Email: chawlap @ giasdl01. vsnl.net.in, Fax: 91-11-3276593

First Floor, N.S. Bhawan, 4th Cross 4th Main
Gandhi Nagar, Bangalore-560 009 Ph. 2204639

Distributors:

UBS Publishers' Distributors Ltd

- 5, Ansari Road, **New Delhi**-110002 Ph. 3273601, 3266646
- Apeejay Chambers, 5 Wallace St., **Mumbai**-400001 Ph. 2070827, 2076971
- 10, First Main Road, Gandhi Nagar, **Bangalore**-560009 Ph. 2263901
- 6, Sivaganga Road, Nungambakkam, **Chennai**-600034 Ph. 8276355
- 8/1-B, Chowringhee Lane, **Calcutta**-700016 Ph. 2441821, 2442910
- 5-A, Rajendra Nagar, **Patna**-800016 Ph. 652856, 656169
- 80, Noronha Road, Cantonment, **Kanpur**-208004 Ph. 369124, 362665

First Published, 1980
Revised and Enlarged Edition 1997

Illustrations by Jamila Verghese

Printed at Kay Kay Printers, Delhi.

Contents

Acknowledgements

I would like to acknowledge the support and assistance I have received over the years from a large number of individuals and institutions, without whose help and continuing support, this book and its update could never have been written.

When I originally wrote this book in the late seventies, Girija Kumar placed the library of The Jawahar Lal Nehru University at my disposal. His constant guidance helped me to get to grips with the subject. The Nehru Memorial Library and the libraries of The Archeological Survey of India, The National Archives of India, The American Centre, The Indian Council of Social Science Research and the Ministry of Law, The Times of India and The Hindustan Times all gave most generously of their facilities. To Padma Ramachandran of the Department of Social Welfare I was particularly indebted for all the help and guidance I received from the Ministry.

Lotika Sarkar patiently explained points of law to me. Jai Mehra, O.K. Moorthy, Zarina Bhatty, Anna John, Vina Mazumdar, Rami Chhabra, Mildred Mashedar, Raisa Begum, Avdhash Kaushal, N.S. Jagannathan and Susy Verghese gave me many constructive suggestions and ideas. Sylva Roy, Mary Haney, Kapila Hingorani, Marilyn Wingard, the late Premvati Thapar, Razia Ismail, Susan Vellapally, P.N. Chopra, and the embassies of the Philippines, Portugal, Greece, and The High Commission of Sri Lanka gave me a wealth of material for which I am most thankful. Mercy Joseph helped me with translation work, and the late Sarla Mudgal whose work continues to be an inspiration was available at all times with information. The YWCA of India supported my work and followed up the letters I received from dowry victims, and Usha's little voice singing me the 'Soldier' song still rings in my ears.

While updating this book after sixteen years, I found old stalwarts and new friends continuing to help and support the venture. I can, unfortunately, only acknowledge a few while thanking the others whole heartedly.

Lotika Sarkar, Danial Latifi, Rani Jethmalani, Alice Jacob, Sona Khan, Kumud C. Rao, Roxna Swamy and Mohan Vellapally helped me in the field of law. The staff of The Indian Law Institute Library, and in particular, Pramod Singh its Deputy Director, who single-mindedly tracked down unavailable judgements for me. Sundari Nanda, Deputy Commissioner of Police of the Crimes Against Women Cell, New Delhi, and Ved Marwah who explained changing attitudes of the Police towards women. The officials of the Vital Statistics Division of the Ministry of Home Affairs, in particular S.K. Sinha Deputy Registrar General and A.K. Sinha Assistant Director Census operations, have been especially helpful. Adarsh Mishra and K.S. Sugathan, Joint Secretaries in the Family Welfare Department of the Ministry of Health and Family Welfare gave unstintingly of their time and thought as did Usha Rai and Leila Caleb. Dr. Badri Narain Saxena, Deputy Director of The Indian Council of Medical Research, Dr. S.P. Tripathi, Director, Research and Family Health in the World Health Organisation, and Dr. Pran Talwar, former Director National Institute of Immunology meticulously explained the intricacies of family planning and related research. The Director of the National Crime Records Bureau and the officials of the Bureau, in particular Kamini Shaw, D.L. Ajmani, S.K.N. Rajakumar and their colleagues in the Statistical section were most generous with material and help. B.K. Samaddar, now retired as Legal Consultant and his colleagues; Mohini Giri and members of the National Commission for Women, supplied me with material and put me in touch with knowledgeable persons in other parts of the country. Razia Ismail Chief of Information, United Nations Children's Fund has continued to make UNICEF material available to me. The library of the American Centre, Reuters, the British High Commission, New Delhi, and the Embassy of Greece have all helped me update my text.

To my many friends in the women's movement, in particular

Mary Roy, Pramila Dandavate, Sadhona Ganguly, Jyotsna Chatterji, Asha Ramesh, Shakuntala Narasimhan, and the Women's Centre in Bombay I owe grateful thanks.

Finally, I would like to thank my sister Dr. Seeta Sinclair whose penetrating mind helped me understand various approaches to medical procedures, and my husband George, whose eagle editorial eye and continuing support have been a great source of strength.

JAMILA VERGHESE

Preface

More than sixteen years have elapsed since this book was first published. There have been a number of changes during this period which have affected the status of women worldwide and that of Indian women in particular. The fulminations against women attributed to *Manu* in The *Manusmriti* should have long since been given a decent burial as they have been superseded by a new awareness of woman as a person of worth with human rights. A new generation of committed persons is working for this cause. Even though die-hard attitudes continue, gender justice is now the yardstick by which old laws are being reviewed and amended. This has necessitated an update which is incorporated at the end of this edition. I have left the original text intact as it forms part of the historical situation of Indian women, and of some of their counterparts in the world at that time.

Within the last few years the telecommunication revolution with its mind boggling sophisticated electronic technology has brought the world into our homes and our thinking. Human situations around the world are becoming more understandable as commonalities begin to emerge. People are very gradually beginning to think globally and to work together on common issues.

A number of United Nations conferences on women's issues have been held : Mexico - 1975, Copenhagen - 1980, Nairobi - 1985 and Beijing - 1995. Womens' issues were first recognised as Human Rights issues at the World Human Rights Conference in Vienna, 1994. With the 1995 Beijing Conference this has been reaffirmed, with Gertrude Mongella its Secretary General saying, 'Today women are demanding political participation vociferously... This is an age when economic development is taking place at the expense of women.... of armed conflict and ethnic cleansing. Therefore women's struggles are more important today than ever.'

Although less emphasis than hoped for was laid on some of these important subjects, the gains of the earlier conferences were protected by the global meet. India for its part, agreed to come up with a national policy for women, the appointment of a Human Rights Commissioner to deal specifically with women's human rights, and the formation of a mechanism for the monitoring of the platform for action contained in the Beijing document. The quota for education has also been raised to 6 per cent of the Gross Domestic Product.

The most invigorating experiences were those of the participants in the Non-Governmental Organisation Forum held at Huairou, some fifty kilometres from the site of the official conference at Beijing. Here, together with academicians, media persons and cultural activists, were grass root workers carefully selected from mass based ground level organisations countrywide. Fisherwomen, vegetable vendors, construction workers and others forming 60 per cent of the representatives of two hundred non-governmental organisations interacted with each other and with their counterparts from around the world for the first time ever, in stimulating encounters, communicating through a host of interpreters. With the South Asian bond almost tangible, Indian and Pakistani women marched together for peace. With ground relationship, hope for future world conferences lies in working out the practicalities of fostering this mutually enriching interaction. The needs of the most disadvantaged members of the global family can no longer be side-lined[1].

With the winding up of The Co-ordination Unit for Beijing, the formation of The National Alliance of Women has given this hope a chance of materialising[2]. A whole new crop of grass root leaders from quiet towns and far flung villages around the country have come together to work towards giving the woman at the lowest level life instead of sub-human existence. Their determination to squeeze out the gap between political promise and performance has a welcome powerful potential for change.

Surveys in recent years have stressed the fact that almost a quarter of the world's women are subjected to violence in their own homes. This is considered the most widespread form of violence against women in the United States. Thailand figures stand at 50 per cent, Pakistan at 60 per cent and Chile at 80 per cent. The surveys note that home violence rises in direct proportion to women's progress which is seen as threatening patriarchal values.[3]

At The International Conference on Population and Development at Cairo 1994, the participants found that 'the empowerment of women is the answer to the alleviation of poverty and to population stability. The improvement of their political, social, economic and health status is a highly important end in itself.'

The problems faced by Indian women at home and at work are gargantuan, enmeshed as they are in archaic attitudes and power structures. Conceptualisation of remedies therefore, must be all encompassing and must include the nurturing of support systems around each point of a multipronged attack. This needs to be made simultaneously on both micro and macro levels–a daunting task indeed!

The Indian woman's unquestioning silence which had begun to simmer during the 1970s, came to a head by the end of the decade. The early 1980s were filled with angry questionings as long repressed agony finally surfaced. The seeds of what is now called The Women's Movement, were sown after the lifting of the Emergency 1975-77. Women began to recognise their own strength as they focussed on one ghastly bride burning case after another. While ultra-feminist bras reportedly burnt in the West, Indian women were still struggling to pick up enough courage to fight a deeply entrenched patriarchal system for a rightful and dignified place in the sun. They were immediately branded frivolous or publicity seeking. Angry demonstrations against criminal violence and murder attracted much jovial comment and patronising tolerance. Even the media, with honourable exceptions, devoted little or no place to thoughtful articles or programmes on women. The few that might have made it, would be elbowed out by salacious or sensational items. Since the real woman existed only in the art, cookery, cinema or glamour pages, how could any other kind lay any claim to being newsworthy?

Gradually women's organisations began to attract liberal minded and concerned persons. Lawyers of repute and theatre persons willingly gave their expertise. Street plays were organised, awareness cells and legal literacy workshops began to proliferate. Cases of women subjected to violence or exploitation were publicised and energetically fought in courts as more and more enthusiastic young women joined the legal profession. A large number of women are entering the media and are now in the forefront of investigative reporting. Many are editors of newspapers and thoughtful journals. Women have entered the judiciary. The Supreme Court had two women judges, one of whom has retired, and 'gender justice' has become a measure of the health of the process of law. Some positive judgements have made their mark, while debates, demonstrations and demands for the plugging of loopholes in laws have brought about a number of positive changes. Laws passed between 1980 and 1995 which affect women are appended at the end of this edition. However, decades of experience have brought about a realisation that laws cannot function in a vacuum. Legislation needs to be strongly supported by basic social change.

The National Commission for Women was set up in 1992 as a direct result of a demand in the 1974 report of The Committee on the Status of Women, widespread debate and the active involvement of women's organisations.

The Parivarik Mahila Lok Adalat (Family Court for Speedy Justice) started in February 1996 by the National Commission for Women provides legal aid and counselling for aggrieved women, and tries to give them speedy justice at no cost. There has been overwhelming response. Non-governmental organisations in the states are being encouraged to interact with judges on long pending cases which may be followed up by the *Adalat* in an informal atmosphere. The Commission is hoping that local NGOs around the country will fill the all-important need for pre-litigation counselling and case follow-up.

The success of this venture will depend largely on quality of training, dedication and long term involvement. The National Commission also plans to diversify the activities of the *Adalat* to include family welfare and the education of the girl child in rural areas.

A number of states have appointed their own State Commissions for Women. Governmental and non-governmental services for women in literacy, health and training in different skills, rural based and urban, function at every level with varying degrees of success. Legal aid and support cells with women police function in major cities. Women form part of the police and the armed forces. Family Courts have been set up in some states to settle marital disputes in an informal atmosphere. These are answerable to their respective state governments.

In a revolutionary step for women's representation anywhere, Parliament adopted the Constitutional 73rd and 74th Amendments stipulating that one third of all members in all tiers of *panchayat* and municipal bodies[4] shall be women.

The relevant Article: 243 D for Part IX and Article 343 T of Part IX A of the Constitution came into force from 20 April, 1993. Further, among the seats reserved for members of the scheduled castes and scheduled tribes, one third shall be women for as long as these reservations are constitutionally provided for, that is, up to the year 2,000, unless further extended.

This mandatory reservation will bring approximately one million women into decision making positions in urban as well as rural governance. There will doubtless be many cases of misuse of this provision with women being used as dummies by powerful men or other vested interests. Even so, for a vast number of women thus far side-lined, the opportunity for articulating gender interests in developmental processes and social change constitutes a remarkable advance. Elected women are trained to discharge their responsibilities. Actual working experience so far is already showing positive results.

By 1995 in Madhya Pradesh alone, out of over four lakh eighty four thousand elected *panchayat* representatives, over one lakh eighty four thousand are women who are beginning to take charge of the community in which they live. They will be directly responsible with the men in the *panchayats* for education, health and employment, directly appointing doctors and teachers.

As far back as February 1989, an excited all woman *panchayat* in Pidhgara Village in Madhya Pradesh immediately set to work on a scheme for much needed tap water and covered toilets for women.

'Let the men sit at home', they said, 'now we shall show them how to work.'[5] In 1994, in spite of a vicious bomb assault and continuing harassment, Kesarbai, *sarpanch* of Sanswari Village has finally won the village and district administration's admiration and support in her unrelenting battle against crime.[6] Thirty two year old Zeenat Naaz who abandoned the veil for public service was voted into power as the municipal chief of conservative Deoband, Uttar Pradesh,[7] and twenty two year old Sudha, a Masters degree holder, blind from birth, is *sarpanch* of over seven thousand people in Changa Village, Kaira, Gujarat, handling major problems with confidence and sensitivity.[8] The only woman to be elected three times to the Lok Sabha from Bihar is sixty year old Bhagwati who continues to work as a stone crusher, living simply in her one-room tenement.[9]

In pursuance of the United Front's commitment to reserve one third of all elective seats for women in all legislatures, the government has introduced a Bill in Parliament (1996) which is presently under consideration. The National Commission on Self Employed Women in the Informal Sector was appointed on 5 January, 1987. The Commission's excellent report *Shramshakti* was made public in June 1988. It is a painstaking, sensitively complied monumental labour which brings the daily life of the invisible poor rural woman and her equally deprived urban sister into sharp focus, highlighting these women's as yet unharnessed potential.

The majority of women workers in the country, over 90 per cent, are in the unorganised sector. Out of these about 76 per cent are agricultural workers. Few laws seem to apply to these women. If they do, their implementation is extremely faulty. Minimum wages are rarely paid, and The Equal Remuneration Act remains on paper. Home based industrial workers get shamefully low salaries which are cut at will, while women workers suffer indignities at work with no hope of legal redress. The National Commission for Women has recommended compulsory registration of all workers and employers in the unorganised sector, as also the regulation of employment through a tripartite Construction Labour Board with women as members. They have also recommended that such workers should be encouraged to form unions.[10] As of February 1996, a government notification has brought stone breakers and stone crushers under the The Minimum Wages Act.

In recent years the large number of highly committed women who have joined the journalistic profession has brought about a mini revolution in the media. Women now make news other than the sensational. There is hardly a newspaper, magazine or programme in the electronic media worth its salt that does not provide sizeable space for women's issues. The problem now is how to offload unwelcome travellers who present archaic patriarchal ideas as ideal family values, and extreme violence, perversion and vulgarised sex in the garb of progress for their own crassly commercial ends. Inviting investment shares for a daughter's marriage many years later, or playing the passion merchant selling expensive desire in a condom in the name of family planning are only two of their many ploys.

There is an almost imperceptible change in society's general attitude toward women's problems. A realisation that a woman's problems could be the responsibility of the whole community is beginning to dawn, and women's issues now form an important part of the national agenda. The Eighth Five-Year Plan covers a broad spectrum of development programmes aimed at gender sensitisation and a recognition of women not merely as beneficiaries, but as equal partners in development. Women's studies in the domestic, socio-economic and political spheres are now recognised in academia. They form part of The University Grants Commission's approved courses in the universities, and are gradually beginning to be viewed as human rights issues.

Human Rights as a subject is sought to be introduced in school curricula. The recent upsurge in crimes against women, as also the increasing exposure of children to explicit sex for its own sake being high-lighted through the print and electronic media together with the alarming incidence of HIV Positive and full blown AIDS cases reported in the country, have started a heated debate for and against the introduction of sex education in schools. Some schools have already taken an initiative in this matter. However, this subject needs extremely sensitive treatment.

It might be useful to consider the introduction of Human Relationship as an umbrella subject into school curricula, which would include every aspect of the human condition and its inter-relationships. This would obviate the necessity for preparing for major battles over each component of the course. These separate components could then be explored and presented in an interesting, informative manner, by trained and sensitised personnel. Such an umbrella subject would naturally include Human Rights and Sex Education as part and parcel of the fundamental right of every child to acquire knowledge which will help him or her to grow into a responsible and knowledgeable citizen.

With all this input however, ground realities reveal a very different picture. Statistics of recorded crimes against women spiralled from 67,702 in 1989 to 83,954 in 1993, and to 98,948 in 1994.[11] A data sheet of The Department of Women and Child Development, Ministry of Human Resource Development, New Delhi, worked out a break up of 1987-1991 violence against women data into the following projection: One dowry death expected once every one hour and forty-two minutes. One rape every fifty-four minutes, one criminal offence against women every seven minutes.

There has been a shocking increase in the rape of children below ten years of age, some of whom are barely one year old, with figures standing at 727 cases in 1994 as against 369 in 1989.[12] The Draft National Policy on Women which aims at eliminating violence against women and girls, and the promotion of a positive portrayal of women is presently being scrutinized by the government and by women's organisations. It is due for discussion countrywide.[13]

With the minutes ticking inexorably on to the watershed year 2000 A.D., India is in the grip of a robust money culture which is fast replacing the more stable but slower approach to establishing a solid base for living. Acquiring instant riches is the name of the game. Old fashioned notions of hard work and high quality achievement are quite passé. Oppressive attitudes culled from tradition join hands with money and power in a grip that will not easily yield to all the humane legislation in the world. Without the sorcerer's magic potion—attitudinal change—nothing will change the brew. The challenge for the Indian woman today is twice as great as ever before. Her one step forward needs to be strengthened to ensure that she does not slip the traditional two steps back.

NOTES AND REFERENCES

1. Devaki Jain and Asha Ramesh.
2. Doughty Dozen, Usha Rai, The Indian Express, 13 December, 1995.
3. Roxanna Carrillo : Battered Dreams - Violence Against Women as an Obstacle to Development, United Nations Development Fund for Women, New York, 1992; and Lori Heise with Jacqueline Pitanguy and Adrienne Germain : The Hidden Health Burden - discussion paper, World Bank Population, Health and Nutrition Department, Washington D.C. 1994, quoted in the State of the World's children, United Nations Children's Fund, 1995, Oxford University Press.
4. Rural and urban governing bodies respectively.
5. We Want to Outdo the Males, Manjeet Singh in The Sunday Observer, 12 February, 1989.
6. Free Press, Indore, 14 October, 1994.
7. Zeenat Takes Over, Deoband Rejoices, M.V. Rao, The Indian Express, 2 December, 1995.
8. Girl Born Blind Has grand vision for Her Village, Milind Ghatwal, The Indian Express, 11 March, 1996.
9. From Stone - Crushing to Parliament, Usha Rai, The Indian Express, 22 May, 1996.
10. 'Laws for Working Women Inadequate,' The Times of India, 4 September, 1995.
11. Crimes Against Women, from Crime in India, 1993 and 1994, National Crime Records Bureau, Ministry of Home Affairs, New Delhi.
12. Crime in India 1993 and 1994, National Crime, Records Bureau, Ministry of Home Affairs, New Delhi.
13. Draft Policy to Eliminate Violence Against Women, The Statesman, 27 November, 1995.

Introduction

'Daughters!' laments an Indian father blest with six girls. 'They even sweep out the ashes from the hearth and take them away when they leave us! Why do they give us daughters?' He glares balefully up at the skies.

To understand his problem we shall have to view it in its global context. Only then will we find that his is a universal complaint: one that has plagued mankind everywhere at some time or other in history.

Even childrens' nursery rhymes can have more than a prophetic real life ring. Here, for instance, is a Western jingle sung with tremendous gusto by a seven year old Indian girl:

" 'Soldier, soldier, will you marry me
    with your musket, fife and drum?'
'Oh yes, sweete maide, I shall surely marry thee,
    but I have no hat to put on!'
So she ran to her grandfather's chest,
    and pulled out one of the very very best;
    and the soldier put it on.
'Soldier, soldier, will you marry me
    with your musket, fife and drum?'
'Oh yes, sweete maide, I shall surely marry thee,
    but I have no shirt to put on!'

Needless to say, she ran to her grandfather's chest and pulled out one of the very very best, and of course the soldier put it on. He goes on to equip himself from tip to toe in the contents of the 'sweete maide's' grandfather's chest, and when he has squeezed everything out of it, he says *'I would have surely married thee, but I have a wife of my own.'*

The guests at the little girl's birthday party clapped and laughed at the plight of the 'sweete maide.' I did not laugh, because just a year ago I had seen the same story enacted in real life in my very own neighbourhood.

It was a splendid wedding. The groom as a wonderful 'catch' as he had a good job in a foreign country as a Chartered Accountant. His family was one of the 'very very best' and the gently bred bride was being supplied with as good a dowry as her doting parents could give her with all their love and affection. Everyone was happy. The parents on both sides had known each other fairly well for some years and Surinder was considered an up and coming boy.

Surinder left for the foreign country two days later. It was only natural that he should take the money that came with his bride as he had plans for investing it in a little cottage 'out there' where the young couple would live. Since he wanted every comfort for his bride, he also took most of her heavy jewellery to deposit it safely in the bank near the little cottage. He left her the few jewels she would have to wear to keep up her new status as the bride of a prosperous young man living abroad. He was all concern for his new parents-in-law. He touched their feet as he left, torn asunder at the thought of having to part with his lovely bride. He would send for her as soon as all arrangements had been completed, he promised tearfully. She stood, her head covered in the gold and red brocade sari his parents had given her, love and hope shining from her glistening eyes.

Four months later I saw her again. She was expecting a baby. The light had gone out of her eyes. No letter had come from her husband. Her parents decided to collect their savings and send her to him. They sent Surinder a cable. The young mother to-be arrived in an alien land only to find that she was to function as a servant in the home where she had pictured herself reigning as a wife. Surinder's foreign girl friend and their baby boy needed a worker in the house.

And that was not all. It was a sordid tale of cigarette butts stubbed out on her arms, and more threats under cover of darkness. She managed to run away to the local church since her captors saw to it that she never came in contact with any Indians of her own community. The priest contacted her family. Yesterday's bride is today's unwanted working mother who will not divorce the father of her little daughter. In the tradition of Indian wives of long ago she has begun to keep the fasts ordained for the well-being of the husband whom the sacrament of marriage has made her other half in a rite that had been witnessed by the gods. In their eyes the bond is indissoluble. While she lives, she hopes that some day Surinder will acknowledge his daughter and his legally married wife.

Her mother is worn to a shred with worry, and her father has little ready cash left to pay for the ailments of an advancing old age. His Rs 25,000/- insurance policy and his provident fund have both been used up for his daughter's wedding. He spreads his palms outward in an age-old gesture of resignation. 'Who can fight *Bhagwan*?'[1] he says. 'It is His will.'

'He' of course, has always been at the bottom of it all. It is according to 'His' will that oppression and suffering which are to be borne uncomplainingly, come into this world. 'He' operates the laws that force a wife and her parents to be silent under the severest provocation, and it is in accordance with 'His' wishes again that wives occasionally end up in morgues, burnt to death, 'by accident' of course, at the kitchen stove.

In this book I have attempted to put the Indian parents' dilemma in correct perspective, fitting it as far as possible, into a larger world frame.

I make no claims to erudition or scholarship. I have written a simple book in every day language which will try to expose the cancerous social diseases which feed on the patient sufferings of women, inflicted on them by an active traditional tyranny and an acquiescent society.

This book will have served its purpose if it can save one unwanted wife from torture and death, and jolt her tormentors into seeing her as a human being instead of as a means of extortion: if it shocks even one girl who willingly offers herself as an adjunct to a heavy dowry into a realisation of her own personal dignity, and if it can persuade even one future bridegroom to throw his dream of living comfortably-ever-after on his bride's dowry out of the window.

To try and understand this special kind of discrimination, you and I shall together undertake an exploration into the human mind to try and find out how a woman's body has been exploited for gold, and the interrelation of this exploitation with the subject of marriage. Through this exploration spanning eras of history and recognising no geographical boundaries, I hope we shall be able finally to get to the root of how the giving of gifts of money or goods to a daughter at her marriage deteriorated from being gifts of affection to becoming a means of extortion and exploitation.

I have juxtaposed incidents, utterances and writings of yesterday against those of today to demonstrate the existence of exploitation in strikingly similar if not even more perverted forms.

The dowry problem cannot be tackled in isolation, simply because it does not exist in isolation. To fully comprehend its nature and growth into a system, we shall have to trace the tenuous thread of the sort of thinking from which it could have sprung, and touch briefly on the various regions of experience between the banks of which the stream meanders.

This will of necessity take us through the strange but fascinating world of female infanticide, child marriage, widowhood and *sati*[2], prostitution, bonded labour, open sale and other forms of exploitation of women: the various types of giving and taking connected with the different forms of marriage, bridewealth to dowry, woman as property, the inheritance and property which clothe her person in desirability, and on to social and legal pointers to positive thinking.

All or most of these may seem extraneous to our subject at first glance, but eventually tie in with the larger picture of exploitation of woman, her body and her property.

Much has been and continues to be said on the subject of dowry; still I feel most of us have not realized its full impact and implications. This may primarily be due to the fact that the system's deleterious effects have by and large been felt by the least vocal people of our land—the middle and the lowest income group. Although there are quite a number of cases among the higher income group, one does not often come to hear about them as family prestige and influence usually moves in to hush them up.

This being the case, I intend to lay the emphasis mainly on the low and middle income groups in India, and less on the more affluent sections of our society.

Also since the Hindu community in general and some sections of the Christian community—of the South in particular, are some of the worst sufferers of this system, other less affected communities would necessarily have to take a back seat in the scheme of this exploration.

The characters in this semi-fictional work are fictitious only in name. The words they speak or write and the situations they find themselves in are authentic, being based on research papers, or are a composite of several similar cases—as in the story related in the first chapter. Often I have written a story as I have found it reported in a publication. In this case I quote the source and give authentic names. In an occasional example I may have chosen a common Indian name for a character which may in actual fact fit a similar situation. The resemblance in such a case would be purely coincidental.

I have quoted extensively from the *Manusmriti* as translated into English by G. Buehler and edited by F. Max Mueller, *The Sacred Books of the East*, vol. XXV, Banarsidass, 1964. I have tried to avoid involvement in controversy regarding the apparent contradictions in some of the verses, Max Mueller feels that the *smriti*[3] only reproduces ancient opinions but omits possibly for metrical reasons to mark them as belonging to different authors or schools.'[4] For example, while Manu condemns the *Asura*[5] form of marriage among the Hindus in no uncertain terms, rules are simultaneously laid down for the purchase of a bride; a situation which may show that while the existence of the custom may be acknowledged, the practice could be condemned in the same collection of writings. So it is quite possible that for every quotation from the *Manusmriti* which appears in this book, there may be another saying the exact opposite. Since however, I am not in a position to make a study of The Laws of Manu, I shall only be quoting those sayings of the great lawgiver which may seem to have relevance to my subject.

My material has been gleaned from books, research papers,

periodicals, newspaper reports, random personal interviews with people on buses, trains, and in villages and towns from Punjab to Kerala: also from the many anxious letters from agonised parents of boys and girls from all over India who wrote to me in response to a letter in the newspapers, supplying me with personal material concerning dowry and related problems.

It is impossible to enumerate the many friends, travelling companions and involved persons who have helped me understand situations or gone out of their way to put me in touch with concerned individuals: nor can I thank them sufficiently for opening my eyes to problems of which I was so far only vaguely aware. I can only hope that these pages may pave the way for free and open re-thinking on the subject so dear to their heart—basic human relationships: so that men and women may stop exploiting each other, and marriage may once again become closer to what 'He' intended it to be—a complete and evenly balanced partnership based on mutual respect.

NOTES AND REFERENCES

1. God.
2. Immolation by fire or the burying alive of a widow. The word *sati* denotes a chaste and virtuous woman.
3. What is remembered and passed down by tradition.
4. The Institutes of the Sacred Law, Max Mueller, *The Sacred Books of the East*, Vol. XXV Banarsidas, 1964 (reprint) Oxford University Press: Delhi, vol. XXV, p. XXXI.
5. *Asura* marriage : a marriage in which the bride is purchased by the groom.

1

The Scream

It is the strangeness of the sound that makes your hackles rise. A strangled scream—the kind of gurgle a child might make if you shoved a knife into her and turned it around inside.

Everything else is normal in the dark little square between the small cluster of the three storeyed buildings; normal, dark and cold.

Suddenly a blaze of orange lights up a second storey window—That one there!

The peculiar sound wakes Dipti Chowdhry from a restless sleep. Tiptoeing fearfully between her mother-in-law's string cot and her husband's, she reaches the window, putting her eye to the crack in the shutter.

Transfixed with horror, she feels rather than sees Neena aflame by her kitchen window opposite, screaming the blood-curdling scream that had awakened her. A man's dark form outlined in the nightmarish orange light bends over her. With a shock Dipti recognises Parkash Arora. For two or three agonising seconds Neena hangs, gasping and shrieking; clutching the window sill, while he hits her charred fingers with some sort of a stick.

The next second she is hurtling down grasping at the air, to land with a sickening thud on the bricks below...

Dipti's eyes feel as if they are being torn from their sockets. Her lungs burst with the gasp she dares not take. Neena, she wails silently—O Neena!

Suddenly she is thrown back, straining against the open window, her arms pinioned behind her. Gnarled old fingers dig deep into her already constricted throat as the all too familiar gag fills her swollen mouth.

'Go jump also—take your poverty-stricken parents and yourself to hell!' Whispers the foul-breathed witch at her shoulder sharply. 'That's the sort of future I want for you, my dearest daughter-in-law!' The vicious fingers claw eagerly at her shrinking flesh. 'Do you want some more treatment, you accursed one, or are you going to get your misbegotten parents to send us a refrigerator for summer?'

Dipti's eyes bulge above her gagged mouth.

'Shameless creature!' whispers her tormentor; 'I'd rather you lived! I want you to live through my kind of hell! Pretending you were rich! Ah, scared, my beauty? How I would love to gouge out those white white eyeballs; but how would we explain that to your school children? No, no,' she grinned horribly, 'It's the hidden places that are best for school teachers!'

'No! No! please—Oh *Maji*![1] moans the struggling Dipti, her gagged mouth bursting while her inert lord and master snores on loudly and evenly.

'*He Ram*![2] shrieks her brain as the iron pestle falls rhythmically and noiselessly again and again...

'What's this stench, Rommy?' murmurs Babli sleepily. 'Smells like burning rubber or something!'

She stretches like a lazy kitten—well creamed fingers aflash with rings, feeling for the bed-side lamp.

There is also a peculiar sound which seems to accompany the odour—like a jackal crying: but there haven't been any jackals here ever since daddy bought Rommy his job and her this second floor flat and everything in it!

The only thing Babli has always held against the place is the neighbourhood. The people are so depressingly middle class. She always feels a little embarrassed wearing her best sets of jewellery out here. Rommy is okay. He appreciates his well hung wife. His family also duly eats out of her hand. Too bad his old Ma has to live with them though!

'Whatever is that smell, Rommy? Please see what's burning at this hour of night! Really, the municipality here stinks!' Babli having delivered herself of her views on the state of the world, rolls over in her beautifully sprung bed.

Ramesh pads bleary eyed towards the window and flings it open.

'Babli! B-Babli! Oh God! Babli!'

'What is it?' Babli leaps out of bed, a nameless fear in her voice. The sight of her husband crouching against the window, white as a sheet however, puts her in control of the situation again. 'What cowards men are', she mutters.

She reaches the window and follows Ramesh's limp finger pointing unbelievingly at what his lips refuse to formulate.

Babli's heart leaps into her mouth as her stomach turns.

She shuts the window with a bang and runs retching to the bathroom.

'Put that telephone down Rama!'

Ramaswamy Aiyangar stands facing his father, the telephone receiver in his hand, the right hand's index finger poised above the dial. He trembles slightly with suppressed emotion.

'Father,' he says, controlling the trembling with an effort. 'We have witnessed a murder. It is my duty to inform the police.'

Lakshmi stands framed against the open window—an immobile spectator of the drama between her husband and her son. Her hand, frozen in the act of suppressing a silent scream into a deeper silence, seems eternally engraved against her mouth.

Narayanaswamy Aiyangar towers above his son; his dark face harsh in the light of the naked bulb. 'You have witnessed nothing!' he says sharply. 'We have smelt something burning and heard some sounds. That does not add up to witnessing a murder. Put the telephone down this instant. It is no concern of ours what happens in someone else's family.'

Lakshmi's dried up throat makes a rasping sound.

Rama glares at his father. 'Father, you saw Arora throw his wife out of the window. Isn't it your duty as a fellow citizen to report the matter?'

'Arora is my colleague in the Ministry,' roars Narayanaswamy. 'I have to think of the society we move in. I refuse to have my family name dragged through the mire; involved with courts—reporting murders we are not even sure about. I have a daughter to marry off...'

Rama watches uncomprehendingly as his reliable authoritarian father crumbles before his eyes into a caricature of himself. He hears him bluster on trying to get back on the pedestal from which he can feel himself falling, trying desperately at the same time, to keep his position as lord and master of the household secure in the glazed eyes of his bewildered wife.

'How will I hold up my head in society,' he shouts, 'when my own son has cut the family tree from the roots?'

Rama begins to dial, disgust and rage writ large on his face. For the first time in his twenty years of life he feels master of a situation.

'The Ministry is full of North Indians,' his father continues. 'Do you want me to lose my preferment? Will *you* supply the dowry for your sister then? Do *you* have the responsibility of this household?'

Rama's disgust turns into pity. 'Father,' he says, 'I am only doing my duty. We shall all have to face the consequences. I am prepared... Police station? I am speaking from...' with his hands cupped around the mouthpiece he quietly and clearly gives the details of the murder as he saw it. The rest of his words are drowned in a howl from his father. 'Get out of my house. I have nothing to do with you any more. Do not expect anything from me and mine. I disassociate myself and my family from your actions. Get out!'

Lakshmi jerks into activity. All her life she has accepted her husband as her God-given lord and dispenser of her destiny—but her son—He is throwing out her son. He is throwing her own son out of her house!

'My Rama!' she screams; 'You have no right to...' but years of conditioning catch up with her, and suddenly limp and accepting, she falls in a semi-conscious heap at the feet of her master as her son gives her a long sad look and walks briskly out into the night...

Murder or Suicide?

'Where is that consumer of husbands?[3]

'Neena had turned to stone. She decided she was not going to answer. She was not going to answer ever. It was just not worth the effort. She was not going to make any more efforts ever.

'Oh where are you? May a snake bite you![4] Go, my darling son, and see where your beautiful wife is hiding herself; and when you find her, bring her to me. I'll know what to do with her! She's not even a woman. She's witch! May she die!'

Neena stood in the kitchen and carefully bolted the door. She smiled to herself. It was so peaceful now that she had made up her mind. It had been terrible before when she was'nt sure, but now.. she smiled again. 'I suppose,' she said aloud,' this is what Sister Teresa had meant when she spoke of the peace of God that passeth all understanding.' She lazily pulled out the kerosene tin from the shelf under the stove. She opened it, and slowly anointed her whole body with it. Voluptuously she rubbed it like an ointment into every aching joint. Far off she heard Parkash call, 'Neena! 'Neena! Where the Devil has she gone off? Don't worry *Bhabiji*.[5] I'll get her if I have to twist her neck for it!'

Neena smiled. How childish he was—thinking she was a mud toy to be broken and remade according to his wishes.

He could'nt get her; no one could get her now—ever! She wondered vaguely if it would hurt. It would be like a wonderful *jauhar*[6] cermony—where she would join beautiful Queen Padmini and the other Rajput wives all dressed in their bridal best. They would walk into the orange flames together, and their gallant men would don their saffron robes, and go off to battle to fight to the death!

'Neena! Open up, 'Neena! How dare you bolt the door?' Parkash was pounding on the kitchen door. Neena laughed. It was the same bubbling laugh she had had long ago—Oh so very long ago. He was such a boor—that husband of hers! 'He'll never be able to make it,' she said aloud. 'It's quite safe!"

'My God! She is in there with a man!' howled Parkash. 'I heard her, *Bhabiji*. I'll kill her—the bitch!'

'You can't!' tinkled Neena melodiously. 'We're off now! There are three of us here; me, myself and I, and you are all alone, poor Parkash! Not even your darling mother can help you now! Ha! Ha! Ha!' she laughed.

Now, she thought solemnly, now is the great moment—the moment of death and re-birth. I'd like to be a bird, dear God—A beautiful, free, flying bird. She wished Parkash wouldn't shout so much, but he couldn't ruin the magic moment for her. This moment was hers, and they could not take it from her. The door, hammered on and heaving, still stood firm between her life and theirs...

'Who is it? Lord Krishna wants me for a bride? Does he really think me beautiful enough?' Or was it the mass the nuns used to celebrate in the convent with those lovely white candles on either side of the white altar? She would be a bride of Krishna, she decided. She would get married to him, at the beautiful candle-lit altar of the convent.

She opened the window and lit the match. The air was suddenly filled with the strains of the wedding *shehnai*,[7] 'I am Joan of Arc,' she shrieked, 'I am free! *He Ram*! I am free!'

The door caved in as Parkash and his mother fell panting into the kitchen.

'*He Parmatma*[8]' shouted Karmo Devi, 'the witch has killed herself!' She ran shrieking back through the broken doorway into her husband's sick room. 'Do you hear, O father of Parkash, the consumer of husbands has set fire to herself! Our family name will be mud. God's curses fall on her worthless head! *He Ram* that I should have lived to see this day!'

Parkash, rushing in like a battering bull fell backwards at the sight of Neena aflame like an angel of vengeance framed in the open window. She was pointing at him accusingly and shrieking and cackling horribly. His hair stood on end. Oh God! What could he do? The neighbours—they would blame him for this. He had to get rid of her. He had to get rid of her in a hurry! But first he had to stop this howling hell-cat. He pulled the dish cloth from the pan and stuffed it into her mouth, fighting the flames that threatened to engulf him also. Neena's blazing, bulging eyes bored holes through him. He had to get rid of this terror fast; this cackling, flaming bride of hell. He steeled himself to face her, and then, shutting his eyes, pushed her with all his might through the window and out of sight; yet the witch clung to the window ledge with blazing fingers making the most horrible muffled sounds as her hideous eyes seemed alternately to plead and accuse. He took the rolling pin from the shelf and hit those clawing, sizzling bones again and again, until at last it all disappeared, and she plunged down, oh God, a burning gurgling ball of fire, to the floor below.

Parkash stood shaking like a tree after a forest fire. He was sweating from every pore. He had thrown Neena down! He had thrown Neena to her death! No, no! She had killed herself. She was on fire when he got there. '*Bhabi*!' he called piteously from the dark cold room.

Karmo Devi came rushing into the kitchen and clasped her son to her sagging breasts. She sat down on the floor and rocked him to and fro murmuring soothingly the while, 'Why should you cry, my darling, my jewel, *mere lal*![9] Let your enemies cry! What have you done? That creature was a bitch and she deserved it all. What you did was quite right my son, my dearest son. I am glad you are safe. That witch has gone to the hell she was intended for by the gods. Don't you worry, I am here. What am I for if not to take care of you? Don't you worry, I'll protect you!!'

The blood surged back again through Parkash's veins. 'The body—' he shouted suddenly, 'the neighbours! *Ma!* What shall I do? The police will come!'

'*Ekkhan*![10] The police! Let them come. What will they find out? Who will say anything? She was good for nothing. None of our neighbours will report, don't you worry. Come, let me bandage your burns, my poor darling child. She deserved every bit of what she got. She and that family of hers! Let them hold up their heads now!' Karmo Devi cuddled her huge lumbering son, half carrying him out of the kitchen, and laid him down comfortably in his bed. She covered his shivering body with his soft warm quilt and sat on the floor by his side attending to his burns as if nothing had happened.

'*My Wife, My Queen!*'

'Be a queen to thy father-in-law,
    a queen to thy mother-in-law,
a queen to thy husband's sisters,
    and a queen to thy husband's brothers.[11]

Ashok Kumar Arora turned restlessly in his sleep. He stretched out his hand in the gesture that had become a habit, feeling along the bed at his side for Sheila's warm hand. He found and held it, relaxing again into deeper slumber...

Sheila cuddled her baby closer under the warm *razai*[12]. She could hear Babloo snoring gently through the open door. Wrapped in warmth, she soothed her husband's hand gently, feeling its reassuring pressure. The baby whimpered, and Sheila automatically put her breast to his mouth. He sucked desultorily and mother and child drifted into sleep tied to each other by need and love.

It was the hair-raising scream that wasn't quite a scream rather than the thud that jerked Ashok and Sheila awake. The baby set up an annoyed howl, and Sheila automatically started rocking him, her senses alert the while to the sudden strangeness around her. Ashok was already fumbling with the catch of the window. Sheila wide awake now, leapt off the bed and reached her older son's door in a single bound. The blood rushed back to her face as she saw Babloo fast asleep, his face to the wall. She turned to the window. Ashok looked as if his eyes would start from his head. Following his transfixed stare, Sheila saw the burning flailing body on the stones outside their window, lit horribly by the orange flames while the stench of burning flesh seemed to pervade the whole atmosphere.

'*He Ram!*' she cried, 'Run, Babloo's father, run!' Jolted into motion by his wife's reaction, Ashok Kumar ran out, pulling his best green Dhariwal[13] blanket with him. In a second he was by the burning body smothering it in the blanket and slapping the flames. Sheila switched on the porch light and gasped, the bucket in her hand sloshing to the ground. Somewhere behind that blackened hole of a face was Neeno!

'*He Parmatma,* It's Neeno!' She shrieked. Ashok clamped his hand on her mouth and spoke softly but firmly, 'Sheila *Rani*[14] go empty my bed quickly. Put the child in Babloo's room, and lock his door.' Sheila ran back into the flat automatically following her husband's instructions. She balanced the howling baby on her hip and lifting Ashok's bedding, dragged it to the floor of the older child's room. She slumped on to the floor patting the baby mechanically to sleep on the bedding, her senses numbed with shock.

Ashok looked around desperately. In the darkness around, all the windows of the flats in the cluster of three-storeyed buildings seemed shut tight. An occasional shaft of light would appear only to be immediately blacked out. It was a weird sensation—almost as if a ghost colony was alive and whispering around him. As he bent over what remained of his nephew's moaning wife, he saw a man walk determinedly towards him from the building opposite. 'Quick,' whispered Ashok, 'help me, please!'

Between them they lifted the groaning bundle and laid it gently on Ashok's bed. Sheila came hurriedly out of Babloo's room. 'The doctor,' she whispered sharply, 'call the doctor!' 'I'll go,' said Ashok, dashing for his coat and slippers. He had suddenly realised he was barefoot in the cold. 'Please,' he looked at the young man. 'Oh Rama, how good of you—' Rama cut him short. 'I have already phoned the police,' he said, looking out of the window in embarrassment. 'Of course,' said Ashok, his jaw suddenly hardening, 'then I shall stay as they may want to ask questions.'

Sheila was standing helplessly by Neena's head. Anything she could do would have hurt poor Neeno. The room smelt of burning flesh and her head swam as the gorge rose inside her. She half covered the gaping hole that was a face with her softest *duppata*[15] and bent down. Unintelligible sounds seemed to come through the cloth.

'Please come and listen, do!'cried Sheila. Ashok and Rama bent close to the hideous face. A strange cavernous voice groaned, 'Harkash...O...I...khill...' The blanket convulsed once, twice, and the overwrought body lay quiet.

With Neena dead, the world sprang alive about the three humans in the room. Unspoken thoughts, unacknowledged dreads leapt hydra-headed from the shadows. Rama felt more than awkward. He had provoked the whole situation and brought the dreaded police into the life of this serenely happy family for no fault of their own. He didn't feel as determined as he had felt when fighting his father. He felt embarrassed and out of the picture. Why ever had he come in to help this man whom he didn't even really know? Why had he left his weeping mother crumpled at the feet of her husband—What had he hoped to accomplish by asserting himself in this way? He stood staring out of the window. He had nowhere to go anyway, and a strange quirk of fate had bound him to this charred body...

Ashok Kumar saw red. That damned family of his! He clenched his fists as he stood looking down at the pathetically small bundle that had once been the gay and vivacious young Neena. He would see Parkash hang or burn. He waited, the blood pounding in his temples—and his sister-in-law—God! That was no sister-in-law—she was a hell-hound! Thank God he had kept Sheila well away from them all. Heaven permitting, he took a silent oath—'On your body, I swear, Neeno, I shall get you avenged, even if I have to drag my family name through the courts!' Oh he would make them stink! A flaming tear stung his eyes and fell into the ghastly hollow eye socket of the charred skeleton...

The police will be coming, thought Sheila as she drew the red[16] *dupatta* over the head of the body. Red blood... sizzling black blood. 'Oh Neeno,' she wailed aloud, 'they got you at last! Oh Babloo's father, how will we tell her mother? How will we tell her that her dearest child...' She sat down on the floor beside the corpse, holding herself tightly, rocking backwards and forwards in a paroxym of grief. 'Go and telephone them—phone her father now!' She shook with sobs.

Phone Neeno's father? The red haze was clearing from Ashok's befuddled brain. Yes, of course, that's what he had to do. He grabbed his coat again. 'I'll go,' he repeated once more. He pulled on one sleeve... but where would he telephone from at this hour of night, and whose house would he go to? What would he say? That there had been an accident? 'May I use your phone please, my nephew has just murded his wife?' What, Oh God, was he to do? 'Rama,' he turned suddenly, 'you have a phone. Please can I telephone her parents from there?'

Rama's shoulders twitched with embarrassment. 'I—it's—Mr. Arora, it's out of order. I-I'll go and ring from the station for you. Please give me the telephone number.'

Ashok turned to look at Rama for the first time full in the face. He caught him by his shoulders and looked at him for what seemed an age to the younger man. 'Rama,' he said at last. His brain was quite clear now. He saw before him a bewildered young man who had tried to do his duty by his neighbours and reported a murder to the police, and didn't know how to continue his role in the drama, nor indeed did he understand what it was. 'Rama,' said Ashok again, 'I understand everything. Please do us the kindness of ringing this number for us. It will be a trunk call. I shall be ever grateful to you. Ambala—Mr. Rajinder Varma. Please tell them—tell them their daughter, Neena, has died as a result of an accident in the kitchen. Will you be so kind as to help us?'

Somewhere in the back of Rama's mind a stone flint struck a spark. Here was this marvellous man—faced with disgrace for his innocent family: still determined to root out the murderer and face the police and the courts, even if it meant death for his brother, nephew or sister-in-law; and he had no harsh words for a rank outsider's interference in his family's affairs! Rama's embarrassment melted into admiration. He could not let this man down. He took the number and ran into the night.

'*My Daughter, O My Daughter*!'

'Suniti, Oh God!'

Mrs Suniti Varma leapt out of bed, her heart in her mouth. There was such a strange note of urgency in her husband's voice—who could have phoned at this hour of the night? She ran to the bare living room from where everything had been sold off. The only luxury left them was the telephone.

Her husband stood slumped over the table, his face pale and drawn. Suniti could only look at him. The question formed itself and died on her lips.

'Neeno,' he whispered, 'Neeno!'

Suniti was suddenly galvanised into action. 'What is it?' The words came out like pistol shots. 'Tell me. Why don't you tell me?'

'Killed her! They've killed our little girl.' Rajinder Varma stared uncomprehendingly at the wall as his wife grabbed the receiver from him, listening to the unknown voice that went on mechanically, 'Hello! Hello! Mr. Varma? Hello...' She put the receiver back and looked at Rajinder. 'Burnt her,' he said with difficulty. 'I'll go, you stay'.

Suniti nodded and moved towards the little bedroom to collect the necessities for her husband's journey. Her knees seemed to have turned to water. She didn't feel anything; only the pit of her stomach seemed unusually hollow. The train left very early. He would need some tea. Like an automaton she occupied herself with comforting normal daily things. The kerosene stove had to be lit, and the tea kettle put on it. Suddenly little details became all important. Only two-thirds of the kettle must be filled as it would only waste kerosene if she heated more. Everything was so expensive these days. The interest on the wedding debt never seemed to get paid. She wondered apathetically whose wedding had landed them into this terrible debt. Oh, of course it was Neeno's! What a lovely, dutiful little darling she was. She really must make up her mind to get those in-laws of hers to send her back home soon. She got up from the small wooden floor level stool on which she always did the cooking, and moved towards the bedroom. She opened the tin trunk that contained everything they owned, and took out a carefully folded shirt, trouser, coat and tie. The vests were all gone and the underpants in shreds, but it didn't matter as long as the top clothes looked good. After all he was going to their *samdhis*[17] and he had to make a good impression otherwise they wouldn't treat her Neeno well! She smiled vaguely as she picked up the carbolic soap from the bathroom. Neeno's father was a good man. Everything would be all right if she left it to him. Hadn't he chosen this family for Neeno? Of course they were hard on her now and again, but then, she smiled blankly again, mothers-in-law had a right over their daughters-in-law, 'and that is why we gave them so much—in fact just whatever they asked for,' she said aloud. 'That is why they respect Neeno so much!'

Rajinder stood looking strangely at his wife packing his things in the battered old Air-India case meticulously, even happily. "I'll not need the tie," he said.

Suniti was shocked. 'No tie? What sort of impression will you make? Our family's nose will be cut, and God forbid, my *samdhan* will take it out on my poor Neeno! No, no! you must take it.'

"Oh God!' breathed Rajinder softly. 'The water is ready,' he said aloud. 'Make me some tea.'

'I wish you had given me some notice. I could have made some *halwa*[18] for Neeno's Kuky. She would have loved the *halwa* her *nani*[19] would have sent her; but that's always the trouble with you. You never give me enough time. Always at the last minute you start thinking of doing things!' Suniti got up from the *morah*[20] near the box and walked to the kitchen to make his tea. She wondered why her knees kept giving way at every step. She must go to the *vaid*[21] and get this strange sick feeling also checked up. She laughed aloud! It wasn't even as if she was at an age when the sickness would have been something to start knitting for! She smiled coquettisly at her husband as she passed him in the doorway.

Suddenly she felt Rajinder grab her by the shoulders. He looked deep into her eyes and shook her hard. 'Suniti, Suniti, Neeno is dead! Our Neeno is dead. Don't you understand? She is killed. They have killed her. She has no child. The baby was born dead. They are both dead, and I have killed them both. Do you understand? You are married to a murderer—a man who is unnatural enough to have killed his own child with his own two hands! Don't smile at me as if

I am mad, Suniti, or I swear to you that I shall kill you also! Face it! Face it! Suniti! I am not going there to make any impressions. I am going there to get Neeno's burnt body back—God forgive us all! Now do you understand, Suniti?'

Suniti's eyes widened. She gazed blankly up at her husband. He had never been violent with her before. He had always been a good man. Even now, it wasn't as if he had raised his hand to her. Something had upset him very much. If she bore it quietly, he would be all right. She decided to humour him. He was saying something about murder; but she understood her man. She would show him that she could stand shoulder to shoulder with him as she had always done. Something was worrying him very much. May be a friend was involved in some murder case. Anyway whatever it was, it concerned her Neeno's father's welfare, and she must be strong enough to help and support him.

She smiled up at him. 'Of course I understand. Haven't we stood together in the hardest times? Don't you worry. Whatever it is, it will blow over. *Parmatma* is above all. His ways are known to Him alone. Don't let anything get you down. You just have your tea and get yourself ready for the train. I shall be here waiting for you three when you return with Neeno and the baby; bless them both. Will you come with them in a day or two? That should give me enough time to get things in order.' she bustled off into the bedrooms. 'What a lot of dust collects here,' Rajinder heared her say: 'So much to be done with a married daughter coming home again. I must borrow a cot from Nirmal for the baby.'

Rajinder stood before his shaving mirror studying the lines on his forehead which seemed to have grown deeper since he last looked at his face. He decided he didn't like the face in the mirror and wondered in an abstracted manner whether it belonged to him at all. He shut the door with a bang. He couldn't bear to hear Suniti humming the lullaby she used to put Neeno to sleep with. The face in the mirror clenched its teeth. Rajinder looked at his watch. It had stopped at three thirty. He drew the worn out blade viciously across his jagged chin, and slapped the icy water into the cuts...

The train was almost empty. Rajinder found a seat by the window, and wheel and whistle combined to lull his consciousness...

'Don't be ridiculous, *Sethji*,'[22] he found himself saying... 'All this is loose talk! The Muslims are all our friends. Nothing can ever happen. This is Lahore, not Timbuctoo!'

Seth Makhhan Das was trembling uncontrollably. 'You don't know *beta*,[23] they may be rumours, but what would you say if you found your house and all you have worked for in your life suddenly blowing up in flames before your eyes? You young people can never understand what it means to slave all your life for something and then see it go up in smoke. Your father put land, house and position in your lap and left this world, may his abode ever be in *Swarglok*.[24] I am an old man and have no courage to face this division of the country.'[25] Rajinder smiled at him and called out to his shy little bride. 'I said, *ji*![26] send out some tea!' She came out five minutes later, feet a-jingle, head dutifully covered with one of the many gorgeous gold-embroidered *saris*[27] she was expected to wear throughout the first year of her marriage else people would cast aspersions on her parents' status in life. Her gold and red bangled arm daintily placed the tea and *pakoras*[28] on the table. Rajinder's cup of joy brimmed over. This lovely package was his. He noted the Seth's approving eye. He seemed to have momentarily forgotten the division of the country. 'Sit down, I said,' Rajinder said gently to his wife as she made as if to go back into the house, 'and remove your *ghungat*,[29] *Sethji* is a very dear friend.' Suniti sat on the third chair and began pouring the tea, her lovely face shyly exposed to the sun and to her husband's elderly friend.

Next morning Seth Makhhan Das was dead, stabbed in the back while going to his office, and Shahalami, a busy crowded area in Lahore was aflame...

The train jolted to a stop at Karnal. Rajinder jerked awake and dozed off again. That had been a nightmare journey. How they were alive at the end of it was nothing short of a miracle. The maddened crowd had reached their house at eleven. He still remembered the drum beats, the inhuman howls, and the shrieks. Suniti was wonderful. She acted while he hesitated. She seemed to have instinctively assessed the situation before its full impact hit him. Darting to the Godrej steel almirah she swept the contents of the cash and ornaments drawer into a bag, threw him his best suit and said,

'Quick—the back door is still open.' She pushed him out through the vegetable garden just as the mob spilled over into the house. They slid along the darkest shadows and bribed their way with fast dwindling resources through fearfilled days and hungry nights until at last, totally bereft and alone they stumbled into India.

No one had wanted them there at all. The local people openly cursed the Punjabis calling them *jaanwar*[30]. How they had lived through those early nightmare years, he would never know. Just as well his mind had rejected the entire shattering episode and wiped it out from his consciousness... If it hadn't been for Suniti... Suniti working her delicate fingers to the bone, saving every *paisa*,[31] eating nothing and smiling while he ate; washing, cleaning, taking in sewing... and then the child... Little Neeno ...What a happy little butterfly she was...

Rajinder's head jerked with the sudden stopping of the train.

The platform was alive with porters and anxious passengers shovelling their families and luggage into little manageable mounds of trunks, suitcases, babies and winter bedrolls. Rajinder picked his way through the welter of people.

'*Baba*!'[32]

Rajinder jerked to an unbelieving standstill.

'Neeno?'

He swivelled around in the direction of the voice, his mind agog with amazed expectation. A young girl ran into the extended arms of a large man directly behind him. Drained of feeling, he walked on bumping into an irate plantain seller...

'*The Mills of God...*'

'What is the matter, Parkash's mother? Why are you making such a noise?... and who is hammering at the door at this hour of night? I wish you would realise I am a sick man and need a good night's sleep!'

The voice from her husband's bed was querulous and complaining, like a child kept in a constant state of dependence. Karmo Devi's mind was working very fast as she rubbed her son's head soothingly on the bed next to her invalid husband. The police would be here. She had to do something very fast to save herself and her son.

She got up quickly from the bed, opened the windows wide and switched on the light so that the neighbours could see and hear her clearly.

'Whatever could have happened?' she wailed, working herself up to a shrieking crescendo. '*He Parmatma!* What am I to do? Now my daughter-in-law has killed herself! *Hai Hai*! I always told you she was a no-good, lazy, over-educated hussy, and she has gone and proved me right! My poor darling gem of a boy is left with a corpse on his hands!'

The old man lifted his frail body from the bed, his rheumy eyes squinting against the light from the naked bulb. 'Oh stop shrieking you bitch! Who has killed herself? What are you screaming your head off for? The neighbours will hear you. Close the windows. Do you want me to die of cold tonight?'

'*Hai Ram*! Let my neighbours hear me! They know we are a good family! What had I ever kept from her? She ruled this house as if she was a queen on a throne! *Git-mit-git-mit* in English is all she would talk when I told her to do some work in the house. *Ram Ram!* What a curse on our family honour!' Karmo Devi wailed piercingly, tearing at her clothes, pulling at her hair and beating her breasts standing in full view before the window. Her son lay listless on the bed, his arm covering his eyes—the warm *razai* shutting off the terrible sounds from his ears. His father dragged himself cursing from the bed. 'Put off that light, you... you... before I beat the life out of you! Put it off and shut the windows!' He advanced tottering towards his howling wife, his shoe in his hand.

'Come on, beat me!' screamed Karmo Devi. 'I am twice cursed. Beat me–you were always on her side. Who did all the housework, I ask you? I kept her like my own daughter. I gave into every fancy of hers, and this is the way she repays me! *Hai hai* that I was ever born to see this day!'

Jagdish Kumar Arora collected his scattered wits. He had to stop this she-devil from making a fool of him and his family before all the neighbours. He had to take charge of the situation somehow. He reached for the switch, and with an effort pressed the button upwards, plunging the room into darkness. The wailing suddenly ceased. Karmo Devi was taken aback. Was this the same invalid she had nursed every day of her married life; nursed and cursed from morning to night for being responsible for all her woes? This husband of hers who had thrown the whole responsibility of the household on her shoulders so early in her life that she both feared his possible death and longed for it? She shivered at the thought of being left a widow; but then if it hadn't been for this *churail*[33] daughter-in-law of hers, curse her; she would have had her son wholely and solely for herself for her old age... and now...!

'Nobody Move!'

It was a sharp crisp voice that had taken over. A bright torch blinded her and the switch flooded the room with light again. The horrified woman looked in the direction of her husband and saw instead the heavy boots and khaki uniform of a policeman. Before she could shut her open mouth, the room was swarming with police. Parkash was hauled out from his protective *razai* and stood blinking in the light looking piteously at his mother. Jagdish Kumar had collapsed into a chair, his determination to control the situation shattered. It was only Karmo Devi whose mind was still clicking. Who could have informed the police? A mental procession of neighbours passed before her mind's eye, each one ticked off as incapable of such an unneighbourly act. She collected herself and started where she had left off, her face resuming an expression of sad bereavement.

'Have you seen her?' she cried, addressing the tallest policeman. The light has gone out of our house! My poor son! Our *Lakshmi*[34] *Rani* has gone forever! *Hai*! *Hai*! and she rocked to and fro shrieking, and tearing at her hair.

'Stop it this instant!' The boots were right in front of her. She whimpered to a stop, and looked up.

'Jagdish Kumar Arora, Karmo Devi and Parkash Arora, I have a warrant of arrest for you. You are to come with me to the *kotwali*.'[35]

'Arrest? Arrest? For what? We are respectable people, officer *sahib*,[36] please don't do this to us.' Jagdish Kumar's frail wrists were manacled to his son's. Kindly get up *bibi*.[37] You will have to come with us!'

'Come to jail? *Hai hai*! How will I survive this day?' The implacable officer stood coldly by as her wrists were locked together...

Rajinder Varma leapt into the three-wheeler hardly noticing whether the man had turned the flag of the metre down or not. 'Motinagar' he said curtly. The scooter responded like a horse to its master's kick and they roared off into the early dawn.

'Neeno,' he said aloud, 'Are you really gone?'

The scooter driver turned around. 'Yes?' he asked. 'No, nothing,' said Rajinder. As the scooter sped on, he hardly felt the biting Delhi cold. Who could have telephoned him? He had asked but the voice had only said he was a neighbour. It was a young man's voice, and it had a Madrasi accent. Could someone have tried to play the fool? Why should they want to do that? Perhaps Neeno was actually all right and... NO! Neeno was dead, as dead as her baby. How well he remembered that day—the day Parkash had brought her home, his little Neeno with her face puffed with weeping, a small suitcase with a few summer clothes in his hand.

'Daddyji', he had said in an embarrassed voice, 'Neeno is not very well, so *bhabiji* said she would get well when she saw her mother and father. I shall be coming to get her soon.' He had gone before he could offer him a cup of tea... and then Neeno's dead little voice, drained of tears, quietly repeating again and again, '*Babbo*,[38] she beat me... I was tired and the baby was dead... I was very tired *Babbo*... She slapped me and Parkash stood by the window biting his nails. He said, '*Bhabhi* leave her alone.' She beat me again and said I was not capable of bearing a son to look after her in her old age, and then it all became black. I have not had any food for so long.. but don't tell *maji*. I am quite well.'

How he had clasped her—broken in mind and body—his darling daughter. How many trips he had made over the past several months to ask them to take her back... and then there had been that terrible letter...

How greedy they were! First the table fan, then the Godrej almirah, the 'fridge, the motorcycle... the list was endless... and it was all his fault... the blue-black marks on her delicate skin and her hollow cheeks—his fault...

'Don't send her back, please. Listen to me also sometime. Don't I have a heart? Don't I know how my daughter is suffering? Please don't send her back. I feel somewhere inside of me that she will suffer more...' Suniti's eyes had looked pleadingly up at him.

'Even if we empty our house and sell every article we own, it will not fill that *churail's* mouth!' Suniti said. 'She didn't give her anything to eat, made her work like a slave. Naturally the baby was born dead! She has taken everything we own and the best daughter anyone could ever ask for, for her worthless son. She will surely kill her, *Parmatma* forbid! Leave her with me. I'll keep her in the house. No one need know she is here!'

It had not worked. He had taken her back with two gold bordered saris for her mother-in-law and a woollen suit for Parkash. He was still paying for those things. Poor Suniti... poor Suniti. His fault!... his fault!

The scooter drew up with a jolt and Rajinder got down, paid the driver and walked like a sleep-walker into Jagriti Housing Colony in Motinagar. The foggy morning was beginning to emerge from the shadows. Rajinder found himself suddenly in the midst of a crowd of curious people surrounding the all too familiar building. A police van and jeeps were parked at the entrance. Something made him stay where he was—nameless and faceless in the crowd. A long low murmur rippled through the crowd as three shrouded figures walking awkwardly between police escorts came through the door and were hustled into the waiting van. Jagdish saw Sheila run out screaming, 'Please, please leave my poor brother-in-law. He is an old man. He is ill! He has nothing to do with this!' Ashok came out quickly and gently drew her quietly back into their ground floor flat.

Suddenly Rajinder felt as if someone had pressed a knee into his stomach. His breath was suspended between throat and chest. Something was being carried out covered with a white sheet. There was a horrified gasp from the onlookers, as it disappeared into the van followed again by Sheila weeping and stretching her arms out as if to hold what could never be held again. Ashok brought her back indoors tenderly, chatting calmly with a policeman the while. Bulbs flashed everywhere. Newspapermen talked quickly and intensely with Ashok and the police officer. Rajinder Varma passed a hand over his eyes. He decided he did not want to get out of the wonderful anonymity of the crowd. He pressed against it gratefully. He could not go and face it all. He was not strong enough. He would go back to Suniti. There was no one here for him now. Neeno was gone where she belonged—she was shining among the rays of the morning sun. Yes, he would go back. There was no reason for him to stay here... He would go to Suniti and find peace again.

NOTES AND REFERENCES

1. Mother.
2. Oh God!
3. *Khasmaanu khaaniye:* a Punjabi curse.
4. *Tainoo Sap laṛay:* a Punjabi curse.
5. Sister-in-law. Mothers are often affectionately called *Bhabiji.*
6. Collective immolation by fire, historically connected with widows of the martial Rajputs.
7. A wind instrument.
8. Oh Great Spirit!
9. My ruby.
10. Let them try.
11. Marriage of Surya, Verse 46, Rig Veda X : 85 from Abinash Chandra Bose, Hymns from the Vedas, Asia Publishing House, Calcutta, 1966, p. 139.
12. A quilt.
13. A city in the Punjab famous for woollens.
14. Queen.
15. Veil.
16. Hindu brides generally wear red. The colour of sacrifice and joy.
17. Relatives by marriage.
18. A sweetmeat.
19. Maternal grandmother.
20. A Cane Stool.
21. A practitioner of indigineous medicine.
22. Term respectfully used for a businessman.
23. Son.
24. Paradise.
25. The partition of India into India and Pakistan in 1947.
26. A term of respect. Traditionally Indian husbands and wives do not take each other's names.
27. An Indian woman's dress.
28. Salty fried delicacies.
29. Veil covering the face.
30. Animals.
31. One-hundreth of a rupee.
32. Father.
33. Evil Witch.

34. Goddess of wealth and fortune.
35. Police Station.
36. Sir.
37. Lady.
38. Baby word for father.

2

Why?

I close the book and look out of the window. It is 1979. We are steaming into a station. Anxious faces swim past: men and women straining to catch a glimpse of a relative, or trying to locate an empty seat—faceless, anonymous people—characters exploited by novelists... Somewhere in that teeming crowd is Rajinder Varma waiting for a train to take him back to a lonely life with a shattered woman and memories of a bright young girl's laughter...

Was this just another story dreamed up by someone who wanted to sell a book with a hot title? How could Neena's death fit into the picture of a country with five thousand years of civilization behind it and a three hundred million strong electorate, with a constitution that guarantees equality of the sexes and prohibits discrimination? What of India's religions that elevate a woman to the sacred position of goddess and mother?

Taking a very long view of Neena's doomed life, let us shut ourselves, you and I, into the Time Machine, and allow it to spin us right into the cave of earliest man....

Looking out at the unfamiliar landscape around us, we shall discover our primeval ancestor—a speck of fiercely assertive life surrounded by unpredictable and all-enveloping nature. His life is a daily battle for survival against incomprehensible natural forces completely beyond his control.

There, outside the cave, is the terrible sky—deceptively blue and smiling one minute, growling and sabre-toothed the next. There also is the hot sun that comforts with its warmth, but can also set giant forests ablaze. From our vantage point we try to understand his reactions. What his mind cannot grasp, we decide, must frighten him very much indeed.

Ages pass like minutes in our Time Machine. We see our man now more in possession of himself. He involves himself in the happenings of nature. He sits enthralled watching a miracle unfold before his eyes. A seed is transforming itself into a springing plant whose baby tendrils reach upwards for warmth. He feels the nurturing earth with wondering fingers..

Back home in his cave there are three little incessantly bawling miracles also. The warmth and milk which flows from his mate's body gives them the nourishment they need just as the little plant outside gets it from its earth mother. Where did these little creatures in his cave come from? This amazing fact of birth seems to confuse him most of all. Pressing a button in our machine, we get a deeper close up of his mind. It is agitated and convulsed by conflicting thoughts and emotions. Something very important seems to be eluding him. What is this inexplicable Earth-Mother-Creation Power which is given solely to the creature he has won by the strength of his great right arm?

We see his mind equating this unknown power with the riddles of nature. He puts it in the same pigeon hole in his mind as the sun's heat, the force of flash floods and the earth's inscrutable nurture power. The creature who satisfies his physical urges and makes him comfortable, he decides reluctantly, is in some mys-terious fashion, superior to him.

The more he cogitates on the miracle of birth, the more we can see him feel that these little creatures in his cave are a one-woman effort, and that he has nothing at all to do with their production. He can fight. He can kill, but try as he may, he cannot produce another cave man. We watch two thoughts begin to seesaw for ascendancy in his mind:

The first and foremost thought that is driving him mad is that he—First Man—Mighty Hunter—should be in any way inferior to any living being—least of all, to his mate. The nagging sense of inferiority pricks him every time he sees her and her three little creatures. To convince himself of his own superiority, he dreams up a scenario in which he is invincible.

He can always beat her and her creatures down, he tells himself. In fact, come to think of it, he can even kill them if he so wishes. This is a pleasant thought and we watch him relax. A reassuring stream of warmth flows comfortingly up and down his system. There is no immediate threat to his status as Lord and Master. He has solved the problem in his own inimitable fashion and is in complete control of the situation. These creatures are after all, his possessions. He looks up at the ceiling of the cave and laughs at his baseless fears.

He mellows towards them. Poor helpless creatures! They need his protection and his strength so desperately! He even begins to look lovingly at them. He will guard them with his life, he decides because they are his own.

Suddenly the see-saw plunges this picture of primeval domestic bliss into the depths, and fear gains ascendancy once more. The 'something-strange' which his mate has, raises her several notches above him whether he likes it or not. Her Earth-Mother function frightens him. Hasn't he experienced the pleasant warm earth suddenly splitting open and disgorging hot death from its mouth? What of the fearful rumblings and tremblings that accompany this terror? Although he has managed to subjugate her physical presence in his cave, could not that 'something-strange' fall on him like snake-tongued lightning and utterly destroy him?

But now, our confused ancestor stumbles on a truly ingenious plan by which he can simultaneously guard his supremacy and placate this unknown power. He has already found that building altars to the strange powers that govern his existence gives him a sense of security. He prays fervently to the sun, the heavens, the earth and any other power he feels needs to be pleased, for his own protection. Impending disaster finds him cowering in the shadow of an altar in anxious communication with the concerned power. He now adds his mate's 'Something-Strange' to his list of imponder-ables, and builds an altar to Mother-Power.

From our Time Machine we get a private eye-view of the first appearance of the dichotomy which is one of the many factors that will together culminate aeons later in Neena's death. Through the ages that will follow, woman will be worshipped as goddess and mother while being battered into mental or physical submission at home and at work; discriminated against and excluded from fields of self-expression other than those assigned to her by tradition and usage.

Often however, the mother goddesses win the day:

Ishtar of Babylon and Assyria—a goddess not only of beauty but also of divine motherhood, was worshipped by the Arabs as the god Athtar.[1] The mother goddess 'was the secret inspiration of the growing soil, and the creative principle everywhere.'[2] Even the many breasted Diana of Ephesus who together with the Roman Venus and the Grecian Aphrodite, came in direct line from Ishtar, was in her original form the embodiment of nurturing motherhood.

Ishtar was addressed as 'Virgin Mother'—not necessarily implying chastity, but that her love was bestowed freely, unsullied by the bonds of marriage.[3]

'Supreme is thy might, O Lady, exalted art thou above all gods...

Unto thee are subject the laws of the earth and the laws of heaven...

Shining Light of Heaven...goddess of men...'[4]

...And so altars to goddesses proliferated the world over—the Chinese *Kwan Yin*, the Egyptian *Nut*, the Indian *Durga*—and nurture-power took precedence over sex-for-pleasure-alone.

Mother was God long ago, and the suffragettes of the early twentieth century who called on people to 'trust in God, She will not let you down!'[5] were only trying to re-establish her on the pedestal off which she had been so rudely pushed.

Today our cave man's descendant still smarts from the Almighty's discriminatory ruling against him. Although by now he has scientifically dissected and analysed every aspect of the mystery of the first germ of life, the divine spark still eludes his grasp. It riles him to feel that the signal honour of being the receptacle and food supply for all future generations of Man is still reserved for woman alone. Even if she has to contend with the test tube, at any time, she will still reign supreme as the Mother.

Unlike his earlier ancestor, man is now quite aware of his role in the act of creation, but he has had to grudgingly admit that it is minuscule. His ego has taken several thousand years of painstaking labour to build up, but the hurt has been accumulating. He tries not to acknowledge the pain and laugh the whole thing off. Obliging image builders including willing masochistic members of the opposite sex, weave a web of myth and legend around the ever present thorn until he is finally able to convince himself that he has become the Legend Incarnate.

'So,' says Margaret Mead, 'it is safe to deduce that woman and her nurturing power was originally the most widely respected and acknowledged power, and later man *learned* to make himself superior.'[6]

To make himself superior effectively, he has had to put up a consistent act—'a theatrical mime, which would fall to the ground in a moment...if its true constituents were known—a shaky structure, protected by endless taboos.'[7] To this end men had to group together against the common threat of erosion. So a young Iatmul boy from the Lower Sepik River in New Guinea, separated from the influence of his mother and sisters at an early age, walks through an entrance significantly enough called a womb, and through a crocodile passage with its Freudian overtones, into the Men's House. Here alternate humiliations and rigours make a 'man' of him.[8]

'Women it is true make human beings, but only men can make men,'[9] they say, hoping thereby to try and usurp as much as possible of woman's role in the making of a human being.

Meanwhile, the unwitting cause of man's inferority complex is portrayed in traditional lore the world over as a pliable, clinging creature whose very life hangs on the whims and fancies of her lord...

She must at all times subject herself to his wishes—

> 'A wife should take her meals after her husband...sleep after he sleeps. If he assaults her, she should not lose her temper...If she has to offer a suggestion, she should say, Sir, this looks advisable, but do what you think is right...She should never sit in an elevated place and never look angrily at her husband. She should wash his feet, shampoo them, fan him.'[10]

At the same time, Manu the great law-giver of ancient India reveals the double think that has woven itself into the social fabric of our country, and acquired sophistication with the lapse of time. Revered as goddesses ...

> 'Women must be honoured and adorned by their fathers, brothers, husbands and brothers-in-law who desire (their own) welfare. Where women are honoured, there the gods are pleased; but where they are not honoured no sacred rite yields rewards.. The houses on which female relations, not being duly

honoured, pronounce a curse, perish completely, as if destroyed by magic...'[11]

So many a screen heroine weeping glycerine tears before a symphathetic goddess pleads for strength and courage to help her man tide over his latest crisis; to help her bear her sad lot, or to give her a son, so that she may win the affection of her estranged lord and the appreciation of his kin. The celluloid goddess obliges with an appropriate miracle and generally provides an edifying lecture on the duties of a good wife and mother; or smilingly showers gold and silver on the bowed head of a girl whose parents are too poor to afford the necessary dowry for a good marriage. Never ever, does a goddess so far forget herself as to reprimand an erring husband, or in any way lower his stature as a Man. Even in modern Hindi films, it is quite common for the dying heroine to totter through lengthy footage interspersed with mournful songs, to draw her last faltering breath with her head resting against her lord's unphotogenic hairy feet.

So even the honourable goddess-mother picture is circumscribed. It is subject to long distance male control. The superiority of the goddess is never absolute. She is goddess only inasmuch as she can use her superior powers in the service of her greatest creation—Man.

It was not always so.

As elsewhere in the world, the Indian woman of early history seems to have had it very good indeed. Between about 2,500 and 1,000 B.C. her status could have been the envy of her sisters anywhere in the world.

Although less welcome than a boy at birth, she was treated on par with her brother. She received the same training and was subject to the same disciplines. The *upanayana* ceremony[12], an initiation into the wonderful world of knowledge, was meant for both of them without any discrimination. Among other subjects, she studied philosophy, theology and medicine. It is interesting to note here that as late as the Middle Ages, no woman in England could enter the medical profession.[13]

Spinning and weaving, teaching and practising medicine assured the Vedic[14] woman of India economic independence, while philosophy and theology gave her confidence and poise when she stood in the general assembly debating abstruse points with the greatest minds of the age. Yajnavalkya[15] the celebrated sage and law-giver of ancient India was bested in argument by Gargi, a remarkable woman dialectician at a philosophical tournament, while Maitreyi, one of Yajnavalkya's two wives, taught philosophical doctrine by her husband, achieved great eminence in that line. In fact a Jataka[16] refers to the four daughters of learned Jain parents who toured the country challenging one and all to philosophical debate.

There was no special premium on early marriage, so it was possible and indeed auspicious for young virgins to be included in the list of eminent persons who gave Sri Rama[17] a ceremonial bath at his coronation:

'The Ritvijs[18] and the Brahmins with sixteen virgins, counsellors, warriors as also the merchants, were full of joy and Rama was sprinkled with pure water...'[19]

Kings had women guards and some of the old Vedic hymns were written by women.[20] Since parents were not hounded into marrying their daughters early, stress was laid on their education, and equal partnership was possible between men and women. Marriage for a girl came as late as at the age of sixteen and even later. The early Vedic woman approved of the man she married and was invited soon after she was married, to address the *Vidatha*'[21] a religious assembly—an invitation coveted by the most learned of sages. She was addressed as '*Subhage*'—O Graceful One,[22] a form of address whose masculine form was specifically reserved for the gods. A god was described as '*Him whom your sacrifices clothe, even as a woman her robe*.'[23] Even the purity of the mighty god of fire Agni was compared with the chaste wife, '*like as a blameless dame dear to her husband*.'[24]

It was only later when Vedic studies became too complicated and the ritual more and more involved, that girls found it impossible to spend fourteen years in mastering the intricacies of religious education. Add to this the scare that the slightest mistake in performance of the ritual was fraught with danger for the performer, and we begin to see why women gradually gave up Vedic studies. The *upanayana* ceremony was performed as before, but began to lose its meaning for girls as their studies were discontinued with marriage. The situation drifted along with the boys' *upanayana* initiating them into studentship at eight years and most of the girls marrying later as they had been doing before.

Finally Manu declared the *upanayana* ceremony unnecessary for girls, equating it with marriage:

> 'The nuptial ceremony is stated to be the Vedic sacrament for women (and to be equal to the initiation) serving the husband (equivalent to) the residence in (the house of the) teacher, and the household duties (the same) as the (daily) worship of the sacred fire.'[25]

This pronouncement spelt disaster for the free Indian woman whose being debarred from the initiation ceremony is described by A.S. Altekar as 'spiritual disenfranchisement.' Since marriage by now had acquired the same significance for a girl as the *upanayana* for a boy, it seemed quite appropriate that these two ceremonies should be held at the same time in a household. Also since the boy's *upanayana* was generally held when he was about eight years old, this began to be looked on as the approved age of marriage for a girl. The Indian woman's brief dream of freedom was over. She now found herself beginning to be bracketed with those whose origin was considered to be lower than that of the Brahmins, the highest in the hierarchy of the caste system. The existence of this discrimination is acknowledged in the *Bhagvadgita* in Krishna's discourse where he refers to the prevalent view concerning women at the time:

> For those who take refuge in Me, O Partha' (Arjuna), 'though they are lowly born, women, Vaisyas,[26] as well as Sudras,[27s] they also attain to the highest goal.'[28]

As memories of her *upanayana* ceremony fade into the past, woman becomes gradually more and more unlettered, and less and less able to stand on her own feet. The arts become the preserve of the courtesan, and girls from good families become increasingly more uneducated and dependent on their men. With such a bright beginning behind them, they finally join their dominated and browbeaten sisters the world over. Custom and usage present them with the daily tyranny of child-bearing, kitchen and servitude. Slowly but surely, community approval or censure has driven the young brides of the world, their brains teeming with untapped possibilities, into narrower and still more narrow confines, leaving the pedestal free for the deification of the husband.

The shrew, the libber, the articulate and the demonstrating woman—all products of centuries of frustration, become figures of fun. Ridicule poured on their doings very often has the desired effect. The women shrink back into their historically familiar role and fit once more into the grey and brown background tones of the attractively coloured portraits of their men...

My Son! My Son!

'*Allah*[29] be praised! The All Merciful has granted you a son!'

'*Narayan*[30] is great!'

'*Laddoos*![31] *Laddoos* for my son!'

In the little house oil lamps are lighting happy faces. The young father is beside himself with joy as he gazes enraptured at his newborn son...

Himself incarnate! My son will inherit my twenty square yards of mud hut! My son will inherit my kingdom!

My son will see me into the next world and make my name eternal! He will impregnate his wives with my imperishable energy so that a million more of myself spring from his loins to inherit the earth!

My son will perform the sacrifices, for is it not common knowledge that a sacrifice performed by women or eunuchs is an abomination unto the gods?[32] My son will establish a link between me and *Allah, Yahveh,*[33] *Wahe Guru,*[34] *Parmatma*...And so—*machismo*[35] comes into the world...Virility incarnate is my son. I am he and he is I...

A survey carried out in Chile between 1968 and 1970[36] revealed that 27 per cent Chilean men admitted that their reason for getting married was to affirm their masculinity.

Around the proud mother the women are singing, Her husband cannot contain his excitement. '*Arri*[37] Champa,' he says. 'They say that a mother of sons becomes two fists taller when she has her first boy. You are still the same!'[38] His nineteen-year old sister is shooed away from the window. She is a widow, and her inauspicious shadow must not fall on the man-child's first day in his world.

The young mother's parents have come with gifts of money and clothes for their son-in-law and his kin. 'Thank you,' they whisper to the invisible gods who have granted their daughter a son. Now at last, her life will have meaning and security, She has fulfilled the purpose for which she was born. She will reign a queen.

NOTES AND REFERENCES

1. *New Larousse Encyclopedia of Mythology*, New York, Hamlyn, 1968, 10th impression, 1974, p. 58.
2. Will Durant, *The Story of Civilization: I: Our Oriental Heritage*, Simon and Schuster: New York, 1954, Ch. IX, 1954, pp. 235-36.
3. *Ibid.*
4. Robert Briffault, *The Mothers*, Vol. (iii), N.Y., 1927, p. 88 quoted by Will Durant, *Ibid.*
5. Sylvia Pankhurst.
6. Margaret Mead, *Male and Female*, Victor Gollancz Ltd, London, 1950, p. 95.
7. *Ibid.*, p. 103.
8. *Ibid.*, pp. 93-94.
9. *Ibid.*, p. 103.
10. From the *Skandapurana* as quoted by Vimala Veeraraghavan in *The Weekly Round Table*, 16 September 1973.
11. Manusmriti: III: 55, 56, 58 from Max Mueller, *Sacred Books of the East*, Vol. XXV: The Laws of Manu, Motilal Banarsidass, reprint 1964, p. 85.
12. *Upanayana:* An initiation ceremony at which the sacred thread is tied around the young Brahmin novice.
13. Will Durant, *op. cit:* 1950 The Age of Faith, Ch. XXX, p. 826.
14. Vedic: From '*Veda*'. The *Vedas* are sacred writings which are the fountain-head of the Hindu religion. It is impossible to affix a definite date to them. The oldest hymn in the Vedas is believed to have been sung about the thirty first century before the birth of Christ. The generally accepted opinion is that the Vedic Age was somewhere between that time and about one thousand five hundred years before Christ.
15. *Yajnavalkya:* The White *Yajur Veda* and the code of law called the *Yajnavalkya-smriti,* among other writings, are attributed to this ancient sage. The *Mitakshara* law (mentioned in Ch. 6) is a commentary on the *Yajnavalkya-smriti*. John Dowson, *A Classical Dictionary of Hindu Mythology*, Routledge and Kegan Paul Ltd., 1968, pp. 372-73.
16. *Jataka*: A birth story relating to the previous births of the Bodhisatva before he was eventually born as the Buddha. Here the reference is from *The Jataka*, ed. E.B. Cowell, vol. III, Luzac and Co. Ltd, London

1956: *Jataka* no. 301 *Cullakalinga—Jataka*, Book IV - *Catukkanipata*: pp. 1-2.

17. Vishnu's seventh incarnation.
18. Sacrificial priests.
19. *The Ramayana of Valmiki*, translated by Hari Prashad Shastri, London, Shanti Sadan, 1959, Vol. III, pp. 368-69.
20. The Prayer of Ghosha, the daughter of Kakshivat, to Asvins is an example, *Rig Veda*, X: 40.
21. *Ibid.*, X: 85: 26 and 27.
22. *Ibid.*, X: 10. 12
23. *Ibid.*, VIII: 26. 13. Translation R.T.H. Griffth, *The Hymns of the Rgveda, Motilal Banarsidass*, Delhi, 1976, p. 417.
24. *Ibid.*, I: 73.3, p. 48.
25. *Manusmriti*: II. 67 as in Max Mueller *op. cit:* 1964, p. 42.
26. *Vaisya*: The third caste: traders and agriculturists.
27. *Sudra*: The fourth caste.
28. *The Bhagwadgita* IX, verse 32, translated by S. Radhakrishnan, London, Allen and Unwin, 1949, 252-53.
29. Arabic for God.
30. Another name for the god Vishnu.
31. Sweetmeats for auspicious occasions.
32. *Manusmriti*, IV, verses 205, 206: in Max Mueller, 1964, pp. 160-61. Contrast this with early Vedic times when woman was a necessary partner in sacrifice. Some sacrifices were even performed by women alone.
33. The Jewish name for God.
34. A Punjabi phrase meaning God to Whom be all praise; generally used by the Sikh community.
35. All - Manism.
36. *Machismo*: 'Latin America's Myth-Cult of Male Supremacy' by Hernan San Martin in *The Unesco Courier*, March 1975.
37. Hey!
38. From the Hindi film *Sadhana*.

3

It's A Girl!

Universal lamentation proclaims the birth of a girl.

The Jew, like Plato, daily thanked *Yahveh* that he was not born a woman. Downcast parents the world over implicate the Almighty in the whole sorry business. A sigh of resignation follows. Friends gather to sympathise: 'It is His will,' they say sadly, and the announcement goes out that the worst has happened.

During the Mughal period — from the sixteenth to the eighteenth centuries, the *Jat*[1] father pacing the floor anxiously expecting news of a son's birth found his hopes dashed to the ground on hearing that he had fathered 'a stone.' If however, the planets smiled on him the lugubrious announcement that a 'mere girl' had been born, would send him rushing home so that he could hold his beloved son in his arms. The message, everyone knew, had been carefully couched in code language to fool the malignant powers that lay in wait to pounce on every newborn boy. A Muslim father would often find his little son dressed as a girl to further confuse the evil ones.

To this day a compliment to a baby boy will bring you dark looks from his female security guard and his moonlike face will be covered from your inauspicious gaze. Cries of 'a black face for the evil eye' will show you how *gauche* you have been...

It is 1927: An air of expectancy hangs over the *Jhandewali Kothi*[2] where my mother is in the final throes of a difficult labour. Her mother-in-law bustles about the room, her every breath a prayer to Allah to please be personally responsible for the safe delivery of this boy. He knows how much her son needs an heir. What will happen to the family inheritance if... Who will look after her in her old age if this one too...

A puny cry heralds my birth. My mother turns exhausted but smiling to the older woman: 'Your third grand-daughter, *Bebeji*,'[3] she whispers...

'Just her luck!'

'Poor woman!'

'She was born under an unlucky star!'

Only a girl! The desperate cry still comes from the world's labour rooms as exhausted mothers turn their heads away from what should have been a son.

No. It is not *Durga, Lakshmi, Devi*[4] or any other goddess that is born to be respected and revered: only an ordinary Mehr, Rebecca, Rani or Rita who will snatch the morsel from the deserving mouth of a son. A mere girl who cannot even carry on a name or a lineage: who cannot touch the lips of her dying parents with the holy Ganga water that will cleanse their souls from every sin and assure them a place in heaven. Only a girl! She has no identity of her own until it is breathed into her nostrils when she is united with her lord and master. So necessary has marriage been for a girl that sometimes the wedding ceremony was read over her dead and bedecked body before it could be consigned to the flames.[5]

The baby girl is only luggage marked 'Virgin—Handle With Care—Keep Until Called For'—Chastity to be guarded against the day the dowry wrapped package is eventually passed on and all rights on it satisfactorily transferred. It does not end there, as Rajinder Varma and his wife know only too well. Every function and every festival preceding and following a daughter's wedding burns larger and yet larger holes in her parents' budget.

The fact that the unwelcome little girl is growing into an affectionate and accomplished little person helps her only in so far as it may buy her a better husband; but few grooms are enthused by qualities of head and heart alone.

Looking away from India, we find the medieval Jew's problems began with Baby Rachel's birth. He knew marriage would not be considered valid without the 'family house' he was supposed to give her. He had to start collecting the 200 *zuza*[6] needed for it straightaway. Even after her marriage, his problems would not be over as he was expected to support the young couple who would live under his roof for quite a number of years after the wedding.[7] Ah well, *Yahveh* knew best!

Centuries later, twenty six year old Omana's little Mariamma poses the same problem for her parents in India. The scrimping and saving start with her birth. Extra tuitions and daily school teaching between husband and wife will still find them short of the one lakh rupee[8] dowry expected by a good Syrian Christian[9] bridegroom's family in Kerala. Then although education is free, specialisation is expensive, and there is the problem of joblessness. She looks up desperately at the palm-fronded sky. Who will look at a bride without these qualifications nowadays, and which boy's family would ever dream of compensating her parents for a lifetime of sacrifice?

The shoe is always on the other foot. The demand from them is invariably cash compensation to cover the money spent on their son's education.

Kill! Kill!

Omana has not told her husband of the baby now forming in her womb. She prays quietly that she may be forgiven for the sin of wanting to abort it: for whatever would they do if, God forbid, it should turn out to be another girl?

The ancient Spartan father's right to infanticide was upheld by the law of the land, but his was a case of killing a weakling whether boy or girl. In India various causes combined to produce a favourable climate for the killing of baby girls.

Turbulent times, attacks and constant fear of invasion made it increasingly difficult for families to care for a tender defenceless little girl. Strong boys were family assets particularly in the wide plains of the Punjab where invading hordes were constantly pouring through the passes in the high Hindu Kush. A boy could wield a sword, while a girl needed protection. Furthermore, she was always in danger of losing her most valued possession—virginity. She had to be guarded by her harassed parents, who became so obsessed with keeping her chastity intact that they seemed only to live for the day when they could pack her off lock stock and barrel to become someone else's responsibility. This objective was becoming more and more difficult to attain without an offer of monetary inducements to accompany the goods.

The Rajput clans lived in islands of security surrounded by warring clans. There were restrictions on whom their daughters could marry, as the families of the same clan considered each other's women—mothers or sister.[10] A marriage between them would naturally be considered incestuous. Bridegrooms therefore had to be sought from among 'outsiders' and cultivated assiduously without compromising the family honour. Add to this the Rajput's pride in his noble ancestry, and his problem can be easily appreciated. In an effort to 'bag' an outsider who was also as high born as themselves, the family found itself involved in an unseemly scramble with other parents equally anxious to gain a true blue connection. Constant warring would also leave few friendly clans to choose from. The groom's family of course, held all the cards, and bestowed their son on the family that gave the most for the honour of the association.

'Face' among the Rajputs has always had to be kept at all cost, and the 'honour of the turban' even now continues to demand larger and flashier dowries. In those days Bhats[11] and Charans—bards and genealogists, were maintained as status symbols in wealthy Rajput families. These marriage vultures had to be stuffed with luxuries else they were likely to satirise the bride's father in public bringing dishonour to the family.

'Their exaction have sometimes amounted to three quarters of the year's income'... 'and threw insurmountable obstacles in the way of future marriages in the same family.'[12]

'Even now,' writes Col. Tod in 1829, 'The Rana of Oodipore in his season of poverty, at the recent marriage of his daughters, bestowed "the gift of a lakh" on the bard who sang in praise of his munificence... The Chundawat[13] of Saloombra... expended on the marriage of his daughter a sum even greater than his sovereign could have afforded... to have his name blazoned by the bards and genealogists...'[14]

Even as long ago as Alexander the Great's invasion of India in 326 B.C. Greek historians commented on the custom among indigent parents in Punjab of 'exposing' their unmarried daughters for sale in the market place. When the young blades of Taxila had collected in the square, the maidens' necks and shoulders would be bared for inspection, and bargains struck.[15]

Small wonder then that the little baby girl was refused nourishment, and her mother's nipples coated with poison for her to suck.[16] 'It was a custom,' says Firishta.[17] 'as soon as a female child was born, to carry her to the market-place and there proclaim aloud, holding the child in one hand and a knife in the other, that any one wanting a wife might have her; otherwise she was immolated.'[18]

In an investigation carried out in 1852, it was discovered that the Bedis who claim descent from Guru Nanak were known all over Punjab as *Kuṛi Mar.*[19] The only Bedi who had at that time been courageous enough to preserve two daughters, was ostracised and humiliated by his compatriots.[20]

Before the advent of Prophet Muhammad, Arabia was hell on earth for women. Baby girls were buried alive even though the *Quraish* and *Kurdah* tribes ironically enough addressed angels as 'Daughters of God.' If we look closer, we shall perhaps be able to catch a glimpse of early man again and the double standard he handed down to male posterity:

> 'When any one of them has tidings of a female child, his face is overclouded and black, and he has to keep back his wrath. He skulks away from the public for the evil tidings he has heard;—is he to keep it in disgrace, or bury it in the dust?'[21]
>
> 'It is said the only time at which Usman shed a tear, was in the days of ignorance, when his little daughter, whom he was burying alive, wiped the dust of the grave-earth from his beard.'[22]

Female infanticide was also very common among the Australian tribes and the Todas of the Nilgiri Hills of Tamil Nadu.[23] Although in ancient China woman had been as elsewhere, regarded as nurturing mother, and was considered synonymous with happiness and creative power, later Chinese classics make many references to female infanticide.[24] In fact, it is by no means something that existed in the distant past. The author Han Suyin says,[25]

'Under the Confucian system, the husband had the right to kill his wife. Female infanticide was common. I saw it myself when I was a midwife during the war against Japan... In poor families it was not unusual for girl children to be sold as slaves or concubines... My own daughter Yung-Mei was purchased from a mother who had four girls...'

'*Hukum*'[26] says my neighbour's Rajasthani servant women, 'what do you city ladies know? It happens now and again in my own district—Where all will the law go? It is a big country!' She looks enigmatically up at the sky.

'Female infanticide is one manifestation of male supremacy.' writes the American anthropologist Marvin Harris in his stimulating books, Cows, Pigs, Wars and Witches. 'The Yanomamo expects his first baby to be a male. So his woman strangles her baby girl with vines or by 'standing on both ends of a stick placed on top of the baby's throat, by banging the baby's head against a tree or by simply leaving the infant to fend for itself on the jungle floor.'[27]... And here, in modern India, I picked up the following news item concerning prenatal tests conducted on three hundred rural women at the All India Institute of Medical Science in Delhi from *The Statesman* of 17 April, 1977:

'*Doctor Kill It If It's A Girl:*'

'...Ever since a report in this newspaper disclosed that it was possible to identity... whether the foetus was male or female... The AIIMS has been flooded with requests for such tests to be done... But of the 300 women so tested last year, almost everyone wanted termination of pregnancy if it was found that the foetus was female...'[28]

If by some strange miracle the baby girl survives, she is tolerated but never allowed to develop at the expense of her brothers. Throughout her life it will be her unique privilege to watch the men and the boys eat before her...

'My dear woman,' says the lady with the tinted glasses sitting before me sipping a lime juice in the club lawn, 'when we were small, it was a matter of Feed the Men. Whenever we had enough money for meat, it was literally apportioned out among the men. I remember my father always had the two bones with the largest amount of meat on them, then my four brothers got two cuts of meat each, and we girls were given a good helping of gravy and potatoes. My grandmother used to say that we would be of no use to our mothers-in-law if we got used to luxury. Grandmother and mother took whatever was left. We never gave it a thought! There usually was very little!'

In 1971 children under 14 years accounted for 42 per cent of India's total population.[29] Since India is predominantly rural, we shall look at the infant mortality rate for rural India. The 1969 figures show a death rate of 148.1 for girl babies as against 132.3 for males in the same age group.[30]

Contrary to popular expectation, the newborn girl is stronger than her male counterpart. She is better equipped by nature to withstand the rigours of the world outside the womb. This is borne out by figures which show that baby boys die in larger numbers than baby girls in the first few days of their lives:[31]

Once the numbing shock of having produced a daughter is over and the parents' blood starts circulating again, love and attention are poured on the male child and the nourishment is literally taken out of the baby girl's mouth and given to him.

In the weeks and months following her earliest days of life, the little girl is a victim of death by neglect. Available figures show that such deaths are on the increase.[32]

Contrasted against the chances of her peers elsewhere in the world, the Indian baby girl has a much lower chance of survival, except in Sri Lanka where the 1961 figures show conditions somewhat similar to those in India.[33]

As she grows the little Indian girl finds out from the stories her grandmother tells her, that her wedding day will be the culmination of all her hopes, and motherhood her crowing glory. Her ultimate fulfilment will be in becoming a grandmother of males. Apart from these great events in her life, she can expect nothing more than an occasional smile of approval from the lord she was born to serve. She knows that she will follow him through her successive lives, as the great goddess Lakshmi followed her lord through his incarnations.[34] She will set a pattern for all dutiful Hindu wives to follow. Whatever the courts may say, she knows in her mind that for good or for ill, the marriage is indissoluble.

Religion brands the father who has not done his duty by his daughter, and has left her unmarried until 'the proper time' is past 'reprehensible'. Ever since Manu declared that the marriage ceremony should take the place of the *upanayana* ceremony for a girl, the marriage age for girls dropped steeply from the fairly reasonable sixteen years or so of the Vedic age to eight years—that being the age at which the boys went through their *upanayana* ceremony.[35] This was how the 'proper time' for a girl's marriage came to be understood as meaning 'before she is marriageable.'

In fact Yajnavalkya very specifically stated that if a girl was not married before puberty, her guardian would be held entirely responsible for the murder of an embryo with every month that passed.[36]

From about the eighth and ninth centuries A.D. marriages between different castes began to be looked down on and the preservation of caste purity forced parents to choose bridegrooms from their own caste alone. The choice of eligible males got considerably narrowed down and parents in their anxiety to catch and reserve the best, married their daughters off as soon as a good groom was discovered. The wedding day arrived all too soon for the expensive little luxury who was transferred from her parents' laps to the cradle in her new home, virginity satisfactorily intact.[37]

Various attempts have been made to check child marriage. The Civil Marriage Act of 1872 declared marriage illegal for a girl before she was fourteen. The Age of Consent Act of 1891 prohibited consummation before she was twelve. This age was raised to thirteen in 1925. Finally the Sarda Act—*The Child Marriage Restraint Act of 1929* fixed the minimum age for marriage at fourteen for girls and eighteen for boys.[38] This was amended in 1949 to fifteen years for girls. In 1976 a Bill was introduced in the Lok Sabha to raise the age still further, but it lapsed with the Lok Sabha's dissolution in December 1977. Another Bill was introduced in the Lok Sabha in the same month. A later amendment to this Bill raising the girl's minimum age for marriage to eighteen years and that of boys to twenty-one years has finally been passed.[39]

Children, however, are still married off almost in infancy. In 1971, 13.6 per cent of girls in rural India were married between the ages of ten and fourteen, while 0.1 per cent in the same age group were already widowed.[40] The death toll in the same year taken by the Indo-Pakistan conflict left several young girls under fifteen, war widows.[41]

The Emergency (26 June 1975 - 20 March 1977) showmen who organised mass dowryless weddings were occasionally embarrassed by the ages of their *protegés*. On 15 October 1976 *The Indian Express* reported a mass wedding of seventy couples where 'most of the couples turned out to be minors... " There is hardly a family with an unmarried daughter over fifteen years here," remarked the lawyer responsible for the show.

Diaries of village level workers in Haryana show that young girls of ten and twelve are often married to men twenty or thirty years of age. They are mostly 'bought' with bride price and generally harshly treated by their husbands' families.

...And Sarda Act or no Sarda Act, Rajasthan has never stopped marrying off tiny children at annual festivals. *The Times of India* of 25 April, 1961 reported 'ten thousand child marriages performed in the Jodhpur Division on the Akha Teej Day. About 200 of the crying baby brides and bridegrooms had to be carried to the marriage "*pandals*" by their parents.'

In the summer of 1976 sixty to seventy couples were married at this Rajasthani festival. The ages of the little brides and their bridegrooms ranged from two to twenty years.[42] The air was rent with cries of 'J*agte raho*!' (stay awake) as the little ones were carried around the sacred fire, asleep in their parents' arms. There will be two more ceremonies in the years to come before the young bride is finally led away to her husband's home, a symbolic rope tied to her veil.

Ralph Fitch, an English traveller, came across many instances of child marriage during his travels through sixteenth century India. He was told that since *sati* had become quite prevalent, many children were orphaned if their father happened to die when they were small. Child marriage in these cases acted as a safeguard for them.[43]

Often the new groom was very much older than his child wife. Among the elderly grooms of history, Humayun, the second of the great Mughal emperors of India has a prominent place, being thirty years old when he married Hamida Bano the fourteen year old girl destined to be the mother of Akbar the Great.[44] Marriages betwen old bridegrooms and young girls caught the Italian traveller Manucci's attention. He notes that 'ordinarily the marriage is between a little child and a grown man.'[45]

'A man aged thirty years shall marry a maiden of twelve who pleases him,' says Manu: 'or a man of twenty-four a girl eight years of age: if (the performance of) his duties would (otherwise) be impeded, (he must marry) sooner.'[46]

Today the groom in rural India is also as a rule considerably older than his wife.[47] We may infer that he has seen something of the world, and may also have received some rudimentary education. He finds his innocent bride interesting at first, later an irritant and then a positive incubus. His thoughts race with his ambitions and he plans on marrying again. The fact that she may produce only daughters may add to his annoyance and precipitate a second marriage. It will not matter to him that The Hindu Marriage Act of 1955 has made monogamy universal. His young wife meanwhile is subjected to every indignity. Her little world frowns on divorce and the word carries a stigma far greater than widowhood. So she continues a twilight existence, either living with her parents if they allow her, or working for her uncaring husband and her co-wife, denuded of all self-respect.

A Maiden for A Song

Maya's father is an agricultural labourer and lives in Uttar Pradesh with his three daughters and an ailing son. Whatever he earns goes almost entirely into keeping his son alive, the remainder being scraped up by the rest of the family. Ram Dhan is a religious man. He knows he is failing in his duty by his fifteen year old Maya. The neighbours are already commenting on her having come of age, but who will marry the girl without any dowry at all? Even if he sells the few rags and broken utensils they possess, it will not get her a groom. He looks sadly at his beautiful daughter as she brings him a glass of hot tea...

That evening a friend of a friend drops in. Maya is called to give her father his *huqqa* — hubble-bubble. She brings it in, her head covered, her baby brother balanced on her hip, then runs off to cook and clean...

The very next week her fate is sealed. She sits tear-stained by the marriage fire. By her side sits Buṛhaoo the village's lecherous fifty-year old widower. He rises to embrace Maya's grateful father. The old bridegroom's eyes linger over Maya's draped body. Who wants a dowry when a man can get a warm-blooded young beauty with no questions asked about himself?...

And who is there to point a finger at Ram Dhan?

With the emphasis on virginity and pre-puberty marriage laid so long ago, Ram Dhan cannot find it in himself to fight his caste and community's censure. He seriously believes that he has done a very good thing for his beloved child, and if there is a single nagging doubt anywhere in his mind, he will find, if he refers to *Yama* the seventh century A.D. law-giver, that what he has done deserves a pat on the back. 'If no suitable husband is available,' says Yama, 'it is the father's duty to marry his daughter to whomsoever he can find, even if he is unsuitable.'[48]

This is where Manu rises from the hoary pages of his *Smritis* to lend his blessings to that most acceptable of all Hindu marriages—the Brahma rite,[49] where a daughter is gifted in the ceremony of the *kanya daan*—the precious gift of a virgin.

There is little difference between the virgin, *kanya*, offered as a worthy gift, suitably accompanied by socially acceptable and tradition blest accessories at a marriage witnessed by the gods and the sacred fire, and the unspotted lamb tied to an ancient Jewish altar, or the one awaiting the Muslim *Kalimah* (literally the 'word'—the Muslim creed of faith) and the sacrificial knife today.

The sacrificial lamb purified by fire established a hot line between the suppliant and the Almighty who rewarded him with religious merit and often temporal blessings. The blameless *kanya* sacrificed at the altar of convention and married off before the all-purifying fire with symbols of earthly pomp and circumstance, is the necessary conductor through which social merit and prestige pass to her family. They will now revel in the reflected glory of the connection, but far too often at the expense of lifelong stinging condescension from the bridegroom's family.

In early Vedic times when gods and goddesses formed a very real part of every day living, the institution of *kanya daan*, where the bride was received by her future partner in the presence of the gods, was considered the best guarantee for her against the possibility of ill-treatment in her new home. 'I take thy hand for good fortune,' says the Hindu bridegroom, repeating the age-old marriage vow, 'that thou may'st attain old age with me thy husband. Bhaga. Aryaman, Savitri, Purandhi have given thee to be my household's mistress.'[50]

Today's husband is no longer afraid of heavenly retribution and the divine control implied in the sacred vow has lost its impact.

The child bride has a bleak future ahead of her.[51] If her marriage is consummated at all, her elderly husband is almost certain to die long before her. If she escapes a life of permanent widowhood, she is faced with a long reproductive period with many still births and complicated pregnancies. By the time she reaches her peak productive period, the girl wife's death rate shoots up.[52]

There is a definite connection between early marriage and death due to childbirth in the peak productive period. '208 per thousand deaths are due to child bearing and complicated pregnancy, i.e. one fifth of all deaths,' writes Seeta Sinclair.[53]

If the child bride manages to reach the age of thirty, she will have at least five children to feed and will be left with a body drained of energy and a mind that died before ever it could open and touch the world.

In 1948, a survey showed that the average age of widows was twenty years—their ages ranging from eight to fifty-four years. Of these only 16.5 per cent had had their marriages consummated, and only 14 per cent had lived with their husbands for a full year. The average married period was found to be only seven years.[54]

Since a widow is ill luck incarnate, the child widow has been doomed to a life of despair and more often than not *sati* came almost as a welcome relief. The immolation of a widow with her husband by burial or by fire was a pre-Vedic idea for which the Aryans[55] seem to have had no use, as there is no mention of the practice in Vedic literature between about 1500 and 400 B.C.[56] In fact, although the widow was expected to lie symbolically by the side of her husband's corpse on the pyre, she was exhorted to rise and lead a full and happy life:

'Rise, woman, come to the world of the living:
Come, the man by whose side thou liest is lifeless:
Be united with this man as his wife,
Who holds thy hand and seeks to be thy husband.'[57]

'Where are you *Asvins*[58] in the evening? Where at morn?
Where do you sojourn? and where do you dwell?
And who brings you into his presence as the widow
a second husband to her bed, or the bride the groom?'[59]

In this beautiful Vedic hymn written by a woman—Ghosha, the daughter or Kakshivat, the word for second husband is *devara* which also means husband's brother. The *Niyoga* marriage—with the dead husband's brother seems to have begun very early in the history of marriage all over the world, and in India it helped take the widow off her dead husband's pyre.

The ancient Greeks commenting on the Indian scene of the fourth century B.C. were convinced that the reason for *sati* was that the thought of such a horrible death would keep a wife extremely interested in her husband's longevity and clear her mind of any thoughts she might have entertained of poisoning him.[60]

Sati, when it did come back in the later Vedic period, was still an optional custom, mainly practised by the higher castes. If the young wife was terrified by the flames and changed her mind, she was free to return to her relatives and undergo a penance for having flagged in her purpose, or else she could give the price of a cow to a Brahmin.[61]

By about 700 A.D. however, the idea of *sati* had fired peoples' imagination and Harita says that a wife, by committing *sati*, would cleanse her husband of the deadliest sins and what is more, earn for both herself and her husband an assured seat in heaven for three and a half crore years.[62]

It was not easy to attain the signal honour of becoming a *sati*, and the faint-hearted child or mature widow was occasionally doped, or if she tried to escape, she was hit over the head with poles and pushed shrieking back into the flames.[63] Several ingenious method were devised to keep her resolve firm. In Gujarat and Northern Uttar Pradesh wooden huts were built over the dead man's bier and his wife chained to a pillar before the hut was set on fire. In the Deccan and in Western India deep pits were excavated in the centre of which the funeral pyre was lit, so that there was no escape from the furnace.[64]

When it was all over the relatives heaved a sigh of relief. Only they knew what a problem it would have been to have had to look after her all her life. They were glad it had all passed off so honourably. After all it was a great honour to be related to a *sati*. The many *sati* stones dotted all over Rajasthan depicting a woman's hand with the bangles of a happily married wife on it bear gruesome testimony to the high incidence of this custom. Soon, even mothers were burning themselves or having themselves buried alive with their dead children, or with articles representing them in the equally gruesome custom of *ma sati*.

Later on, it became a prestige issue with the Sikh community who prided themselves on being as much a martial race as the Rajputs. So much so that when Maharajah Ranjit Singh died on the 27th of July 1839, 'his four wives, all very handsome, burnt themselves with his body, as did five of his Kashmiri slave girls... Nine living beings... perished together without a shriek or a groan.'[65]

The vicious system has continued well into our time in spite of the Bengal Sati Regulation of 1829. Mrs. Indirabai Madhav Udgaonkar, sister of Dr. A.S. Altekar deciding to commit *sati*, immolated herself within twenty-four hours of her husband's death on 17 January 1946, as she considered it her sacred duty.[66]

As early as the seventh century A.D., Bana had openly criticised the custom of *sati*, dubbing it 'a custom followed by the foolish' and sent those who followed it 'to the hell reserved for those who are guilty of the sin of suicide.'[67] The sixteenth century emperor Akbar did his best to stop the custom and to restrict the prostitution that claimed young widows who could not face the flames. He built *Shaitanpura*—The Devil's abode, outside the city limits to house prostitutes. He attempted to protect the very young girls, by having the court screen all requests for virgins, and kept a check on anyone wanting to avail himself of the services of the women.[68] Aurangzeb's puritanical solution to the problem of prostitution some two hundred years later was far simpler—marry, or clear out of the realm.[69] In 1254, Louis IX of France had been plagued by the same problem. He banished all prostitutes from France, but found himself ultimately beaten by the oldest profession in the world. He was forced to allow them to practice 'under supervision.'[70]

As for *sati*, despite efforts to control it, only the Portuguese managed to suppress it in the areas under their control by the simplest expedient of arresting all relatives and bystanders. Although the British recorded five thousand one hundred cases of *sati* in Benares alone between 1815 and 1928, it was not classified as homicide until the next year—1829 by order of Lord William Bentinck.[71] 'No church for me today,' exclaimed William Carey, dedicated missionary and orientalist when he was called upon as official translator to the British Government to translate the ban order. 'A day's delay may cost the lives of many more widows.'[72] That very night the order was in circulation.

But despite everything, an orthodox society still continues to revere the ideal of the chaste wife—the *sati* who follows her husband in life and death. Even today an occasional small item tucked away in the daily newspapers screams for attention:

'Timely intervention by the police prevented Badami, a 60 year old woman of Raghunathgarh village in Sikar District, from committing "*sati.*" Badami had made known her intention to burn herself along with her husband, Jhuntha...'[73]

'A 45 year old woman committed "*sati*" on Saturday at Hathidath village, 100 km. from here. She is alleged to have jumped into the pyre of her husband, Mr. Hira Lal Chaudhary, in the presence of a large number of people of nearby villages. The Nimkathana police have arrested two villagers... Residents of Hathidath have decided to erect a memorial to the woman.'[74]

And so the adult bride of 1500 B.C has become a pawn. She has been robbed of all she possessed—her free will, her future and her life itself, all for someone else's benefit. Compulsion has firmly entrenched itself in the business of marriage, and fear of censure and the necessity for the bride to be 'pure' for an ideal *kanya daan* has so perverted the mind that there have even been instances of pregnant woman going through an entire wedding ceremony on behalf of their unborn embryos just in case they should turn out to be of the correct sexes. Such a ceremony was binding on the promised children.[75]

'Three cases of wedlock between the unborn were reported from the Marwar area on the Akha Teej Day last week. The interested parties have placed complete faith on astrologers' predictions about the sex of their forthcoming issues.'[76]

The whole issue ultimately boils down to merit earning—religious or social—at any cost. Nothing and no one is too precious to be sacrificed.

So marry her off—the earlier the better. If you offer a chaste *kanya* in marriage, your sacred duty will be accomplished. If the gift wrapping is good, she will be eminently more acceptable. Then you can encash your cheque in the Approval Bank. When you become a husband, guard your wife's purity so that she may give you unblemished offspring. Now zealously guard their purity so that their virtue may ensure your own religious and social security[77] in this life and for ever and ever, Amen.

'*Aloo le lo*! *Baingan le lo! Timatar le lo*!'[78]

The Rajasthani vegetable woman's raucous voice shrills through the air. Usually she comes with her eleven year old Rani. this time, as I help take the basket off her head, I find only nine year old Omvati and a tiny four year old clutching their mother's skirt.

'Where is Rani?' I ask.

'Married, *bibiji*. I've married them all off!' She bursts into a flood of tears. I stand awkwardly by, mouthing inanities, playing with the vegetables. Suddenly the horror of it strikes me. 'All? I look aghast at the little four year old. She nods wordlessly.

'Ten thousand rupees I took from the *sahukar*,[79] *bibiji*! I had to give their mother-in-law and sister-in-law clothes, brass utensils.. I had to give silver jewellery. I filled their laps with cash, *bibiji*! They are married to three brothers from our people, so it is much cheaper; but I have to borrow two thousand more when Rani leaves next month at her *gona*[80] for her new home. I'll have to give more clothes and jewellery then... my baby son died...' she adds with pathetic irrelevance. *Parmatma* only helps the rich, *bibiji*,' she says dully, holding up the scales. 'We poor people have to carry on living somehow.'

'But dowry is prohibited by law since 1961,' I say. 'You shouldn't give so much when you can't afford it.'

She wipes her nose in her voluminous veil. 'Then who will marry my poor daughters, *bibiji*? Am I to see them die virgins? My man fell from a tree and broke his neck two years ago. I am left paying through my nose for these poor stones around my neck. Here, take some chillies. They come free with the vegetables. *Kismat*[81] hounds our poor girls through life... *Parmatma* took away my son...

'*Aloo le lo! Timatar le lo!...*'

'*Bibiji*, I am an old man. Allah may call me any moment. I have an obligation to these grandchildren of mine. Am I to leave them to beg for food when I am no longer there to fill their mouths? Am I to die with the thought that my dead son's little pearls will have to walk around in the world of men with their faces uncovered, pleading for a morsel of food?'

He holds up his needle with gnarled fingers close up against his rheumy eyes. He can barely see the spit stiffened thread as he pokes at the needle's eye.

'He was my only son, *bibiji*. It was Allah's will. He left me these three flowers to tend. *Allah* is Great, *bibiji*! I shall somehow scrounge together enough money for a cycle, a wrist watch and a few utensils. These are their minimum demands for Farhat. Then, perhaps out of your bounty, you will bestow on me some of your old torn *saris* that I could turn into *ghararas*[82] for her. Then I shall only have to drag myself around working for just another two years, if the All Merciful gives me breath, for my Habiba and Sultana.' The old Muslim tailor dabs his eyes with the petticoat he is sewing and gives a racking cough.

'But *Baṛe mian*.'[83] I venture, absolutely shaken, 'Farhat is only 10, and the others you told me, are 6 and 5!'

Muhammad Qassim looks wordlessly up at the sky, his unthreaded needle in his eloquently upraised hand. 'His will,' he murmurs, 'His will!'

NOTES AND REFERENCES

1. The *Jats* are a race claiming descent from the princely Rajputs.
2. Flagstaff house.
3. Mother dear.
4. Durga; Devi : Forms of Parvati, consort of the god Shiva.

5. Vern L. and Bonnie Bullough, *The Subordinate Sex*, 1974, University of Illinois Press, Chicago, p. 235. Also A.S. Altekar, The Position of Women in Hindu Civilization, Delhi, Motilal Banarsidass, 1962, p. 33: Baudhāyana Sūmarta Sutra, V. 9.
   Subhru, the saintly daughter of the sage Kuni, having remained unmarried all her life, died. She found the gates of heaven closed to her as her body had not been sanctified by the sacrament of marriage. She, therefore, returned to earth, persuaded the sage Sringavat to marry her and spent a night with him. It was only through this marriage that she finally gained admission into paradise.
6. *Zuza*: (Plural). In the time of Sennacherib, the *zuzu* was an Assyrian coin equal to half a *shekel*. It later came into the Christian era as a very small coin.
7. Will Durant, The Story of Civilization, Simon and Schuster, New York: 1950, *The Age of Faith*, Ch. XVI, pp. 380-81.
8. A hundred thousand.
9. The Syrian Christians of Kerala claim conversion to Christianity at the hands of Jesus Christ's disciple Thomas Didymus, traditionally believed to have established seven churches in these parts in the first century A.D.
10. James Tod, *Annals and Antiquities of Rajasthan*, Routledge and Kegan Paul Ltd, reprint 1950, Ch. XXXV: 'Festivals and Customs of Mewar', p. 505.
11. The Bhats of Rajasthan 'have now taken to puppeteering and doing odd jobs. Some even catch stray dogs and sell them'. Report in *The Times of India*, 6 July 1978.
12. Lalita Panigrahi, *British Social Policy and Female Infanticide in India*, Munshi Ram Manoharlal, New Delhi, 1972, p. 9, quoting J. Ludlow, Political Agent, Jodhpur writing to Colonel J. Sutherland, Agent to the Governor General for States Rajputana, 29 June 1842, 294, India Political Consultations, 28 December 1842.
13. One of the Chiefs of the clans of Mewar.
14. James Tod, *op. cit.*, 'Festivals and Customs of Mewar', p. 506.
15. J. Talboys Wheeler, 'Greek and Roman India', in *Ancient India*, Sushil Gupta (India) Ltd., Calcutta, 1953, Ch. X, p. 108. quoting Aristobulus in Strabo, India, sect. 54, 62.
16. R.C. Majumdar, H.C. Raychaudhuri and Kalikinkar Datta, *An Advanced History of India*, Macmillan, London, 1946, p. 822.
17. Muhammad Qasim Firishta: a sixteenth century historian.
18. Tod, *op. cit.*, Ch. XXIV: 'Festivals and Customs of Mewar;' p. 505, f.n. (i).
19. '*Kuṛi mar*': girl or daughter killer. From Lalita Panigrahi, *op. cit.*, 1972, p. 26; quoting a communication from P. Melville, Secretary to Chief Commissioner, to J.P. Grant, Officiating Secretary to Government of India, 8 July 1853: Board's Collections 1853-54: Vol. 2566. No. 151171.

20. H.B. Edwards, Deputy Commissioner, Jullunder Doab, to D.F. McLeod, Commissioner and Superintendent Trans Sutlej States, 30 June 1852: Selections from the Public Correspondence of the Administration for the Affairs of the Punjab, 1853. Vol. I: Nos. I-IV; as it appears in Lalita Panigrahi *op. cit.*, 1972 p. 25.
21. From the Quran: XVI: 60, 61, as quoted by Thomas Patrick Hughes, *A Dictionary of Islam*, London, W.H. Allen and Co, 1885, (Women) I, p. 677.
22. Ibid.
23. Edward Westermarck, *The History of Human Marriage*, Macmillan and Company Ltd, London, 1921, reprint 1971; Johnson Reprint Corporation, New York, London, Vol. III, p. 166: (Curr: *Recollections of Squatting in Victoria*, p. 249).
24. *China Report*, Vol. XI, Nos. 5 and 6, September-December 1975. Emancipation and Enslavement of Women in China: Sources of Inequality: Morality and Law: Confucian and Communist Variations, Krishna Prakash Gupta, p. 53, note 19.
25. An Interview with Han Suyin by Claudia Dreyfus, 'Third World Woman', *UNICEF News*, July 1976.
26. Literally, 'command', here it means, 'I am at your service.'
27. Marvin Harris, *Cows, Pigs, Wars and Witches* (The Riddles of Culture), Fontana/Collins, Glasgow, 1974, 'The Savage Male', p. 75. The Yanomami are an American Indian tribe who live on the border of Brazil.
28. The doctors of The All India Institute of Medical Sciences have since decided to restrict the chromosomal analysis of the amniotic fluid of the uterus to identifying sex-linked, genetic and other disorders with a view to their prevention.
29. J.E. Parks, *Text Book of Preventive Medicine*, 4th edn, Jubbulpur, Bhanot, 1974, quoted by S. Sinclair, *Vital Statistics*, 1975.
30. Vital Statistics Division, Office of the Registrar General of India, Infant Mortality in India: Sample Registration Survey Analytical Series No. 1: 1971. (Sinclair: 1975)
31.

Infant Mortality: 1968-69					
Year	Sex	0-7 days	7-28 days	29-6 months	7-12 months
1968	Male	46.0	33.4	35.7	20.9
	Female	40.4	27.9	42.5	26.9
1969	Male	44.4	29.4	38.1	20.4
	Female	41.0	34.9	47.7	24.5

Vital Statistics Division, Office of the Registrar General of India: Infant Mortality by Age: Sex Composition in India: S.R.S., Analytical Series No.4, 1972.

32. **Table 1: Death Rates 1993**

Estimated age-specific death rate by sex, 1993 (abridged)

(per 1,000 live births)

Age-group	*Total*			*Rural*			*Urban*		
	Person	*Male*	*Female*	*Person*	*Male*	*Female*	*Person*	*Male*	*Female*
0-4	23.7	22.7	24.8	26.6	25.3	27.9	13.4	13.4	13.3
5-9	2.2	2.0	2.5	2.8	2.6	3.1	0.5	0.4	0.5
10-14	1.4	1.2	1.6	1.5	1.3	1.7	1.2	1.1	1.3
15-19	1.9	1.6	2.2	2.2	1.9	2.6	1.1	1.0	1.2
20-24	2.6	2.1	3.0	2.9	2.4	3.4	1.7	1.4	2.1
25-29	2.7	2.3	3.0	3.0	2.6	3.5	1.8	1.6	2.1

INDIA (excluding Kashmir & Jammu)

Table 2: Sex Differentials in mortality 1990-93

Mortality Indicators	*Total*			*Rural*			*Urban*		
	Male	*Female*	*M-F*	*Male*	*Female*	*M-F*	*Male*	*Female*	*M-F*
Death rate	9.80	9.60	0.20	10.60	10.70	0.10	7.00	6.20	0.80
Infant mortality rate	77.75	78.94	-1.19	84.03	86.07	2.04	50.95	49.05	1.90
Neo-natal mortality rate	52.19	47.88	4.31	56.46	52.63	3.83	33.95	27.94	6.01
Post neo-natal mortality rate	25.22	30.75	5.53	27.16	33.04	5.88	16.96	21.13	4.17
Perinatal mortality rate	37.62	33.74	3.88	40.39	36.95	3.44	25.79	20.25	5.54
Still birth rate	12.16	9.98	2.18	12.49	10.19	2.29	10.75	9.08	1.67

INDIA (excluding Kashmir & Jammu)

Definitions:

Infant Mortality Rate : All deaths occurring in the first year of life per 1,000 live births.

Neo-natal : birth to one month.

Post Neo-natal : 4 weeks to less than 1 year of life.

Peri-natal : 28 weeks of pregnancy to 7 days after birth.

Still birth : born dead.

33.

Table 1.

World Life Expectancy at Birth 1951-81 (Projected): Selected					
1969	USA	Male	67.0	Female	74.0
1951-60	Japan	Male	65.3	Female	70.2
1961	Sri Lanka	Male	61.9	Female	61.4
1951-60	Thailand	Male	53.6	Female	58.7
1966-71	India	Male	48.2	Female	46.0
1976-81	India	Male	53.2	Female	51.8

Definition

Expectation of Life at birth: The average number of years a new born is likely to live.

References quoted in Sinclair: Vital Statistics, in Newer Horizons in Tropical Paediatrics, ed. Suraj Gupte, Jaypee Brothers, 1977.

Table 2.

World Life Expectancy at Birth: 1995 (Selected)	
Pakistan	59
Nepal	54
Bangla Desh	53
India	61
Myanmar	58
China	71
Sri Lanka	72
United States	76
Australia	77
United Kingdom	76
Japan	79

The State of the World's children 1995, UNICEF: Oxfored University Press, 1995, Table 5.

34. As Seeta, wife of Rama, Vishnu's seventh incarnation; as Rukmini, wife of Krishna, Vishnu's eighth incarnation.
35. *Upanayana* ceremony note 12, Ch. 2.
36. A.S. Altekar, The Position of Women in Hindu Civilisation, Motilal Banarsi Dass, Delhi, 1962, p. 56 quoting *Kathasaritsagara,* 34, 229.
37. An obsession with chastity was responsible for the introduction of the chastity belt into Western Europe. An occasional story of the medieval period spoke of wives locked into these iron girdles languishing in discomfort until their jealous husbands released them.
38. *Towards Equality*, Report of the Committee on the Status of Women in India, New Delhi, 1974. Government of India, Ministry of Education and Social Welfare, Department of Social Welfare; p. 111.
39. The Child Marriage Restraint (Amendment) Bill of 1978 has been published as Act No. 2 of 1978 in The Gazette of India, 14 March 1978. It also provides that police officers are competent to investigate offences under the Act, but not to arrest without a warrant or an order of a Magistrate. It has come into force with effect from 1 October 1978.
40. Government of India, Ministry of Education and Social Welfare, Department of Social Welfare. *Towards Equality, op. cit.*, 1974.
41. *The Times of India*, 9 November 1977, Editorial: 'Marriage Age'.
42. *Youth Times*, June 24—7 July, 1976, article by Jai Gaur.
43. 'In many places where wee passed', he writes, he saw marriages 'of boyes of eight and ten yeares, and girles of five or six yeares old. They both so ride upon one horse very trimly decked...they marry their children so yoong, because it is an order that when a man dieth, the woman must be burned with him: so that if the father die, yet they may have a father in lawe to helpe to bring up the children which bee married: and also that they will not leave their sonnes without wives, nor their daughters without husbands.'
    Richard Hakluyt, *Principal Navigations* London, 1599, vol. II quoted by R.C. Prasad in *Early English Travellers in India*, Delhi, Banarsidass, 1965, p. 57.
44. Ila Mukerjee, *Social Status of North Indian Women* (1526-1707), Agra, 1972, p. 19.
45. Niccolao Manucci, *Storia Do Mogor* (or Mogul India: 1653-1708), translated by William Irvine, John Murray, London, 1907. Edited by The Royal Asiatic Society, The Indian Text Series—1, Volume III, p. 155.
46. *Manusmriti*: IX, 94; F. Max Mueller, The Sacred Books of the East, (translation: G. Buchler) vol. xxv, The Laws of Manu, Varanasi, Motilal Banarsi Dass, 1964, p. 344.
47. In a strange reversal of roles, one occasionally comes across wives several years older than their husbands.

'In Mao Tse Tung's own province', says Han Suyin in an interview with Claudia Dreyfus (*op. cit.),* 'it was customary for women to be much older than their husbands. This was because a young girl of eight or ten was sent to work as a servant for a few years in the household of the boy she was going to marry, who was usually much younger than she.'

In 1929-30 the KMT banned among other things, the 'taking of a daughter-in-law in anticipation'. (K.P. Gupta, *op. cit.*, (c) Change in the Pre-Modern Period, p. 59: The KMT Period Revaluation and Reform.

Rural India today has many such cases. Not much imagination is required to appreciate the plight of a growing girl blossoming into womanhood, saddled with a child husband who grows too slowly, and very much at the mercy of her father-in-law and brothers-in-law.

Yet another aberration was prevalent in Punjab at the turn of the century—a custom called '*chakri*.' Here the mother of a prospective bridegroom served the eldest woman of the household where she hoped to place her son as an acceptable *ghar jawai* (a-son-in-law who sets up house with his parents-in-law.) If the arrangement did not find favour with the girl's family, her services were unceremoniously terminated and the proposed deal called off. *Chakri* was particularly in vogue among the *Khatris* of Lahore. (Parkash Singh Jammu 1976, quoting Harkishan Kaul in his thesis—The Problem of Dowry in Punjab, 1976. Department of Social Anthropology, Punjabi University, Patiala.)

48. *Yama*, c.600 A.D., *Smṛitichandrikā: Samskārakānda*: p. 216 quoted by A.S. Altekar, The Position of Women in Hindu Civilization, Motilal Banarsi Dass, Delhi, 1962, p. 56.

49. *Manusmriti*: III: 27, Max Mueller, *op. cit.,* 1964 p. 80. *Kanyadaan*: gift of a virgin girl. *Kanya:* virgin/young girl; *daan*: offering.

50. Marriage vow taken by the Hindu Bridegroom, from The Rig Veda X: 85: verse 36; as quoted by Abinash Chandra Bose in *Hymns From The Vedas*, Calcutta, Asia Publishing House, 1966, p. 135.

The deities mentioned here are Vedic: *Bhaga* is the bestower of wealth. He presides over marriages. *Aryaman* is chief of the spirits of ancestors, *Savitr/Savitri* (masculine form as distinguished from Savitri the devoted wife of Satyavan), is the personification of divine influence, and is the universal vivifying power of the sun. *Purandhi/ Puramdhi* is the mother of 'the golden handed' Hiranyahasta.

51. *Option of Puberty Among Muslims*: If a minor girl who has attained puberty wants to repudiate her marriage before the act of consummation, she is at liberty to do so and the marriage will be declared invalid.

Before 1939: traditional Muslim law as practised in India held that she could not do so if she had been given in marriage by her father or her paternal grandfather.

With the passing of The Dissolution of Muslim Marriages Act in 1939: a young Muslim wife received the right to exercise her 'Option of Puberty' and have her marriage declared invalid whoever may have been responsible for her marriage. This is however, subject among other factors, to the non-consummation of her marriage.

The courts in India have applied this law very liberally, benefitting many girls. Even the non-consummation clause has been waived in certain cases. (*Towards Equality*: *op. cit.*, 1974: IV: Divorce: Muslim Law: 4.98: p. 120.) With Muslim girls often marrying at a tender age, the element of force in consummation is a very real problem. Legislation for the removal of the non-consummation clause in Section 273 of The Dissolution of Muslim Marriages Act of 1939 would go a long way towards helping these girls.

52. **Table 1.**

Deaths Per Thousand Per Year				**India**
Age Group	*1968*		*1969*	
	Male	*Female*	*Male*	*Female*
15-19 years:	1.99	3.34	2.09	4.22
20-24 years:	2.65	5.09	3.88	5.54
25-29 years:	3.19	6.92	3.73	5.50
30-34 years:	3.76	5.08	4.07	6.35

Vital Statistics Division: Office of The Registrar General of India: Age Specific Death Rate by Sex—Rural—1968 and 1969: Sample Registration Survey Analytical Series No. 4: 1972: (Deaths per one thousand in particular age groups for one year).

Table 2.

Expectation of Life at Birth* by sex and residence, India (excluding Jammu and Kashmir) - abridged.					
Residence	*Period*	*Mid-year*	*Male*	*Female*	*Person*
Total	1970-75	1973	50.5	49.0	49.7
Rural	1970-75	1973	48.9	47.1	48.0
Urban	1970-75	1973	58.8	59.2	58.9
Total	1988-92	1990	58.6	59.0	58.7
Rural	1988-92	1990	57.2	57.4	57.4
Urban	1988-92	1990	62.8	65.5	64.1

Occasional paper no. 4 of 1995. SRS Based Abridged Life Tables 1988-92 Statement 1, Registrar General, India, Ministry of Home Affairs, New Delhi.

* The average number of years a person is likely to live per one thousand live births.

I reproduce below all India figures concerning marriage and widowhood in the age group 10 to 29 years, from The 1971 Census of India: Part II-C (II): Social and Cultural Tables: Office of The Registrar General and Census Commissioner of India: Series I:

Table 3

Marriage and Widowhood in India: 1971 Census			
Age Group	Total Female Population	Married	Widowed
10-14 years	32,281,631	3,722,773 (11.53%)	17,521 (0.05%)
15-19 years	22,246,454	12,325,666 (55.41%)	74,525 (0.33%)
20-24 years	21,527,935	19,122,792 (88.83%)	189,331 (0.88%)
25-29 years	20,481,079	19,447,045 (94.95%)	397,033 (1.94%)

Office of the Registrar General and Census Commissioner of India, Series 1.

Table 4.

Widows, Widowers and Divorced in India : 1981 Census						
Age Group Years	*Widows & Widowers*		*Divorced & Separated*		*Total Population*	
	Male	*Female*	*Male*	*Female*	*Male*	*Female*
10-14	9,768	12,304	2,713	12,027	45,265,292	40,646,075
15-29	31,399	61,880	25,486	130,077	34,026,988	30,111,819
20-24	109,179	191,541	91,912	235,936	29,000,075	28,337,783
24-29	204,385	368,622	123,788	223,620	25,754,744	24,969,871
10-29	354,731	634,347	243,899	601,660	134,047,099	124,065,548

The Registrar General, India, Ministry of Home Affairs, New Delhi : Social and Cultural Tables, 1981 Census: Vital Statistics Division:

Although marriages of children below 10 years of age are still prevalent, figures concerning this do not appear in official documents. It is therefore difficult to obtain reliable documentation on child widowhood in this age group.

53. Dr. Seeta Sinclair, Vital Statistics India 1976-77; writing in *Newer Horizons in Tropical Pediatrics*, p. 218, edited by Suraj Gupte, Delhi: Jaypee Brothers, 1977.
54. Vern. L. Bullough, *The Subordinate Sex*, A History of Attitudes Toward Women, Urbana, Chicago, 1974, p. 243.
55. The *Aryans*: an immigrant, race which came into India, displacing the original inhabitants, the *Dasyus*. The *Aryans* are mentioned by the poets of the *Rig Veda* as 'men of their own stock and religion' (J. Dowson, A Classicial Dictionary of Hindu Mythology..; London, Routledge & Kegan Paul, 1968, p. 24.)
56. Altekar *op. cit.*, (1962), p. 118. The concept of the wife accompanying her husband after death was fairly widely known in ancient times. It existed in New Guinea, The New Hebrides, The Solomon Islands and Fiji. (Will Durant, *op. cit., Our Oriental Heritage* (1954), p. 34, quoting Havelock Ellis, and others.
57. The Funeral Hymn: *Rishi Samkusuka*, son of Yama, *Rig Veda*: X. 18: verse 8: in Abinash Chandra Bose, *Hymns from the Vedas* 1966, *op. cit.*, p. 345.
58. Twin Vedic deities who bring the earlest light at dawn.
59. Ghosha's Prayer to *Asvins*: *Rishi Ghosha*, the daughter of *Kakshivat*: *Rig Veda*, X. 40, quoted by Abinash Chandra Bose, *op. cit.*, 1966, p. 143.
60. J. Talboys Wheeler (quoting Strabo, India, Sect. 30) in *Ancient India*, Chapter X—Greek and Roman India, Gupta Publishers, 1953, p. 112, f. n.
61. P.N. Bose, *A History of Hindu Civilisation During British Rule*, II, New Delhi: Asian Publishing Services, first Indian reprint New Delhi, 1975, first published in 1894, pp. 67-68.

    'The widow must *voluntarily* ascend and enter the flames to destroy her existence allowing her at the same time, an opportunity of retracting her resolution, should her courage fail from the alarming sight or effect of the flames, and of returning to her relatives, performing a penance for abandoning the sacrifice, or bestowing the value of a cow on a Brahman.' Ram Mohan Roy's "English Works": Calcutta, 1885, Vol. I, p. 356.
62. Thirty-five million. Altekar, *op. cit.*, 1962, p. 126.
63. 'They are soon choked by the smoke, while the men surrounding the pyre raise a great noise with drums and gongs and loud shouts, while the burners skillfully force them to lie down by thrusting at them with poles.' Manucci, *Storia Do Mogor: op.cit.* Vol. III, 1907, p. 156.
64. Altekar, *op. cit.*, 1962, p. 134.
65. W.G. Osborne, *Ranjit Singh*, Calcutta, Sushil Gupta (India) Ltd., second edition, 1952, extract of a letter, p. 80.
66. Altekar, *op. cit.*, 1962, p. 137.

67. *Ibid.*, pp. 124-25: (*Kadambari*, Purvardha: p. 308).
68. Abd-ul-Qadir bin Maluk Shah (Al Badaoni), *Muntakhab-ut-Tawarikh-i-Akbari*, Vol. II, translated from the original Persian by W.H. Lowe, Calcutta, printed by J.W. Thomas, 1884.
'These (the prostitutes) he made to live outside the city, and called the place Shaitanpurah. And he appointed a keeper and a deputy, and a secretary... And a number of well-known prostitutes he called and enquired who had seduced them. And after learning their names, several important Amirs were severely reprimanded and punished or imprisoned for a considerable time.'
69. Niccolao Manucci, *Storia Do Mogor: 1653-1708*, *op. cit.*, Vol. II, 1907. 'Aurangzeb... ordered that they' (dancing women) 'must marry or clear out of the realm. This was the cause that the palaces and great enclosures where they dwelt went to ruin little by little; for some of them married and others went away, or, at least, concealed themselves.'
70. Will Durant, *op. cit.*, *The Age of Faith*, 1950, Ch. XXX, p. 823.
71. Bullough, *op. cit.*, p. 242.
72. J.N. Ogilvie, *The Apostles of India,* London, Hodder and Stoughton, MCMXV, p. 321.
73. *The Indian Express*, 17 October 1977. This incident occurred in Sikar District, Central Rajasthan.
74. *The Times of India,* 19 January, 1978. This incident also occurred in Sikar District, Central Rajasthan.
75. Bullough, *op. cit.*, 1974, pp. 235-36.
76. *The Times of India,* 25 April, 1961.
77. *Manusmriti:* IX: 7., Max Mueller, *op. cit.*, 1964, p. 328: 'He who carefully guards his wife, preserves (the purity of) his offspring, virtuous conduct, his family, and his (means of acquiring) merit.'
78. Come buy my vegetables! I have potato, brinjal and tomato to sell!
79. Money lender.
80. When the young bride finally leaves her parents' home for her husband's.
81. fate.
82. Ankle length divided skirt.
83. Respected gentleman.

4

Catch Me! I'm Worth It!

In the drama of life, the catch-me-if you-can relationship is perhaps one of the most basic.

When the present day Western bride is swept over the threshold of her shiny new apartment in her he-man's arms, does something somewhere in the back of her mind ring a little bell? Does she feel at all akin to that other woman, aeons ago, freshly captured, overwhelmed perhaps by the same emotion as her modern sister, as she was tossed starry-eyed into the cave that would be her new home?

The comparison may be odious to modern Mrs Newlywed, but she cannot escape the hand-me-downs of history which have an odd way of popping up in the most unexpected places. Capturing a mate is one such phenomenon.

When the manly Hiawatha called, the lovely Minehaha followed where he led.[1] From time immemorial, woman has formed part of the spoils of war; but consummate actress that she is, she leads her conqueror by the nose exciting him by alternately showing her teeth and crying for help.

The struggling Spartan bride of 1,000 B.C. being carried off by her future master behaved in much the same way as the Himachal bride of today is expected to behave during the staged capture that precedes a Dab-Dab or 'Darosh' wedding.[2] Although the marriages of both women, thousands of years apart, were almost always arranged for them by their parents, custom has always demanded that they put up a good show of resistance as becomes honourable women. In fact parents have been known to plead with prospective grooms whose weddings have already been fixed, to stage a capture so that their daughters may be given a chance to prove their mettle and to bring honour to their fathers' households by their spirited resistance.[3]

This kind of mock battle for the bride doubtless comes down in history from the days when brides were the trophies of war and were pointed out as such, bringing honour to the husbands who had won them. A woman was at this time a highly prized and useful member of her father's household and he was loth to lose her services. Often therefore, very real resistance was offered by the girl and her relations.

Sometimes the future bridegroom who has been promised the belle of the village finds that several other families are interested in her. His nerves already jangled by the waiting period, he decides to capture her before his rivals step in to stake their claim, and presents the village with a *fait accompli*.[4] This done, the young couple is married by the girl's approving parents in a 'regular' ceremony.

Among the Bhotias of Kumaon, although the women are more liberated than many and choose their own husbands, a pretence of capture adds spice to the proceedings. The groom's party approaches the *Rangbang Kuri*[5] at night. They creep in stealthily and carry her off 'by force.' There is a quickie wedding and messengers of peace proceed to her father's house armed with a token sum of money which is readily accepted and all is good fellowship again.[6]

Stinging nettles greet the Lapcha and Bhutia bridegrooms' party when they come for their wedding. The Sikkimese bride is not to be won easily. The women of her house drive a hard bargain. Usually the stinging nettle thrashing is averted by a '*malak*'—a peace offering of forty rupees; the women are pacified and the marriage is allowed to proceed.[7]

Writing in 1961, Iyer and Ratnam record that cases of capture marriages have been reported among the Nagas, the Malayalis of North Arcot and among the Gonds of Bihar. The Kharias and the Birhors ambush the desired bride, and if they manage to mark the struggling woman's forehead with vermilion, captor and captive are thenceforth considered man and wife. In fact marriage by capture is still carried on in one form or another among at least seven of the tribal communities of Bihar.[8]

Marriage by elopement is quite frequent among the Khawas of the Kameng district of Arunachal Pradesh. The father of the girl searches for his runaway daughter, and if he happens to catch her abductor, the boy is expected to pay a heavy penalty usually in cattle or in useful household goods. After family honour has been satisfied, everyone feasts off pig and rice or millet beer at the groom's house. At most North Eastern tribal festivals, boys and girls pair off and elope in the uninhibited atmosphere of the fair. They return later to be accepted into tribal society as husband and wife.

Capture is still an accepted form of marriage in many parts of the tribal world. In fact among the Yanomano Indians[9] the very words used to describe marriage mean 'dragging something away.[10]

> This compares interestingly with the early Vedic term for marriage: '*udvaha*' meaning 'carrying away.' The *Manusmriti* records the existence of this form of marriage in ancient India, calling it the *Rakshasa* rite, but strongly condemns it.[11]

Working or paying for the bride have existed side by side with marriage by capture. The age of chivalry shifted the emphasis from force to proving worthy of a bride, and brawn was henceforth clothed in gallantry. 'None but the brave' deserved the fair the world over, and many were the knights who won fair maidens through jousts and brave display. Chivalry bound East and West together in quest of romance, beauty and fairplay.

Young Lochinvar galloped through English literature to rescue the fair Ellen from the 'laggard in love and... dastard in war' she was being forced to marry. He spirited her off from under the noses of the gathered nobles and her family, on to his saddle before ever they could collect their scattered wits and organise a chase. 'They'll have fleet steeds that follow,' laughed young Lochinvar.[12]

Halfway aroung the globe the valiant Prithvi Raj Chauhan, scion of the proudest race of Rajput princes, rode into the palace of his sworn enemy Rajah Jai Chand of Kannauj. He whisked the beautiful Sanyukta right out of her *swayamvara*[13] cermony and on to his horse. They were away before the enraged father and discomfitted rivals realised what had happened.

Today's sad white mare that carries the North Indian bridegroom to his wedding seems but a faint shadow of Prithvi Raj's spirited steed, but she enshrines in herself the whole concept of bride capture. Here the wedding steed is always a mare, and as far as possible a pure white one. It is the spotless unablemished *ghori* (mare) decked in all her finery like a virgin bride that carries the conquering male who symbolically subdues the female represented by herself. Around them gyrating dancers try to inject some of their virility into the brocade clad figure of the groom. There are still some parts of the country where the bridegroom carries a sword. Not so long ago wedding processions in Kerala were led by men with drawn swords and shields.

Major Hastings describes a bridegroom's procession in nineteenth century Peshawar on its way to the bride's home 'discharging guns and blunderbusses.'[14]

The Statesman of 3 March 1978 reported the death of a twenty-one year old factory worker who was killed by a stray bullet fired in the air by a marriage party in Badarpur. This firing was described as 'customary' on such an occasion.[15]

In the marriage songs of Gujarat and Uttar Pradesh, insults are showered on the 'marauder' who comes to carry away the daughter of the house. Similarly, the wailing of the Punjabi bride as she leaves her parents' home is the cry of a well-loved daughter whose future is shrouded in uncertainty. 'They are carrying me away, dearest father!' cries Heer as she leaves after her marriage, in Punjab's most famous love story—Heer Ranjha.

While the daughter of the house was working full time at home tending the sheep, cows or camels, drawing water from the well twenty times a day, spinning yarn and weaving the family's clothes, selling the field's produce in the market, cooking the meals and looking after the little ones, she was an economic asset sought after eagerly by men in need of just such an all round administrator. Her price at this stage of the marriage game was literally 'far above rubies.'

Purely in economic terms, the loss of such a valuable helper would have serious repercussions on her parents' household, and it would be only fit and proper for them to be adequately compensated.

So it was hard labour for the bridegroom to be...

Seven Years for Her

When Jacob, son of Isaac the Jewish patriarch, saw the lovely Rachel at the well, he decided on having her for himself. He promised her father Laban, that he would be willing to work seven years for her. When the seven years were up, the wily Laban subsituted Rachel's older sister Leah for her at the wedding. Jacob nothing daunted, worked another seven years, and finally won Rachel after fourteen years of hard labour.[16] If only he had had access to the *Manusmriti*, he would have found he could have claimed both women for the price of one:

> 'If, after one damsel has been shown, another be given to the bridegroom, he may marry them both for the same price; that Manu ordained.'[17]

'It was not uncommon in nineteenth century Bengal for a pretty girl to be displayed during the preliminaries and then to be replaced by a plain bride.'[18] However, plain or beautiful, she is an asset worth striving for, and work for her still continues among the tribals of India.

From the hard reality of labour for a working partner, a glamourised version of the theme entered the world's myths and fairy tales. Princes bent their backs under impossible tasks set them by their prospective fathers-in-law for the pleasure of winning not a working wife, but an adornment for their homes. For the love of Shirin, Farhad the celebrated Persian lover made a canal of milk flow where none had ever existed, and the 'Pig Sty Prince,' a knight of King Arthur's Round Table, uprooted a hill, levelled it, planted and harvested the wheat and baked bread from the grain—all in one day, to be served at his wedding to the lovely Olwen.

The prospective bridegroom's troubles were legion. Among many tribal societies he had to prove he was man enough to stand up to physical torture which was sometimes carried to an unbearable degree. Westermarck writing in 1921[19] mentions the case of the Macusis of Guiana among whom the young hopeful had to allow himself to be sewn up in a hammock full of fire ants. If he survived this ordeal, he had to prove himself capable of maintaining his future wife by clearing enough space in the forest single-handed, for cultivation for the family's needs.

Among the Yukaghir tribals of the frozen North[20] a young man who aspires to the coveted position of son-in-law, has to undergo severe endurance tests. He stays awake in his father-in-law's home at night while the family snores. He is fed the scrappiest of meals, and in this state, he has to prove himself a mighty hunter before he can plan on raising a family.

The *Lamsena* boy from the Gond areas of Jabalpur district in India enters his father-in-law's household to work for him as Jacob did for Laban: 'Tonha Dewar and his wife lived in Madangarh. They had one daughter. As the girl grew to maturity her parents said, "Let us sell our daughter in marriage to someone and then we will have a little money." The Dewar went out... to Mahakasur Deo with his only son, whose name was Lamsena. Mahakasur Deo said, "Do not sell your daughter, *samdhi*. You may keep my son for twelve years in your house. Then I need not pay you anything and your daughter and my son will live with you... and the two of them will feed you and look after you." This is how the custom of keeping a Lamsena boy in the house began. In those days he had to work for twelve years, but now it is only for three.'[21]

Writing about eighteenth century Burma, Sangermo an Italian priest wrote:

'In this country... the man... goes to the house of his bride's parents, and must take with him a dower according to the resources of his family... If (the girl's parents) and their daughter consent... the bridegroom... goes to the house of the father-in-law where he continues to reside for three years.'[22] The Burmese bridegroom also brought with him the wherewithal for the setting up of their house. If he was unhappy over the arrangement however, he was at liberty after a stipulated period, to take his wife away from the fold and live apart from her family. The Burmese marriage system today is extremely liberal, being in the nature of a contract with as little ceremony as possible.

Working for the bride was a general custom in nineteenth century tribal Zambia. Young Narwimba was won by a suitor who worked in her father's field for three years, gave her parents gifts after his work period was over, and also built them a house—it was only then that he could claim her as his bride.[23]

Today's Khawa bridegroom in the Kameng District of Arunachal in India also works in his father-in-law's household for a stipulated period. During this time, the couple is allowed to live together in anticipation of the *Maphori* wedding they will celebrate when the waiting time is over. The girl's parents help the couple set themselves up when the boy's working period is completed, arranging a house for them and giving them a few modest necessities of life: a cow, a pig a small iron hearth stand, a hen and a few clothes.[24]

For the tribal youth working himself to the bone for his bride the magic days of helpful *dijnns* and fairies are over. Since canals of milk and golden castles cannot be made to materialise in a day without supernatural aid, our sympathies are entirely with the young man of unimpressive physique who realises that it is simpler to scrape together enough money or get some cattle to impress his father-in-law, than to slave for a bride until he is long past the age when he can appreciate her charms.

Somewhere, at such a point of time, the system of bride price payment must have come into its own and begun to take precedence over working for a bride, although both customs still co-exist in tribal areas. The people of the Himalayan belt have long been known to accept the price of a captured bride to 'save their noses,' even if the capture was staged with the knowledge or even at the instance of the bride's kinsfolk. Often enough a bottle of the local brew has salved a troubled conscience in the tribal world, while cash anywhere from twenty to five hundred rupees helps ease it further.[25] The Melanesians occasionally stole their wives from their parental homes and legalised the transaction with a negotiated settlement.[26]

The practice of paying for the bride was so common among South Indian Brahmins of the fifteenth century Padaividu Kingdom that King Deva Raya II of Vijayanagar (1422-49) was compelled to enact a law which forced a father to give his daughter to her bridegroom without receiving any fee from him. He anticipated our anti-dowry legislation by several hundred years, and went a step further. He made all money transactions connected with marriage legal offences and had the giver and the receiver excommunicated.[27]

Among unusual bride price tales, one of the strangest must surely be that of the famous Old Testament musician king David, whose prospective father-in-law King Saul decided to use David's enthusiasm for the discomfiture of his enemies—the Philistines. He sent word to David that if he was anxious to marry his daughter Michal, he should produce one hundred Philistine foreskins as bride price. David obliged by sending Saul double the number. The delectable Michal, needless to say, was won.[28]

The battle against extortion of bride price is still on. A Pravda report of February 1977 quotes the case of a Turkmenian mother-in-law who was given a three year jail sentence for exacting 'thousands of rubles and expensive gifts in payment for her daughter's hand in marriage.'[29]

Prices of brides have shot up so much in the recent past that the tribals of Kerala have begun to rebel. A girl who could once have been acquired for a mere Rs 1.50, could not in 1976 be purchased for anything under Rs 5.00, with prices rocketing as high as three hundred rupees. The men have decided they simply cannot afford this kind of luxury. They plan to carry on where Jacob left off, working for their brides for a specified period, after which they will have won their women fairly.[30]

The Hos of Chhota Nagpur have a tale to tell about how woman first became a saleable commodity:

Any member of the tribe who so far forgot himself as to yawn, found himself in trouble. Yawning being considered the mark of a *were-tiger,* the poor man was immediately pounced upon by his erstwhile friends... and transported to the nearest tiger's lair. There he had plenty of time to ruminate over his social lapse until the tiger returned to his cave for dinner. Once a Munda maiden[31] was caught yawning. She was immediately taken to where all good yawners went and abandoned by her tribe. A herdsman watching the proceedings decided she might make him a good wife. He descended on the tiger, killed him and carried off his dinner. Living together as man and wife, they were soon discovered by the irate tribals. The herdsman had to surrender a he-buffalo and three cows before the social taboo was lifted from him and his hard won bride. This princely sum paid for a 'useless girl' set the pattern among the Hos for bride price payment.[32]

Manu acknowledged the existence of bride price transac-tions, but made no secret of his aversion to the practice. He described it as *blamable* of which only 'blamable (offspring) would be born.'[33] 'Nor, indeed, have we heard,' he said, 'even in former creations, of such (a thing as) the covert sale of a daughter for a fixed price, called nuptial fee.'[34]

But whether the great law-giver approved of it or not, the *Asura* form of marriage[35] had come to stay, and exists to this day in India mainly among tribals and in the lowest income group.

Saunder's Settlement Report written in the late nineteenth century mentions the prevalence of bride price marriages in Punjab at that time:

'Marriages are seldom effected without payment of money;' he writes; 'and daughters are popularly supposed to fetch from Rs. 100/- to Rs. 500/-...'[36]

Small wonder then that there were so many bachelors among the poorer agricultural labourers of Punjab. Wherever there was lack of confidence in the bridegroom's party, the amount to be paid for the bride was mentioned in full assembly and given in two installments: one at the betrothal, and the other when the marriage had been consummated. Among the upper *echelon* however, the practice was regarded with distaste as it was considered a thinly disguised sale of a daughter.

In the remoter and more inaccessible areas of the Philippines the prospective bridegroom still combines labour with *bigay-kaya*—bride price paid in gold or land. He was to serve the girl's family for months, sometimes years: chopping wood, fetching water and generally doing the house-hold chores. Earlier, conversation between him and his lady love was frowned on. 'Only their eyes met occasionally to exchange mute messages of love!'[37] It was only when her parents were satisfied with their assessment of their future son-in-law, that they consented to the marriage; but first the *bigay-kaya* had to be handed over. Next the eager lover had to give his lady's mother money for her 'nocturnal efforts in rearing the girl to womanhood.'[38] Even the girl's wet-nurse got money for breast feeding the baby bride-to-be. For having fed her in infancy, the groom would then have to reimburse her parents to their satisfaction. Presents were also generally given to her other relatives. Even then it was not quite over. After the wedding, she refused to ascend the stairs in her new home unless the father-in-law gave her a present. Having ascended, she refused to sit down, and was given another gift. Having sat down she would not eat until cajoled into doing so with another present—all this before the actual marriage ceremony. Very few of these ceremonies appear today in the marriages of the Filipinos who generally choose their own partners.[39]

In modern Laos, the birth of a girl brings great good fortune as the minimum price for marriage continues to be 5 *khuns*—beautiful ornamental slabs of silver, each the approximate equivalent of fifty dollars. Even the poorest father will have such wealth tucked away under a tree on his land or in some other secret place, waiting to be pulled out for a son's wedding. These pieces of silver—it is only the extremely rich who can afford gold—may be bought for weddings. A family of many sons will find itself in great straits during the marriage season. Dowry coming with the bride has not crept into Laotian thinking yet. Enlightened families often waive the *Khun* payment, and ask nothing of their sons-in-law to be.[40]

'Old ways die hard in China,' writes *Asiaweek* in an article on marriages in communist China.[41] The magazine article quotes a recent letter in the Chekiang Daily from a frustrated suitor—a member of a commune whose future in-laws demanded US$ 7.2 from him for every year of his fiancée's age as 'engagement money.' Other demands included gold ornaments for her grandmother, six urns of wine and eight expensive suits for her father and mother. 'My betrothal alone cost me 500 yuan' ($300), he wrote, 'but that was only the first rake-off. The second came upon my request for marriage: they asked for high class furniture and banqueting costing a full 1,000 yuan. Finally, as I could not meet their demands, the girl backed out of the engagement.'

Stories pour in from the mainland, the article goes on, about extortionate demands for, 'interview money' for the man's first meeting with the woman's family, 'face money' to create a favourable impression; 'birth-pang money' for the prospective mother's future travail; and 'sedan chair' and 'door' packets to bring the girl home... That is why,' concludes the article, 'a peasant couple usually begins saving up for their son's nuptials as soon as he is born.'[42]

All the one hundred and sixteen tribal groups of India covered by the 1961 Census Report give their daughters in marriage for bride price in cash, kind, or in both.[43] The African tribal pays for his bride in cattle, goats, shell money, agricultural implements, cash, or in anything considered valuable by his society. His Indian counterpart does exactly the same, exchanging pigs, rice, local wine, poultry, bead or coin jewellery, and sometimes cash as well, for a wife. In the snow-capped hills of Kinnaur in Himachal Pradesh, a deed witnessing the handing over the land to the bride's father, together with a house or a room, is signed and confirmed. The list of articles handed over includes an enumeration of utensils, all weighed and valued, to be returned in case of divorce.[44] The returnability of bride price varies from culture to culture.

The richer Idu Mishmis of the Lohit District of Arunachal Pradesh pay in *mithuns.* for their brides.[45] Each *mithun* is a highly prized animal and costs between two and four thousand rupees. A man's standing goes up in direct proportion to the number of *mithuns* he owns, and, it naturally follows, to the number of wives he has been able to purchase with them. In fact there is a charming tale which has been in circulation since the mid-fifties, concerning a certain tribal chieftain of Arunachal Pradesh who offered Jawaharlal Nehru several of his precious horde of *mithuns* for the hand of his daughter Indira in marriage.[46]

The institution of bride price as a marriage by contract helped raise the woman from being considered part of the spoils of war to being appreciated as a partner worth paying for. The amount paid gave the bride a certain status in her new home. In areas where it is still practised, it works as a check on her new master's roving eye. If he plans on divorce, he is in trouble in more ways than one. First, he will have to find more wealth to pay for a new bride. Although his ex-father-in-law or the new husband will compensate him at the time of divorce or remarriage, the amount will never be enough, with escalating prices, to be buy a new bride. Meanwhile, between wives he faces a complete collapse of his household economy. So he usually takes the line of least resistance. Drowned happily, as he often is in rice, millet beer or any other local brew, he lets things slide until the suggestion for another wife comes from the lady of the house herself. She realizes soon enough that another wife will be a much needed help, may provide some company for her and of course also help bear some necessary children for the family; besides she can always be hired out as a wet-nurse.[47] However, the tribal husband finds himself at the losing end again in the deal, as it is usually the first wife who sets herself up as a one woman selection committee to decide which woman shall enter her home.

The gifts received by the bride's family at such weddings range the world over from articles of use in tribal societies like shell money, jewellery, household goods, household animals and the local brew—to goods which fit in with a modern setting—cash, modern jewellery and luxury articles for the young couples' home. Indonesian wedding gifts called '*sesarahan*,' fall mainly in this second category. Here the groom brings his contribution to the bride's home five days before the wedding.

Historically, these gifts have appeared in various forms in most parts of the world: sometimes as 'morning gifts' given by English bridegrooms to their brides in the Middle Ages[48] or as the modern '*vari*' given by a North Indian groom and his family to the bride. Every day Indian newspapers carry advertisements in every language saying: '*saris* for *daj*' (dowry) 'and *vari*.'

The ancient established practice in the case of bride price marriages from Africa to South East Asia has been for the girl's father to return all or most of these gifts together with the bride price, to go with his daughter as a special gift of love to her new home. In India this grew into her *streedhana* — women's wealth, known in the South as *streedhanam*, which is her very own to use as she pleases.

In the last twenty or thirty years, we in India have managed to convert this custom into yet another headache for the bride's harassed parents. These gifts are now *expected* to be returned to the groom's kin in the form of jewellery, cash, fruit, clothes, utensils, etc. which will accompany the bride *as part of her dowry* which usually goes straight into the hands of her parents-in-law. There have been reported cases where even the keys of the jewellery and clothes cupboards are kept by the husband and his mother. The new wife is grudgingly doled out a *sari* at a time to wear until it is worn to a shred, while the rest of her trousseau is earmarked for her sister-in-law's wedding.[49]

The tribal however, is still happy when his wife produces a wealth-earning daughter. The good price she brings gives her a claim to maintenance by her parents in case of desertion by her husband. She is also much freer than her dowry laden sister in the matter of moving on to a better or more desirable husband, since her wedding ceremony is a contract and not a morally binding sacrament.

The 'cattle bringing maidens' of Homeric Greece of 1300-1100

B.C. mentioned in the *Iliad*[50] brought prosperity in the form of oxen into their fathers' homes with their marriages, but their provident fathers saw to it that their daughters took substantial dowries also with them to their new homes. These were useful girls—they attended to all the carding, spinning, weaving, grinding of the grain and the rearing of the children, very much like their eonomically prized sisters in tribal India today, with one notable exception: the Greek men took over the kitchen.[51]

The African bride who brings cattle wealth to her father's house as she leaves for her husband's home, does not add to her father's wealth thereby. She only brings in live capital that must remain untouched but well looked after; as it is in the nature of a circulating marriage bank. It will go on in toto with her brother's marriage, to his bride's household as bride price. It passes clean over the young peoples' heads, moving from kin to kin at each marriage, and is used only for buying more marriages. It becomes a kind of equaliser as the wealth that comes in with a daughter's marriage goes out with the son's. So that although the actual wealth in the family's control is not increased, the family does not lose on a wedding deal.[52] On the other hand, it may sometimes help a warm blooded father to enter the marriage market himself:

> 'Wolu, Madume's only wife bore him four daughters—a most annoying thing, despite the dowries (i.e. bridewealth) he knew he would collect when they got married. But who would bear his name when he died? The thought of his elder brother's sons inheriting his houses and lands filled him with dismay. But there was enough time to marry another wife and the problem did not bother him unduly. Moreover, the daughter's marriages would provide him with the money for another wife.'[53]

So every father from the Gusii tribe in Central Africa keeps track of the latest bride price rates to keep himself from losing on the transaction. When the cattle roll in with his daughter's marriages, his nerves are constantly on edge wondering whether their numbers will tally with the rate in force when his sons are old enough to marry; or as Madume planned, for his own marriage. Hence his demands go up whenever he hears of other fathers demanding more for their daughters. This increases the general rate all round, making it increasingly difficult for a poor man to afford a marriage.[54]

With the advance of civilisation, the African tribal is finding it difficult to keep his circulating marriage bank stocked. Earlier, depleted herds from this bank-on-the-hoof could have been easily replenished by convenient raids on unwary neighbours, as used to be the case with the Zulus of South Africa.[55] It is not so simple now. The 'bank' has to be set aside even more strictly and given much greater care. As a result more and more marriage business is understandably transacted in money.

The debt implicit in the exchange of wealth at marriage makes the bride's brother her debtor, since the wealth that came into the house because of her marriage made his marriage possible. This unique debt carries through to the next generation. Among the Lobedu tribe of South Africa, a sister can lay claim to her brother's daughter for her son in settlement.[56] At the wedding of their children, the brother is released from any further obligation to his sister's family.[57]

Scarlett Epstein who conducted a study in two little villages of Karnataka describes an occasion in 1955-56 at a time when the wedding display was still the concern of the bridegroom's father.[58] The son of a 'middle' farmer was firmly encased in an expensive, obviously imported woollen jacket and a pair of closed shoes for his wedding. This made his father one-up on his social rivals, but in the sticky heat of little Dalena and Wangala it must have been a heavy price to pay for a skin used to free air, and feet conditioned to open sandals. Honour and respect can only be won the hard way.

...And what of the women? How do they react to being bought and sold? Instances from around the world throughout history reveal that by and large they lap it all up. In this inverted form of womens' lib, depending on the price paid for her, the bride gets a certain edge over her in-laws in bargaining power. However, try as she may to shut her eyes, she knows she has become a barterable commodity—howsoever valuable.

But feminine nature being what it is, she manages to extract immense satisfaction from the high price she has fetched, and looks down her pretty nose at the misguided creature who gives her all to the male chauvinist pig for love and love alone.

NOTES AND REFERENCES

1. Henry Wadsworth Longfellow, 'The Song of Hiawatha' a poem on the life and times of the early American Indians:
   'Comes a youth with flaunting feathers
   ...Beckons to the fairest maiden.
   And she follows where he leads her;
   Leaving all things for the stranger.'
2. M.D. Mamgain, *Kinnaur Gazetteer* (Himachal Pradesh), Ambala, 1971, p. 100.
3. T.C. Das, *The Bhumijas of Seraikella*, p. 12; as quoted in *The Adivasis*, Government of India, Publications Division, 1955, p. 113.
4. M.D. Mamgain, *op. cit.*, p. 100.
5. *Rangbang Kuri*: A community hostel for unmarried tribal girls.
6. Prakash Krishen, "Bhotias of Kumaon," article in *The Illustrated Weekly of India*, 2 June 1974.
7. 'A Sikkimese Bride Comes Home,' article in *The Times of India*, 6 May 1971 by Veronica Pereira Kamath.
8. L.A. Krishna Iyer and L.K. Bala Ratnam, Anthropology in India, Bharatiya Vidya Bhawan, Bombay, 1961, p. 136.
9. Marvin Harris, *Cows, Pigs, Wars and Witches,* Glasgow: Fontana/Collins, 1974, p. 69.
10. *Ibid.*
11. *Manusmriti*. III, 33, F. Max Mueller, (ed.) The Sacred Books of the East, translated: G. Buehler, Vol. xxv, The Laws of Manu, Varanasi, Motilal Banarsi Das, 1964, p. 81.
12. Sir Walter Scott, 'Lochinvar.'
13. *Swayamvara:* A ceremony in which a Hindu bride chose her husband-to-be from among the gathered aspirants to her hand, by garlanding him with the *jai mala*, the victory garland.
    Hindu brides still garland their bridegrooms with the traditional *jai mala*, but the choice is not always theirs.
14. Quoted by C.L. Tupper, *Punjab Customary Law*, Vol. II, 1881, p. 92.
15. Killed by a Bullet out of the Blue.' *The Statesman*, 3 March 1978.
16. The Bible, Genesis, Ch. 29.
17. *Manusmriti*, VIII, 204, Max Mueller, *op. cit.*, 1964, p. 204.
18. '...As Handsome Does,' editorial, Statesman, Delhi edition, 30 September 1976.
19. Westermarck, *The History of Human Marriage*, Macmillan & Co. Ltd., London, reprint, 1971, Vol. I, p. 51, quoting Im Thurn, *Among the Indians of Guiana*, London, 1883, p. 221.
20. *Ibid.*, Vol. II, p. 373, quoting Jochelson, *Yukaghir*, p. 93.
21. Verrier Elwin, *Myths of Middle India*, Madras, Oxford University Press, 1949, pp. 476-77.

22. Sangermo quoted in Jack Goody and S.J. Tambiah, *Bridewealth and Dowry* London, New York, Cambridge University Press, 1973, p. 150.
23. Meli's Story in "Women in Peril" by Marcia Wright, *African Social Research Journal*, No. 20, December 1975.
24. Resarun, Vol. 2, No. 3, July 1976, p. 14.
25. M.D. Mamgain, *op. cit.*, p. 100. This is a common custom among many tribals. Here the reference is to the *Dam Tangshis* form of marriage.
26. Will Durant, *Our Oriental Heritage,* The Story of Civilization, Simon and Schuster, New York, Vol. I, p. 42 quoting W.G. Sumner and A.G. Keller, *Science of Society*, New Haven (iii), 1928.
27. C.P. Ramaswamy Aiyar, *The Cultural Heritage of India*, Vol. II, The Ramakrishna Mission Institute of Culture, Calcutta, (reprint: 1969), p. 631.
28. The Bible, 1 Samuel, 18: 25 to 27.
29. Pravda Report in *The International Herald Tribune*, 8 February 1977.
30. 'Bachelor Brawn Meets Tribal Challenge', report in *The Patriot*, 15 July 1976.
31. Tribals living in Bihar.
32. Verrier Elwin, Myths of Middle India, Oxford University Press, Madras, 1949, Ch. XXII: 'Custom and Taboo', pp. 469-70.
33. *Manusmriti,* III, 42, Max Mueller, *op. cit.,* p. 83.
34. Ibid., IX: 100, p. 345.
35. *Asura* originally meant 'spiritual.' It later degenerated into 'enemy of the gods.' (*Manusmriti*: III, 31, Max Mueller, *op. cit*., p. 81)
36. Saunder, Settlement Report quoted by C.L. Tupper, *op. cit.*, p. 194.
37. A. Agoncillo and Oscar. M. Alfonso, *A Short History of the Filipino People*, University of the Philippines, 1961, pp. 34-35.
38. *Ibid.*
39. *Ibid.*
40. Keo Kaufman.
41. *Asiaweek*, 1 September 1978: Life and Mood: Marriage: The Wages of Wife-Taking.
42. *Ibid.* An interesting contrast is provided in Ch. 3, little Mariamma's birth.
43. *Towards Equality*, Report of the Committee on the Status of Women, New Delhi, Government of India, December 1974, p. 69, f.n. 25.
44. M.D. Mamgain, *op. cit.*, p. 98.
45. Tapan Kumar Barua, *The Idu Mishmis*, NEFA: Shillong, 1960, p. 51.
46. The *mithun* is an animal resembling the bison.

    This little snippet may well be apocryphal, since the number of mithuns offered grows with every telling of the story! It has been finally traced to the chieftain who now denies it. There are however, many officers who have been posted at Ziro who need little prompting to relate this tidbit.

47. *Sirmur Gazetteer*, 1969, p. 114.
48. Will Durant, *op. cit., The Age of Faith*, 1950: Ch. XXX: III, Marriage, p. 823.
49. A friend told me that the clothes that went with her in her trousseau were made to fit her bridegroom's sister whose wedding was next in the family.
50. Homer, *The Iliad*, XVIII: 593 as quoted by Will Durant *op. cit., The Life of Greece*, 1939, Ch. III, p. 51.
51. *Ibid.*
52. Jack Goody, *op. cit.*, (1973) p. 5.
53. *Ibid.* The Givers and Receivers, pp. 7-8, quoting Elechi Amadi's novel *The Concubine.*
54. *Ibid.*, p. 5: quoting Philip Mayer, Gusii Bridewealth law and custom: Rhodes—Livingstone Papers No. 18: 1950: 19.
55. *Ibid.*, p. 5: quoting E.J. Kridge, *Property, Cross-Cousin Marriage and the Family Cycle Among the Lobedu*, 1964, p. 160.
56. *Ibid.*, p. 7.
57. The '*tara*'—an equivalent of bride price, customarily given in the villages of Karnataka until the advent of dowry set up a spirit of competition among the farmers. It is still given in token form as part of the wedding ceremony. Scarlett Epstein, *South India, Yesterday, Today and Tomorrow,* Macmillan, 1973, p. 194.
58. *Ibid.*

5

Today He Is Good–Tomorrow...?

In the tribal world contractual marriages based on bride price have a socially levelling influence. Cattle and goods flow in an opposite direction to brides. Daughters are profitable workers and bread earners. They also attract working sons-in-law. To beget more daughters, there is no bar on marrying many wives. More so since wives themselves suggest another alliance. Any individualism and any separatist tendencies therefore that might have threatened to creep into the family are submerged by the influx of wives, the resultant hordes of children jointly owned and the many heirs of both sexes. Tribal economy based on this kind of working partnership cannot tolerate elitism or leanings to aristocracy.

A bride price oriented society's mainstay is interdependence. The tribe is more important than the family. Kinsfolk come to the immediate aid of a family or a single member in distress. For instance, in places where cattle and not land form the chief ingredient of a man's wealth, an epidemic or a freak turn in the weather may make a rich man a pauper overnight. This is when he finds the bonds of kinship a great source of strength.

Every silver lining however, turned inside out is a thunder cloud, and the practice of bride price is no exception. The good goes with the bad, and in some cases the bad overrides the good in the system.

From its inception bride price has given lecherous old grooms society's sanction to bring young brides to their beds provided they can pay enough. The bride is conscious that her value is only in her being a commodity of barter and exchange. She is married off earlier and earlier as the quicker she marries, the sooner and earlier bride-wealth flows into her father's coffers. For the opposite reason a son is married as late as possible, to keep the wealth in the family.

Unless there are daughters to attract an equal amount or more back into the paternal fold, the wealth that goes out with a son will have gone forever.

What Price Self-Respect?

A woman's price varies, depending on her looks or on her utility. Among the people of the submontane tracts of the Himalayas, the more backward areas of Uttar Pradesh and Bihar and among the tribals of Madhya Pradesh, one comes across a strange twist to the custom of bride price. *Reet* literally means custom. This is the money—the value of clothes and ornaments plus other wedding expenses given to the husband of a divorced woman by her next husband-to-be. It is never given at the marriage of a virgin. At a first marriage, payment anywhere between one hundred to two thousand rupees or more, depending on her charms, is made to the girl's father by her bridegroom.[1]

In the Sirmur District of Himachal Pradesh, *reet* carries a negative connotation, as it is not a regular recognised form of marriage. Parmar describes it as a kind of divorce.[2]

In these areas a woman may be cruelly treated or otherwise find life with her husband intolerable, but she may not divorce him until her next husband has managed to pay him his *reet*. She may go back to her father's house however. He welcomes her return as she will attract suitors who will work in the house for either her hand in marriage, or for the privilege of being allowed to live in hope.[3]

Among other tribals, the custom of repayment of bride price when the woman leaves her husband is a recognised practice, but nowhere has it been so perverted into a continuous exploitation of women as in these parts. Her father and husband have full authority to sell and re-sell her indefinitely. Quite often she may have to leave her husbands one by one against her will. In these successive transactions everyone profits except the woman.

One look at the recorded customary laws of the various districts of Punjab prevalent at the turn of the century will show how widespread the practice was:

> The custom of selling wives is on the increase among all castes especially among the *Khatris*.[4] If it was not for fear of the courts...the girl's people would often keep the money paid at the

> betrothal, and then sell the girl elsewhere... The people are becoming more prone to invoke the dangerous aid of the law courts to save themselves from the risk of losing money.[5]

During the regime of the princes, some states levied a 15 per cent tax on the *reet* changing hands at every wedding. A woman who was married into every single family in the village of Thanga in Sirmur in succession, was alone responsible for a sum of three thousand, three hundred and thirty-three rupees being paid into the State treasury by her various husbands as tax on the *reet* they paid for her; which of course means they were in debt to the same tune for their marriages.[6]

If a woman is pregnant at the time her marriage is dissolved, she goes from the frying pan into the fire. Not only is she to undergo several future sales of her body, but even the child in her womb is not to be hers. It goes to the husband she is leaving along with the other children already born. Even if her husband waives his claim to the unborn, a value is set on the embryo and the amount added to the *reet* payment.[7] This makes the next husband think twice before he takes the plunge that will land him in such heavy debt.

Among the African Sonjo tribals, the husband, when abandoned by his wife, also claims repayment of the amount he paid for her from his successor. This amount like the *reet*, has to be paid in full before the second marriage can be held valid.[8]

Reet's easy come, easy go attitude to marriage, plus the fact that there is no stigma attached to divorce, produces an atmosphere most conducive to broken homes, since the binding links are so fragile. Often the man suffers by the system as well. The woman being the kingpin around which the entire economy of his household revolves, can ruin him overnight by leaving him suddenly, plunging him into a debt that will cling to him and his family for generations.

Meanwhile the woman flits from husband to husband either of her own volition or what is far more usual, being sold and re-sold until she is literally squeezed dry and her market value plummets to zero. Recent research conducted at The Lal Bahadur Shastri National Academy of Administration demonstrates how this practice still continues.[9]

In Jaunsar-Bawar and the adjoining regions of North West Uttar Pradesh, this bride price-gone-wrong is called *chhoot*.[10] Trade in women is a roaring business here. The journal of the Administrative

Academy at Mussoorie cites the case of a *sarpanch*—village headman, of Kuan Village in the Purola Block on the Damtha-Naugaon Road. The village headman had at the time of the publication of the report (1975), sold and re-sold Paano, a low caste girl 'into prostitution on four separate occasions. Each time he collects the bride price from the man to whom he sells the girl. The whole transaction is called a marriage in each case.'[11]

'At Thaddiyar in the Dehra Dun district, the local forest officials have settled a few poor Harijan families on forest land. The daughters of these families are used for prostitution by the department in this region...'[12]

Phullo is a Kolta girl. Her people are among the lowest of the low, beaten in misery only by the Doms. Living in filth and subjected to humiliations of all sorts by high caste Brahmins and Rajputs who have the whole area in their grip, they manage to survive in the blessed belief that they are descended from the great Pandavas of the Mahabharata. To marry Phullo, Suppa has had to borrow two thousand rupees at an interest of 35 per cent from Kunwar Singh, the Rajput for whom he works twelve, sometimes fourteen, hours a day. He is working off the interest on a loan of three hundred rupees his grandfather had taken from Kunwar Singh's family.

From the moment thirteen-year old Phullo walked into Suppa's life she has not known a single day's rest. She is expecting her first child now but still does all the work in the little hut where she lives with Suppa and his three brothers as their collective wife. She also fetches and carries for the landlord and works on his fields.

The baby arrives. she is a sickly girl and the local quack expects money. No matter how hard they all work, there is never enough to repay the Rajput *Thakur* — chief. The interest keeps mounting and the debt seems endless. The young father swallows what little self respect he has left, and borrows more and more for the newborn: for medicines, food for the ever empty cooking pot, and above all for the religious ceremonies attendant on the cycle of birth, marriage and death in his little circle.

At the fair, Phullo with her baby whining at her breast, watches Suppa and his brothers, their tatters covered with hides of goats and dogs, beings forced to leap about for the entertainment of their landlord and his high caste friends.[13] Suppa tries to do his best to please his master. He is overwhelmed at the interest Kunwar Singh begins to show in him. Kunwar Singh calls him aside and talks to him in a very amiable manner. Suppa is almost in tears with gratitude. The landlord is the embodiment of sweet reasonableness. He sees Suppa is at his lowest ebb, and makes a suggestion.

'Why should you have any problem?' he says. 'I am here to help you. Your wife is good looking. I have contacts in the big city. Let her earn you your liberty. What have your married her for? Let her serve you!'

Sleeping naked under one coverlet that night with his brothers and his wife, Suppa turns the idea over in his mind. The more he thinks about it, the better he likes it. What's wrong with her earning money in this way? Don't we share her here? It's only a matter of her going to some more men, and then we shall have her back, and the money as well. That debt at least will be paid. What a wonderful man the Thakur is. He has shown so much understanding.

So young hill bred Phullo finds herself installed in a Delhi brothel. If they are lucky, her looks will fetch three thousand rupees, out of which two thousand may go to the husband,[14] and the remainder will be split between Kunwar Singh and the agent. Kunwar Singh also of course, gets the two thousand, and Suppa realises that his complete debt to the landlord will never be paid in his lifetime. However, things seem temporarily a bit easier, and Phullo is given a new name in the brothel. She is now Champa Rani. This will make it more difficult for any case registered in her home town against her abduction to follow her down here. Phullo settles down to her life in the brothel as Champa Rani. She has to please every customer. She may have to oblige as many as twenty to thirty men a day. She barely gets time off for food, and goes to sleep in the crowded dormitory around 1 a.m. The earliest callers are at her door by 6 a.m. The customer pays a minimum of ten rupees to the brothel owner, out of which Phullo receives one rupee. From these meagre earnings she is expected to pay for room rent, electricity, laundry and sundry bribes which might help make her hard lot a little easier to bear.[15] Often by the time she has worked enough to earn her liberty, she has nothing but the clothes on her back in which to go home again...

Budh Singh, a resourceful Rajput, is a professional bridegroom. Old Kualoo has spent a lifetime in his family's service to repay a three hundred rupee debt he had incurred to pay for his eldest daughter's marriage. Budh Singh, who has plans for Kualloo's youngest daughter, offers to free the old man from serfdom in exchange for his daughter's hand in marriage.[16] Kualoo, overwhelmed by the honour done to his family, readily agrees. Budh Singh then approaches two other Kolta or Bajgi,[17] families, and 'marries' another two wives, offering the poor low caste parents a tidy one thousand five hundred rupees for their daughters. After dispensing his favours among his new wives, the bridegroom leaves with his catch for the brothels of Meerut, Saharanpur or Delhi. He sells them at a profit and returns home a prosperous man. Meanwhile, the girls grow old sending their earnings to their lord and master. When they are no longer attractive to the city men, Budh Singh will settle them in the village from where they will continue to provide for his sons until they can earn no more.[18]

Often the brothel owners use these girls as agents to entice other disgruntled girls to their houses in the big city. These women return home hung about with flashy fake jewellery, riddled with syphilis and gonorrhoea, their nails gleaming with cheap nail polish. They paint life in the city in glowing colours and help keep up a steady flow of fresh recruits to the brothels of North India.[19]

The most significant part of the story is that having lived at the lowest level of poverty in subhuman conditions for so long, one scrappy meal a day comes before any metaphysical questions of morality. There is also the startling fact that this trade in women has been given a boost not only by the village *patwari*[20] who commands more respect than the local deity, but also by educated priests, school teachers and local petty officials.

Chhoot increases with the number of divorces a woman has survived. A fifty year old woman may fetch as much as four thousand rupees or more, while a ten year old child would cost very little. [21] Since the little wife would not be able to put in very much work, it would be economical for her husband to buy another older wife as well. In these areas the strange phenomena of polygamy and polyandry exist side by side. The rich can afford more wives, and the poor can only share one wife among many brothers.

I was told by a local official that when he asked the husband of a woman shot through and through with venereal disease why he did not get her treated, he was told that the treatment would cost too much. He could buy himself two wives for that much money. The ailing woman turned towards the official from her corner in the room. 'I am only a mule,' she said fatalistically. 'I was bought for fiften hundred rupees. I can't complain.'

For the economic rehabilitation of freed bonded labour in these areas, the Uttar Pradesh Government earmarked a sum of twenty-four lakh rupees for 1976-77, and a future sum of twenty-six lakhs for 1977-78.[22]

The greater part of this vast amount of money has gone into maintaining the top heavy establishment created for the purpose. The office is in an unrealistically elegant part of town. Salaries of officials and all the paraphernalia of bureaucracy allow little gain to trickle through to the men and women for whom this money is intended. Red tape ties the rest into neat little inaccessible bundles.

The machinery oils itself and gleams on red letter occasions to distribute some animals among the freed bondmen under the approving gaze of a visiting VIP. There is, however, a general awakening in the area, and young Koltas are being educated and taught how to deal with problems which affect their lives. Under the Suppression of Immoral Traffic in Women and Girls Act of 1956, only an officer of the rank of Deputy Superintendent of Police is empowered to search houses or conduct raids. In Jaunsar-Bawar there is no regular police. The Chief Revenue Officer is the Chief of Police, and therefore naturally, there is no Deputy Superintendent of Police. However, to make the recovery of abducted girls easier, the magistrate has been given powers to issue search warrants to fathers or relatives of missing girls, who then look for their women in the brothels accompanied by police.

But no amount of police patrolling will do the trick, says a battered old inmate of a brothel. 'Buy freedom for our men', she says. 'Give them land and only land. It is this land, these green fields which will contain their girls. Nothing else can.'[23] But although the land she pleads for is now coming their way, it is often uncultivated and on very high atitudes. It needs tremendous effort and money to make it cultivable enough to maintain a family. With hope of promised help receding, thoughts of borrowing from the *thakur* recur, and square one is always standing by, waiting to be re-occupied.[24]

In a small out of the way village in Sangrur District lives Amrit Kaur. Her people are Jat Sikhs.[25] They have very small landholdings and eke out a hand to mouth existence tilling the land and harvesting its meagre crop. Amrit has just got married to a kinsman. On the outskirts of the village lives Asa Singh whose father could not find him a girl from his own clan, and so he has had to buy 'an outsider' for a wife. Amrit knows it is taboo to mention their names among her people.

Amrit's bridegroom is poor, but he is Seventh Class Fail and manages his father's land better than any of his four brothers. His father has scraped up enough money to enthuse Amrit's father with his proposal of marriage between Amrit and Harmik. Amrit is one of the few women in Sangrur District whose ratio to the men in the area is 839 to 1,000 (1971 Census). She is therefore much sought after.

Ever since her marriage to Harmik, Amrit has become tight-lipped about certain things. Used as she has always been to working for an entire family of men, she has discovered that although she is ritually married to Harmik who is the eldest of the brothers, she is expected to allow his four brothers to share her favours. Even before her marriage her friends had told her that this was the done thing, but she hadn't quite visualised herself in such a situation. However, she is a fatalist and has resigned herself to life with her five men. She washes their clothes, cooks their food and calls them *Devar* or *Jeth* — brother-in-law, which is an affectionate way of giving a compliment.

Amrit realises that the other villagers know what's going on in the family, and that they look down on them for it; but also understands the pressures that have driven her father-in-law into the situation. She realises that he just does not have the kind of money that will buy a wife for each son. She feels she is helping the family in her own way, and as a worker she knows there will be few who can compete with her.

Amrit, however, is not all sweetness and light. Having been hurled into a difficult situation, she wants to make the most of it. She and Harmik know very well that for all the love and affection they show his brothers, all their property will eventually go to Harmik's children.

Amrit's sons are growing into fine men. During the past years she has seen many changes come into their society. Money is coming in a bit easier these days, and the agriculturist's lot is better. Most fathers are now able to give their sons a wife each, and she has hopes of a better life for her children.

While Harmik Singh's brothers have had to make do within the family itself, the African second and third brothers usually leave home to seek their fortune in town. This results in a large influx of poor tribals into urban areas. Also, once the bride price has been paid and the bride installed in the house, many African husbands from rural areas leave for the cities in search of work. 'From Cape Town to Tunis millions of women have experienced what it means to be father, mother, husband, wife even though they are not widows. The drift to urban areas and mines leaves women without the protection and assistance of their husbands.'[26] They see their husbands two or three times a year. With little or no money coming in, they learn to produce food and money to feed themselves and the children gifted to them by their visiting husbands. These are the market mammies of Africa, who, like their Indian counterparts, seek no divorce as orthodox society the world over shuns a divorcée but may sometimes sympathise with a widow. So the women take on the unwieldy load of responsibility uncomplainingly.

In the midst of all this gloom however, things are happening... unspectacularly, slowly. Perhaps the patches of blue in the sky are small ones, but they are there, hopefully to stay. Let us look at one little patch no larger than a hand, very close to home.

Shera is one of the four hundred and seventeen villages that make up the polyandrous tract of Jaunsar-Bawar. The villagers remember 10 January 1974 very clearly as Murder Day. Shri Puri who had been trying to stop trafficking in their women, had been carried into their village, dead—killed by those who made money on the villagers' women.[27]

It is 4 November 1976.[28] There is a strange new excitement in the air. Almost a thousand workmen, freed at last from a lifetime of bondage and over thirty ex-prostitutes have trekked into little Shera, their beddings and food on their heads. Something new is beginning. Centuries-old traditional customs are examined and decisions taken to convert the old order in what bids fair to being one of the most unusual assemblies ever witnessed in these parts.

Chhoot is the first casualty. The age-old practice has come under heavy censure. Men and women together fix a ceiling of three hundred rupees on the amount to be paid. The wedding party which used to be composed of an entire village coming from the bride's home to wine, dine and stay at the expense of the hapless groom is the next to be axed. Not more than fifteen persons they say firmly, are to accompany the bride. Next—the senseless frenzied butchering of one animal per family at every festive occasion. Not only are the animals expensive, but a poor man's inability to pay one rupee towards their purchase is likely to land him into further bondage to work off even this small debt. The assembly decides that only one goat will be sacrificed per village at the January festival.

If Phullo had been at this amazing conclave, she would have heartily concurred with the decision taken on prostitution. Men who had never given the practice a second thought, are now being told in no uncertain terms by the very women they have been light-heartedly packing off to brothels, that within the month their wives and daughters are to be recalled, or they will face a social boycott they will not easily forget. For the first time the men begin to realise this may be a bad way of earning money.

Co-operatives were formed on this red letter day which are still working, manned by enthusiastic workers. Young Koltas are playing volley ball in their youth groups. The slaughter of buffaloes for superstitious reasons is beginning to disappear after stiff resistance, and best of all, the ex-prostitutes have formed themselves into the Kolta Mahila Labour Co-operative Society with thirty-three women as a nucleus.[29]

8 February 1979 brings another red letter day into the lives of custom ridden and long suppressed Malhar Kolta tribes of Maharashtra.[30] Four couples are getting married at a common marriage cermoney at Durves, a little over a hundred miles from Bombay. This ceremony has cost them altogether thirty rupees each.

Old Barku stands on the outskirts of the wedding crowd. In his mind he sees himself smiling confidently at his shy young bride so many years ago. How confident he had felt that day, and how warm and friendly the *Seth Saukar* had been when he had gone to ask for a four hundred rupee loan! He remembered the forty painful years of labour he and his wife had had to put in to repay the bond... and then the pipes had begun to play for his eldest son's wedding. The *Saukar* had smiled again as Barku took another loan from him. The young couple smiled shyly at each other, and then they went to work for the lord *Saukar*. Soon they had two children who are still cutting the long green grass that brings such huge profits to the *Saukar*... And then the cruel pipes and drums had begun to sound yet once more for Barku's younger son's marriage. They played as he wept. He had to go to another *Saukar* for another loan, and yet another smiling couple have become bonded slaves for life with the *Saukar*.

But now, at Durves, these young people are smiling. They have not taken any money from the *Saukar*. Who knows, thinks Barku. Others may follow...

'O *Adivasi*'s[31] son, what need have you for a wrist watch?' they sing. 'This expensive wedding is not ours, it is the *Saukar's*. We are the kings of the jungle. We are no man's slave. We shall not allow anyone of us to become a slave!'

Modern roads have brought a number of formerly inaccessible areas of tribal India in contact with the world of today. The young tribal is now going to school and college and being respresented in Parliament. He is beginning to look at the problems in his world. He will hopefully keep the good discarding the evil. Perils strew his path to modernity, and the fear is that old skills, simple living and the customs that guarded a way of life may be replaced by a plastic mug and transistor civilization.

Bride price and dowry are members of the same family, often going hand in hand wherever giving and taking are involved in a marriage transaction. Sometimes the seesaw of economic factors combined with social approval throws up the one while the other plummets down, and vice versa. Since everywhere in the world behaviour patterns adapt themselves to what the upper stratum of society thinks and does, the little man who dreams of marble palaces and slaves every night adds another fantasy to the scene—a daughter laden with jewels, sitting by the sacred marriage fire, with gods and neighbours showering blessings on her father's head...

The ordinary mortal in the streets of Mughal India could not help but be dazzled by the dowry that came from Rajah Bhagwan Das when his daughter was married to the future Emperor Jahangir.

> 'With the quantities of gems and gold that were scattered around,

Mens' hands were aweary of gathering them up.[32]

However the great Akbar realised that although a rich dowry of such dimensions was possible for his son, such an example might make life very difficult for his poorer subjects. So he appointed *Tui-begs* to keep a strict check on those who might demand exorbitant dowries from them.[33]

Although in India the dowry system has been the bane of Hindu society for long, it has never found religion a barrier. Even the most orthodox of Muslim emperors, Aurangzeb, was not averse to demanding the fortress of Ramgiri when his son Prince Sultan Muhammad was to wed a princess from Golconda.[34]

Apart from the dowry accompanying a Mughal bride, even the presents given to the groom were not the sort the receiving party could have displayed in one room. These were the Mughal equivalents of today's *varadakshina*—presents given to the *vara*—the groom, by which the girl's family honours the bridegroom's family and makes sure of their consent to the proposed marriage. This sets the final seal on the lowered status of the bride and her family. From proud takers they have become cringing givers who are glad to lick the hand that slaps them. The family's honour has begun to trickle away from their home and wealth in cash and kind has begun to flow in the opposite direction, in a steady stream into the coffers of the groom's family. No wonder it was only the rich earlier who could afford the doubtful privilege of giving substantial dowries. The common man who so far had opted for the more practical marriage by purchase of the bride is now beginning to climb the slippery social ladder on the top of which the sun smiles. In Bengal this kind of climbing on the necks of daughters had already established itself as an accepted practice by the 16th century. In Punjab however, by the close of the nineteenth century, bride price marriages were prevalent among the common people and dowry existed only at the very top.[35] Ironically enough it is in Punjab that dowry has made such a quick come back. It now ranks high on the list of states, where young brides are often reported to be tortured to urge their luckless parents to snowball their way into permanent indebtedness by giving more and more from their fast diminishing store.

Among the poor of the world, love and companionship have played little part in the choice of life companions. For them the daily battle for survival is the only reality. The ancient American-Indian sun god gave the Sapa Inca many wives and much gold, while the poor labourer married solely to acquire a strong domestic animal. The Indian construction labourer of today marries also mainly to become the owner of a healthy wife who will churn out breadwinners by the quiverful and still be strong enough to carry head-loads of bricks continuously up and down shaky bamboo structures.

The reverberations of the industrial revolution in Europe in the last century produced an echo in India. With modernisation we have also imported a desire to keep up with the progressive West at all cost. Unfortunately what we often succeed in acquiring is the outer shell. The green and white revolutions[36] combined with the ingenuity of our people and the greater availability of scientific know how, have produced a new rich class born about twenty to thirty years ago, which is now thriving. Its entire aim in life is to devise new ways of making bigger and better piles of riches.

The village and all it stands for is falling in comparison with the bright lights and the new glitter. The loudspeaker has replaced the temple bells and the *muazzin's*[37] call. The educational system is totally unrelated to the student's daily living. Especailly, is it alienated from the life of the economically weaker members of our society. It brings with it a whole set of flimsy values that titillate the palate but cannot fill an empty stomach or train the mind in directions of lasting value.

According to Scarlett Epstein,[38] Beregowda, one of the most enterprising peasants of Wangala in Mysore was responsible for the shift in the marriage pattern among the farmers from bridewealth to dowry. The demands of a changing society expected him to acquire an educated son-in-law, it did not matter how. His higher status consonant with his newly acquired wealth had made it a disgrace for him to allow his daughter to work in the fields any more, but most of all, it was the magic of *sanskritisation*.[39] that brought change to Beregowda's life. To copy the *Brahmins* in every detail was to acquire a passport to immediate social recognition. The 'Gowdas' of Wangala quickly changed their names and became characters from the old epics—Rama or Lakshmana. Since the *Brahmins* had always given dowries with their daughters, and selling a daughter was considered evil by them, Beregowda resolved that he would be as Brahmin as he could. His new wealth helped him to top an offer for an eligible son-in-law by three hundred rupees, earning his daughter her educated bridegroom for a round thousand.[40]

Bride price payment is by no means confined to the underprivileged of the world. The custom is prevalent in many South East Asian countries, where it is an acceptable marriage transaction in the best society. The poorer members of the world community carry on paying for their brides, quite oblivious of the exalted company they are in. Bride price continues to exist side by side with dowry giving, but it is fighting a losing battle. The Joneses of the world, backed by religious sanction, have decreed that receiving payment for a daughter's marriage is not the done thing. For the entertainment of the world there is nothing to beat dowry demand and giving...and so the circus goes on and on...

NOTES AND REFERENCES

1. Y.S. Parmar, *Polyandry in the Himalayas*, Delhi, Vikas, 1975, p. 63.
2. *Ibid.*
3. *Ibid.* p. 78.
4. Punjabi Kshatriyas, the warrior caste.
5. The Customary Law of Ambala quoted by Parkash Singh Jammu, 1976, p. 7. of cyclostyled manuscript.
6. Y.S. Parmar, *op. cit.*, p. 43.
7. Thakur Sen Negi, *Sirmur District Gazetteer*, Aligarh, 1969, p. 105.
8. S.J. Tambiah, "Dowry, Bridewealth and Women's Property Rights," in Goody and Tambiah, *op. cit.* 1973, p. 64, quoting R.F. Gray, Sonjo Bride-price and The Question of African "Wife Purchase," *American Anthropologist,* Vol. 62, 1960.
9. Journal of The Lal Bahadur Shastri National Academy of Administration:Vol. XX, No. 2, Summer 1975.
10. *Chhoot*: The price of freedom.
11. *Journal of The Lal Bahadur Shastri National Academy of Administration, op. cit.*, p. 880. 'From The Green Hills of Purola to the Brothels of Delhi and Meerut' by Rabindra Nath Gupta.
12. *Ibid.*, p. 881.
13. Nergis Dalal, 'Koltas of Jaunsar-Bawar,' *The Illustrated Weekly of India*, 5-11 June, 1977.
14. Adapted from the *Journal of The Lal Bahadur Shastri National Academy of Administration, op. cit.*, p. 876.

15. *Adapted from ibid.*, p. 884: 'Inmates of a brothel also have to pay the following fixed sums on a monthly basis: Rs 10.00 for the use of a fan; Rs 10.00 for the laundryman; Rs 15.00 to pay the combined bribe to the policemen who patrol the area.'
16. Nearly 5% of the total agricultural labour in India are debt-serfs. More than 90% of India's bonded labour are not allowed to leave the village or seek alternative employment. National Survey on the Incidence of Bonded Labour—A Preliminary Report, November 1978.
17. *Bajgi*—traditional musicians and barbers. A caste a rung higher than the Koltas.
18. Adapted from: 'National Survey on the Incidence of Bonded Labour—A Preliminary, Report' : November 1978, V. Sarma Marla, Gandhi Peace Foundation, and R.N. Maharaj, National Labour Institute.
19. *Journal of The Lal Bahadur Shastri National Academy of Administration, op. cit.*, p. 877.
20. *Patwari*: Lowest revenue official with powers of a police constable.
21. Occasionally such a transaction gets a mention in the daily newspapers, as witness a despatch from Dholpur entitled 'Held On Charge of Selling Wife' in *The Times of India* of 8 January 1979, which mentions that Pritam a resident of Shivpuri was caught red-handed selling his sixteen year old wife through a broker on 7 January and was arrested together with the broker.
22. Field report on Jaunsar-Bawar by Avdhash Kaushal Youth Co-ordinator, Nehru Yuvak Kendra Dehra Dun, presented at a workshop on bonded labour organised by the Gandhi Peace Foundation and The National Labour Institute at Delhi in November 1977.
23. *Journal of The Lal Bahadur Shastri National Academy of Administration, op. cit.*, p. 882.
24. From field report on Jaunsar-Bawar by Avdhash Kaushal, presented at a workshop on bonded labour held at Delhi, November 1977: (National Labour Institute and The Gandhi Peace Foundation).
25. This story is adapted from 'Polyandry Among the Jat Sikhs' by Ramesh Kapila—an article based on a study conducted by Mrs. K.P. Singh of the Punjab University's Sociology Department, and Dr Y.S. Parmar's thesis on polyandry in *The Sunday Standard*, 3 April 1977.
26. Thelma Awori, 'For African Women Equal Rights are not Enough,' *The Unesco Courier*, March 1975.
27. Judgement delivered by the Sessions Judge Moti Babu, Session Trial No. 92 of 74: State Vs. Paddu and another:
    In the court of The Sessions Judge, Dehra Doon, 29 January 1976.
28. 'Comprehensive Plan for Jaunsar-Bawar Area, Uttar Pradesh Hill Areas Newsletter, December 1976. Vol. 1 No. 5. Also *The Times of India*, 16 Nov. 1976 'Comprehensive Plan for Jaunsar-Bawar Area,' and *The Patriot*: 'Making Destitutes Self-reliant,' 2 November, 1976.

29. Avdhash Kaushal.
30. Adapted from 'Marriage and Bondage' an article by Pamela Philipose, *The Times of India*, 25 February 1979.
31. Original inhabitants, generally tribal in character.
32. *The Tabaqat-i-Akbari* of Khwajah Nizamuddin Ahmad translated by B.De, Calcutta, 1936: The Royal Asiatic Society of Bengal, *Akbar Badshah*, p. 599.

    Khwajah Nizamuddin Ahmad gives an account of the marriage festivities. *Ibid:* 'Rajah Bhagwan Dass passed so much of vessels of gold and fine fabrics and rich stuffs, and stabelfulls of horses, and one hundred elephants and slaves and slave girls, Abyssinian, Circassian, and Hindustani before the noble eyes, that the accountants of imagination and thought were unable to take account of them..pearls and gems were scattered all the way from the Rajah's mansion to the threshold, as a thank offering.'
33. Emperor Akbar: 1556-1569.

    'His Majesty disapproves of high dowries for as they are rarely ever paid, they are a mere sham, but he admits that the fixing of high dowries is a preventive against rash divorces'.. (here the emperor presumably alludes to dower as given or promised by bridegrooms).

    'He has also appointed two sober and sensible men; one of whom inquires into the circumstances of the bridegroom, and the other into those of the bride. These two officers have the title of *Tui-begi*, or masters of marriages.,' (*The Ain-i-Akbari* of Abu'l Fazl Allami translated by H. Blochmann, third edn. 1977, p. 288).
34. Aurang-Zebe' who 'married his son Mahmud to the king's (of Golconda) 'eldest daughter, exacted a promise that the young prince should be nominated successor to the throne of Golconda, and received, as the princess's dowry, the fortress of Ramguyre, with the whole of its appurtenances.' *Travels in the Mogul Empire* by Francois Bernier translated from the French by Irving Brock, London, William Pickering, 1826, Vol. I, p. 23.
35. Customary Laws of Ambala, Mianwali, Moga, Zira, and Firozepur as mentioned in Parkash Singh Jammu's thesis: p. 8. of cyclostyled manuscript.
36. (*i*) Agrarian: (*ii*) Milk and dairy products.
37. One who calls Muslims to prayer.
38. Scarlett Epstein, *South India Yesterday, Today and Tomorrow*, 1973, Macmillan p. 197.
39. *Ibid.*, p. 193. Sanskritisation: coming under the influence of Sanskrit culture.
40. *Ibid.*, p. 197.

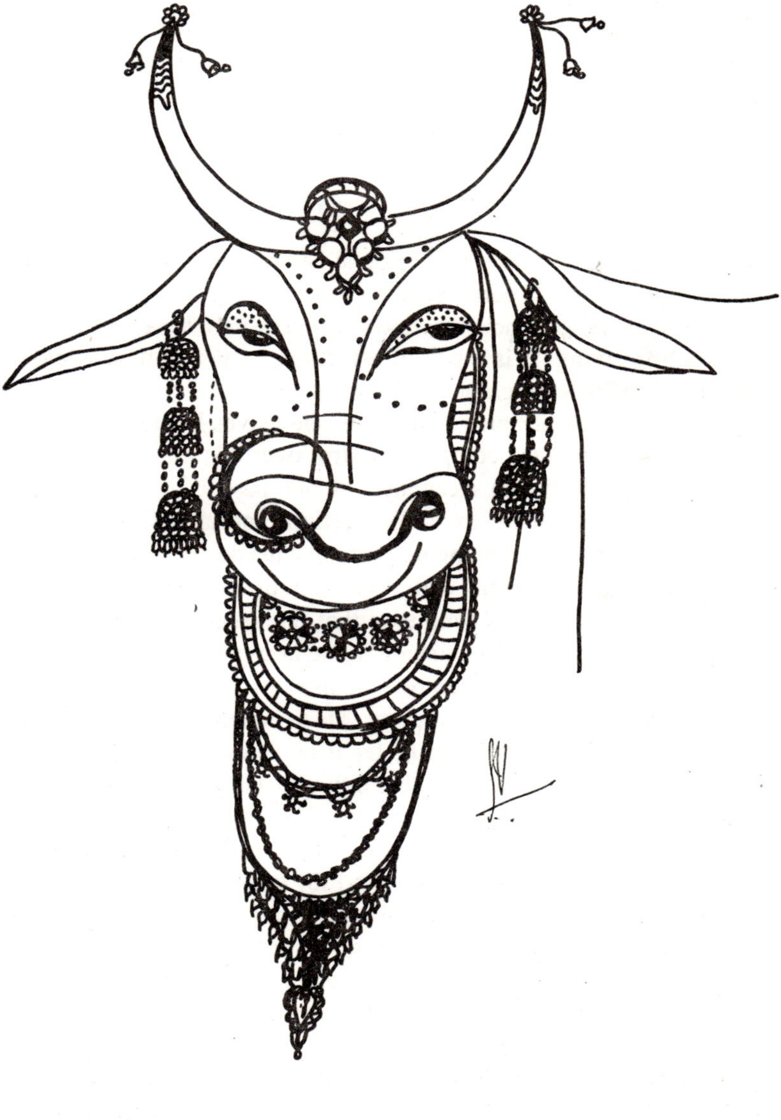

6

Her Gold

Is the wealth handed over to a bride at her wedding the result of the promptings of a guilty conscience?

How could it be? Ancient scriptures everywhere have approved of this kind of giving. It is a gift of affection, they say. It is as old as parental love for a daughter. Her parents are naturally anxious, even duty bound to see her provided for as she leaves her home for new territory. She will have complete control over this gift. She will live wrapped around by the assurance of her parents' love and their understanding of her needs. It is a definite moral obligation and a religious injunction which the parents must needs obey.

And what of their son? Well, that's another matter. He is a boy, and she is a girl. It's as simple as that. He gets his share and she hers. Why does she not get a share in the house and land also? Well, the law allows it, and there are a number of communities who do give their daughters landed property. There is nothing to stop a father from giving his land to his daughter if he so desires...But does he? Well, the son will carry on the father's name and line, and so naturally, he is the obvious heir in that sense. Naturally.

In most early societies the bride was an equal partner with her future husband. If anything, she had an edge over him. She was valuable and her family was the dispenser of his fortunes. He was in no position to demand anything to go with the bride. On the other hand, he was expected to recognise her full ownership of whatever she brought with her, and he promised to return it to her father if she died childless.

In India, woman has theoretically always been free to do as she pleases with her *streedhana*—woman's wealth. Every law-maker down to the present day, has upheld her right over it.

Even though high society in ancient India generally frowned on the custom of taking money for a bride, it was fairly widely practised, and even Queen Kaikeyi's guardian was not averse to taking bride price — *shulk* for her at her marriage with King Dasaratha.[1]

It was about the third century A.D. that the idea of *streedhana* began to be spelt out. Manu described it as:

> What (was given) before the (nuptial) fire, what (was given) on the bridal procession, what was given in token of love,[2] and what was received from her brother, mother, or father, that is called the six-fold property of a women. (Such property), as well as a gift subsequent and what was given (to her) by her affectionate husband, shall go to her offspring, (even) if she dies in the lifetime of her husband.[3]

It was the general prejudice against giving the daughter a share in ancestral property that started some re-thinking on the subject. Since a daughter passed from her own *gotra*[4] to another family with her marriage, it caused the fragmentation of property, and the old ones were against the whole idea. So were the men who would have otherwise inherited undivided land. Not only was her own family perturbed, but her husband's family too spent sleepless nights as gifts given by their son in token of his affection began to swell his newly acquired bride's *streedhana.* Since this reckless giving could sometime or the other include his portion of their joint family property, it would be disastrous if she were to be allowed to will it all away as she pleased.[5]

Learned heads clashed, tempers were frayed, as seventh and eighth century jurists discussed the powers a woman should be allowed to have over immovable property. Manu had already said that she had no right to bequeath even what was hers, without getting her husband's consent.[6] After much altercation and discussion, a woman's *streedhana* was divided into two parts: *saudayika*: gifts under her complete control; *asaudayika*: what could neither be bequeathed, sold, nor in any way used up by her. All she could do with this part of her *streedhana,* was to invest it and use the interest from it while she was alive.[7]

Since in ancient India, the goddess of good fortune was supposed to dwell in the person of the unmarried daughter, her presence in the house was considered an excellent omen. After the sonless *pater familias* had recovered from the initial shock of having fathered a girl, he rose gallantly to the occasion. He decided he would rather give his landed property to his Appointed Daughter—his *putrika*,[8] than adopt an outside male who would not be of his blood. The *putrika* would be treated for all intents and purposes as a male heir. Her son would then take over the inheritance directly from his grandfather, thus keeping the continuity of the line intact. His father would be part of the household and live in his wife's home.

The later *Smritis*[9] recognised well defined areas over which husbands and wives had control. Even their debts were not to be a burden on the other partner.[10]

Be that as it may, it has invariably been the wife's exclusive property that has pulled a family out of its monetary troubles. Victorian novels are full of instances where the mistress of the house defrays her husband's recklessly acquired debts by selling the linen she had so lovingly embroidered as a girl, and allowing her silver service to fall under the auctioneer's hammer.[11]

With the boundaries of control over the *streedhana* becoming fuzzier all the time, although she is upheld by the law of the land, in practice more and more of the actual control over her private wealth shifts to her husband and to his family.

How did this 'gift of love' become transformed into the terrifying and insatiable *Mahapralaya*[12] that we see nowadays in India? At what point did a woman's wealth, meant for her exclusive enjoyment become dowry?

The army wife came from Rajasthan. The other ladies were complaining loudly about how difficult it was to get a good servant to look after the children. Smiling serenely, she told the astounded women that this had never been a problem in her family, as she had been given two 'slaves' in her dowry. 'Of course, they are slaves, but they are used to it. We keep them well. Their family has always worked for us, so naturally their two daughters are with me.' Naturally!

Earliest references to dowry show that it was mainly a preoccupation of kings and of the very rich who could indulge in luxurious display. Fairy kingdoms and wealth which could only be measured in terms of golden chariots and palaces full of jewels went with a beloved daughter to her new home...

Parvati, consort of Lord Shiva, ideal wife and goddess received 'slaves, horses and elephants, cattle and vehicles, grain, jewels, clothing...gold vessels....'[13] Not to be outdone by the gods, King Janaka, father of the beautiful Seeta[14] destined to be the wife of Rama, sent with his daughter a dowry of 'a hundred thousand cows, woollen cloths, countless silken robes and richly decorated elephants, horses and chariots...male and female attendants, numberless golden coins with quantities of pearls and coral. All these and many other gifts....'[15]

Among the more memorable dowries of history was that given by the Queen Regent of Portugal to England's Restoration monarch Charles II. Being as ambitious as she was shrewd, she married her daughter Catherine of Braganza to the English king, wrapping up as added inducement, Tangiers and the city of Bombay—two of Portugal's private possessions. She also promised her royal son-in-law a large sum of money which she conveniently forgot to despatch. As a result, Catherine was forced to stay on in England, putting up patiently with an unsatisfactory husband whose attentions seemed almost entirely concentrated on Mistress Nell Gwynne, the charming orange vendor and Louise de Keroualle, Duchess of Portsmouth. He was forgetful of his wife to such an extent that he sometimes even omitted to dole her pocket money out to her. Catherine finally left, and the dowry cash never touched the shores of England.

The dowry system, like every other institution, has had its own complement of saints and do-gooders. Who would have thought that the world famous little old man in red with his sack of goodies who is loved by children all over the world as Father Christmas, could also have been the patron saint of unmarried maidens in search of a dowry?

Santa Claus—in his original form as Sank'ni kolaus—was a bishop of Myra, a seaport town in Asia Minor — Turkey. He lived during the reigns of three Roman emperors—Diocletian, Maximilian and Constantine. He died in 326 A.D. The good bishop was a rich man, and like the fabled Haroun-ul-Rashid spent his fortune in helping people anonymously. Once an Asian merchant,[16] father of three girls, became a pauper overnight as his ships sank in a storm.

Bishop Nicholas came to hear that the poor man was so overwhelmed by his bad luck, that knowing no one would marry his dowryless girls, he had decided to sell them into slavery as there was no other way for the family to survive. The bishop's fortune was almost spent by now, but three bags of gold remained. That night a bag of gold whizzed through the merchant's window, and a possibly apocryphal story tells us that it lodged itself mysteriously in a stocking his eldest daughter had hung by the fireplace to dry. Needless to say the miraculous gift came in very handy for a handsome dowry. In due course the second daughter came of age and also discovered her dowry in her stocking. When his third daughter was ready for marriage, the merchant could contain his curiosity no longer and sat up the whole night to find out who his benefactor was. He caught the bishop red-handed in the act of aiming a bag of gold at the lone stocking hanging expectantly by the fireplace. Ever since then, not only have children hung up their stockings on Christmas Eve and found them full of good things in the morning, but Western maidens dreaming of good marriages have prayed to Saint Nicholas to make their dreams come true.

Helping maidens in distress to secure husbands was the main preoccupation of a number of highly placed ladies of history. Livia,[17] the wife of Caesar Augustus, and the thirteenth century French queen, Blanche of Castille,[18] wife of Louis VIII of France, who earned the sobriquet 'Blanche La Bonne Reine,' — Blanche, the Good Queen, were both known for their generosity to dowryless maidens.

The capable and beautiful wife of the Mughal Emperor Jahangir, Empress Nur Jahan who lived in the seventeenth century, was known to be 'liberal and just to all who begged her support. She was an asylum for all sufferers, and helpless girls were married at the expense of her private purse. She must have portioned above five hundred girls in her lifetime, and thousands were grateful for her generosity.'[19]

The early Vedic woman, free and independent minded as she was, is personified in the *Rig Veda*, as *Surya*,[20] daughter of the sun. She goes to her wedding accompanied by her 'treasure box' eloquently equated with heaven and earth. *Surya* was so beautiful, that no embellishments or accompanying wealth could make her more attractive to her lord, the Moon.[21]

'Intention was the pillow, sight was the ointment, heaven (and) earth were the coffer (koça), when Surya went to her husband.'[22] The *Rig Veda* says more poetically:

> 'Thought was the pillow of her couch,
> and sight the unguent of her eyes,
> heaven and earth her treasure box,
> when Surya went to her husband.'[23]

Perhaps the 'hope chest' of a Western bride stacked to the brim with hand monogrammed linen, the treasure chest of the Grecian bride filled with her trousseau and the *pitara* of the Indian bride had a common ancestor in Surya's wonderful poetry wreathed box.

Alluding most probably to a rich dowry, the *Atharva Veda* says:

> 'Not on his couch lies a beautiful hundred-bringing (*vahi*) wife....'[24] This has been taken by some writers to mean a hundred cows being brought in dowry.[25] In these matters, the 'cattle bringing maiden's, of ancient Greece[26] were definitely better off than their Indian counterparts, as the cattle that came to their fathers' homes with their marriages, did not go out to another.

By the epic age, the face of the Indian woman has begun to change. The mature Vedic woman who not only approved her future partner before her marriage, but was an intelligent life companion for him has become Seeta. She still holds the victory garland of marriage.[27] She is mature enough to take part in decision making, but her position has changed greatly. Although she serves her lord faithfully with self-effacing love, even following him voluntarily into fourteen years of exile and hardship, she finds when she needs his support most, she is repudiated by her lord, even though the gods openly vindicate her honour.[28] Woman is now fast slithering down the hill and changing to a dowry laden bride who will by the twentieth century be sweeping out all her parents' carefully garnered savings, to leave her home for another with the blessings of gods and society.

Definitions of dowry are as varied as the people of our land. The members of the Committee on the Status of Women 1974 admitted as much when they wrote that there are 'baffing regional variations in peoples' understanding of dowry.[29]

They finally defined it as:

'i. What is given to the bride, and often settled beforehand and announced openly or discreetly. *The gift though given to the bride, may not be regarded exclusively her property.*' (emphasis mine.)

'ii. What is given to the bridegroom before and at marriage.

'iii. What is presented to the in-laws of the girl.

The settlement often includes the enormous expenses incurred on travel and entertainment of the bridegroom's party.'[30]

It is obvious from this that the already fine line between *streedhana* and dowry has become almost completely obliterated in the plethora of grandiose demand and obsequious giving.

Laws concerning property ownership in India have been very varied. The Mitakshara Law[31] limits ownership of joint ancestral property to three generations of males. This joint heirship is called a coparcenary—an all male club whose membership is restricted to the father, his son, his son's son and his son's grandson. 'Ownership by Right of Birth' says the sign on the door, 'Women Keep Out!' Property in this coparcenary is never divided until a member of the club decides to break away and set up separate house. Only then can he claim to have a share in the property which would be exclusively his own.

The Hindu Succession Act of 1956 made an inroad into this system which tries to help the women of the family get a toe in the door. According to the letter of the Act, the Hindu women is to be given equal rights with her brothers in movable as well as immovable property, allowing married daughters a share in their patrimony as well.[32]

Opposition from the die-hards however, was so strong that some of the basic inequalities of the Mitakshara system which tilt the scales heavily in favour of the male side of the family could not be erased from the new law. Hence the mens' club remained intact.

In practice it works out as something like this:

The father of a family composed of a wife, two sons and a daughter, dies. During his lifetime, no one has broken away from the homestead, so the property has remained undivided. On his death, the law makes a notional partition, dividing the property equally between the late father and his two sons. The father's share is now equally divided between all the living members of the family—widow, daughter *and the two sons again.*

This means that over and above their continuing ownership in the coparcenary the sons get even more. Their mother and sister however, get infinitely less.[33]

If the father is evil-minded enough to want to cut the women right out of the family property, he can do it in at least two interesting ways that we know of, apart from the simple expedient of leaving them out of his will. He can give up his right in the coparcenary, so that when he dies there will be nothing left which could have been divided among the women, as his share has already been renounced. He can also convert any property he may have acquired into coparcenary property, knowing that the women would have otherwise had an equal share in his acquired property by law, with all his other heirs.

The Dayabhaga system on the other hand, which was mainly prevalent in Bengal and Assam, states that during the father's lifetime, all joint family property belongs to him alone. Neither his wife nor any of his children can have any ownership rights in it until his death, when the entire family wealth will be divided equally among his widow and the children without any discrimination on the basis of sex or any other consideration. It is only if he has the good sense to die before his children are too old to enjoy their inheritance that it can be of any use to them at all. Even here, as in the Mitakshara system, the father is lord of all and can will anything away as the spirit moves him.

Matriarchal communities however, still continue their own traditions with the inheritance following the mother's 'blood' line.

To add to the legal merry-go-round, apart from the various personal laws which govern people of different religious persuasions, a variety of other laws governing other communities have further tangled the inheritance and ownership scene. This was the mess that the Indian Succession Act of 1925 had sought to bring under some kind of cohesive control.

The Hindu Succession Act of 1956 still has a long way to go

before it can provide the kind of equality it aims at giving the Hindu woman.

One of the main grievances the traditionalists have against the Hindu Succession Act is that it was passed without due thought being given to traditional institutions and social *milieu.* Daughters they say, should definitely not inherit on par with sons. Property given to a daughter leaves the family and goes to another; besides, what earthly use can property be to a woman? Is'nt she mistress of her husband's wealth?

They would much rather she took the cash and jewellery to which everyone knows she is entitled. Who can forecast the endless litigation bound to involve brothers and sisters when the latter start claiming a share in landed property, they say.

One such gruesome case was reported on 1 November, 1977[34] where a woman bequeathed 8 acres of land in Khillaur village (Rajpura Subdivision) in Punjab, to her daughter, a young school teacher. The teacher's angry brother, his two sons and daughter-in-law are alleged to have viciously attacked her with *kirpans*[35] and sticks. As a result of the injuries she sustained, the young woman has lost both her arms which had subsequently to be amputated. According to the same report, she has also lost her hearing and walks with a limp.[36]

However there are very few women even now, who, given the possibility of claiming and receiving their rightful share in their father's estate, would ever lay claim to it. Girls brought up as they still are, to be dependent, are almost always only too ready to surrender their share of land to their brothers. They usually take what is given or promised them by the brothers they trust.

Before the passing of The Hindu Succession Act of 1956, a Hindu widow had only a life interest in her share of joint family property which lapsed with her death. Often this 'share' supposedly owned by her, stayed firmly in the hands of her dead husband's male relatives. With the passing of The Hindu Succession Act, she has become a full owner of her share.[37]

In the case of women inheriting after 1956, the law poses no problem. They are automatically declared complete owners in their share of joint family property, with full right to lease, mortgage or sell it without having to ask their men for permission.[38] If they remarry, the share will continue to be theirs and the law will uphold their right. Here again, there are few widows who would take recourse to law, to be upheld by it, against the traditional usages of their caste or community.[39]

According to the letter of Islamic law, the Muslim woman was on a much better wicket than her Hindu sister long before the Hindu Succession Law was passed. In actual practice again things were less rosy.

In several detailed verses, the *Quran* explains the Laws of *Miras*:[40] inheritance

'With regard to your children, God commandeth you to give the male the portion of two females, and if there be females more than two, they shall have two-thirds of that which their father hath left: but if she be an only daughter, she shall have the half... Without loss to anyone. This is the ordinance of God, and God is Knowing, Gracious.'[41]

Father, mother, wife, sister, grandmother—all share in the patrimony—the woman getting half the man's share.

The *Mahr* or dower, is a sum of money promised by a Muslim bridegroom to his bride. The amount and category of *Mahr* may be mentioned in the wedding contract or decided upon later. *Mahr* is the bride's by right. Its upper limit is the sky. It rockets in direct proportion to the bride's beauty, family connections and other assets: also according to the groom's family's assessment of what their own honour is worth in terms of a high sounding *Mahr*. According to Islamic law, the minimum *Mahr* has been fixed at 10 *dirhams*[41(a)] or their equivalent. It need not necessarily be in currency. 'Everything, except carrion, blood, wine and hog. Also the bridegroom's own labour if he is a free man, being held by the law to be a good dower.' The *Mahr* is usually divided into two parts—Prompt, (*Mu'ajjal*): which may be given to the bride at the time of marriage or before or after consummation of the marriage, and Deferred (*Muwajjal*). Deferred *Mahr* may be demanded by a wife if the marriage is dissolved or if her husband dies. It can be demanded within three years of either happening.[42] The marriage contract may also be made on the basis of *Mahr* to be paid on demand—Prompt On Demand — *Mu'ajjal ind-ul-talb* — that is, *Mahr* which has not been paid immediately at the wedding, but has been postponed until demanded by the wife.[43]

Although the Prompt *Mahr* is almost never given or demanded at a wedding, strictly according to Islamic law, it will remain due to the wife until she demands it. *Mahr* like bridewealth, was originally intended as an insurance for the young bride against ill-treatment, and also to work as a brake on her husband's wandering fancies. It was regarded as an honourable welcome for the new wife entering her husband's home.

These laudable objectives often tend to stay enshrined within the pages of law books and sacred writings. Although the *Mahr* can be demanded by the wife at any time, it is usually given if the husband himself divorces her. This leaves several openings for a twisted mind to function in, particularly where the wife is illiterate, or whose modesty or ignorance of her rights keeps her from showing her face in a court of law. A husband anxious to rid himself of such an encumbrance cheaply will begin to ill-treat her and bring her to such a pass that either she or her family will be constrained to ask for divorce. He knows that his wife cannot divorce him easily. She can only ask for it on certain grounds enumerated and recognised by Muslim law.[44] The process is so difficult that the promised *Mahr* will almost certainly continue in his own possession. Often in the interest of hanging on to the amount of the *Mahr*, he can simply discard his wife and marry again.[45] He can then offer the new bride another large *Mahr*, and if she should at any time incur his displeasure, he can start all over again. If she should ask for a divorce, he can pose as the aggrieved party swearing that he loves her dearly and is willing to keep her for ever; but since she is the one who has taken this painful decision, it is understandable that the poor man should not have to give her the *Mahr* also.

'*Behn, kya bata-ein*?[46] Where shall I begin my tale of woe?' said a Muslim lady living a secluded life in the shadow of the mosque. 'My poor Aziza has suffered. We had thought the family such an excellent catch, but Allah knows how he beat her. Even then, being from a respectable family, she never opened her mouth. We had them fix a large *Mahr* so that we would have some sort of surety for our Aziza who is like a piece of our heart. You see it would hurt them to return so much money as it is her right to get it if, *Allah* forbid, he should want to divorce her. Marriage is such a gamble *behn*! What can you do with the male tribe? Our lives are in their hands. Finally, when she came home my poor little flower was unable to walk. I forced her to show me what he had done. *Ya Allah*! She was black and blue. Her father wanted to ask for divorce, but of course he does not want to drag our family name through the dirt of the courts. We had to think of Aziza's future also. So he got off free as the wind. He has married again. May the justice of *Allah* fall on his evil head! Everything is in the hands of these men. My daughter is thrown away like a suit of old soiled clothes and she may not marry again until he is prepared to say the word. Ah, *behn, Taqdeer*[47] is like a stone. What is written on it will happen. A stone has no heart!'

It is easy to scare an illiterate bride into waiving her right over her *Mahr*[48] Zahida's was one such case. Her knowledge of her religion and the laws that governed her life was limited to verses she had learnt by rote from the *Quran Shareef*.[49] She knew she was born to be married one day. Her friends and the local know-alls had told her that a marriage was not valid unless crowned by the act of consummation,[50] and that then and then, alone would she become a *real* wife. These were the thoughts in her mind as she stood by the flower-decked bed waiting for her bridegroom. The door opened softly and closed behind the man who was to put the seal of his acceptance on an honourable marriage. Zahida stole a look at him through the strings of threaded marigolds, 'Waive the *Mahr*,' she heard him say with a smile. '*Mahr-mu-af kar do*,' he repeated, 'or I shall not lay a hand on you!'

Zahida trembled. She suddenly saw herself weeping on her mother's shoulder sobbing, '*Ammi jan*,[51] he never touched me!' She shut her eyes tight. 'It will be as you say,' she murmured.

There was no need for witnesses. Remission of dower by a wife is valid under Muslim law.[52] There must be no compulsion however; but who was present when Zahida waived her claim over her *Mahr*, and who would swear in a court of law that she had not been a free agent when she gave in to her wily husband? Even if the law were to stand by her, could she or her family stand the shame and disgrace of speaking about such personal matters as consummation of marriage in public?

If Zahida had asked for a *Khula-nama*[53] which if accepted by her husband would have got her a divorce, she would in all probability have had to forgo the *Mahr* payment to buy herself freedom.

As long as polygamy is allowed to a Muslim husband and does not figure in the list of grounds for divorce, his wife's future will continue to hang in the balance. Turkey has completely banned bigamy.[54] Prior permission from court is required for a bigamous marriage in Syria,[55] Iran,[56] Iraq,[57] Singapore[58] and Sarawak.[59] A wife in Jordan and Morocco can stipulate in the marriage contract that she will have a right to pronounce a 'delegated divorce' if her husband marries again.[60] Sri Lanka gives the widest publicity to a forthcoming bigamous marriage. Thirty days' notice to the *qazis*, judges of the areas in which the husband, his present wife and his prospective wife live, is required to be given.[61] The *qazis* then publicise the matter, posting notices in the mosques and on the residences of all three parties.[62] This gives plenty of time for re-thinking and persuasion. A Pakistani husband planning another marriage has to present his case to an Arbitration Council headed by a Civil official on which representatives of his first wife and himself will sit.[63]

In spite of the reforms made in India on this subject by The Dissolution of Muslim Marriages Act of 1939, there is a great deal more to be accomplished. The voice of orthodoxy is far too loud and the Muslim woman is still very vulnerable.

Old Muhammad Qassim, the tailor with three grand daughters waiting for a good marriage is in misery. The promise of a sizeable *Mahr* has not helped alleviate his distress. He still has to provide the girls' future in-laws with cycles, transistors, wrist watches and gold.

It is not Muhammad Qassim alone who suffers. The Hyderabad Muslim who has barely enough to feed himself and his large family has to supply his son-in-law to be with *joray ke paise*..[64]

'*Ya Khuda*![65] sighs Haseena's mother. The girl has come of age already! What will the neighbours say if we can't find a husband for her soon! The family's nose will be cut right off, and we will never be able to raise our heads in the neighbourhood!'

Haseena's father is a wayside cycle repairer. His eldest son Zubair works with him. Between them they earn three hundred and fifty rupees a month. Little Haseena feels the sun has gone out of her life with 'youth' having overshadowed her. There must be something wrong with her, she decides, since no husband has come her way as yet. She slinks apologetically about their two-roomed house, helping her mother with the chores and sewing shiny borders on to her wedding clothes which one day, perhaps . . .

She wonders what exactly is wrong with her. Three sets of people have been to the house to see her. Her mother has housed and fed them. Expensive food which they can ill afford, has been cooked for them, but they always seem to go away again. She is beginning to wonder whether she will ever get a husband.

At last one day two ladies arrive. She comes out, as always, with the tea tray, not raising her eyes. She sneaks a glance at the older one who is looking appraisingly at her. The two women, whisper among themselves. 'It will be two thousand and five hundred rupees for the *joray*, says the older one finally. Haseena's mother is stunned. She had hoped the demand would be nearer three hundred and fifty rupees, but after all they have heard that the boy is a government servant in a *pakki sarkari naukri*.[66] Permanent government service is too good to lose. There is no help for it. The deal is clinched by Haseena's father who will take a loan from the local *Marwari*.[67] The money lender gives twenty six rupees, fifty paise less on every hundred rupees he loans; so asking for five hundred rupees they will actually receive only three hundred and sixty eight rupees, fifty paise. Haseena's family will pay back ten rupees on every hundred borrowed as interest. These payments, like those of bonded labourers elsewhere in India are likely to carry on in their family for generations.

The great day dawns. A *Mahr* of five thousand rupees has been announced. Sitting with her mother and the other women behind a curtain, Haseena hears the announcement. What a marvellously rich family she is going into, say the women. Haseena lowers her *kohl* rimmed eyes under her shiny bordered veil...

For the first two weeks of their marriage, Haseena's new lord relaxes at home and does not go to 'office.' When the cash given him at the wedding by his friends is exhausted, he decides to start work again. It is then that Haseena learns that he pulls a rickshaw up and down the streets earning four rupees a day.

Haseena is to be a mother soon. They live on her husband's meagre earnings. They eat in two of the twelve plates and six glasses she brought in her dowry. Her five copper vessels contain the little they have to cook, and they sleep on the double four poster bed her father is still paying for. A China tea set and her seven sets of clothes are still locked in the large tin trunk. Occasionally Haseena gets two rupees from her husband to get a little vegetable and sometimes some rice for him. She often goes hungry herself. The rest of the time he drinks the remaining one or two rupees in country liquor and comes home at night to beat her and fall dead asleep. She lives in constant dread that he will carry out his threat of bringing home another woman. Haseena's father and brothers will never allow her to divorce him as they know it will be very difficult for her to marry again, even though educated people say that the *Quran Shareef* allows such things. As for the *Mahr*, well, *Allah* knows such a sum will never even be within smelling distance of their family...

Haseena's friend Tahira can read Urdu. She has told Haseena about some societies which help women like her; but where to go? Each society wants people to think it is the only one in the whole city, and at their meetings, give only their own name and address. How can Haseena who is in purdah go to a far away address. "Why can't they all join hands and put a full list of names and addresses of all societies in their Urdu papers," sighs Haseena. This way, at least Tahira could have helped her slip out quietly to one which was close enough for her to go to without fear of being seen by her in-laws.

Haseena wishes she had her sister Bano's strong mind. Bano was beaten with a big stick by her brother. She left home and he threatened to beat her within an inch of her life if she returned to ask for her share in the house. He could not bear the thought that she did not want to marry the boy they had chosen for her. She is now earning a hundred and fifty rupees a month, working with a family in Delhi who look after her as if she were their own daughter. She sweeps, cleans, cooks and minds the children—jobs which would be a disgrace to her family if they ever told anyone about it: but Bano sends forty rupees regularly to her mother which the brother takes with a bad grace. She is even learning how to read and write Hindi although she gets someone to write her letters home in Urdu. What a wonderful life, sighs Haseena.

NOTES AND REFERENCES

1. Queen Kaikeyi: the epic hero Rama's step mother who was mainly responsible for his ouster from his father's kingdom and for his fourteen-year exile.
   Hari Dutt Vedalankar in his *Hindu Vivaha ka Sanskshipt Itihas* (Hindi) *Hindi Soochna Vibhag*, Lucknow, 1950, p. 193, says that Kaikeyi was married to King Dasratha — Rama's father, and he gave '*shulk*' (bride price) to Kaikeyi's father. This reference also appears in Altekar, *op. cit.*, p. 40.
2. By her husband.
3. *Manusmriti*: IX: 194 and 195: F. Max Mueller, The Sacred Books of the East, translated G. Buehler: Vol. xxv, The Laws of Manu, Motilal Banarsi Dass, Varanasi, 1964, pp. 370-71. All this was of course movable property 'obtained by a woman as a maiden or at marriage or after marriage from her parents or the family or relatives of the parents, or from the husband and his family (except immovable property given by the husband.),' P.V. Kane, (1946) *History of Dharmashastra*, Vol. III, pp. 779-80; Government Oriental series, Poona, as quoted by S.J. Tambiah, Goody and Tambiah, 1973, pp. 85-86.
4. Family in the largest sense of the term : clan or blood relationship.
5. (*i*) Compare with the Bedouins of Cyrenaica (Libya), who do not allow their women to inherit (in direct contravention of Islamic law) as they feel their cattle wealth partitioned between sons and daughters, would then be irretrievably lost to them. Jack Goody, and S.J. Tambiah, Bridewealth and Dowry, Cambridge University Press, London, 1973, pp. 27-28.
   (*ii*) In some South Indian communities however where first cousin marriages with the mother's brother's child are common, and sometimes even with the mother's brother, there is no fear of the property going out of the family. Therefore, often in these communities, dowry includes land as well.
6. *Manusmriti*: IX: 199, Max Mueller, 1964, *op. cit.*, p. 372, foot note for verse 199: 'according to Narayana and Nandana the translation should be as follows:
   "*Wives should never take anything* (for their private expenses) *from* (their husband's property, destined for the support of) *their families, on which many have a claim, nor from their own property* (which is not *stridhana*), *without the consent of their husbands*." '
7. A.S. Altekar, The Position of Women in Hindu Civilization, Motilal Banarsi Dass, 1962, p. 224.
8. *Putr*: son; therefore *putrika*: a daughter appointed in place of a son.
9. *Smriti*: See Introduction note 3.

10. Compare with the Lo Daaga tribe of Ghana, where a final calculation and settlement of debts between husband and wife forms an integral part of the funeral ceremony of either partner. Jack Goody, *op. cit.*, p. 38.
11. For example in *The Mill on the Floss* by George Eliot.
12. A total dissolution of the universe - a symbol of total destruction.
13. *The Ramayana* of Tulsidas rendered into English verse by A.G. Atkins, Vol. 1: Childhood and Youth, *chaupai* 101, Marriage of Siva and Parvati, p. 136, *The Hindustan Times*, New Delhi, 1954.
14. Seeta is the ideal Indian woman - generally regarded as the incarnation of the goddess Lakshmi.
15. *The Ramayana* of Valmiki translated by Hari Prasad Shastri, *Shanti Sadan*, London, 1959, Vol. I, Ch. 74, pp. 139-40.
16. This story is one of many told of the Bishop of Myra who later became famous as *Saint Nicholas*. 4000 Years of Christmas, Earl W. Count, New York; Henry Schuman, 1948, *God into Saint*, pp. 59-60. See also Elizabeth Hough Sechrist, *Red Letter Days*: Macrae-Smith Company, Philadelphia, 1940, p. 211. There are many versions of this story.
17. Livia—The third wife of Augustus: Ist Century B.C. and 1st Century A.D., Will Durant, *op. cit., Caesar and Christ*, 1944, Ch. XI, pp. 229-30.
18. Will Durant, The Story of Civilization, Simon and Schuster, New York: *The Age of Faith*, Ch. XXV, 1950, p. 690.
19. Muhammad Hadi as quoted by Lane-Poole, *Medieval India, under Mohammedan Rule (AD 712-1764)*, Delhi, 1963, p. 224.
20. Surya, daughter of Savitri (masculine: the universal motive power as represented by the Sun).
21. Soma—The Ultimate Being; worshipped also as the moon god and the life-giving nectar of the gods.
22. *Atharva-Veda Samhita*, Vol. II: translated by William Dwight Whitney, Banarsi Dass, 1962, Ch. XIV, verse 6. This is exactly the same as the reference in *The Rig Veda*: X, 85.7.
    Here the 'treasure box' appears as a '*koça*' which according to Ralph T. Griffith in *Hymns of the Rgveda*: 1976, p. 593, means 'probably trousseau or bridal outfit. According to some, the box or body of the chariot is intended.'
23. A.C. Bose, Hymns from the Vedas, Asia Publishing House, Calcutta, 1966, p. 129 (7).
24. *Atharva-Veda Samhita*, Vol. I (Whitney's translation), 1962, Book V, Ch. 17, verse 12, p. 249.
25. S.L. Hooja, *Dowry System in India*, Asia, 1969, p. 15.
26. Compare with the 'cattle bringing maidens of Homeric Greece: Will Durant, *op. cit.,* The Life of Greece, chapter III, 3, Sexes, p. 51.
27. See Ch. 4, note 13, *Swayamvara.*

28. Valmiki : *Ramayana* translated by Hari Prashad Sastri, London, Shanti Sadan, 1959, Vol I, Ch. 48, pp. 529-30; and Ch. 97, p. 617.
29. *Towards Equality*, Report of the Committee on the Status of Women, New Delhi, Government of India, 1974, p. 71.
30. *Ibid.*
31. See Ch. 2, note 15 on Yajnavalkya and the Mitakshara Law. Also *Towards Equality*, *op. cit.*, pp. 135-36.
32. *Ibid.*, p. 135.
    It is a sobering thought that as long ago as the first millennium before Christ, the Egyptian woman owned, bought and sold property and could testify in a court of law. Under the Ptolemies a daughter had an equal share in her father's inheritance and a widow was awarded one third of her dead husband's possessions; the remaining two-thirds being divided among his children and his brothers and sisters. (Bullough, *op. cit.*, pp. 32-33)
33. *Towards Equality*, 1974, pp. 136-38.
34. *Morning Echo*, New Delhi, 1 November 1977 and *The Times of India*, 8 January 1978.
35. Swords worn by the Sikhs.
36. The Court has since awarded her brothers, his son and a relative ten years' rigorous imprisonment and a fine of three thousand rupees each. They have also to pay the young teacher nine thousand rupees as compensation, R.I. for Trying to Kill Sister, *The Times of India*, 11 March 1978.
37. The Hindu Succession Act, 1956 (Act No. 30 of 1956); Ch. II: *Intestate Succession* : Section 14: *Property of a Female Hindu to be Her Absolute Property.*
38. (i) *Explanation*: - 'In this sub-section, "property" *includes both movable and immovable* property acquired by a female Hindu by inheritance or devise... *or in any other manner whatsoever*, and also any such property held by her as *streedhana* immediately before the commencement of this Act. (Emphasis mine).
39. Sujata Manohar, 'Breakthrough in Inheritance Laws', article in Femina: 3 - 16 December 1976.
40. Inheritance.
41. *Ayat-ul-Muvaris*, verses dealing with inheritance in the Quran, as quoted by T.P. Hughes, A Dictionary of Islam, W.H. Allen and Co., London, 1885, p. 207.

41(a). (i) A *dirham* is a silver coin resembling a date stone.
    (ii) As a matter of interest, 10 *dirham* were presumably the equivalent of 100 *misqal*, or £ 50 sterling in 1885, at the time of compilation of the dictionary: equal to 9,600 barley grains in weight.
    (iii) 10 *dirham* are the equivalent of three or four rupees according to Mulla's Principles of Mahomedan Law (Hidayatullah and

Shankardass: 1968, p. 270. This has been worked out by the author on the basis of information supplied in Hughes *op. cit.*, pp. 84-85.

42. T.P. Hughes, *op. cit.*, 1895, p. 91 Dower.
43. Dinshaw F. Mulla, Principles of Mahomedan Law (Ist. edition 1906, 16th. edition by M. Hidayatullah and R.K.P. Shankardass, Bombay, N.M. Tripathi Pvt. Ltd; 1968, Ch. XV' Dower'; S. 290 : 'Prompt' and 'Deferred' dower, p. 272.
44. *Ibid.*, Ch. XVI, 'Divorce', B - Judicial divorce at suit of wife. S. 323, p. 298: ***Grounds for Divorce Initiated by Women.***
    These grounds include, among others, cruelty and lack of maintenance. Contrasted with this, the Muslim man is free to divorce his wife as and when it pleases him. 'Any Mahomedan of sound mind, who has attained puberty, may divorce his wife whenever he desires without assigning any cause.' *Ibid.*, Ch. XVI: Divorce: A Divorce by husband. Section 308, p. 286.
    Three Supreme Court judges made legal history by their judgment on 6 October 1978 in the case of Bai Tahira v, Ali Hussain Fissalli Chouthia and another (S.C.): Criminal Appeal No. 332 of 1977.
    The judges were V.R. Krishna Iyer, V.D. Tulzapurkar and R.S. Pathak. The judgement summed up by Justice Krishna Iyer stated that 'Law is dynamic and its meaning cannot be pedantic but purposeful.' It was decided that the amount due to a divorced wife can be reviewed by the court, even if she had signed a marriage contract accepting the amount and conditions of *Mahr* stipulated in it as final settlement thus absolving her husband from any further financial obligation towards her.
    If the court considers the promised amount of the marriage contract inadequate to provide for a divorced wife, it may stipulate a more realistic sum and/or make further demands on the husband's estate to enable the woman to live in dignity.
    Taken from The Matrimonial Law Reporter, April 1979, p. 128 ff.
45. Mulla (1968) *op. cit.*, XIV: A—Marriage: S. 255; p. 251:
    'A Mahomedan may have as many as four wives at the same time, but not more. If he marries a fifth wife when he has already four, the marriage is not void, but merely irregular;' he is however, enjoined to treat all his wives with equal justice.
46. Sister, what can I tell you?
47. Fate.
48. Zarina Bhatty, 'Status of Muslim Women and Social Change, in Indian Women: From Purdah to Modernity, New Delhi, Vikas, 1976.
49. The Holy Quran.
50. The following are references from Islamic law and from the Hadis concerning *Mahr*. It is quite possible that these have trickled down to the illiterate and less privileged sections of the community in garbled

form, making them believe that consummation makes a Muslim marriage valid:

(*i*) '*Dower becomes immediately payable*: If the marriage was consummated, the wife is entitled to immediate payment of the whole of the unpaid dower, both prompt and deferred.

'If the marriage was not consummated, and the amount of dower was specified in the contract, she is entitled to half that amount.

'If no amount was specified all that she is entitled to is a present of three articles of dress.'

(Hedaya, 44-45; Baillie, 96-97) taken from Mulla, Principles of Mahomedan Law — Hidayatullah and Shankardass, 1968, Ch. XVI: Divorce: C—Effects of divorce: Section 336(2), pp. 309-10.

(*ii*) 'After consummation, the wife becomes entitled to full dower; and before consummation only half, or a mere present in case of separation before consummation.'

(Al-Hadis, Vol. II; an English translation and commentary by Al-Haj Maulana Fazlul Karim, published by the author: 1939, Ch. XXVII—Dower, p. 957 (d).

51. Mother dear.

52. *Validity of remission of dower by the wife:*

'The wife may remit the dower or any part thereof in favour of the husband or his heirs. Such a remission is valid though made without consideration (e) (Baillie, 553). But the remission must have been made with free consent.'

(Mulla, Principles of Mahomedan Law, Hidayatullah and Shankardass 1968, Ch. XV, Dower—pp. 273-274, Section 291. Remission of Dower by wife).

53. *Ibid.*, Ch. XVI, Divorce—pp. 295-96: Section 319. Khula and Mubara'at:

2) "A divorce by Khoola is divorce with the consent, and at the instance of the wife, in which she gives or agrees to give a consideration to the husband for her release from the marriage tie...and the wife may, as the consideration, release her *dyn-mahr* (dower) and other rights, or make any other agreement for the benefit of the husband..." A *Khula-nama* is the agreement for such a form of divorce.'

54. Tahir Mahmood, *Family Law Reform in the Muslim world*, Delhi, N.M. Tripathi Pvt. Ltd, 1972, p. 278: Article 93 of The Turkish Civil Code of 1926.

55. *Ibid.*, 276: Law of Personal Status 1953: Article 17 (Syria).

56. *Ibid.*, Family Protection Law 1967: Article 14 (Iran).

57. *Ibid.*, Law of Personal Status 1959: Article 3 (iv), (Iraq).

(According to an INA report in *The Times of India*, 17 February 1978, Iraq has further amended its marriage laws).

58. *Tahir Mahmood, op. cit.,* Muslims Ordinance, 1957: Section 7 A (Singapore).
59. *Ibid.*, Undang-Undang Mahkama Melayu: Section 37 (Sarawak).
60. *Ibid*: (*a*) The Ottoman Law of Family Rights 1917: Article 21
    (ii) Anti-Bigamy Stipulation in the Marriage Contract (Jordan).
    (*b*) p. 276: Moroccan Code of Personal Status 1958: Article 31.
    Note: The delegated divorce (*Haq Talaq-ba-Tafveez*) has been recognized in India from as far back as the thirteenth century, about the same time as the Magna Carta was signed in England. The Al Hedaya of Sheikh Burhan-ud-Din of Farghana (A Commentary on the *Mussalman* Laws) which contains the above information on p. 87 has been in use in Indian law courts since then. This reprint (1963) was translated by Charles Hamilton, Premier Book House, Lahore.
61. The Muslim Marriage and Divorce Act 1951: Section 24 (1) (Sri Lanka). Tahir Mahmood, *op. cit.,* p. 277; Also Judicature Act No. 2 of 1978, certified on 2 November, 1978. Published as a Supplement to Part II of The Gazette of the Democratic Socialist Republic of Sri Lanka, 10 November 1978. (Courtesy: The High Commission of Sri Lanka, New Delhi).
62. Tahir Mahmood *op.cit.,* Section 24 (3).
63. Muslim Family Laws Ordinance, 1961: Section 7. (Pakistan). The Council is constituted under The Basic Democracies Order 1952. *Ibid:* pp. 249-50. Section 6(v), *Ibid.*, p. 281.
    Note: According to a report in *The Statesman* of 28 November 1978 entitled 'Dowries Limited in Afghanistan,' the Afghan government has introduced, among others, 'sweeping reforms relating to marriage, limiting to a modest sum the size of dowries,' and forced marriage was declared abolished.
64. Money for sets of clothes: here bridegrooms' clothes.
65. Oh God!
66. Permament government service.
67. A man from Marwar in Rajasthan in this context, a money lender.

RS.10
MILLION

7

The Gimmee

'But *Padri Sahib*,[1] we Christians in the North don't ever have dowry troubles. Why did you give so much for Mariam's wedding?

'*Beti*,[2] you don't understand. The air is different these days. When you were married your parents kept to our free tradition, but if you want a good Christian boy these days, they demand everything from you. You know our little Pyari. She is being used to extract radios and cycles from us—things a poor *padri* can ill afford.'

It was the same old story all over again, but this time it was not in a Hindu family. Few parents who give or demand dowry will admit that this custom is seeping into every faith in our country through a process of sheer osmosis. However, since we are trying to understand the background and the why and wherefore of this form of exploitation, we must take a trip back to Manu to understand the religious sanctions behind the institution of dowry.

Eight forms of Hindu marriage are enumerated in the *Manusmriti*. Of these, by far the most prestigious and the most prevalent today is the *Brahma Rite*.

The Brahma Rite

'The gift of a daughtr after decking her (with costly garments) and honouring (her by presents of jewels) to a man whom (the father) himself invites is called the Brahma rite.'[3]

Manu lists the other forms of marriage as: *Daiva, Arsha, Prajapati, Paisacha, Rakshasa, Asura* and *Gandharva*.

The Daiva Rite

'The gift of a daughter who has been decked with ornaments, to a priest who duly officiates at a sacrifice during the course of its performance.'[4]

The *Daiva* marriage died out with the Vedic sacrifices. Cultured and accomplished priests were invited by the head of the family to live in his house over the many weeks the sacrificial rites would last. During this time, father and daughter would be in a position to observe them and select the one to whom the girl would eventually be given. She went as a sacred gift. The presentation was witnessed by the sacrificial fire which was the hub of all activity in Vedic times. The later *Smriti* writers however, disapproved of this kind of marriage as it encouraged secular thoughts of marriage during religious sacrifices.

The Arsha Rite

'When (the father) gives away his daughter according to the rule, after receiving from the bridegroom, for (the fulfilment of) the sacred law, a cow and a bull or two pairs...[5]

Although the implication here is that a daughter is being gifted away not for sale, but in exchange for animals to be used strictly for the performance of religious rites, it is difficult to disassociate this in one's mind from the custom of bride price.

The Prajapati Rite

'The gift of a daughter (by her father) after he has addressed (the couple) with the text, "May both of you perform together your duties," and has shown honour (to the bridegroom)'[6]

Here the bridegroom is honoured, and 'a honey mixture' is offered to him which he accepts even though no gifts accompany the bride.

These four forms of marriage are regarded as 'blameless' from which 'spring sons radiant with knowledge of the Veda and honoured by the Sishtas.'[7]

From the four *blamable* marriages that follow however, '*spring sons who are cruel and speakers of untruth, who hate the Veda and the sacred law*.'[8] The most despicable of these four is the *Paisacha*.

The Paisacha Rite

'When (a man) by stealth seduces a girl who is sleeping, intoxicated, or disordered in intellect, that is... the most base and sinful rite...'[9]

Altekar concludes that this rite has been included in the *Manusmriti* only as a relic of a prehistoric custom. He also feels that at a time when virginity was at a premium, such an enforced marriage helped the seduced woman who would otherwise stand no chance in the marriage market. Healthy fear of this impending marriage might even have acted as a curb on a possible seducer's appetite.[10]

The Rakshasa (*Kshatra*) *Rite*

'The forcible abduction of a maiden from her home while she cries out and weeps after (her kinsmen) have been slain or wounded and (their houses) broken open...'[11]

The Kshatra form of marriage was not always condemned. Women were won as prizes of war without blame or censure. Even Arjuna carried Subhadra away forcibly.

Sri Krishna justified his action by saying, 'Since Subhadra had fallen in love with him, to carry her away, relying upon the power of his own arms was the only honourable course left open...'[12]

The Asura Rite

'When (the bridegroom) receives a maiden, after having given as much wealth as he can afford, to the kinsmen and to the bride herself, according to his own will...'[13]

'According to his own will,' and not 'according to the sacred law'—there lies the rub. The transaction by which a father exchanges his daughter for wealth makes this form of marriage 'blamable.'

The Gandharva Rite

'The voluntary union of a maiden and her lover, one must know (to be) the Gandharva rite, which springs from desire and has sexual intercourse for its purpose.'[14]

This marriage although generally regarded as *blamable* is extolled by the *Kama Sutra*[15] as it also implies adult choice. No rites were necessary in this marriage. Consummation followed choice. It was only many years later that it was stipulated that a couple married according to this rite, should later go through the 'regular' marriage ceremony. The only difference here would be that the word *kanya* (virgin) would be understood to imply 'bride' in the ceremony.[16]

Even a cursory glance at these eight forms of marriage will show that the first four emphasise the role of the father as protector of his daughter and dispenser of her destiny. He has a say in the kind of home she will go to, and can also have a reasonable chance of safeguarding her future. This is not the case at all with the 'blamable' group of marriages where the girl may be seduced, forcibly abducted, sold or may marry irresponsibly 'for love.'

Together with the good comes the bad. The father's role in the approved list of marriages, is that of the owner of his daughter. She is his property to gift away as he pleases, and he can do this, irrespective of her wishes or hopes for her own future. Tradition has blessed the acceptable gift of a virgin. We have already explored all the evils attendant on early marriage. A father with no one to challenge him can easily use his prerogative to his daughter's detriment. Decking the bride with 'costly garments' and covering her with jewels brings out the gleam of avarice in her future in-laws' eyes. Demand and extortion are natural corollaries, and here is where dowry steps in to complete the sorry picture.

In Mughal times, often a younger sister was an item on the dowry list of a bride. She became the bridegroom's property thereafter.[17] Sister exchange; another form of marriage found not only in the Indian subcontinent but also formerly practised fairly widely in Australia, still exists among some African tribes and among the Yanomami.[18]

In India, this custom dating from ancient times, still continues among the lower income groups since it is more economical than carrying on money transactions with more than one set of in-laws.

In Sri Lanka however, sister exchange occurs among the well-to-do also as the following matrimonial advertisement will show:

> Govi Catholic parents seek well employed person for accomplished daughter with one brother, 29, very fair, pretty.

Passed O Level, and convent educated. Substantial cash dowry with gold jewellery available. Intermarriage if so desired for brother considered.[19]

The dowry giving parent in India generally looks for a bride-groom from a higher placed family than his own, hoping to buy his daughter a comfortable future and social approval for himself and his family. This sets the More-and-More ball rolling. The-more-he-gives-the-more-they-want. He borrows more and more, but is able to give less and less. As the in-laws' property, the bride may be tortured if it pleases them. Blackmail squeezes her parents dry. When she is of no future use to her husband's family, she may be killed or be driven to kill herself.

It is this insidious thread of dowry giving and taking, involving a woman's person, that has woven itself in and out of the whole fabric of Indian society. Even the uninhibited societies of the tribals are coming under its influence. At a time when more advanced countries are laying stress on human relationship as a foundation for marriage, our society is sinking deeper into an institutionalised system of exploitation which establishes an entirely commercial relationship between the kinsfolk of the young couple.

The story of dowry is a tale of men and women striving against heavier and heavier odds to 'keep their respect' in a relentlessly apathetic society where the price demanded is high in money, values and life.

'We will buy our grooms, isn't it?' Twenty year old Lata, a medical student from Vijayawada bursts out angrily. 'Haven't they got any self-respect? She spits suddenly and viciously out of the train window. 'These men!'

Two thousand years ago Euripides' Medea had given vent to the same feelings when she said:

'Of all things upon earth that bleed and grow,
A herb most bruised is woman. We must pay
Our store of gold, hoarded for that one day,
To buy us some man's love; and lo, they bring
A master of our flesh! There comes the sting
Of the whole shame. And then the jeopardy,
For good or ill, what shall that master be...[20]

Her sisters in twentieth century Greece still fight for personal dignity.

'Woman: 38—with moral principles—dowry 200,000 *drachmas* cash and 300 olive trees...'[21] says the matrimonial advertisement in a Greek newspaper in 1977. The bride carries her jewels in a casket as she goes to her wedding. In Crete a mule train carries the dowry which has won another bride a desirable husband. This dowry is the 'open seasame' to the glitter of life in the big city. The groom's relatives pose for a photograph, and proudly display the wealthy bride's dowry—silver articles, a carved chest, a huge bed, pots and pans.

'Customs are deep within our country's soul,' says Professor Andrew Gazis, Chairman of the Governing Committee that has been drafting the Anti-Dowry Bill. 'There will be no way to stop a father offering a daughter a gift when she marries. The big difference now is that she will be able to manage her money herself.'[22] Legislative pressure is on from the seven women in Greece's three hundred member parliament to do away with compulsory dowry.

The scene could so easily have been set in India where the very same problem exists after thousands of years of development, and where legislation still fights a losing battle against massive illiteracy and lack of education.

The Dowry Prohibition Act of 1961 comes at the end of a long line of efforts by kings, queens and social reformers to elevate the long-suffering, uncomplaining Indian woman from handmaid, back again to the trusted companion she once was.

With the advent of the British and the impact of Western thought on the Indian scene, Indian scholars and thinkers began to re-examine social and religious values—Raja Ram Mohan Roy, Keshab Chandra Sen, Pandita Ramabai, Karamat Hussain, Jotiba Phule, Behramji Malabar, Ishwar Chandra Vidyasagar and Hamid Dalwai—to mention only a few in a galaxy of eminent names.

Mahatma Gandhi's condemnation of the dowry system was forthright:

'Any young man who makes dowry a condition for marriage discredits his education and his country and dishonours womanhood. Young men who soil their fingers with such ill-gotten gold should be excommunicated from society.'[23]

> Jawaharlal Nehru appealed to college girls:
> 'Our marriage laws and many of our out-of-date customs which hold us back and especially crush our womenfolk—will you not combat them and bring them in line with modern conditions?... I charge you to keep that torch of freedom burning brightly till it spreads its lustre all over this ancient and dearly loved land of ours.'[24]

But in spite of everything, the buying and selling goes on:
'My face is my fortune, sir,' she said...
'Then I can't marry you, my pretty maid!'
'Nobody asked you, sir,' she said.
Now that is the kind of answer that would have done a world of good to many an Indian groom who puts fortune before bride, and there is the occasional woman who is courageous enough to refuse a money hungry wooer.

Mrinalini's father is a Gandhian who believes that he has no right to choose a husband for his daughter. Living in a small village in the most orthodox part of Uttar Pradesh, Mrinalini is twenty-four years old—well past the age considered marriageable anywhere in the country. She has been educated and trained to think independently and given the right to decide whom she will marry. Tiwari, a young engineer, attracted by the possibility of acquiring a highly educated bride comes to 'view' her. He comes from a middle class family and is well aware that Mrinalini's father is not planning on providing her future husband with a dowry. Tiwari comes with his mother and maternal uncle fully expecting the usual tea tray carried in demurely by the bride to be. To his surprise, the host calls out to his daughter, 'Mrinal, *beta*,[25] would you like to have a word with this young gentleman?' He then retires, taking the surprised mother and uncle with him, leaving the astounded young hopeful alone with his daughter. The object of the visit hangs awkwardly in the air between the composed young lady and the embarrassed man.

He clears his throat. Could she cook, sew, embroider? he asks. She answers politely with a twinkle in her eye, that she could. 'Had she written any novels? Could she sing and dance? Did he want a *nach gane walee*[26] for a wife? asks Mrinalini. He smiles awkwardly, ill at ease. Perhaps she could drive a scooter? Was she prepared to teach and work? She can do all this, she answers in growing disgust. 'And what about dowry?' he asks at length. 'My dowry,' says Mrinalini getting up, 'is what my parents have blessed me with—an educated mind and an open outlook.' She smiles. The interview is at an end. He leaves with an uncomfortable feeling that somehow, somewhere he has blundered ....

Excitement is in the air in a small town tucked away in the heart of Punjab on the Grand Trunk Road ... *Diwan Sahib's*[27] son, an up and coming *vakeel* — lawyer, tipped to go abroad has agreed to come with his family, and look over the local beauty, Shanta. The only trouble is that the school teacher's family, although of extremely respectable stock, might not be able to honour them with a suitably expensive wedding and a 'decent' dowry. However, they feel there is no harm in adding this girl to the list of the many they have already seen.

Ever since Shanta was a child, she has seen her father and mother working ceaslessly. She is the apple of their eye and their only child. She has been brought up to be married one day and she constantly lives with the thought. However, she has seen the humiliations her friends have been through before and after their weddings, and she is determined that her parents, come what may, will not suffer on her account. Her father is a retired school teacher and her mother has saved every *paisa* for 'my golden bird's dowry,' denying herself the barest necessities in the process.

The great day dawns. The *mohalla* — neighbourhood, is agog. Envious looks follow her. What a great family *Masterjee* has managed to attract! Shanta is excited but keeps her own counsel. The best lace work, cross-stitch table cloths and cushion covers are pulled out of the big tin trunk. The *halwai* — sweet vendor, sends over a plate of his best *laddoos* with glimmering silver foil on them to help *Masterjee* who has, after all, taught two of his sons. At 3.30 p.m. the great ones arrive. They note the threadbare carpet and the well worn sofa set. They delicately put their handkerchiefs to their noses as the overpowering smell of moth balls is borne in on them by the table fan. *Masterjee* and his wife are most solicitous for their comfort. Pleasantries are exchanged.

Diwan Sahib's wife looks languidly up from her polished nails. '*Aap ki reet rasam kya hain*?' — what are you customs?. In other words, 'Let's have it straight. How much are you willing to pay?'

Masterjee thinks hard. They had already decided that it did not become them nor their beloved daughter to give less than twenty-five thousand rupees inclusive of course, of wedding expenses. So he says as much, adding that he is a poor retired school master whom *Diwan Sahib* has shown great honour by deigning to consider his daughter for his illustrious family. *Diwan Sahib*, his wife and her brother go into a huddle. The prospective groom looks vacantly at the ceiling. His uncle speaks up, 'Well, *Masterjee*, there is a certain party from Bombay who has already offered us two lakhs. So...'

Masterjee, thunderstruck, looks at his wife. Perhaps if he mortgaged the house, he could raise another five thousand. He looks pleadingly at *Diwan Sahib* while addressing the uncle who had spoken earlier. 'I might be able to raise another five thousand rupees', he says. The glances from the other side are cold. They have two other girls in mind anyway, and they had only come here because they had heard she was worth a look.

'Shanta Beta!' calls Masterjee's wife.

Shanta is shaken. She has heard every word of the bargaining from behind the curtain. She can feel without having to see, her parents' discomfiture. She comes in, her eyes lowered—a picture of feminine charm and simple beauty in a plain pink *salwar qamiz*[28]—a plate of *laddoos* in her hand.

Diwan Sahib sits up, his eyes gleaming. The up and coming lawyer is galvanised. He leaps up from his chair. His uncle and mother forget about the fictitious two lakh deal awaiting them in Bombay. Why, this one is a prize! The mother already sees her elegantly attired, standing beside her son, easing him into the good books of his superiors and up the prestige ladder. Well if they don't have the money, it can't be helped. She would have to set her up somehow herself. Aloud she says, 'What is your name, *beti*?'

'Shanta' answers the girl offering her a laddoo, her eyes still on the plate.

Masterjee and his wife pray inwardly that all may yet go well for their child. Shanta sets the sweets on the table. 'I'll get the tea,' she says as she leaves the room.

'*Manzoor! Manzoor!*'[29] whispers the man. 'I agree! I want to marry only her.'

Masterjee looks anxiously from one parent to another. Diwan Sahib smiles as his wife's bony elbow pokes his side.

'Yes, Masterjee, we accept your daughter, and we shall settle it at thirty thousand rupees; but perhaps you would like to give a little more cash, because as you can see we shall have to get her used to our ways and introduce her into society, and so...'Masterjee sends up a silent prayer of thankfulness. He bows his head, 'Yes, I shall add another three thousand to that somehow,' he says softly.

The curtains part and Shanta re-enters with the tray. She slowly sets the tea things on the table, and looking her prospective in-laws full in the face, says quietly, 'But I do not accept. You have dishonoured my parents and made me feel like a sack of wheat on sale. You have seen other girls before me. God knows how many others will be ruined before they get a judgement from you on their future. Please have some tea and go to your two lakh proposal. We are simple people and we do not accept you or your highly placed son!'...

'What is your fortune?'

'This woman is mine, but I do not accept her without the wrapping. What is thine is mine, and what is mine is mine!'

Among some South Indian communities the number of gold chains around a prospective mother-in-law's neck proclaims the family's status to the girl's relatives during the negotiations without their having to utter a word. This ensures a better dowry than they might otherwise have been offered. Among the Chettiars, particularly those belonging to the middle income group, the *mamyar saman*—money, jewellery, gold, brass vessels and *saris*—is an essential part of the bride's dowry. This is meant solely for the mother-in-law. Even if the bride gets no *streedhanam*, the *mamyar saman* is absolutely necessary to keep the status flag flying.[30]

A good dowry has hooked a good 'catch' everywhere in the world, and girls who will stand up and be counted like Mrinalini and Shanta are few and far between. Passiveness has been beaten into their system for far too long.

Spartan women inherited, and were at liberty to bequeath landed property, and a great deal of Sparta's riches were theirs to do with as they pleased. In classic Greece marriages were made for profit, but a woman's dowry was her own property and returned to her in case of divorce. Needless to say the Greek husband was as a result, a self-controlled if not always model husband. In India today, dowry is supposed to be returned to the woman in case of divorce and to her family in case she dies childless,[31] although in practice the picture is often very different.

'Return the dowry? What are you saying, *behnji*? The day I entered their home, my mother-in-law took away all my jewellery from my body and said it is to be kept in the bank for safety. My fifty one beautiful saris and my all clothes—They are still with them. One key "she" had and one key "he" had. I have lived in my these four *saris* which I am washing for past three years.' Sarla turns sharply away so that I may not see the tear that cannot be held back any more. She has just obtained a divorce on grounds of cruelty and desertion.

Between 506 and 202 B.C. a Roman matron had no rights either in the use of her dowry or in her husband's estate; nor could she have recourse to law; but by 148 B.C. Cato was complaining, 'We Romans who rule over all men, are ruled by our women!'[32] The Roman woman had become rich enough to be suddenly desirable to all ambitious bachelors. An advantageous marriage with a substantial dowry eased Cicero into politics[33] in much the same manner as our ambitious Indian bachelors these days are helped up the social ladder, given an entry into the business world, or educated in foreign countries all on the strength of a 'father-in-law' scholarship.

It was only by about 30 B.C. that the Italian courts took over from the Roman *pater familias* and ruled that an adulterous wife would lose half her dowry and one third of her fortune, and of- course, could never re-marry. Her husband, needless to say, invariably got off scot free.[34]

The medieval Jew set aside a marriage settlement to be paid to his wife in case of divorce. This was based on the same principle as the Muslim *Mahr* which forms part of Islamic law to this day.[35]

The Jewish widow received the full 'marriage settlement' as well as her dowry after her husband's death. The Jewish daughter, like her Hindu counterpart in an Indian joint family before the passing of the Hindu Succession Act of 1956, inherited only if there was no male to continue the line. She was otherwise entirely dependent on the dubious bounty of her brothers and their wives.[36] This is comparable with the predicament of the Syrian Christian girls in Kerala today.

In medieval England marriage was a matter of property adjustments and financial deals. A husband was made in the image of God, and as such he had full control over any property his wife may have brought with her to her marriage. He could invest it and use the interest or do as he pleased with it. His wife's word on the other hand, could not be admitted in court because of her 'frailty.'[37]

The bridegroom however, gave his bride a one-third right in his estate and also a 'morning gift.'[38]

As in most countries, the brunt of meeting the dowry expenses fell heavily on the bride's father who apart from supplying his daughter with a dowry and clothing, was also expected to present the groom's parents and family with gifts, as well as provide the young couple with linen, utensils, furniture and wherever possible—landed property. A wife was her husband's bondwoman and until the passing of the Married Woman's Property Act in 1882, all her movable property continued to be in her husband's possession, unless a trust had been established which kept him from using up the capital. It was only with divorce that a wife could even begin to think that her belongings might possibly return to her.[39] Man's inventive brain is forever devising ingenious methods of keeping property within the family. First cousin marriages sometimes celebrated in the Muslim community in India and elsewhere, as also maternal uncle and niece marriages occasionally performed in some South Indian Hindu communities and elsewhere in the country often help in ensuring control over consolidated family property.

Such marriages continue in spite of well publicised medical research which has clearly demonstrated that the nearer the relationship between marital partners, the greater the risk of mental retardation in their offspring.[40]

Marriages in ancient Egypt between half-brothers and sisters were fairly common.[41] Although there is some controversy about whether brother/sister marriages were common there or not, it is an established fact that by the time the Ptolemies began to rule Egypt, the Pharoah was expected to marry his sister. This may have been because 'The Great Wife of the king was the heiress' and the throne went to the Pharoah only by marriage with her,[42] since a princess could not rule in her own right and needed a husband to give her the seal of authority. So the beautiful Cleopatra married her younger brother Ptolemy XIII[43] to keep the royal blood blue. By this time however, brother/sister marriages seem to have become a far more general practice there. So much so that lovers addressed each other as 'brother' and 'sister'.[44] In ancient Persia even father/daughter marriages have been recorded.[45]

Polyandry also helps keep this well-loved property together.[46] The desire to preserve an estate intact makes it quite the done thing for several brothers to share a common wife. Any of the brothers wishing to bring another woman into the family has to await the green signal from the ruling lady of the house. If he decides to set up house elsewhere, he loses all rights in the family property.[47]

Polyandry in hilly areas where the soil is rocky, and cultivable land limited, joint ownership and cultivation ensure maximum returns. Fragmentation of this land would be a highly uneconomical proposition.

For the woman in a polyandrous family, it is a hard life. She does a herculean job of work from crack of dawn to long after midnight, hours after her menfolk are asleep She sees to it however, that she gets her due. Polyandry ensures her protection at all times by at least one of her husbands, even if the others have to involve themselves in various occupations connected with their property which may take them long distances away from the homestead. Had she been the wife of one man alone, she would have been entirely unprotected in his absence.

The long day over, the queen of the household comes into her own. She is the sole dispenser of the comforts of her men. She decides whom she will favour for the night, and quietly lies down by his side. Her views are respected by the others.[48]

In Lahaul and Ladakh, an unmarried girl controls her father's property as long as she is alive. If she marries, she may bring her husband to live in her father's house[49] as a *magpa* a son-in-law in the house[50] and thus keep her inheritance. The moment she leaves the homestead for her husband's house, she forfeits all claim to it.

Polyandry occurs where there is a scarcity of women perhaps due earlier to female infanticide, internecine warfare or other causes. The bride is married to one brother and paid for. The others, as we have seen, stand in the queue. So when your gardener who hails from such an area takes leave three times in the year because his 'father has just died,' his tears may well be genuine. It is quite possible that three out of his four or five Uncle-fathers, have been stricken in the same year. By the same token, it would be quite in order for him to want to run home and congratulate his wife on the birth of a son conceived in his absence. The time to sit up and take notice, however, might be when his wife dies more than once.

Desire for landed property has ruled mankind ever since someone discovered that possession is power and a means of becoming eternal. Mahatma Gandhi was convinced that 'the root of the evil lies... in man's greed for power and fame... Ownership of property gives this power. Man also hankers after posthumous fame based on power. This cannot be had if property is progressively cut up in pieces, as it must if all posterity become equal co-sharers: hence, the descent of property for the most part on the eldest male issue.'[51]

Property is the mainstay and prime concern of the joint family. The people who live on it enjoy certain rights in it only because they are closely related. Three generations of males who have inherited it, their immediate relatives and their extended families have varying rights in it. Those closest to the nucleus, of course, get the lion's share. The outer circle composed of widows, unmarried daughters of immediate relatives and *ghar jawais* are entitled to maintenance on the proceeds of the land in varying degree.

It is not the patriarchal society alone that is plagued with this hankering after property. The emasculated *ghar jawai* is a direct product of a matriarchal society's desire to keep the property in the family. Even the tribal world is afflicted by this disease. Among the Garos of Meghalaya where the property follows the maternal line, a son-in-law is even expected to marry his widowed mother-in-law who is the owner of the property to keep her from developing outside interests.[52]

When little Grace de Saleby was married off to an influential and rich medieval nobleman, surrounded as she must have been with dolls and fairy stories, she could never have suspected she was being used as a pawn in the inheritance game. She had been married twice before—once at the age of four and again when she was six, to one lord after another. These marriages were mano-euvered so that the estate remained intact.[53]

Nor could the full blooded Eleanor of Acquitaine, owner of the prize revenue producing port of Bordeaux, have guessed that Louis VII's passion for her was prodded not by her personal charms, but by her dowry.[54]

So here is our Indian bride, coming in an illustrious tradition of dowry carriers—a bejewelled cow surrounded by all the status symbols of high living, waiting to take the seven auspicious steps around the sacramental fire, to walk up the aisle to an altar or to sign a marriage contract. A bride who will become a Mother of Sons who will continue their father's line and provide the eternal permanence his soul craves: 'Look at them,' men will say long after he is no more. 'How well they have cared for the property their father provided them with! Worthy sons of an honourable father!'

...And here is the process by which the bride reaches this coveted position:

'Wanted: Aggarwal, Jain—really beautiful rich family girl for handsome, 24 practicing Advocate, only son, millionaire family...'[55]

'Wanted: an excellent convent educated match for Arora boy... having flourishing independent export business with turnover in millions. Owns bungalow in posh colony and other properties. Standardised modern living. Income high. Five figures per month. Maintains cars...'[56]

'Wanted: Well placed Hindu/Sikh Defence Executive or businessman... for Sikh graduate working girl earning four figure salary. Father retired Gazetted Officer...'[57]

Dowry is banned by law. So devious methods have to be devised to get the message across for under the counter dealings.

Here is everything the parties would like to say but cannot publicly proclaim:

In the first two advertisements, the boys' parents are trying to show that their families are used to a high standard of living. They are rich and expect to receive replies from girls whose families if not equally well off, are at least prepared to set themselves and their sons up in the standard they are all accustomed to, with all the trappings of highly connected living. Those who cannot afford such a relationship, say the advertisements loud and clear, need not waste our time by replying.

The third advertisement is the bait the father of a would-be bride throws. He clearly says, 'My daughter will be a never drying source of money. A four figure salary will flow regularly every month into your home. It will be for you to use as you wish. Our family is well placed. Although I am retired, I still have one of the best classes of government service against my name. So what with one thing and another, we can have a good, high class wedding also, if you so desire.'

The advertisement scanners now get down to the serious business of analysis: That the girl is educated is a good sign; nowadays of course, they would like to know whether she is convent educated or not. This would be a feather in their family's cap. Gone are the days when education was considered a disadvantage. She should not however be 'uppish' in her new home. Working girls are just fine. Doctors are the best bet as they can always be relied on to keep their son and themselves in money. The next important consideration is whether the girl's family is 'Well-Connected and Highly Placed' or not. This is essential as if the girl's earnings should flag, her family could be a continuing source of strength in the uncertainties of modern living. Without this support their darling son would, God forbid, be constrained to fall back on his own resources to maintain his wife and her children! An ideal connection should pour into the receiving family an unending river of modern luxuries from TV, 'fridge and cooking range down to car, scooter or cycle and wrist watch—depending on how high up the social ladder they aspire to ascend. If respectability and a good name are their goals, their attention can be discreetly drawn to the gaping hole in the bedroom wall made specially to accommodate the airconditioner which they had doubtless planned on giving their daughter. Then the bridegroom's mother would certainly need a change of *sari*, now and again, and the wedding suit stitched for the groom would naturally have to be of the best quality, as these other varieties fray so fast and are only worn by the kind of people who cannot afford the best. Incidental mention could also be made of the fact that the bridegroom's sister was about to be married, and the tailor could supply her measurements should they feel inclined to present her with suitable outfits...

Such a family once hooked would naturally be asked to see that a 'decent' wedding is celebrated for their son-in-law. Since his family lives in Delhi, the bride's people surely would not object to having a huge party at one of the biggest hotels there.

A little inconvenience in coming a few hundred miles to the capital with all the wedding paraphernalia would be nothing compared to the honour and respect they would gain from the whole community.

Sometimes the tensions of the matrimonial columns in the daily papers are relieved by insertions like the following:

'An innocent divorcee, paragon of beauty.'[58] — the person referred to is obviously an unusual gentleman — or a surgeon who works in New York and is 'worth $40,000.00 per annum. He is milky white, teetotaller.'[59]—'a healthy pious boy without any bad habits'[60]—or again, a man 'who won't smoke, chew, booze, or see cinema.'[61] What a remarkable breed of men!

In Sri Lanka dowry is out in the open. Although the ancient Hindu tradition describes dowry as being mainly movable goods, the Sri Lankan tradition includes a house and lands as well. This is by no means confined to the Hindus:

> 'Respectable Govi Catholic parents seek partners for only daughter 21 year, 5 feet; convent educated, passed O Level in Science. Doing ATCL in Piano music.
> *Dowry*: New house and property worth over a lac.
> *Jewellery*: Over Rs. 30,000/- New Piano: Rs. 15,000/- and cash Rs. 10,000/- Apply with full particulars.'[62]

Old values are undergoing a sea change. The farmer's sights are set on the big city. Bombay and Madras films churn out heroes who zoom about in flashy cars, smoke expensive cigarettes, live in incredible palaces among statues and fountains and cuddle obliging foreign women or their Indian counterparts. These things become desirable to him. He begins to slosh through his mud caked fields in floor length bell bottom pants, a transistor slung from his shoulder, shrieking his newly acquired status to the skies.

Ancient tradition has always been the arch enemy of modernity. They can only work hand in hand when the mind has been trained to build on the good inherited from the past, and to look ahead into the future with clear undistorted vision. Our caste and community pressures take advantage of the absence of educated minds to enslave men and women in their group control, to abide by their attitudes and behavioural norms. Man being a social animal is unable to live in isolation, and his very life hangs on his community's approval.

Having recently come into good money, therefore, he is warned that society will point an accusing finger at him if his womenfolk do any manual work. This would mean that he has not progressed. He has been found wanting. He has not been capable of earning enough to keep his women deliciously and respectably idle at home.

'Why are you working in your fields? Don't you have servants? Doesn't your master earn enough to get a tractor? Do you mean to tell me that you even bathe the buffaloes yourself? *Hai hai hai*! He has made good money from this harvest. What a shame for the family! You shouldn't let anyone see you sweeping your courtyard. God be praised your grandfather has gone to heaven and cannot see the degradation that has come to his family! *Hai hai hai*!

So our healthy young girl—who enjoyed equal status as a working partner with her husband, is reduced to an incubus. Not being allowed to take an active part in work, she begins to glean her ideals from the cinema, the TV and the few magazines she may be able to read or see pictures from.

Here she finds that heroines spend their entire time in trying to look glamorous, singing or jerking in contortions that go by the name of dancing. She also notes that in spite of doing nothing at all, they still seem to win the admiration of the hero and the respect of society. They never lack money for a change of outfit in which they seem to float diaphonously through every film. This concerted attack on our future bride's senses leads her to suppose that it is old fashioned and beneath her dignity to want to involve herself in the manual labour she had earlier enjoyed. She refuses to work in the fields, and gradually, even in the home. Her world has progressed. Richer girls no longer need to, and poorer ones no longer want to work. 'Face' and 'nose' have to be kept from being blackened or cut off in a changed society. From a much sought-after asset, she has turned into a worthless liability—a 'milk white complexioned' (a necessary qualification for a bride—according to matrimonial advertisements) ornament, educated only as much as strictly necessary. If she gets a degree against her name or becomes a 'teacheress,' she may want to marry above her status. If her family's daily living is just above the poverty line, this would be most inadvisable, as the higher the rung of the marriage ladder, the more extortionate the demands.

Her education should only be marriage oriented. If the demand is for doctors, whether this is her inclination or not, that is what she should aim for. If the marriage market wants her convent educated in an English medium school, it does not matter whether her family has never spoken one word of English in their lives. That is where she is bound. Tutors will be kept and 'B-A-T bat' and 'C-A-T cat' will be dinned into her head. She has to be trimmed to fit the currently popular frame. To sell this mass produced portrait brought out by the marriage merchants, her father will have to smother it in alluring accompaniments...

Marriage is the time when the bridegroom's family makes up all its losses and plans to live the good life on the demands they make from the bride's kith and kin. After all, are they not relieving them of the millstone around their necks? 'This stone will now hang around our son's neck, and we expect to be adequately compensated for our pains,' says the canny mother-in-law.

The girl's family has no choice. The shoe is now on the other foot, and whether they can afford it or not, a 'good' marriage has to be made, otherwise 'what will people say!'

So it works like this:

When economic necessity dictated that a working partner be brought into the household, bride price was paid to compensate the bride's father for the loss of a valued labourer, and the bride went to her new home. Money and valuables flowed into her parents' home as she moved in the opposite direction. Approval of the caste and community remained with her parents. Side by side however, the nagging feeling existed that the whole operation amounted to the covert sale of a daughter and was therefore not to be openly indulged in by those who might know better. It left a slightly acrid taste in the mouth and the idea of paying for a bride gradually began to lose favour. Add to this the human desire to appear as rich and prosperous as those in the highest circles and the constant attack on the old value system by every arm of the media, and the stage is all set for the drama of dowry.

In this drama, the parents of the hero, and often the hero himself are the chief actors. The parents have come to recognize the fact that they own the goose that lays the golden egg. So they invest in a foreign education for their eldest son, somehow putting enough capital together. This prize bull will on his return from 'foreign' be auctioned off to the highest bidder. The huge dowry he fetches will be re-invested in another 'foreign' education for the second son, whose takings will provide the dowry that will accompany his sister at her marriage. Thus the final harvest will be well worth the initial investment.

The idea has caught on, and the 'father-in-law scholarship' books a bridegroom in many parts of our subcontinent. Here for instance, is a marriage advertisement from Sri Lanka:

> 'High caste Hindu bachelor 28 years, technically qualified, presently employed in a leading firm drawing an attractive salary, seeks very good charactered, homely attractive girl below 23 years. Those who can afford to help in my studies abroad only need apply.'[63]

And another from Kuwait asking for 'Christian youths' from Kerala for a girl who is employed in Kuwait....'If the boy is interested, help could be extended for employment or higher studies abroad.'[64]

It is of interest to note here the role of the mother-in-law in the business of her son's marriage. She has given birth to a son. This has saved her from a fate worse than death. As a mother of daughters no one could have guaranteed her a secure place in the family hierarchy. As it is, she is transformed from an apprehensive bride to a reigning queen—A Mother of Sons, who gradually becomes the very person she dreaded when she stepped hesitantly into the house as a young bride—an authoritarian mother-in-law.The change is gradual, borne in on her with the realisation that this son is uniquely hers—her husband incarnate, given to her by a benign Providence...

'The husband, after conception by his wife, becomes an embryo and is born of her,' says Manu.[65] Since her being is inextricably interwoven with her husband's, it follows that it also forms a mystic part of her son's. Therefore, his health, wealth and future are her old age insurance and anything that concerns his life must of necessity be her affair, and cannot be left to the vagaries of chance or 'love.'

The next inexorable step is the selection of a bride worthy enough to be not only his wife, but a suitably docile, and useful daughter-in-law. How much is she worth—in land, in social status, in clothes and jewellery, in hard cash—or in everything weighed together? Will her kith and kin keep the home fires burning long after the sacramental wedding fire has died out?

Wrapped around in sugary layers of mother love, an eagle eye angled to assuring a beloved son's future comfort, the calculating glance sizes up the future bride, reducing her relentlessly to cold cash. Greed having once got a foothold, latches on, and like the proverbial camel, edges out the original inhabitant of the tent—humanity.

Having found fertile soil and fed daily on a diet of general acquiescence the all devouring and still hungry 'Gimmee'[66] now takes over as the principal actor in the dowry drama.

Laxmi Ramaswamy quotes two letters from a prospective Hindu father-in-law in an article in Roshni magazine of January-March 1975, long after the Dowry Prohibition Act of 1961 was passed:

'Dear....

1. We accept your offer of contribution of Rs. 5,000/- as dowry.
2. But we want another Rs. 2,500 for meeting the train fare etc., of our own family members including children which will be about 23 in all.
3. Dress for the bridegroom about Rs. 1,000/-
4. Beddings, etc.
5. Vessels—silver, stainless steel, brass. Please state how much for each item.
6. Sarees. etc.,—how many and for which occasion? Please state clearly.
7. *Vadhyar Dakshina*[67] etc., and the safe conduct of the marriage. Please state whether I should contribute anything towards the same.
8. Finally—ornaments—gold about (30) thirty sovereigns you will have to put for your daughter.
9. Diamond ear ring pair, each of seven stones.

I have done all these things satisfactorily for both my daughters, and their relatives are expected to attend the marriage. So please see that I command my respect among them as regards my son also.

Sd/-.....

'Dear...

The details of the final break up are as under.

Jewels	Rs. 8,000	consisting of 30 sovereigns of gold ornaments apart from the ear ring and the nose screw.
Vessels	Rs. 5,000	We can decide the break up of this into silver and stainless steel when we meet in Madras as in any case you will be buying the vessels here.
Marriage expenses	Rs. 12,000	If this amount is slightly exceeded, I am sure you will not mind it.
Dress and ring	Rs. 2,000	You can pay us this in cash when we meet so that we can make our own choice.

Sarees for the girl and dhotis for the boy Rs. 1,500/-

The other expenses mentioned by you being your personal ones, I have no comments to make and therefore excluded these from the marriage expenses.

I might also add that an amount of Rs. 1,500/- towards cots and beds may be paid in cash so that we may make our own choice. Your wife has already agreed to this.

Sd/-....'[68]

The 'Gimmee' is now riding the heady wave of popular approval. Religion has sanctified his demands. Family, caste and community are acquiescent if not actively aiding and abetting the destruction of the bride's self respect and her family's fortune. The 'Gimmee's cavernous mouth is wide open and his insatiable appetite takes him through one wedding after another demanding, demanding...

'Jewellery of the value of 30 sovereigns
diamond earrings and nose screw for the bride
ring for the groom
silver vessels not weighing less than 5 kg.
brass and stainless steel household utensils in adequate quantity
"decent" marriage celebration.'

(A list of demands made by a laboratory assistant whose monthly salary does not exceed three hundred rupees.)[69]

NOTES AND REFERENCES

1. Respectful form of address for a clergyman.
2. Daughter.
3. *Manusmiriti*: III: 27: F. Max Mueller, (ed.) The Sacred Books of the East, translated: G. Buehler: Vol. xxv, The Laws of Manu, Motilal Banarsi Dass, 1964, p. 80.
4. *Ibid.*, verse 28.
5. *Ibid.*, verse 29.
6. *Ibid.*, verse 30, Max Mueller, *op. cit.* pp. 80-81.
7. *Ibid.*, verse 39, Max Mueller, *op. cit.* p. 82.
   Sishtas: good men.
8. *Ibid.*, verse 41, Max Mueller, *op. cit.* p. 83.
9. *Ibid.*, verse 34, Max Mueller, *op. cit.* p. 81.
10. A.S. Altekar, The Position of Women in Hindu Civilization, Motilal Banarsi Dass, 1962, p. 36.
11. Mansmriti III, 33, Max Mueller, *op. cit.* p. 81.
12. *Mahabharata* I : 245; 5-6, as quoted in Altekar *op. cit.*, p. 37: The *Rakshasa* or *Kshatra* form of marriage.
13. *Manusmriti* III: verse 31: Max Mueller, *op. cit.*, p. 81.
14. *Ibid.*, verse 32.
15. Kama Sutra: A treatise on sexual love. *The Kama Sutra of Vatsayan*, translated by Burton & Arbuthnot, Allen and Unwin, London, 1963, Part III, Ch. V. pp. 190-93.
16. Altekar, *op. cit.,* 1962, p. 43.
17. Rekha Misra, *Women in Mughal India,* (1526-1748): New Delhi; First Published, 1967: Allahabad. Munshiram Manoharlal Oriental Publishers, 1967, p. 131 (Dowry) quoting T.C. Das Gupta, *Aspects of Bengali Society*, p.3.
18. J. ,Goody, and S.J. Tambiah, Bride wealth and Dowry, Cambridge University Press, London, 1973: Sister Exchange, p. 35 and Yanomamo: Marvin Harris, Cows Pigs, Wars and Witches, Fontana/Collins, Glasgow, 1974, p. 67: see also : Chs. 3 note 27, and 9: notes 42-45, *Sister Exchange*: Exchange marriages also occur among the *Patidars* of Central Gujarat and among the *Brahmin Pundits* of Kashmir. In places where there is a dearth of women, an exchange marriage arranged for a daughter by her father will provide an honourable marriage for her brother as well, and will be less expensive. Klaas W. van der Veen, I Give Thee My Daughter, A Study of Marriage and Hierarchy Among the *Anavil Brahmans* of South Gujarat, Assen, Van Gorcum and Company. N.V. the Netherlands, 1972, p. 47.

19. *The Sunday Observer*, Sri Lanka, 27 February 1977.
20. Euripides: Medea: 410 f. translated by G. Murray Oxford, 1912, p. 15 as quoted by Will Durant, 1939 *op. cit.*, *The Life of Greece,* Ch. XVII, p. 403.
21. 'Greece: Should Men Be Bought?' Article in *Time* Magazine, 17 January 1977.
22. *Ibid.*
23. Mohandas Karamchand Gandhi, writing in *Young India*, 21 June 1928.
24. Jawaharlal Nehru, message to the Prayag Mahila Vidyapitha, Allahabad, 12 January 1934.
25. Son: often used as on endearment for a daughter who would normally be called '*beti*'.
26. Nautch girl.
27. An honorific title.
28. A Punjabi outfit consisting of loose pantalooms, a long shirt and a veil.
29. I accept.
30. The *Chettiar* bridegroom's parents pay for the entire wardrobe of their daughter-in-law for the first three years of marriage. The *mamyar saman* is often a help during this period.
31. The Hindu Succession Act, 1956:
    Section 15: *General rules of succession in the case of female Hindus:*
    (2) (a) any property inherited by a female Hindu *from her father or mother* shall devolve, in the absence of any son or daughter of the deceased (including children of any pre-deceased son or daughter)...*upon the heirs of the father;*
    (b) any property inherited by a female Hindu *from her husband or from her father-in-law* shall devolve, in the absence of any son or daughter of the deceased (including children of any predeceased son or daughter)...*upon the heirs of the husband.* See also Chapter 17: His Share, or Mine?
    (emphasis mine)
32. Plutarch, *Cato the Elder*, as quoted by Will Durant, The Story of Civilization, Simon and Schustar, New York, *Caesar and Christ*, 1944, Ch. V, p. 89.
33. *Ibid.*, Ch. VII, p. 141.
34. *Ibid.*, Ch. XI, p. 223.
35. See Chapter 6.
36. Will Durant, *Op. cit., The Age of Faith* (1950), Ch. XVI, p. 381.
37. *Ibid.*, Ch. XXX, p. 826.
    The British woman is still fighting for equality. 'Neither the inland revenue nor the social security department accord rights to women. For taxation and most welfare payments, the government regards a woman's earnings as belonging to her husband.' (*Reuters, The Times of India, 1 July, 1978.*)

Towards the close of the millenium, the British woman's financial affairs have undergone a change for the better, even though inequalities in pay scales persist with women's gross hourly earnings being 79% of the men's. (*Reuters, June 25, 1995.*)

With the introduction on April 6, 1990 of Independent Taxation, the British married woman has for the first time, a full tax allowance in her own right. Every person, male or female, married or single, has become entitled to a personal tax allowance. A wife's income is no longer taxed as belonging to her husband. Both partners are independently taxed, and a married woman enjoys a larger measure of privacy and independence in tax matters.

(The British High Commission, New Delhi, 1996.)

38. Will Durant, *The Age of Faith*, *op. cit.,* Ch. XXX, p. 823.
39. Bertrand Russell, *Marriage and Morals*, London, Allen and Unwin, Eighth impression, 1948, p. 66.
40. Seeta Sinclair, 'Familial Mental Retardation and Parental Consanguinity,' *Indian Journal of Medical Research:* 60: 1718-23: 1972.
41. Vern L and Bonnie Bullough, The Subordinate Sex, University of Illinois Press, Urbana, Chicago, 1974, p. 32. Jaroslav . Cerny, 'Consanguinous Marriage in Pharonic Egypt,' *Journal of Egyptian Archeology*: 40 (1954) 23 ff.
42. *Ibid*., p. 31 (Margaret A. Murray, *The Splendour That Was Egypt*: rev: N.Y. Hawthorn Books, 1963, p. 102).
43. Will Durant, *op. cit., Caesar and Christ*, 1944, Ch. IX, p. 188.
44. Ivar Lissner, *The Living Past*, translated by J. Maxwell Brownjohn, London, Jonathan Cape, 1957, pp. 78-79.
45. *Ibid*., p. 119.
46. *Polyandry*: This institution, common in ancient Sparta, still exists in some Eskimo tribes, among the *Wahuma* of East Africa, in the less accessible highland regions of Sri Lanka (Krishna Iyer and Ratnam, *op. cit.*, 1961, p. 139), among the lower income groups of Uttar Pradesh, Assam and Bihar, the *Todas* of the Nilgiris, the *Kaniyans* and *Pannikans* of Cochin (Y.S. Parmar, Polyandry in the Himalayas, New Delhi, Vikas, 1975, p. 90) and as we have already noted, it is very much the way of life in Himachal Pradesh and on the Tibetan plateau.
47. Parmar, 1975, p. 84.
48. *Ibid*., p. 91.
49. *Ibid*., p. 90.
50. *Ghar Jawai*:

    The son-in-law who lives in the home of his bride's parents is a guest husband. Property plays an important role in emasculating him. Maternal descent gives the property to daughters. The husband's earnings are absorbed by the household, and his children will quite often carry their maternal grandfather's name. The property remains under the control of the maternal blood line.

The *Nambudiri Brahmans*, the matriarchal *Nayars* and the *Mappila* ('*Moplah*') Muslims of Kerala follow this custom. Although the large joint families in South India are breaking up and change is coming fast to these communities, there are still some matriarchal households among the Nayars and the Mappilas where some three hundred persons live in sprawling homesteads.

The custom is by no means restricted to South India. A number of Punjabi families have sons-in-law living in their wives' homes, and although fast dying out, the institution of the *ghar jawai* or *ghar jamai* exists in scattered areas over most of North India.

The *Kandyan Sinhalese* living in the isolated hills of central Sri Lanka and some *Tamils* of Jaffna also in Sri Lanka, also have their equivalent of the *ghar jawai*. Russia's *ghar jawai* is called a *primak*. Jack Goody, *op. cit.*, p. 26 quoting S.P. and E. Dunn: *The Peasants of Central Russia :* New York, 1967, p. 74.

51. D.G. Tendulkar, Mahatma: Life of Mohandas Karamchand Gandhi, Vol. II, Government of India, The Publications Division, second edition, 1961, p. 366.
52. The Adivasis, Government of India The Publications Division, 1955, p. 112.
53. Will Durant, *The Age of Faith*, 1950, Chapter XXX, p. 823 quoting E. Power, *Medieval People*, 118.
54. *Ibid.*, p. 827.
55. *The Hindustan Times Weekly*, 30 July 1978.
56. *The Hindustan Times Weekly*, 31 December 1978.
57. *The Times of India*, 23 January 1977.
58. *The Sunday Statesman*, 30 January 1977.
59. *Ibid.*
60. *The Malayala Manorama.* May 16, 1978.
61. *Ibid.*
62. *The Sunday Observer*, 20 February 1977.
63. *Ibid.*, 13 November 1977.
64. *The Malayala Manorama*, 7 May 1978.
65. *Manusmriti*: IX: 8. Max Mueller *op. cit.*, p. 329.
66. 'Give me!'
67. Offering made to a preceptor. In this context it means money or goods given to the priest who performs a Hindu marriage.
68. Roshni magazine, pp. 24, 25;
Journal of the All India Women's Conference: January/March 1975 issue.
69. 'A Bridegroom for Sale,' a *Statesman* survey, 17 February 1976.

They wanted to get her married off at any cost.
women carry a price tag
More dowry deaths
Make a marriage vow with a
DOWRY DEFACES WEDDING PARTY
harassed brides
POST GRADUATE DELHI GIRL
UNIVERSITY. FATHER
VERY SENIOR OFFICER
WELL CONNECTED FAM-
ILY VERY DECENT HIGH
STATUS MARRIAGE.
WRITE BOX 70
TIMES
The burning issue
Maruti or else...
Wife burnt alive for Rs20

8

How Filthy is Lucre?

The Christian girl of North India is not generally overburdened with dowry troubles although the status boat is beginning to rock as more 'progressive'. Muslim and Christian families have begun to step into it. The Roman Catholics of Goa have inherited both the Latin tradition of heavy dowry giving as well as the social customs of their neighbours of other faiths.[1]

It is in South India that dowry assumes frightening proportions among the Christians who have for centuries absorbed many of the traditions of the Hindu community from which they originally come. Even though social intermingling among religious communities here is almost non-existent, the Hindu dowry tradition is firmly entrenched among the Roman Catholics of Mangalore and the Syrian Christians of Kerala.[2]

The trouble spot is mainly in the laws governing inheritance. The Syrian Christians are still governed by an antiquated law which was framed when Kerala consisted of two States—Travancore and Cochin. The orthodox argument is that since this religious community already has a special law, the more liberal and therefore perhaps suspect Indian Succession Act of 1925 cannot be imposed on it. To make confusion worse confounded, there are within Kerala itself, various categories of Christians who are not subject to the old Travancore and Cochin legislations; while still others are ruled by the Hindu Succession Act of 1956.[3]

What in fact is all the fuss about?

The Travancore Christian Succession Act of 1916 provides that if a father dies without specifically leaving cash or property to his daughter, she will be awarded by law: *either* five thousand rupees which is the upper limit in cash allowed the girl, regardless of the downward plunge of the rupee since 1916, *or* one quarter of her brother's share—'*whichever is less*'.[4]

What is more, if she has been given or promised any *streedhanam* at all by her parents, she forfeits her claim to even this amount of her patrimony.

The Cochin Christian Succession Act of 1921 provides that if a father has died leaving sons and daughters, each daughter is to be awarded a share which will be equal to one-third the share of a son.[5]

The son therefore is assured a greater right in his patrimony than a daughter. Again, since children in Kerala do not have any inheritance by right of birth, the daughter is left out in the cold altogether. Her future is wrapped up in an extremely chancy piece of paper—her father's will.

This situation causes almost an anxiety neurosis among the girls who are either completely cowed down by their parents or feel that they have to try and squeeze whatever they can out of them in the form of *streedhanam* as that will be all they will ever get.

Earlier, guests used to be invited to the engagement ceremony as informal witnesses of the handing over of the bridal portion to the girl as is the custom among many South Indian Hindu communities, notably the Aiyangars. This custom has often helped a deserted bride to reclaim her money from the ex-husband. Nowadays however, the affectionately given and provident *streedhanam* is undergoing a transformation and has become full-fledged demand dowry. The bride is not only expected to bring with her the traditional *streedhanam* of jewellery, clothes and cash, but also furniture, car, television and other luxuries which cannot be called anything other than dowry. So Kerala Christians join the ranks of parents all over the country who bend the knee before the almighty groom's family, singing paeans of praise and offering worthy gifts.

In 1956 the Kerala Courts were faced with having to decide whether the Indian Succession Act of 1925 could apply to the Syrian Christians in the state. In his judgement, Mr. Justice Joseph Vithayathil said, 'Since the Indian Succession Act was not intended to interfere with the personal laws of communities which have settled laws of their own..' it 'would not apply to Christians in Travancore who were governed by the Travancore Christian Succession Act.'[6]

So it was the decision of a single judge, himself a Syrian Christian, that spelled disaster for the community. His decision stands to this day, causing much heart burning among the women who realise they have been reduced to permanent dependence on their men, begging at their brothers' doors for charity.

It is only an 'aggrieved party' that can remedy matters by taking such a complaint to the Supreme Court, but there are few who would be willing to make the time, screw up enough courage, or put in the money or the effort to get another ruling on this judgement. So the *status quo* continues.[7]

In 1975 when Thomas and Sarakutty stood in court to hear the judge pronounce his verdict on their case, the Kerala High Court was again agog with excitement. This time it was a question of whether the *streedhanam* which Sarakutty had brought to her marriage could be claimed by her as she and her husband were parting company.[8]

Although the judgement was not in Sarakutty's favour, it was the first time that a Kerala court heard a judge come out in the open against the 'inequities perpetrated by the Christian Succession Acts applicable to Travancore and Cochin Christian community...'

'The conscience of the community has to assert itself to get justice in the matter of inheritance to daughters,' said Mr. Justice V. Khalid. 'That the daughter of a millionaire Christian is entitled under the law today also to a maximum of only Rs. 5,000.00 in his assets after his death, is something unthinkable...'[9]

However, he felt he could not direct Thomas to return Sarakutty's *streedhanam*[10] as the *streedhanam* which is the subject matter of the suit falls within the expression "dowry" occurring in the Act.'[11] It would, in other words, be demand dowry plain and simple—given in order to make the bride a more interesting marriage proposition...

'What other definition would you have given it?' I asked the attractive college student. 'Would you have called it a "gift of affection"? Would you yourself ask your father for this kind of dowry?'

Sosamma smiled as if to say, 'What a strange question! Of course I would ask my father for a dowry!' Aloud she said quietly '*Streedhanam* is my right. I would certainly like to have it and also what is my due share in my father's wealth.'

'You see,' chirruped Mariamma, 'here it is different from the

North where there is cruelty in treatment of brides who were bringing less dowry. We do not have that kind of torture here. Of course, there will be some mental cruelty because the mother-in-law and elder ladies will make the girl work too hard or they may taunt her. Sometimes she is even beaten or sent home, but we also have to have our share in our father's wealth, no? After all, we know the law is so outdated and why should we be cut off from our rights?'

'But you remember, Mariamma, how Lily's cousin – that retarded girl, that Susan – She was married off because the parents offered such a huge dowry with a TV set and car and two lacs? The boy is such a good boy and he was simply married off without even seeing her! So greedy his parents were! At least I would not want this kind of treatment for any so-called *streedhanam*! I would rather not take anything and get a job to work for myself somehow!'

'It is all so insulting, no?' said Sosamma. 'Naomi's parents took her for approval to that great man who has come back from Kuwait. He is a doctor or engineer or something big. Poor girl. She was too short and had to buy high heels, and then even she could not walk well. She is so ashamed. She was weeping when she told that he has seen twenty-five girls in two weeks! He only wants a qualified doctor or nurse he says now. He does not mind even a teacher so that he can have permanent and regular dowry, you see? *He* did not want any dowry, oh no! He was too noble for that! Sosamma's eyes flashed fire.

'It is the terrible bargaining just like a fish market that we don't like,' said Akkamma, tossing her heavy curls away from her eyes. 'I, of course, would like to get all the jewellery that is my due and the gold. It is after all the only thing I shall get from my father's house, and my future depends on it. My in-laws will respect me and also they will respect my parents. So I don't mind asking for it. My father will anyway give it without my asking, even though he is not a rich man, but I know he will do it.'

'Apart from the jewellery', I said, 'what about the cash and luxury goods? Would you demand those also?'

The girls looked at me and looked away. Ultimately it was a quiet young girl at my elbow who spoke. I could barely hear her. It is very bad,' she said, 'We feel like cattle, no? They are coming and demanding such a high price, and our parents, poor people, have necessarily to give because they want their daughter to have a good boy. Some girls,' her voice sank to a whisper, 'commit suicide rather than see the trouble they are giving their parents and many become nuns. So many of my friends have gone to Delhi and other far off places to work as nurses or teachers and earn some money for their dowries, and to support their needy parents and young brothers and sisters. So many are never getting married—' She stopped suddenly.

'What do you think is a "good catch"? I asked to dispel the gloom. The girls giggled, lowered their eyes and would not answer. From the back of the room a young man in a spotless white *mundu*[12] and terylene shirt answered, 'The system works in slabs. If I sit for my IAS[13] or IFS[14] examination and pass, I shall be on the top slab in the marriage market for dowry!'

'Oh, no, you will not!' countered Thomachan. 'Doctors and chartered accountants are the rage nowadays. I heard my father say he wished I had taken up medicine instead of the teaching line, because a doctor is never out of job, while any other profession depends on the whims and fancies of someone else. So a doctor is a safe bet for the girl's parents. He will be in great demand and therefore can in turn demand fifty thousand to two lacs plus even a car.'[15]

'Well,' said the Head Master when I met him later, 'that is true. I can vouch for it as I have personal knowledge of girls' parents who first find out from a medical college which boys are on their rolls. Then they approach the most likely boys' parents and offer to pay their full college fees in a lump sum if their sons will marry their daughters. Sometimes it may also happen that such a boy turns out to be a rogue and a duffer and does not plan to study medicine. Then he can very well refuse to marry the girl, or he can just leave the course. The girl's parents cannot publicise the fraud as they would have to admit that they definitely gave money as "consideration for marriage" and they would not only be publicly disgraced but also held culpable under the Dowry Prohibition Act.'

'These days,' said the business executive,' the parents of a boy look out for a well educated girl who can bring in a regular income. A doctor or nurse attached to some institution abroad is a veritable gold mine. In such cases there will be no need to demand dowry. The women will call the tune!'[16]

'You said it worked in slabs,' I asked the young student who had spoken earlier. 'What exactly did you mean?'

'Well, I've made a kind of survey of the problem. It depends on many things: Pre-school teachers and lower division clerks with an earning capacity of about three hundred rupees can demand a dowry of about ten to fifteen thousand rupees. You see they may not get much salary, but here they will have family wealth in coconuts and paddy. They can get their food even if they have no job.

'High school teachers and upper division clerks with an earning capacity of five to six hundred—this would be our middle class—they could get dowry of fifteen to twenty thousand. Of course if the girl is employed, the demand may be less.

'Lecturers and engineers in the scale of five to fifteen hundred rupees would also be middle class, but in a high category, and would easily get at least thirty five to forty thousand rupees, if the bride is a working girl. If she is not working, then the demand will be higher.

'IFS, IAS, doctors and chartered accountants get the highest dowries. I suppose you may call them our upper classes—from fifty thousand to one or two lacs and often times much more depending on the status in society of the families. Of course, for the rich people there is no limit all!' he laughed.

'What advantage would you see in this system,' I asked the business executive.

'Advantage?' he stormed. 'Eligible bachelors are virtually auctioned while the girls' parents indulge in an orgy of bidding higher so that such a wonderful boy may not slip through their fingers! This reminds me of an article I read in the Weekly some time ago about a marriage market which is held once a year in some village in the North somewhere where the Maithil Brahmins assemble to finalise heavy dowry deals.[17] The young lads are literally on the counter for the parents to inspect like chicken or meat. During the Emergency 1975-77, it was not so popular as there were too many spies from the C.I.D.[18] dressed up as Brahmins waiting to catch dowry dealers! Our girls in Kerala are much worse off. This dowry system has driven many girls to prostitution or suicide. Many are duped into brothels or service of doubtful nature outside the country!'

'I am all for the dowry system,' said smart young Varki. 'Why should I refuse a present that my bride's parents are willing to give me? I am not demanding anything and nor are my parents. Surely it would be most churlish to refuse to accept their present—'

'Are they giving a present, or is society forcing them to give?' Sosamma who had been fuming all along cut in. 'If my parents give such a huge present to the boy's family, why can't they also give to my family? After all in European countries both sides' parents are pitching in to help the couple build a new life; why only the girl's people are forced here?'

Varki smiled tolerantly. 'It is expensive to become a doctor,' he said with the air of one who is trying his best to make a child understand something beyond its comprehension. 'It will cost me at least seventy-five thousand to a lac to complete the course these days. With so much unemployment and job insecurity wouldn't I be foolish to refuse dowry?'

'I thought a girl's dowry was meant for her and wouldn't actually be intended as a present for her husband unless he particularly asked for it to be that way,' I murmured.

'There is one thing you have not understood about us here.' It was a well-to-do planter who spoke. 'Without the incentive of dowry, our community would never have prospered so much.' Seeing my bewilderment, he explained:

'You see the father of daughters knows he just *has* to work hard to provide them with good dowries, otherwise they will not ever get married well. His status and family name also depend on this. Since he has to have that much wealth, he strains himself to work towards that object and the community benefits greatly.'

'Dowry is a good tradition,' agreed Jacob heartily. 'The girl is given a present and she should have it!'

Sosamma boiled over. 'Do you hear what he says?' she shouted. 'Does the girl ever see the money? It goes straight from her father's hand into the boy's father's purse when it is the girl's by right! They palm off what is my right as payment for my wedding expenses and call it *streedhanam*! I want my *streedhanam* as the right of a daughter and not to pay for my wedding!'

'Why are you getting excited?' said Korula running his fingers through his luxuirant hair. 'No one is demanding any dowry these days, so the question does not arise.'

'Oh, they are not demanding?' Mariamma was digging deep into her satchel. With a triumphant smile she produced a letter and handed it to Korula. 'Why don't you read? It is in black and white. It is from an *achan*[19] also, to my friend's father whom he has never seen at all. He has simply found out that he has a marriagable girl and has the cheek to write a letter. 'Read it out,' she commanded.

Korula looked through the letter and began to read out the relevant parts rather sheephishly. "... the retired officer is a Doctor (MBBS). I think your daughter is a graduate. If so, we shall arrange a marriage of her with him. The boy is a handsome, tall and very nice one. Dowry not less than 1 lakh. If you are interested please inform me discussing it with your wife... May God bless you and your family. Yours in His service." 'I can't believe my eyes', he said.

'What about us ugly girls?' said a cheerful youngster. 'If you don't want dowry, don't take; but we also want to get married, no? Who will marry us without some incentive? You tell me?'

The girls all rounded on her while the boys smiled. 'Have you no shame, Chechamma? Will you like to get married to a boy who will only think of money?'

'And what about the whole of last few years during Emergency when so many people were signing pledges in colleges and saying they will never demand dowry, oh no!' It was Akkamma, her black curls bobbing fiercely. 'But how could they do anything? Their fathers were demanding, not they! Poor boys! Just like Pilate they were—Simply washing their hands. They are so respectful to the wishes of their parents. Isn't it?'

'What would you suggest, sir?' I asked the venerable old Metropolitan of the Mar Thoma Church[20] as we sat in his airy office one morning. 'Do you think the evils in this system can be weeded out?'

'The law that governs dowry is too old,' said the Bishop, his kindly eyes shining with the fire of battle under the black cap agleam with gold crosses. 'Since the money is the girl's due, as it represents her share in her father's wealth, it is hers by right. It is her *streedhanam*, and the boy who marries her, and the father-in-law who accepts the money from the girl's parents, have no right over it. Even if they separate after years of married life, the woman has a right over her money. Unfortunately, the father-in-law treats it as if this is *his* own right, and her own father gives it as if it is *his* own to gift away when it is really the daughter's *to be kept in trust* by him until she should require it.'

'The reasonable thing,' he continued, 'is for a father to make a record in the marriage register about the amount given to the girl, and the money should then be kept in a bank in her name. What the boy gets,' he said emphatically, 'is the girl, *not the money*!'

His hands busied themselves with a paper knife. 'Then again,' he said, looking up at the ceiling, 'the provision in this old Act that the girl has a right only to one fourth of her brother's share is also very discriminatory. At the time this law was passed, two thousand rupees was the highest and most prestigious dowry; so five thousand rupees were ample; but in these days it is a very unrealistic figure and not at all fair to the girl, especially if her father is a wealthy man...'

I asked the same question of a frail but intense social worker at the club. 'It is only when *streedhanam* which is a girl's right becomes demand dowry that the whole thing becomes a business transaction and lowers her dignity', she said sharply. 'She becomes an adjunct to the main dish on the menu—the money and the property. You see, in early days in our parts, the father-in-law used to look after the money for the immature girl bride. Nowadays, it is ridiculous and humiliating for an educated woman to see her father-in-law appropriating all the money.'

The woman lawyer at her right exploded. 'This old law,' she burst out, 'gives the girl's father sweeping powers over the disposal of his property. His right to cut her out and will away his wealth must have some curbs, mustn't it? This is a curse in most of our traditional systems.' Her fingers tapped out each point so violently on the cane table that the juice glasses leapt with every tap.

'In any case,' she said,' why should we Kerala Christians have such an unusual law? It is not as if these old Travancore and Cochin Acts which govern us Christians here are based on our religion that we should be so concerned about their preservation! We have a right to be brought under The Indian Succession Act of 1925. What is there so different about us? At least we would all be in the same category — Indian Christians. After that we can see to correcting some of the strange things in The Indian Succession Act.[21]

'Indian Christians for some strange reason are not given the benefits stated in the Act; like for instance, if a man dies childless and his property is under five thousand rupees, his widow according to this Act, would get the whole amount. If his property is worth over five thousand and he dies without leaving a will, the widow gets one-third of his property, and the children get the rest divided equally regardless of whether they are sons or daughters. Even these small benefits do not come to the Christian widow. However, once we are all unified under one category, then we can fight for equal application of the law, but what can we do if we are separated from the others as being governed by these old antiquated laws?'

'And what do you think about *streedhanam*?' I asked.

'Streedhanam as a bribe for marriage? No! Not at all!' she said agitatedly. 'The *streedhanam* has been exploited. The bride never sees it and her father-in-law controls it. It should be declared "dowry," but they will say "girl's share". To this "girl's share" there is no limit at all![22] As for the amount of five thousand rupees mentioned in the Christian Succession Act here, I will not comment at all—better not to speak. It is so bad!'

'But what would the orthodox have to say to these sweeping changes?' I asked. 'The church has always asked for a donation at marriages here.[23] Of course, I suppose they have a point when they say that a Christian can only be tapped for giving towards the Church's many social welfare activities when there is a birth, marriage or death in his family and he needs the Church!"

'They consider this a legitimate tax,' said the lawyer as the glasses danced drunkenly on the table. 'The end obviously justifies the means! That is why these changes should be made by the government, treated as social welfare measures in the interest of women who suffer from these ills, without waiting for a demand from either the church or community. You see it may never come from there.[24] The women also are either too complacent, resigned, or dependent on their menfolk to try and organise a show of strength which could move the powers that be! Their very silence calls out for help!'

She steadied the glasses. I looked at her anxious face and then down at the copy of the memorandum she had thrust into my hand. I saw that it had been submitted for 'prompt and urgent action' to the government on the 16th of February, 1975.[25]

'Prompt and urgent action' is still awaited. Conservatism and greed raise their ugly heads wherever there is effort at reform and traditional patterns continue to bestow landed property on a son. The mind is urged to greater inventiveness, and the law is circumvented and defeated several times over...'

'You know I am a progressive man, and I do not want dowry for my very progressive son, but surely you are at liberty to give whatever you like to your daughter. Of course I am sure being fond of music, she will like to have a stereo set. And since my son occasionally takes a glass of beer, I am sure your daughter would like to have a refrigerator.'[26]

'We would never get such a wonderful boy again. He was a green card holder working in USA. We had to give them all their demand.'

'But how did you manage to cover the deal,' I asked.

'One has to find a way,' said the businessman's wife, diamond a-sparkle on her nose.'We went to the shops and paid for everything, and then informed them in which shops the goods were. They collected them from there directly...'

'The boy was very good. He was well educated and did not demand anything. He had no idea that his parents had made exorbitant demands on the girl's family. Under cover of night, two trucks loaded to capacity with "gifts of affection" reached his house. He was furious as he had only wanted an exchange of garlands. His mother was sweet reasonableness itself. "How can you refuse their gifts, son? It will hurt them. After all they have taken such trouble to show their love." The flat is now entirely furnished with the gifts he received that night.'

It was the plain girl and her parents who suffered in a similar case. The prospective bridegroom was in league with his parents. The girl was 'booked and a truckload of gifts received from her parents. The marriage did not take place. No complaint could be made as the 'gifts' were clearly marriage bait.

The Dowry Prohibition Act of 1961 has the dubious distinction of being honoured more in the breach than in the keeping. Meant in all sincerity to curb the cruel extortions made in the name of dowry, it leaves many holes waiting to be plugged. In fact, more lavish dowries, more vulgar display and flashier and brighter lit weddings are becoming the order of the day, despite the many speeches mouthed by politicians and sincere efforts of individuals and organisations.

Even when cyclone, flood and famine stalk the land, and the media highlight the miseries of countless people, weddings flash their gaudy lights over gold ornaments, brocade covered musicians and dishes overflowing with wasted food.[27] There is no social boycott and no official to pull up the respected member of society who is marrying his daughter with such a flourish.

'How can we interfere in their private lives?'

'They have donated generously to all relief funds in the country. Why should we grudge such generous and god fearing people a celebration for their daughter's marriage when *Parmatma* has blessed them with plenty?'

'They are our friends. How can you ask us to boycott the wedding?'

'*Bibiji*, they are such god fearing people, they will give lakhs of rupees when they know their names will be in the newspapers and on everyone's tongue. They will not give me a broken coin to get my wife into hospital...'

No boycott. No censure. Only blessing from a smiling society.

...And then advertisements continue their attack on the girl's beleaguered parents:

'At her wedding, they say, give her our brand of T.V. our special 'fridge.. These luxurious carpets that will make your neighbours' mouths water.. Here are *saris* that will make hosts honourable and guests glamorous, and here are *saris* for goddesses for *Daj* and *Vari*.'[28]

'What does this little girl want to tell her parents?' asks a nationalised bank. She is dressing her doll for her wedding when she will be coverd with fabulous jewellery. Should this bride take with her this expensive watch or another brand? 'Be a guest at your own daughter's wedding,' says a five star hotel, 'we will take on all your troubles.'

The Gujarat Suicide's Enquiry Committee which began its investigations in 1960 made some startling revelations during its four year research.[29] It made the public aware of the large number of newly married women who were tortured by their in-laws and commited suicide. The spate of debate and discussion that preceded this report and the moral compulsion that followed the disclosure of each horrifying detail ultimately helped in the passing of the Dowry Prohibition Act of 1961.

But the fate of an Act without teeth is the same as that of the legislator who on the point of making an earth shattering pronouncement, finds he has spat out his dentures with the betel juice. Ever since this well-intentioned but boneless Act came into force, various states have tried to amend it. Some have made the prison terms longer. Bihar and Himachal have made every offence under the Act cognizable. Bihar has gone a step further and made these offences non-bailable as well.

Goa dowry is heavily weighted with prestige, gold and property in equal measure. Many a young hopeful is 'willing to wait till the age of thirty five to forty years for his expectations of dowry to be fulfilled.'[30] From Andhra and Tamil Nadu to Kashmir and Ladakh the dowry stories are the same. A village headman in Ladakh had to give one lakh rupees to get his daughter married to a doctor,[31] while a Minister in the State Coalition Government in Kerala was reported in the 1976 papers as having 'paid dowry of 3 lacs to his daughter over a year ago; another arranged a sumptuous wedding lunch for about 3,000 people in the temple town of Guruvayoor to celebrate his daughter's marriage at a time when there was strict guest control and the State was facing an acute rice shortage.'[32]

The Lal Bahadur Shastri National Academy of Administration has been described as a 'happy hunting ground' for parents on the look out for sons-in-law with good prospects. They vie with each other to offer the young gods of the Academy the 'minimum outfit... to maintain his position.' Here comes the 'Gimmee' tune again: 'car, TV, 'fridge, radio, furniture, carpets (of some standard), kitchen outfit, the "requisite number" of *saris*, and "some trinkets of gold and silver to keep up appearances."'[33] A young girl sitting for the Indian Administrative Service examination wonders aloud whether 'those who want over a lac for their IAS sons will now pay the same amount for an IAS daughter-in-law.[34]

However the legal scene is not altogether gloomy. Although the West Bengal parent signs a document to say that he has given everything at his daughter's wedding 'voluntarily,' the state's Amendment to the Dowry Prohibition Act does go some way towards giving him a helping hand. The Amendment includes social organisations in the list of those allowed to lodge complaints in cases of extortion or coercion. Since these individuals and organisations would be in close communication with sufferers of the system, redress is made a little easier.

The 1975 newspapers reported even more heartening legislation from Punjab. According to these reports,[35] a 'no suspicion' certificate was to be demanded from the parents-in-law of a girl who died within seven years of her marriage. Until this was produced, they would be under a cloud. The law here also was expected to insist on a thorough investigation into reported cases of such deaths. *The Patriot* of 4 February 1977 reported that the Lt. Governor of Delhi had issued a call for thorough investigation into alleged dowry deaths in the Union Territory of Delhi also.[36]

The Central Civil Service (Conduct) Rules declared in 1976 that a Central Government employee who was found to have either demanded or received dowry would be 'subject to disciplinary action.'[37]

One can only hope that these babies, born in difficult conditions during the Emergency in India, have not all been thrown out with the bath water.

The Karnataka Bill which seeks to introduce sweeping reforms in the State[38] survived stiff opposition. It has tried to safeguard the exploited family of the bride by extending the definition of dowry to include financial help offered to young men as inducement for marriage, to set them up in business, or to pay for a foreign education. This would hit the 'father-in-law' scholarship demanders very hard. It hopes to discourage ostentatious weddings by levying a 'luxury' tax on wedding celebrations, on which more than five thousand rupees have been spent. This tax would increase in proportion to the amount spent on the wedding. Marriage registration has been declared compulsory by it, as also gifts to the young couple, which would only be given them by their parents; but best of all, not only would the act of giving and taking dowry be made a cognizable offence in Karnataka, but the offenders would also be disqualified from further membership of village panchayats, municipalities, local boards and agricultural produce market societies.[39] In other words, the bill has attempted to introduce social boycott of dowry offenders. At the time of writing, this bill had not been passed.

However, even the fact that someone was bold enough to introduce such a measure in the legislature is a hopeful sign as every attempt dislodges another brick from the wall.

The Dowry Prohibition Act's drawbacks still continue to exercise the minds of thinking persons. In its report, the Committee on the Status of Women 1974 comments: 'We are compelled to record our finding that the Dowry Prohibtion Act of 1961... has signally failed to achieve its purpose. In spite of the rapid growth of the practice' (of dowry) 'there are practically no cases reported under the Act.'[40]

'Who will register the complaint?' asks Dipti Chowdhry the school teacher who is daily tortured by her sadistic mother-in-law because her father did not fulfil her dowry demands. 'Since the offences of both giving *and* taking of dowry are non-cognizable, it is only the "aggrieved party" who can report it. My father, therefore, by registering a report against my in-laws for demanding dowry, would have straightaway put his own head into a noose because he would be held as guilty as the ones who demanded the dowry, as he *had* given me some dowry. How would this help me? My father-in-law and the police are also far too friendly. You know yourself what can follow. Just now it is my legs and back—Next it could be my life!'

Smiling a tight little smile she continues, 'And then this Act says quite clearly that the complaint must be made within one year from the date of the offence. Which Indian woman starts counting the dates when offences are made? The dowry giving and taking happens over her wedding of course, but she always keeps on hoping things will change, and she bears everything for years like myself. It is only when we reach the limit of our endurance that we will even think of lodging a complaint in public about such private situations as our family life. By that time naturally, the year's limit will have passed long ago. There should be no time limit set for lodging a complaint to help solve the problems of women.'[41]

'Yes,' says Rajinder Varma 'my happy little daughter is dead and my wife has gone mad and left me. I can make a complaint now without fear. What does it matter if I am also considered guilty of giving dowry, my Neena is beyond their torture now, and I may be able to help other mens' daughters. How strange it is—six months' imprisonment and a five thousand rupee fine for a murderer, and for me perhaps also the same, who knows, plus a dead daughter and a broken home. Will they be interested in my reasons for giving dowry? Would they realise how great was my desire to keep my daughter's body safe from her in-laws' cruel hands? Can I report it now? Is it too late? Can't the courts after hearing the details of torture for the crime of exploiting a girl to get more dowry articles make a case and say that they will presume a crime has been committed, and then make the poor dead girl's in-laws prove that it has not been committed?'[42]

'I never had the courage to report poor Neena's tortured life,' says Dipti putting her own troubles behind her; 'but here again beating a wife and even throwing her out of the house is not a cognizable offence in our cultured Indian society, so even if a neighbour or a good friend wants to report the whole cruel business to the police and bring the police to investigate, he is powerles. All my fellow teachers know what happens to me, but what can they do? Also going to law courts is too complicated and frightening. If they could, I know they would have been only to glad to help me...

'Even my parents,' she continues stonily, 'I know if I go to them they will be afraid of keeping me—apart from the expense, they are afraid of blame. Their hearts are with me, but for them I belong to someone else. They lose face. They — '

'It is our tradition that is to blame, Mrs. Chowdhry,' cuts in Rama the young South Indian boy agitatedly. Rama who had had the courage to report Neena's death. We live like islands—to ourselves alone. My soul and body's salvation is my own concern—mine and my Creator's. All else is unreal. Beings surround me who are going through the motions of living, paying for deeds committed in their past lives, as I am too. This is their *karma*.[43] So why should I get mixed up in someone else's troubles when I have enough of my own? If they can take their punishment now, they will be better off in another existence. Someone dies, someone is killed in an accident. Millions die in floods and famine—battered wives next door shout for help. We will go mad if we take notice of everything. We have to keep ourselves sane in this terrible world! Look at my own father—his respectability would not allow him to even think of telling the police that we had all witnessed a murder with our own eyes! His job and security were at stake! His name would be muddied by the courts. How would his daughter find a suitable husband?'

'Ever since our bright little Neeno came into their home, those devils had made life hell on earth for her', says Ashok Kumar 'I admire you, Rama for your part in this terrible drama and appreciate your position. Sometimes I wonder why we cannot get our people to set up a kind of watchman group of people whom we all respect, in every *mohalla*, who would have some special powers to see that such murders and tortures after being reported, are probed and looked into thoroughly by the police and a regular case made after all investigations are completed and then follow it up to the courts. This is where everything falls flat, because it is not followed up all the way and fizzles out in the middle, mostly with bribes or influence.'

Ashok Kumar nods enthusisastically. 'Yes, and then the *mohalla* committees could do the same work and co-ordinate it with such a Commission,' he says.

'Huh!' says Babli with a clank of gold bracelets and a toss of her well groomed head. 'Who wants all these probes and investigations? I am glad that the dowry offence is not cognizable by law in some states at least. I hope they don't make it cognizable in Parliament. Who can check the harassment we would have if any old nosey neighbour with a grudge against us brings a policeman and just walks into the house and the policeman registers a complaint against a respectable family? Life would become impossible!'Having delivered this Parthian shot, Babli sails out of the room.

Rama's eyes follow her out of the room, disgust writ large on his young face. 'You are quite right, Mr. Ashok,' he says. 'The past few weeks have opened my eyes to problems which never existed for me before. *Mohalla* ginger groups are very necessary, but these suppressed women need a Commission with stronger powers, also, which could function at a higher level—State and National.[44] It should have the right to information concerning anything that may have to do with women, and have the power to suggest new laws and programmes for them. It should have special powers to help people in cases like Neena's. In fact, it should be the voice of all these harassed women, and have the right to go up to Parliament itself and demand answers from the nation's elected representatives!'

No one has noticed a small woman with a worn face who has slipped quietly into the room and sits listening intenly to every word. She speaks softly now: 'How glad I am to hear Ashok Bhai's idea. Big sounding laws are all right, but it is the *mohalla* where we all live. Such people would give us all good advice and explain us the laws instead of our going to the big cities where those vultures will bleed us dry and to the courts where no one will understand us.' She takes a sharp breath something like a sob—'those courts where no good woman will like to enter even to speak about her murdered daughter!'

Rajinder Varma looks as if he has just seen a ghost. 'Suniti! Oh Suniti!' he gasps unbelievingly.

The small woman looks up at him and smiles quietly, 'I've faced it, Neeno's father. It was difficult, but I am not mad any more. I am now working for many other Neenos. We shall work together.'

Rajinder Varma's heart lifts. Suniti is back: the old Suniti who always made the right decisions. Their eyes meet across the room. This time, he promises himself, this time he will not fail her.

NOTES AND REFERENCES

1. The Dowry Prohibition Act of 1961 was extended to Pondicherry in 1968, but not to Goa, Daman and Diu as of 1977 : (Department of Social Welfare, Government of India). Goa has its own Uniform Civil code which has come down from Portuguese times, and is still operational, 1997.
2. See also Ch. 3, note 9. The Syrian Christians.
3. *Towards Equality*, Report of the Committee on the Status of Women, Government of India, 1974, p. 132.
4. The Travancore Christian Succession Act, 1092, Sec. 20 (1916).
5. The Cochin Christian Succession Act, 1092, Sect. 20 (b) (1921).
6. Judgement (12) 1956 KLT 559, delivered by Justice Joseph Vithayathil in the case of Kurian Augusty vs. Devassy Aley.
7. Susan Vellapally, 'The Lamentable Act: Today, *Journal of the YWCA of India*, No. 3 and 4 (1973).
8. 1975 KLT 386: Thomas vs Sarahkutty: V. Khalid J.
9. *Ibid.*
10. *Streedhanam:* as defined in Section 5 of the Travancore Christian Succession Act: *'means and includes any money or ornaments or in lieu of money or ornaments, any property movable or immovable, given or promised to be given to a female or, on her behalf to her*

husband or his parent or both of them, by any one who claims under such father or mother, in satisfaction of her claim against the estate of the father or mother.' Towards Equality, op. cit., 1974, p. 133, f.n. 17. *Streedhanam:* as defined in Section 3 of the Cochin Christian Succession Act 1092: *'means any property given to a woman, or in trust for her husband, his parent or guardian, in connection with her marriage, and in fulfilment of a term of the marriage treaty in that behalf.' Towards Equality, op. cit.*, p.133, fn. 21.

11. The Dowry Prohibition Act of 1961.
12. *mundu*: (Malayalam): A drape used instead of pants.
13. Indian Administrations Service.
14. Indian Foreign Service.
15. 'Alliance invited from Doctors, Engineers (civil) or Chartered Accountants for a fair Catholic girl...Girls's share one lakh. Job abroad guaranteed.' *The Malayala Manorama,* 7 May 1978.
16. 'Correspondence invited from Christian parents of Doctors, Engineers or Chartered Accountants: healthy, handsome and tall...for a specialised nurse (Catholic) employed in USA drawing Rs 12,000/- per month for immediate marriage...' *The Malayala Manorama*, 11 June 1978.
17. 'The Maithil Market,' Janardan Thakur in *The Illustrated Weekly of India*, 10 December 1972; also 'The Match-Making Fair' by P.C. Gandhi in *The Times of India*, 10 June 1979. The concourse, a ten day affair, takes place in the village of Saurath near Darbhanga.
18. Criminal Investigation Department.
19. Malayalam word for a Christian priest.
20. *Mar Thoma* literally means Saint Thomas. This refers to the Christian community in Kerala that claims conversion by St. Thomas. See also Ch. 3, note 10.

    This conversation took place in August 1976. His Grace Juhanon Mar Thoma has since passed away. He was a crusader for womens' rights in Kerala.

    What he says here is quoted from his own notes on the subject of dowry which he gave me.
21. *Towards Equality, op. cit.,* pp. 131-33.

    Indian Christians are not given the benefits stated in the Indian Succession Act. These benefits are also denied to two other categories of persons in an equally inexplicable manner.
22. 'Proposals invited from Jacobite, Marthomite or C.S.I. youths for a Jacobite girl from a well-known family, aged 21, height 5'5", S.S.L.C; medium complexion. *Share* one lakh (cash)...*Malayala manorama*, 28 March 1979.
23. The Mar Thoma Church no longer asks for a percentage of the dowry from the parents of the young couple at the time of marriage. A 'thank offering' however, is still expected and received, thus continuing the

social compulsion as motivation for the 'gift.' Other denominations of the Christian churches of the South still expect a certain percentage at weddings.

24. Certain amendments to the Succession Acts that govern Syrian Christians are presently under consideration by the concerned Churches.
25. Memorandum of the All India Womens' Association of Kerala: dated 16 February 1975.
26. 'A Bridegroom For Sale'—a *Statesman* survey, *The Statesman,* 17 February 1976.
27. At one such marriage during a cyclone in Andhra Pradesh, a twenty lakh rupee dowry was given with the bride.
28. *Daj/Dahej/Jahez*: dowry. (*Daj*: Punjabi: pronounced: *daaj*, *Dahej*: Hindi: pronounced: *dahaij*, *Jahez*: Urdu: pronounced: *jahaiz*).
29. The Gujarat Suicides Enquiry Committee: 1960-64.
    Note: 'According to a police report, 200 women were burnt to death in the capital...primarily over the dowry issue. Most of the dowry victims are in the 20-35 age group. In one police station alone, 45 out of 71 cases of burning in 1978 were in this age group. According to a senior medical officer of a Delhi hospital, 80 per cent of burning cases are fatal. Since...these...occur in the house, there are no witnesses and therefore, because of lack of evidence, cases are finally dropped.'
30. 'When Every Man Has His Price,' a *Statesman* survey, 17 February 1976.
31. *Ibid.*
32. *Ibid.*, *The Statesman* of 9 July, 1979 reported a lavish wedding organised by a Madhya Pradesh Minister for his daughter at which 'scores of workers from the PWD' (Public Works Department), 'Forest and Public Health Engineering Departments, it is said, worked overnight to erect...a hall supported by pillars' (for the wedding). 'Within days the Principal of a nearby college was persuaded to let out the premises' on a working day while angry students ground their teeth at cancelled classes. *The Indian Express* of 10 July 1979 described the event as 'A Wedding Fit For A Princess.' The next day, 11 July 1979, there was a scathing editorial comment in *The Indian Express* on 'The Vulgarity of Power,' and a forthright condemnation of the 'brazen impropriety with which state apparatus had been used and the mentality that turned government officials into "errand boys." '
33. 'A Bridegroom For Sale' a *Statesman* survey, 17 February 1976.
34. *Ibid.*
35. *The National Herald*, 21 October 1975.
36. *The Sunday Standard* (editorial) of 13 August 1978 comments:
    'In 1975, 350 women in Delhi died of burns. But though the police had been instructed to treat all such cases as murder, they have not done so.'

37. 13 A of the Central Civil Service Rules states: 'No government servant shall give or take or abet the giving or taking of dowry, or demand directly or indirectly from the parent or guardian of a bride or bridegroom as the case may be, any dowry.' This clause was inserted in the conduct rules in 1976.
38. 'Karnataka Bill,' *The Times of India*, 26 November 1976.
39. *Ibid.*
40. *Towards Equality, op. cit.*, 1974, p. 115.
41. Recommendation of an anti-dowry seminar organised by the Mahila Dakshata Samiti, Delhi, March 1979.
42. *Ibid.*
43. Consequences for actions in a previous existence.
44. Need for constitution of a statutory autonomous Commission for Women at the national and state levels: A Recommendation of the Committee on the Status of Women in India, *Towards Equality, op. cit.*, pp. 353-54.

    The National Commission for Women has since been set up and is functioning as a statutory body with magisterial powers. It was founded in 1992.

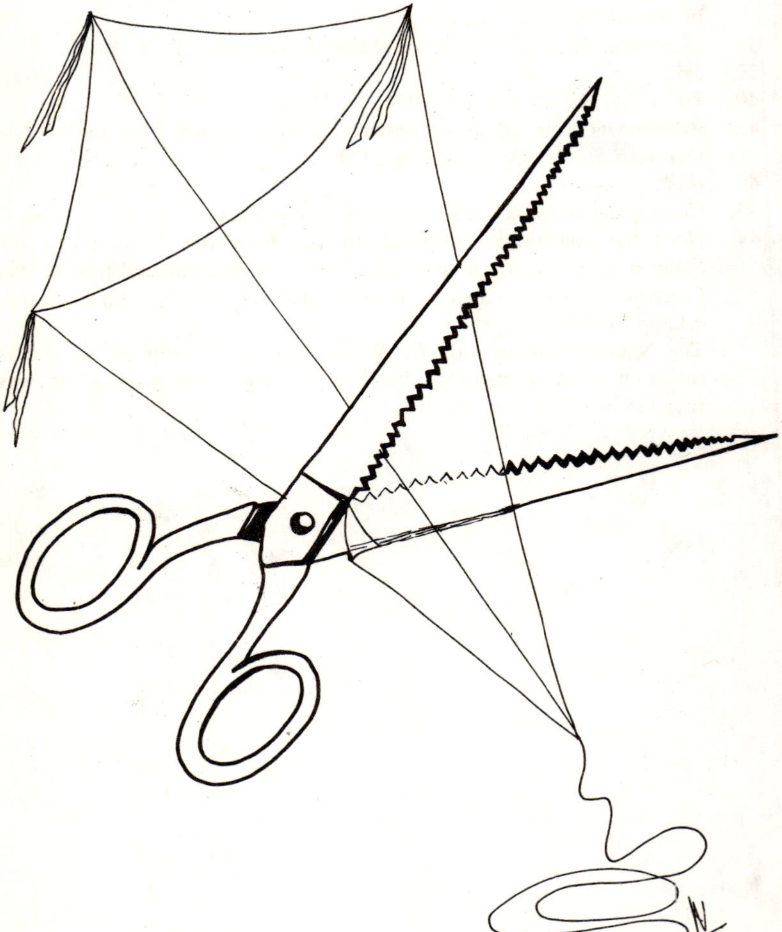

9

Her Body

"It's my kite! Give it back!'

'You gave it to me! I can do anything I like with it.'

'It's my kite! Please give it back. Please!'

'All right! Give me ten paise and I'll give it back.'

'I haven't got any money. Where can I get ten paise!'

'Right! I'll cut up your kite. See!'

'Don't. Don't. I'll get you the money. Please don't!'

Five year old Ramu runs off in an agony of tears and desperation. Looking about him fearfully, he plunges his hand into his mother's tin, takes one of the two coins in it, and runs back.

'Here,' he says anxiously. 'Here, take. Give me my kite!'

'Not so fast, Ramukutty.[1] Not so fast. I'm planning to slash this pretty kite from top to bottom!'

'But I got you the money,' wails Ramu, his eyes fixed on his beautiful kite—the best kite in the whole world.

'If you can find money so easily my little one, may be you can get me a rupee?' Swamy's penknife is poised lightly over the quivering kite.

'Of course,' he continues, 'If you can't do that, I can always burn this beauty. After all it is mine. Is'nt it?'

Little Ramu sits down and weeps. His mother has no money and he has nowhere to get such a vast sum from...

He watches his little world collapse as his wonderful kite goes up in a flash of orange flames...

'She is mine. I can do anything with her. You gave her to me. Didn't you?

'She is my daughter. She is all I have.

If you are so anxious to see her alive and well, then perhaps you could send me—shall we say, four thousand rupees—since you'll appreciate the dowry you gave with her was quite unsuitable... Or would you rather we beat her up some more?

I'll get it for you. My God! Are you human beings or devils? I'll get it if I have to sell my soul for it...

What? Only a refrigerator and a radiogram? What are you thinking of, old man? You insult us with these paltry gifts. My father is a respectable man, my sister and her children are my dependents. I am an engineer. We are not the sort of people you can play about with. Who do you think you people are? She is mine and I can do as I please with her!

... So twenty year old Meera had to die...

She was beaten, strangulated and burnt to death by her twenty-six year old husband, his seventy year old father and his thirtyfive year old widowed sister. The grim judgement sentenced her murderers to life imprisonment.[2]

'Three Face Trial in Dowry Case.'

'First Every Dowry Trial in West Bengal.'

'Murder For Dowry.'

'Wife Tortured by Husband, In-Laws...'

'They always gave me a beating before going to their chemist shop in the morning. After they left, the three women...also did not spare me. They used to force me to lie down on the ground. Shakuntala then used to sit on my chest, and Bela and Renu on my outstretched arms. They also used to pull my hair and strike my head against the ground violently...my neck also used to be pressed...put chillies in my eyes and ask me to stand in the blazing sun...if I closed my eyes they used to give me beating. They did not give me water...My mother-in-law Shakuntala Devi had sat on my chest. Human refuse was forcibly put in my mouth...In addition to slaps and fists, I also used to be hit with *thappis*,[3] *chappals*[4] shoes, etc...Bela and Renu made me stand bare foot in the blazing sun from about 11 am to 5 pm. Thereafter, Bela and Renu removed my clothes and after I had become totally naked they forced me to remain in that position on the roof of the house up to about 11 pm..

'Bela and Renu told the men that I had been treated as they wanted. Words slipped out of my mouth that the Almighty should give them' (Renu and Bela) 'such homes as He had given to me. Immediately the accused, Jagat Parkash,' (father-in-law) 'Anil Kumar' (husband) 'Arun Kumar' (his younger brother) 'Bela and Renu started giving me slaps and blows. I pleaded with them...they forcibly brought me to the railings...beating me all the time. I was crying and pleading...to spare my life. Then they started to throw me down the railings. I had caught the railings as firmly as I could. Then the accused pushed me, and that resulted in my hanging in the air. Then the accused started giving me fist blows on my hands. Thereupon, I lost the grip of the railings and fell down in the courtyard...and became semi-conscious.[5]

Twenty-three year old Kanta Goel was then picked up by her father-in-law's eldest brother who lived on the ground floor and another friend. They telephoned her uncle who took the bleeding girl to hospital.

The Kanta Goel case caused a wave of shock as the morning papers of 7 September 1976 published the horrifying details of her married life in her husband's home. On 6 July 1973, she had brought three thousand, one hundred rupees with her to her marriage. Twenty to twentytwo thousand rupees were spent on 'dowry and marriage arrangements'.[6] Accusations taunts and demands for more followed. Articles like Dunlopillo mattresses, a pedestal fan and electric mixie were extracted from her people. After some months of this living nightmare, she was taken to her relatives and abandoned for a year and nine months. When she was finally allowed to return, she brought clothes worth seven thousand rupees, one thousand rupees in cash, as well as a diamond ring for her husband as demanded.[7]

Within three months the torture started again. The brief honeymoon was over.

Sentencing Jagat Parkash, a chemist of Ambala Cantonment (aged 50 years), his wife Shakuntala Devi (aged 49 years) and their son Anil Kumar (aged 28 years) to seven years' rigorous imprisonment with a fine of two thousand rupees each, the judge observed that they were 'guilty of deliberate and forced starvation, cruelty, maltreatment and harassment,' and that they had behaved in a 'highly shabby and inhuman manner against all decency and norms.'[8]

The Kanta Goel case was barely heard when the papers of

11 August 1977[9] published a little item entitled 'Woman Burnt Alive.' I quote it in full:

'Banda: August 10: A young woman, whose father died before he could fulfill his promise to give a gun to his son-in-law as dowry, is reported to have been tortured and burnt to death in Khushand village, 20 kilometres from here.

'According to a report received here, the woman's husband and father-in-law used to deny her food for days together, insisting that one of her uncles should honour the dowry pledge. She was also allegedly threatened with murder if the promise was not fulfilled.

Yesterday, the woman was subjected to cruel torture by her in-laws and she fled to a relation's house. But she was dragged back home by them and allegedly burnt alive.'

'Lecturer Tortured by Husband,'[10] Woman Held For Murder of Daughter-in-Law,'[11] 'Held For Burning Bride to Death,'[12] 'Dowry Victim Lured to Brothel,'[13] 'Child Falls Victim to Dowry Tussle'[14]....

Lakshmi Devi of Charik village, Renuka Sarna of Naraina, Kanta Goel of Ambala, Krishna Kumari of Gurgaon, Meera of Lucknow, Vasantha Nadar of Kerala, Shanta Rani of Ambala, Alka of Bangalore, Davinder Kaur of Delhi, Tarawati of Kailashpur village, Savitri Sunder, the gold medalist MSc. from Madras University, eighteen year old Manorama of Indore, Kamla, the young tribal Gond mother of two from Nagpur, Kanchan Chopra, Tarvinder Kaur of Delhi, the list is endless...[15]

Mine! Mine! This woman is mine! Mine to do with as I please!

Ever since woman stepped out of her early Vedic Utopia and walked into man's world, he has leaned over backwards to establish proprietary rights over her. Long before she was sentenced to life imprisonment in the protective custody of the men in her family, the Rig Veda had gently but firmly put her man in his place. Woman was divinely protected, her earthly guardian was given the last place in the scheme of things.[16]

'Soma[17] took her up first of all,
    thereafter the Gandharva[18] guarded her,
and thy third protector was Agni[19]
    and the son of man is thy fourth.'

The *Manusmriti* however, firmly thrust her into her new and eternally dependent role:

'Day and night women must be kept in dependence by the males (of) their (families)...Her father protects (her) in childhood, her husband protects (her) in youth, and her sons protect (her) in old age; a woman is never fit for independence.'[20]

The Assyrian scribes of 1100 B.C. had already said the same thing. Woman was expected to be under the rule of her father 'who was free to settle her in marriage exactly as he thought fit.'[21]

Adultery was not a sin which involved conscience or morals, but was regarded as stealing or damaging of property. The husband could leap over his neighbour's fence without let or hindrance, but his wife would be in danger of losing her life if she dared involve herself with an attractive neighbour. Unmarried free women's virginity was their fathers' business. Rape in such cases damaged the virgin's market value and impinged on the proprietary rights of her owner—her father. The rapist's wife was handed over to her father to be used as a prostitute while he himself would be forced to marry his victim. If he was a bachelor, he paid heavily for his moment of pleasure in money, as well as, in being tied to the girl in marriage for the rest of his life. Even this last hung on the fiat of the girl's father, who would of course take the money since it was compensation for his loss. The only way the married rapist could escape giving his wife up to prostitution was by proving that the raped girl came to him of her own accord, but he would still have to pay for the damage he had caused to property.[22]

Early medieval society in Germany acknowledged the husband's complete control over his wife as a right—the right of *mundium*[23] She was passed on from her father's hand to that of her husband. This right included the authority to beat her, but not to mutilate or kill. This was valuable property and the price of damaging it was laid out in the laws of the Alemanni:[24]

If a free woman was stripped above the waist, the penalty was six *solidi*. If she was completely stripped he would have to pay forty *solidi*.[25]

The killing of such property, especially during the productive years—that is between puberty and forty years would have made a saint of a prospective murderer: Either six hundred *solidi* or the equivalent in livestock—three hundred cattle or fifty male horses. The law provided for the payment of installments to continue down to three generations.[26]

So at least in death the woman would have had the comfort of knowing she was valuable.

It is good to read that today's battered wife in Germany has a refuge to which she can go—The 'House of Women,[27] with financial aid and help in training and employment. This measure follows the setting up of a centre in London by Erin Pizzey, and similar projects in the Netherlands and in Scandinavia. The United States have social organisations to deal with this very vital problem.

Society the world over loves a male, but the Indian tradition makes a god of him and a masochist of a woman. She is expected to enjoy being ill-treated, as her tormentor is her lord. Even the word for husband in most Indian languages is the equivalent of 'lord and master.'

'How does he treat you?' ask the newly wed girl's friends; meaning thereby, that if he does not beat her, she is a fortunate woman indeed.

Old records show brutal methods that were used by men to show to the world that the women of their households were their private possessions. In Dahomey when the king died, not only were his belongings buried with him, but his wives' legs were broken so that they could not run away. They were entombed alive with their dead master and 'cautioned to treat their lord well.'[28]

Since wives, concubines and servants formed part of a rich man's property, it would be only natural for him to expect service from them when he migrated to the spirit world. In the timeless pyramids, the royal Pharoah's spirit reigned on, surrounded by the panoply of majesty. Will Durant speculates on the possibility of the idea of possessions—animate and inanimate—having at sometime accompanied the great Pharoah to the other world. Pictures of wives and other possessions painted around him would serve him eternally and be good stand-ins for the real thing.[29]

The divine Inca was not only mummified after death like his Egyptian counterpart, but a golden life-sized statue of him ruled for ever from a golden stool. His women and his servants were given intoxicants to drink. As they danced inebriated before their dead master, they were strangled and allowed the privilege of serving him throughout eternity.[30]

During Confucious' time, if a Chinese husband beat his wife or accidentally caused her death, he was not held guilty, but if his wife happened to do the same, her crime would invoke heavy punishment.[31] 'Women,' said local proverbs of the time, 'are like a suit of clothes.'[32] Although the Chinese woman today has an exalted position as 'one half of the sky,' as late as 1952, 'official reports of infanticide and of selling and purchasing of daughters and wives' were available.[33] The Marriage Law of 1950 has gone a long way in giving the women of China 'equal rights with men in political, economic, cultural, education and social life.'[34]

Tulsidas writing in the Ramayana is all for a little disciplining of women: 'A drum, a rustic, a Sudra, a beast and a woman—all these deserve beating.'[35]...And Manu fully endorses these sentiments:

'On women, infants, men of disordered mind, the poor and the sick, the king shall inflict punishment with a whip, a cane, or a rope and the like.'[36]

Human beings are the same whether born in the East or in the West. Here is a familiar Western saying:

'The woman, a spaniel, the walnut tree
The more you beat them, the better they be.'[37]

Since woman was only one among many animate and inanimate objects owned by a man, killing her was not anything to get hot under the collar about. Of course, you lost caste that way and that could be serious, but no one would have gone so far as to suggest in Manu's day that a man who thus got rid of an unwanted article should be imprisoned for life or have to be executed—that would have been considered most uncivilised:

'Stealing grain, base metals, or cattle, intercourse with women who drink spiritous liquor, slaying women, Sudras, Vaisyas or Kshatriyas, and atheism, (are all) minor offences, causing loss of caste.'[38]

But Manu was an honourable man. 'So are they all—all honourable men,' said Mark Anthony giving his oration over Julius Caesar's dead body. The Roman husband who lived between 508 and 202 B.C. had power of life and death over his wife and children.

He could sell them into slavery or kill them as the spirit moved him. Even for a trivial offence like stealing the keys of her lord's wine cellar, a Roman matron was likely to end up as an untidy mess of blood and guts on the cellar floor. If she was so careless as to allow herself to be caught in adultery, no amount of prayers to Juno could wipe off the insult to her master's ego. His property had strayed from the straight and narrow path. Death was the only way.[39]

The Saxon, not to be outdone by the males of history, formulated laws which gave him the right to kill his adulterous wife,[40] while a Jew in medieval Europe was allowed to beat her 'within reason.' If he happened to injure her severely however, he was fined rather heavily.[41]

Thousands of years have rolled by since the first man put woman on his property list, but woman is still there in one guise or another. Today when a man says, 'this is my wife', it is hard to tell whether the glint in his eye denotes proud possession or appreciation of her as a person.

The Yanomamo Indians of the Brazil border[42] must surely rank highest among modern tribals as wife possessors. Among these people woman is property *par excellence*.

'All Yanomamo men physically abuse their wives. Kind husbands merely bruise and mutilate them, the fierce ones wound and kill.'[43]

In a plethora of violence against what they consider their very own, they yank off ears, chop off flesh from an arm, shoot barbed arrows into buttocks, scorch their women with burning sticks, swing axes at them, or merely chop their heads off. Sometimes an arrow aimed innocently at an arm or a leg lodges itself most annoyingly in a stomach or a heart. The inconvenience of having to look around for another woman is so great that it seems hardly worth the momentary satisfaction of having taught the dead one a lesson.

Dr Judith Shapiro of the University of Chicago who studied these tribals, found that their women expected to be beaten, and proudly displayed their scars as marks of affection. Her own unscarred face drew sympathetic comment. It was obvious to them that the men she met had no tender feelings for her.[44]

A Yanomamo woman realises that she will be discarded the moment her usefulness is over. She understands the full significance of the phrase in her language which means divorce—'throwing something away.'[45]

It's all in the game.

The battle scars of love and marriage are still on display in some of our most civilized societies:

'Recently, some of Japan's ladies themselves have begun to puncture their nation's feminine mystique. The wife of the former Prime Minister Eisaku Sato started it all by accusing her husband of beating her and behaving in ways that would "make a girl of today run away and get a divorce.'[46]

'I'll call daddy to hit you!'

'Women have been raised and socialized to believe they must make their husbands happy, argues Marjory Fields, an Attorney with the South Brooklyn Legal Services Corporation. 'So they not only take the beatings; they tend to feel responsible for them. Their guilt feelings prevent them from getting out... Some police departments have informal "stitch rules": they will arrest a husband only if the wound he has inflicted is severe enough to require a specific—and considerable number of stitches.'[47]

'For many women,' continues MS magazine, 'even arguments over minor items as misplaced cigarettes, unmade beds, or delayed dinners may end in blood and bruises.'[48]

Civilisation is just a scratch away from bestiality....

NOTES AND REFERENCES

1. Little Ramu.
2. *The Indian Express*, 23 December 1976.
3. Wooden rods used for washing clothes.
4. Open sandals.
5. *The Tribune*, 7 September 1976.
6. *Ibid.*, 3 February 1977.
7. *Ibid.*
8. *Ibid.*
9. *The Times of India*, 11 August 1977.
10. *The Indian Express*, 21 September 1977.
11. *The Times of India*, 26 April 1978.
12. *The Indian Express*, 29 December 1977.
13. *The Patriot*, 11 August 1976.
14. *The Times of India*, 17 March 1979.

15.

Lakshmi Devi	:	*The Times of India*, 7 September 1976.
Renuka Saran	:	*The Indian Express*, 11 June 1977.
Kanta Goel	:	*The Indian Express*, 29 December 1976.
Krishna Kumari	:	*The Indian Express*, 15 April 1977.
Meera	:	*The Indian Express*, 23 December 1976.
Vasantha Nadar	:	*The Patriot,* 11 August 1976.
Shanta Rani	:	*The Tribune*,2 October 1976.
Alka	:	*Blitz*, 15 October 1977.
Davinder Kaur	:	*Ibid.*
Tarawati	:	*Ibid.*
Savitri Sundar	:	*Femina*, 15-28 July 1977.
Manorama	:	*Sunday*, 10 October 1976.
Kamla	:	*Ibid.*
Tarvinder Kaur	:	*The Times of India*, 2 June 1979.
Kanchan Chopra	:	*The Indian Express*, 2 July 1979.

16. *Rig Veda*: X: 85. verse 40—from Abinash Chandra Bose, Hymns from the Vedas, Asia Publishing House, Calcutta, 1966, p. 137.
17. Soma: 'The Ultimate Being'.
18. *Gandharva*: Celestial musicians.
19. *Agni*: The deity of fire.
20. *Manusmriti:* IX, verses 2 and 3 as they appear in F. Max Mueller, (ed.) The Sacred Books of the East, translated: G. Buehler, Vol. xxv, The Laws of Manu, Motilal Banarsi Dass, 1964, pp. 327-28.
    This compares interestingly with Confucian thought on the subject of woman: 'To be a woman is to submit' (The Book of Rites). The Three Obediences ordained that a woman was to be dependent on her father as a child, on her husband as a married woman and on her son as a widow, quoted by Krishna Prakash Gupta, *China Report*, 1975.
21. L. Vern and Bonnie Bullough, The Subordinate Sex, University of Illinois Press, Urbana, Chicago, 1974, p. 22.
22. *Ibid.*, p. 23.
23. *Ibid.*, p. 155: *munt* means hand.
24. Alemanni: a name originally given to German tribes of the Upper Rhine and the Danube. Later the word began to be applied to the entire German nation.
25. L. Vern and Bonnie Bullough, 1974, *op. cit.,* p. 154. f.n. *Leges Alamannorum*, ed. by Karl Lehman in *Monumenta Germaniae Historica, Leges Nationum Germanicarum*, Vol. 5, pt. 1. (Hanover: Hahn, 1888), p. 115.
    Solidus: A gold coin of the times of the Roman Emperors.
26. *Ibid*, f.n., *Lex Ribuaria*, ed. by Rudolph Sohm, *Monumenta Germaniae Historica*, Legum, Vol. 5 (Hanover: Hahn, 1875-79), pp. 216-31.
27. Sigrid Latka-Jöhring (In-Press) Social Report 10-76: Women: 111-51.
28. Edward Westermarck, The History of Human Marriage, Johnson

Reprint Corporation, reprint 1971, Vol. I, p. 317, quoting Labarthe (Ling Roth, Great Benin, p. 41. no. 1)

29. Will Durant, The Story of Civilization, Simon and Schuster, New York, *Our Oriental Heritage*, 1954, p. 149.
30. Victor W.von Hagen, *Realm of the Incas*, 1957, p. 132.
31. Krishna Prakash Gupta, *China Report*, Vol I, 1975. Emancipation and Enslavement of Women in China: Confucian and Communist Variations: Nos. 5 and 6, September-December 1975, II. Women in Traditional China: 2 Sources of Inequality: Morality and Law.
32. *Ibid.* 3. Normative Behaviour: Patterns of Institutional Adjustment.
33. *Ibid.*
    IV. 1. Women in Modern China: Evolution and Revolution. 'Womens' Movement: Framework of Analysis.'
    3. 'Womens' Movement: 'Analysis From Without'.
34. *Ibid.*
35. *The Ramayana* of Tulsidas, *Sundara Kanda*: *Chaupai* 59 as translated by Gita Press, Gorakhpur: (1968)—*Sri Ramcharitamanasa:* or The Manasa Lake brimming over with the exploits of Sri Rama.
36. *Manusmriti*: IX: 230; Max Mueller, *op. cit.*, 1964, 382. The word '*whip*' has been explained in the footnotes as '*a rod measuring five fingers*' or *the 'pendant root of a fig-tree*' by Raghavananda, a commentator on Manu.
37. John Taylor, The Water Poet: from Hoyt's New Cyclopedia of Practical Quotations: compiled by Kate Louise Roberts, New York and London: Funk and Wagnalls Company, 1922, 1927 and 1940.
38. *Manusmriti:* XI. 67, Max Mueller, *op. cit.,* pp. 443-44.
    Vaisyas: See Ch. 2., note 26.
    Kshatriya: the second—or regal and warrior caste. Dowson, *A Classical Dictionory of Hindu Mythology*, 1968.
39. Will Durant, *op. cit. Caesar and Christ*, 1944, Ch. IV: Stoic Rome, p. 57.
40. Will Durant, *op. cit.*, *The Age of Faith*, 1950, Ch. XXX, Morals and Manners, p. 825.
41. *Ibid.*, Ch. XVI: The Medieval Jews, p. 381.
42. The Yanomamo Indians.
    According to the anthropologist Napoleon Chagnon, Yanomami tribal culture accords high status to a victorious warrior. He may be rewarded with as many as six wives. This gives rise to the theory that the desire for procreation lies at the root of the Yanomami's violent infighting.* As many as 70% of the tribe have lost close relatives. Added to this is the arrival of gold panners and tin ore and diamond seekers during the eighties, and the resultant depredations on life and old rain forest land. The remaining 9,000 Yanomami are now an endangered people.**

* A Laboratory of Human Conflict, William F. Allman, U.S. News and World Report, April 2, 1988.

** Emissary From the Rain Forest, L.A. Winokur, The Progressive, vol. 57, page 14, March 1993.

43. Cows, Pigs, Wars and Witches. (The Riddles of Culture), Marvin Harris, Glasgow, Fontana/Collins 1974: ch.4.
44. *Ibid.*
45. *Ibid.*
46. 'The Feminine Mystique,' *Newsweek*, 13 January 1975.
47. Battered wives, MS Magazine, August 1976, p. 51. (Wife beating is still not a cognizable offence in India, nor is it considered a cognizable offence if a wife is turned out of the house.) However, with the insertion in 1983, of Section 498A in the Code of Criminal Procedure and other enactments (See Appendix), cruelty to a wife not only attracts severe punishment, but this section also provides for presumption by the Court of abetment by the husband and/or his relatives.
48. 'The Feminine Mystique,' *Newsweek*, 13 January 1975.

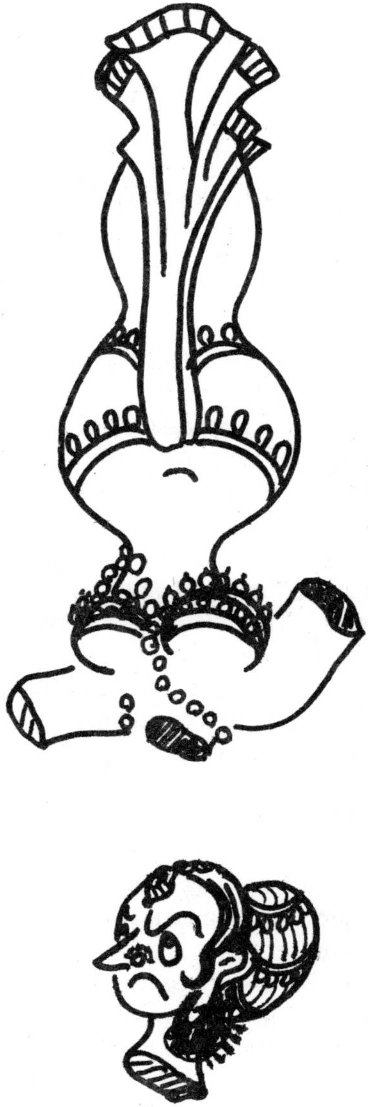

10

What Went Wrong?

'You're my girl.'

'Henry's girl! She smiled. No, she was not Henry's girl. She was Sarah. And that was sufficient.'[1]

Am I myself, or am I a possession? Am I fulfilling myself and giving of myself to those who come in contact with me, or am I just acting out a part dreamed up for me before ever I was born?

'The tragedy, says the wife of an American doctor[2] is that nobody ever looked us in the eye and said you have to decide what you want to do with your life, besides being your husband's wife and your children's mother.' The doctor's wife could so easily have been Hamida, Leela, Sirikit or Eileen anywhere in the world.

Where did we go wrong, I found myself wondering as I boarded the train once again. Was it the conditioning of our minds from birth, or perhaps even earlier, that was wrong? Girls everywhere have been brought up to serve man, to be married and to enjoy perpetual enslavement; to take good treatment as an unlooked for miracle and ill-treatment as a combination of fate and their master's voice. Even if they have gone a long way in some advanced countries towards their own liberation, woman as a universal person has still miles to traverse to discover herself.

Although we have mainly concerned ourselves here with dowry, we have discovered in the process, that this problem cannot be divorced from other forms of exploitation of mind and body. It can only be attacked by a massive all round effort which will take note of every little preconceived idea, however small and seemingly irrelevant, which forms an integral part of the nurture bed of the growing woman...

'You modernised women talk so much about sweeping out our ancient customs! Have you ever read the *Shastras* handed down to us by our great *rishi munis*?'[3] growled the stern looking *pundit*.[4] 'Do you know that Hindu marriage is a sacred *daan* of a beloved daughter? She goes as a gift, which like all religious gifts, is to be accompanied by yet another gift of gold or cash. This is the religious basis of the dowry system which you are so anxious to wipe out!'

'With all due respect, *punditji*,' said a severely dressed lady, 'modern women are right when they say we should do away with dowry. This gift that accompanied our brides in the old *Shastras*, was a mere formality. Nowhere in our scriptures has it ever been used as a bargaining counter as it is today!'

I turned gratefully to her, but she was already immersed in telling her beads, her lips moving in silent prayer...

Prestige conscious orthodoxy of the mind slithers its way into the most enlightened circles:

'Highly educated and well-established non-Shandilya Brahman (even Rarhis will do)[5] groom wanted. Girl, daughter of a retired High Court judge outside West Bengal. Highly meritorious and talented. First class first both in B.A. and M.A. Tall, slim and good-looking. Complexion medium.'[6]

'Intercaste marriages are the only answer,' gushed a mother on her way to a wedding. 'How wonderful it is that young people are going in for this kind of thing these days. No dowries, no flashy weddings and no display! Just a simple wedding with a few of their own friends invited, and a prayer or two if they want a ceremony!'

Wonderful indeed it was, when for fear or gain during the Emergency, college principals and Chief Ministers became one and all zealous champions of dowryless and intercaste weddings overnight. Awards were offered to young men who married without fuss or display. Documentaries were made on the subject. Villages were adopted by colleges to involve rural parents in the great crusade for the establishment of a brave new world....

At the dowryless mass wedding at Bulandshahr on 14 October 1976 nineteen year old Imrat Singh, a labourer earning six rupees a day said, 'My father is still paying back the loan taken over a decade ago from the *Bania*[7] at the time of his sister's marriage.' 'I will never go to a *Bania* again,' smiled a happy Nannu as he watched his daughter take the seven steps around the wedding fire. The organiser of this function said he planned five hundred such weddings in the following six months. 'Let us fight dowry first,' he said. 'Caste and child marriages will be the next victims.'[8]

What happened? Where did all that zeal go?

You see we like our double standards. Intercaste marriages are all very well for everyone else. What happens when the problem strikes nearer home? The newspapers will tell you which the desirable castes are:

> '*Wanted*: Really beautiful Khatri...Jat Sikh...Orthodox Christian youth...Dutt Mohyal Brahman boy, B.Sc; Captain in the army. Arora bachelor... Andhra Brahmin boy working as engineer... For high ranking Class I Gazetted Officer, Hindu Vaish.. Bengali Kayastha... Sunni Muslim engineer'...

And then, someone has the courage to brave community censure and marry into another caste. What happens then?

Omprakash Singh, a young Rajput and Murmila Kumari a Harijan girl[9] registered their marriage in Hajipur on 6 October 1977.

'The local landholders and a former *mukhia*[10] of the village, all of the upper castes, allegedly beat up Mr. Singh and his wife and stripped them. Later Mr. Singh was allowed to leave the village with a towel wrapped round his waist...They were separated ...and she was forcibly detained.'[11]

Is legislation the answer? *The Times of India* of 26 November 1976 had carried the news that the Karnataka Bill[12] hopes to encourage intercaste marriages by offering each party to such marriages a thousand rupees. The Government of Madhya Pradesh is now reviving the thousand rupee award for couples willing to risk community censure by marrying outside their caste. On 2 October 1978 a mass marriage took place on the Marina sands in Madras. These were intercaste marriages where a hundred and fifty rupees were announced as an award for each couple. It was also announced there that the Tamil Nadu Government were considering a grant of five thousand rupees to be given to couples from different castes at their marriage as was the case in Gujarat.[13] This is welcome news indeed.

But with over thirty years of planned development behind us, the women of India have been steadily slipping backwards. Statistics on illiteracy are staggering. The ratio is approximately two illiterate women to one literate man.[14] Of the ones who are considered literate among the less fortunate in our country, the greater part can only laboriously sign their names—to what kind of documents of exploitation, it isn't always the teacher's duty to investigate.

Women's education has never been need based in India. It is completely divorced from reality and is heavily marriage oriented. It is only when Aim Matrimony is taken right out of education that a wholesome search for knowledge can be allowed to develop young minds: an education of the mind that would neither superficially Westernise nor narrowly 'Indianise.' This would equip boys and girls to make balanced assessments and enable them to take a firm stand when necessary.

The ever present 'Gimmee' needs watching. Ever since the Hindu Succession Act came into force placing men and women on an equal footing in the matter of inheritance of property, forces have been at work trying to reverse its key provision.

In 1961 a Punjab Government appointed committee recommended 'abolition of the daughter's share by her own right to the landed property of her father as ensured by the Hindu Succession Act. It granted her instead, a share in her father-in-law's property through her husband's right' in it.[15] The three women on this committee were up in arms saying that 'daughters are as dear as sons to their parents and hence there can be no moral justification to deny the direct right of a daughter to inherit her father's property.' They felt that being given an equal share in it would 'add to her independence and dignity.' They pointed out that co-ownership in her husband's inheritance sounded very good on paper, but would give the husband complete control in practice; for if a wife tried to 'exercise her right of co-ownership by making a partition of the property, it would immediately result in total estrangement of relations between her and her husband.'[16] Also this kind of co-ownership would be more of a privilege than a right. The women on the committee appended a dissenting note to the recommendations, emphatically stating that the passing of such a recommendation would be 'a retrograde departure from the very fundamentals on which the Hindu Succession Act and its contemporary social laws were based.'[17]

These forces are now reportedly at work again, attempting to arouse public opinion in Punjab and Haryana to send the woman back to where she belongs, leaving the undivided land free for the men and the boys again.[18]

Such attacks on the already bereft Indian woman call for vigilance and vocal participation from educated women who understand the insidious workings of the 'Gimmee's' acquisitive mind.

The vast majority of Indian wives bear their lot patiently. Very few dare risk the blaring publicity of divorce. Of course, there is the odd woman who goes in for it, but she has to fight a daily battle against prejudice. She has also to brave complicated court-procedures to squeeze the maintenance that is her due from her former husband, and has also to find the where-withal to keep herself and her deserted children from starving.

If on the other hand, she tries to keep harmony alive in the home, her constant surrender will eventually erode her individuality and self-confidence, enmeshing her still further into permanent subservience to her man for her daily bread. If she has children, she will find the bonds drawn even tighter as 'her' children could quite easily be starved by a heartless father and his relations if she doesn't watch out. Few of us who bring up clinging daughters realise the importance of giving them a trade in hand.

This attitude has been sadly lacking in our traditional upbringing. The woman who works side by side with her man, doing a Herculean job of work as well as bearing and bringing up children often single-handed, needs to be given the honour due to her as an individual in her own right.

"Look at my arm! I have ploughed and planted and gathered into barns...and ain't I a woman? I could work as much and eat as much as a man—when I could get it—and bear the lash as well....I have borne thirteen children and seen most of them sold into slavery...and ain't I a woman?'[19] cried Sojourner Truth, an early American feminist. Remi and Zarina in the remote villages of India say the same thing, but they do not say it aloud. Their cry is muffled by the caste into which they are born and the community that has brought them up. They are offered up on a platter as a gift to be silent slaves who are also expected to be happy ones. Their husbands are at liberty to drink up their meagre earnings, and their parents-in-law may keep the rest as payment towards their keep. They are expected to work for the extended family apart from doing a full day's job outside the home. A break in the routine will invite the family's wrath. The ever useful peg of dowry is conveniently at hand: 'What can one expect from a shameless girl who neither brings a decent dowry nor stirs herself to work!'

We have done little to harness the great potential that awaits release in rural woman power. Given a chance to look outside her home, and certain that her husband and family are being taken care of, woman can perform miracles.

Even though our women are mainly agricultural labourers, little has been done to improve their technical know-how. It would be worth our while to take a leaf from Japan's book where during the harvest season, community kitchens take over from the housewife, preparing the men's food while creches look after the babies. With her mind freed from household cares, the Japanese woman's agricultural productivity has increased threefold. The expenditure for all this does not come as charity—out of the social welfare budget, but from the agriculture budget, thus acknowledging that a woman like any other labourer, is worthy of her hire.[20] The rural woman in India is still bound by house and family before, after and even during her work in the fields.

The urban woman construction labourer is no better off. Pregnant or feeding her newborn, she still has to climb the scaffolding. Her head-load of bricks will earn her the six rupees a day that may buy good seed for the wheat crop back home after construction time in the city is over. Leaving her baby in the occasional mobile creche on the ground floor at the construction site would mean a half hour off from her work, a frown, a cut in pay and even loss of job.

More and more men and women are becoming increasingly enthused with a desire for service and many exciting schemes are being dreamed up and put into practice in pockets all over the country; but India is vast and the irony of it all is that the very schemes that transform deserts into green fields often threaten the very people they aim at benefitting—those on the lowest rung of the economic ladder—the poorest rural and urban working women — leaving them jobless and without hope of alternative employ-ment.[21] Consistent co-ordinated work towards helping this kind of woman gain self-confidence and economic independence has so far been lacking.[22]

The Draft Five-Year Plan for 1978-'83 presented by the Planning Commission to The National Development Council in March 1978 however, promises a ray of hope as it recognises that 'the employment situation confronting women also requires separate discussion.' It puts down in black and white the fact of discrimination against women in the labour market and suggests steps to be taken to change the situation.[23]

It is true perhaps that the Indian woman is a masochist and is the originator and perpetrator of a system that keeps her enslaved, but it is not she alone who can change the established order. The guilt is a collective social guilt. However, it was born and whoever helped it grow, it has been nurtured far too long by a sometimes active and far more often apathetic society. Kanta Goel was beaten and abused according to her own testimony, not by her mother-in-law alone, but by her husband, his father, his brother and even by the two girls in the family. Shanta Rani[24] was thrown from a height on to broken glass by her husband as well as by other members of his family, because their dowry demands had not been met. There is a Kanta Goel and a Shanta Rani behind many a door in our country.

In our excitement over the sensational, don't let us ever forget that the coin has another side. If the harried wife deserves our sympathy, her mother-in-law cries out for even more sensitive handling. Here is a subject that the novelist dropped. She is a product of the society into which she was born. If she happens to come from a poor family, she will have lived a hand-to-mouth existence, cursed by her parents, denied the barest essentials, while she watches the saved *paise* go into the little tin to pay for her brother's nourishment or education, or for her own inadequate dowry. Living with the daily reality of insecurity, she will naturally turn to her son to provide for her old age. Her mind is constantly badgered consciously or unconsciously by the dread of sometime being forced to live alone and unprotected with no one to turn to. So she and her husband provide for their son at the expense of their daughter. He will stay and look after them. She is someone else's property and will leave.

Unfortunately, the New Criminal Procedure Code puts the stamp of legal approval on this kind of preferential treatment in a family.[25]

It provides that indigent parents can claim maintenance from a son by law. No such clause appears in the Code for a daughter. No wonder the son is made much of by fond parents who planning ahead, gift him their house and land, salving their consciences on their daughter's score by giving her cash and valuables at her wedding.

You and I can now understand but not condone the resentment of a mother-in-law from such a background against her son's new wife. The two women approach each other as opponents from the start with mutual distrust. The younger woman is at a disadvantage as her husband's mother sees in her a potential threat to her own future security. This sword of Damocles constantly hangs over her head and she holds her daughter-in-law responsible. She is always on the look out for the slightest hint that her son may want to set up a separate establishment and move away from her, and suspicion raises an impenetrable wall between the two women.

How much more forward looking it could have been if social attitudes and legislation had combined to enjoin the pooling of the affectionate concern and economic resources of both sons and daughters according to each one's capacity. This joint fund would then have set their parents' minds at rest and assured them of their children's love and support as long as they were alive.

Not all mothers-in-law are the gorgons they are made out to be. Quite often it is the daughter-in-law who enters marriage with her boxing gloves on, ready to spar at the first insult, fancied or real.

If the little girl that will one day be a mother-in-law, is helped to gain self confidence, independence and dignity early in life, she will automatically respect another's independence and be a much less tense person by the time her son's marriage comes around. She might even begin to understand the real reason behind her desire to demand more and more articles of status for her son's marriage. Looking calmly at themselves, she and her husband will realise that these demands are not made in the interest of their son alone as they would like to make themselves believe. They are made so that they themselves may be cushioned against an uncertain future by a sense of power which comes from being in a position to demand; and that this sense of power will ensure future control over their son, thus providing for their own lasting comfort and assuring a respected position for themselves in society.

There are many concerned individuals and organisations who could tackle the problem of the girl who has already grown up to be a mother-in-law. Clubs for women of her own age at every level of society can provide creative work and recreation programmes which could help disentangle the knots in her circumscribed mind. These programmes could defuse tense situations, channelising her energies into productive activity which would in turn help broaden the family horizons and not allow pools of hate to form or misunderstandings to develop.

Humanised again, the mother-in-law and her erstwhile antagonist may gain a new insight into each other's problems and become more worthwhile persons. The older woman might even bring herself to acknowledge her jealousy of her son's wife, and the cruel unequal competition have a chance of ending.

So perhaps dowry was not the real villain of the piece after all, I mused as I watched the trees swish by the train window. It had been twisted into a monstrous instrument to protect frightened people from their great dread of insecurity—fear of 'losing face' in a critical society, of having a nose cut off, of 'looking small' in the neighbourhood. According to a survey conducted among working women in Punjab, most of whom were school teachers,[26] the demand for dowry came from the girls themselves and had little to do with their parents or their future in-laws. The women felt dowry was necessary to help them 'extract a greater share from parental property, to get a better husband and earn more honour from their in-laws.'[27]

How, I wondered, could this Frankenstein society be controlled? Society is after all only two persons at base—You and I. Could we not batter the problem from every angle with all the media guns in our arsenal and project a different kind of Indian woman? A woman firmly rooted in all that is good in her tradition, her branches reaching out to dignity, her roots to the distant horizon; conscious of her obligations, unafraid of law courts, police, society or dishonour—Not to be bullied or sold?

'It is necessary security for our daughters,' say the dowry givers. Security against what?

When educated and talented young Rekha was thrown out of her husband's house in the eighth month of pregnancy on one of the coldest nights of winter dressed in a single sari and thin blouse, did it help her that her parents had given the 'good' family she was married into a TV set, a sewing machine and a refrigerator plus innumerable articles of furniture and other household goods?

But does this mean that parents who love their daughters may not demonstrate their affection by giving them a visible sign of their love as they leave their homes for the unknown?

In my mind I was back in a little village sharing the only cot with the *grande dame* of the community, while the other ladies sat on the ground. 'There should be no force,' she was saying, 'but what we want to give, we should be allowed to give.'

Everyone dutifully nodded agreement. I drew her attention respectfully to her indigent neighbours. Might not her standard be impossible for them to reach when their own daughters got married? Wouldn't she be unwittingly setting a norm which would become a social compulsion for all? This was a difficult thing to decide, said everyone, but I still remember the quiet voice of the primary school teacher:

'It is this display and talk about cash and jewels given to the girls,' she said. 'If this was stopped, the dowry would drop at once by 50 per cent. So much dowry is only given for the sake of show and having a big name in society among neighbours. If no one can show it or talk about it, then few would give.'

'Yes,' said a middle-aged mother. 'If we want to give, let us from long before her marriage put the money in the bank in her name. No need to tell all people. When she needs it and is grown up, she may use it for anything necessary not only at her marriage. If we are not sure about her in-laws' intentions, then let us put her father's name with hers also in the bank. Like this they will not take her for greed. She will stand on her own two feet and they cannot say her anything.'

'There is one more thing,' said the regal old lady, 'receiving big money and dowry for a rural boy turns the boy's and the girl's heads and gives them ideas that are not fitting in with the noble thoughts of their fathers and fore fathers. They straight-away want to run to cities and live hollow lives there with friends who are not good for them. What happens to them in the big city? They lose their heads and their money, and our village loses their contribution to its life!'

The old lady's voiced merged with the chugging of the train's engine. The rhythmic motion seemed to merge with another voice I had heard not so long ago in my own house. 'Display of dowry should become a cognizable offence. You will see how this dowry list will end at once!' It was an elderly gentleman, his voice charged with emotion. 'Register every marriage,' he went on. 'What is so difficult about spreading a network of social workers and other dedicated people so that there will be one person per area who can register a marriage? If we can move heaven and earth for political campaigns, why can't we take this simple step? Can you tell me,' he continued, 'why there is no Family Court in India? Personally I dislike the use of the word "court." You know our people are afraid of going there. But these Family Courts are already dealing sympathetically with family troubles in Japan, Australia and in some parts of America.[28] Even Sri Lanka I think, was planning such courts.[29] What is stopping us?

'Every day I see respectable women being jostled about in courts where hardened criminals are awaiting trial. This is absolutely wrong! In a Family Court they would have honourable and private hearings before people who are interested in keeping the family together, and will see the problems of the family as a whole. Nowadays, criminal courts deal with maintenance for wives, another deals with property, and the children are sent to the juvenile courts. It is just like going to one doctor for a disease of the food pipe, another for the stomach and a third for the intestines. All is part of one system, and the actions of one result in good or bad for the others. Husbands and wives will be helped by psychiatrists and counsellers in the court to look for answers rather than await judgements.'[30]

I thought of the flashy weddings I saw everyday—the display of wealth, the easy flowing black money changing hands, the tax evasion, the organisations who have a stake in keeping the display on a lavish scale. I thought of the many men and women who make a living out of the wedding season and thrive on it, and of the vulnerable young couple caught in a net woven by them all. The elderly gentleman's voice faded away. The wheels of the train rumbled soothingly on, and soon I was fast asleep....

NOTES AND REFERENCES

1. 'Sarah and the Seaplane,' *Ladies Home Journal*, February 1949.
2. Betty Friedan, *The Feminine Mystique*, W. Norton and Company Inc. 1974, p. 71.
3. Sages and learned teachers.
4. Hindu divine learned in Sanskrit, philosophy and jurisprudence—A priest or learned man.
5. *Shandilya Brahmin*, *Rarhi*: high castes.
6. *Ananda Bazar Patrika*, Calcutta, 1 July 1973; quoted and translated by D.P. Das in *The Weekly Round Table*, 26 August 1973.
7. *Bania*: A business community caste. Here it implies moneylender.
8. 'Many Minors Figure in Dowryless Weddings' Ashwini Sarin, *The Indian Express*, 15 October 1976.
9. *Harijan*: God's people: A name given by Mahatma Gandhi to persons belonging to a caste traditionally considered low in the Hindu community.
10. Headman.
11. *The Indian Express*, 3 November 1977. 'Woeful Tale of an Inter-caste Marriage.'
12. The Bill has since been passed. The Karnataka Marriages (Registration and Miscellaneous Provisions Act 1984. See Chapter 15.
13. *The Times of India*, 4 October 1978: 'Mass Marriage of 40 Harijans, Caste Hindus.'

    The Statesman of 27 November, 1978 reported a five-point resolution passed by a concourse in Rewari which urged Government to give preference to employees who have the courage to marry outside their caste. The *Mahasammelan* composed mainly of marginal farmers and landless labourers undertook to organise a public reception for ten couples every year who had contracted such marriages.
14. 1971 Census figures put the literacy rate at 39.5% for males and 18.7% for females. According to the 1991 Census figures male literacy is 64.20% and female literacy 39.9%.
15. *The Times of India*, 24 April 1961: 'Daughter's Right To Property.'
16. *Ibid.*
17. *The Hindustan Times*, 11 May 1961: 'Punjab Women Assail Bid To Modify Hindu Succession Act.'
18. Rami Chhabra, Feminist Viewpoint: *The Indian Express*, 3 December 1977.
19. Betty Friedan, *op. cit.*, p. 96.
20. Mrs. Anjani Dayanand, Ministry of Education and Social Welfare.
21. *The Indian Express*, 3 December, 1977.
22. Government of India set up a twenty-six member national committee on women in January 1978.

23. (*i*) "...special consideration should be given to the admission of women students to all educational and training programmes on a strictly non-discriminatory basis." (4-92: p. 88 of Draft Plan, 1978-'83).
    (*ii*) "...to promote female employment...all those industries and occupations which have been identified as 'women-preferred', be specially stimulated by the government investment programmes...it is recommended" that in these occupations and industries "preference be given to qualified women" (4.93: p. 90 of Draft Plan, 1978-'83).
    (*iii*) "A reasonable share...in the allocation of co-operative and commercial bank credit and other aid (training, technical assistance, marketing facilities, hire/purchase of machinery, sheds in industrial estates etc.)" be "available for potential women entrepreneurs and women's co-operatives employing a majority of women workers." (4.94: p. 90 of Draft Plan, 1978-'83).
    (*iv*) "...female labour force" should be included in area development plan manpower budgets and "the schemes included in the plans should be carefully designed to offer a variety of training and work opportunities to women." (4.95: p. 90 of Draft Plan, 1978-'83).
24. Shanta Rani, *The Tribune*, 2 October 1976.
25. Order for Maintenance: The Code of Criminal Procedure: 1973.
    Section 125: (i) 'If any person having sufficient means neglects or refuses to maintain (d) his father or mother, unable to maintain himself or herself, a Magistrate of the 1st class may, upon proof of such neglect or refusal, order such person to make a monthly allowance for the maintenance of his wife or such child, father or mother, at such monthly rate not exceeding Rs 500/- in the whole, as such Magistrate thinks fit, and to pay the same to such persons as the Magistrate may from time to time direct..'
26. Parkash Singh Jammu, 1976, p. 77 of cyclostyled manuscript.
27. *Ibid.*
28. Kapila Hingorani, senior advocate, Supreme Court.
29. According to the *Lankadipa* of 14 July 1979, 'The Government' (Sri Lanka) 'has decided to appoint thirty Family Court Instructors from among persons having very wide knowledge in the field of Social Service.'
30. Proposal for the setting up of Family Courts in India: a recommendation of The Committee on the Status of Women: 1974 (*Towards Equality*, 1974, New Delhi, Family Courts, 4. 227-33, p. 141).

11

Travellers

The train shrieked to a stop. She came into the compartment, wrapping the hand-embroidered shawl tightly around her thin shoulders. Her weatherbeaten face proclaimed her an outdoor worker. The well turned out woman opposite us gave her a sympathetic look. 'You must be tired,' she said.

'Yes, a village *gramsevika*[1] doesn't gets time to look after health!'

'What are the problems you generally come across?' I asked.

She smiled indulgently. 'Not your ladies' kind of problems,' she said. 'Woman's problems—illiterate women, poor people, beating for bringing less dowry. That one is 80 per cent of cases.'

'But I thought that the woman in rural areas is a valued worker and dowry was paid by the bridegroom to get her.'

'That is all changing now!' said the *gramsevika.* 'Everybody is wanting false honour and respect. Those people who gives dowry is honoured, and those parents who takes money for own daughters is condemned. So whatever the high ups do, the poors will follow surely.'

'So then you are implying that it is for the rich to set the trend for dowryless weddings otherwise it will get from bad to worse?'

'Certainly,' she said, warming to her subject. 'Look at all the cinemas! See the expensive weddings and brides dressed in gold and silver and looking like *devis*, covered in richest jewellery. Money is flowing like the Ganga water and she is welcome with greatest respect by in-laws. What do you expect a poor father to do? He wants his daughter to have good reception by in-laws, and so he is drowned up to three generations in debt to give his daughter good dowry like the high ups.'

The well turned out woman smiled. 'My father gave me a priceless dowry,' she said quietly. 'I was given a high value system, discipline and a sense of humour. I took no jewellery from my parents. My husband and I are happily married. We only exchanged garlands at my marriage.'

The *gramsevika* gave her a sour look. 'In one of my villages,' she said, 'all through her life, the girl is wearing clothes, even shoes etc. sent to her all the time from her father's house. Even at her death her parents and relations have to give clothes and turban to her husband, and clothes to children plus cash also to the pundit who performs the ceremony. Even they are giving food when they are standing before the dead body of their daughter. 'Yes,' she said caustically, 'it is good for you that you are not born in the families that are suffering with this dowry giving, all time giving. For the girl's parents it is always pouring out the money. Even at times her shroud is sent from her father's house also.'

The enlightened woman looked out of the window embarrassed. There was an awkward pause. I tried to fill it.

'*Behniji*,'[2] I asked the *gramsevika*, 'What do you think is at the bottom of all this trouble?'

Pat came the answer, 'Bad education. I am not meaning the girl should be a B.A. or M.A., but she should get education to know who she is even if she is a sixth class fail.' The *gramsevika* was fully engrossed in her subject again. 'She must not be told from childhood, "You are nobody without husband." Because of this talk she is always ready for suicide when nobody is marrying her. She should be made strong by her parents. They can say her, "You are a good woman. You stand on your two feet. We help you to get training for job, and we also help you to get the training like the men for the *judo* to see to your self defence. You have got God-given brain; *Parmatma* has given you dowry of two hands and two feet." ' She turned to the educated woman trying to make amends. 'Then only can she say to the one who taunts her, "I am earning woman. I am not frightened. You beat me and I call the *vakeel*. Yes, I call lawyer! What you will do to me and my child? I will see to it." Then you will see them coming running with their tails between their legs.' We smiled at her graphic idiom.

'No no,' she went on earnestly, 'it is quite true. They are big bullies you see. When the girl has no defence in training, she has to depend on them for her bread. Then they are strong and trouble her very much. When she is standing on her own two feet, they cannot trouble her. Government should make many centres where unmarried girls can get training in villages, given jobs after.'

'Of course, one of the main things we really have to fight is the orthodox way of considering it a sin if a girl is unmarried,' said the enlightened woman who had recovered from her original embarrassment. 'The sin is laid at the door of the father and he is forced by circumstances to get a dowry somehow, marry her off and become a slave to her in-laws. Education is so necessary!'

'Humph!' grunted a crotchety little old woman I had not noticed so far. 'Educate daughters? Who educated us? What education does a girl need? After all she will only get married! She only needs to know how much food she must make for her husband and family. All this education is giving them foreign ideas! They only want to break up the joint families and live in big cities to be a selfish small family. Only want to put on lipstick and fill up their husbands' heads with stories against his parents who have spent all their earnings on him to set him on his own two feet. They don't want him to support his old parents. Oh no! Nylon saris and bell bottom pants are all they want to have. Humph! Education!'

'But *mataji*,'[3] I ventured. 'In matrimonial advertisements you ask for convent educated working women, preferably doctors or women employed in foreign countries. A girl's education is valuable even for her in-laws, isn't it? Doesn't her income help the family?'

Before the old lady could reply, a young student shouted, 'They live on our earnings! They never allow the girl one *paisa* for herself or for her children, especially if the child is a girl. Even if she is ill or pregnant she is forced to keep on working. My own friend is suffering in this way. They forced her to work in a factory. They take her money as soon as she brings it home. Her baby girl is left with them and she cries hungry and uncared for till her mother returns. Then when my friend is tired they make her do the housework and beat her if she sleeps.'

'Young women are butterflies nowadays, *behnji*', said an elderly gentleman as he hobbled into the compartment from the corridor and sat down next to the old lady. 'Everyone blames the father and mother-in-law, but has anyone ever spoken of the training that a daughter-in-law should be given to be unselfish and dutiful?'

'Who thinks of moral and religious duties now brother,' said the old woman. 'All these big stories about dowry deaths in the newspapers! They will always pick up anything people will read. Who has ever written about the problems of the mother-in-law? These modern girls are becoming tyrants for us old people! My sister-in-law was murdered—murdered I tell you, by her heartless daughter-in-law. The day my poor brother died, she demanded the house keys from her mother-in-law. One month later the poor widow was dead—starved to death, and who lifted a little finger of blame against the stone-hearted daughter-in-law? No one!'

The train clanked rhythmically in the silence. The hustle and bustle of a station filled the pause. The enlightened woman turned to me, 'But seriously, you know,' she said, 'the evil of dowry giving and demanding can only be stopped by a social boycott. This is the greatest trouble with our society. We expect to be fed from above. The government is expected to impose laws on us, and when they don't work, we grumble. How *can* they when our own people circumvent them all the time? Our parents bend the knee before the boy's family, "Kindly accept my daughter, great ones," they say, "We make you a gift of her mind and body. These little gewgaws of dowry will make the dish more palatable." Shame on us that we smile at people who sell their daughters. Shame on us that we invite such givers and receivers to our homes!' She stopped suddenly flushed and breathless, embarrassed once again.

'You see,' said the elderly gentleman, 'this is exactly what I was saying. If you ladies had not learnt so much English, you would not talk against our ancient traditions like this. Nowadays educated girls who are newly married are taking processions to demand equal rights with men and going to ministers' houses saying abolish mother-in-law, complaining against husbands etcetera.'

'They did not say "abolish mother-in-law etcetera," exploded a young student. 'You think we should take everything lying down quietly like a good traditional Indian woman? Why should we? All over the world women are demanding to be given equal treatment with men. We are not trying to be women libbers. We are only demanding basic equal opportunity. From birth a girl is treated worse than a third class citizen in India!'

'Well,' conceded the elderly gentleman, 'it is true that there is this discrimination. I think there should be for some years some allowance made for women like a handicap they given in races, to help the weaker section of society to catch up with the men, but still I feel—'

'What do you mean "allowance"? We don't want your charity! And what do you mean, "weaker section?" ' flounced the young girl. 'Who is weak? It is the man who is weak! The woman works all the time in the house and outside, and even if she is ill, still she continues to carry on the family. We don't want to be called weaker. We only want to get the same pay for the same work as men. We don't want the prop of a dowry. We—'

The elderly gentleman interrupted her smiling. ' I am sure you, young lady, will not have parents who will arrange a marriage for you. You need not worry. Neither will you need a dowry, nor will your parents have to give it; but mark my words and be careful. Boys do not marry the girls they say they "love" and move about with. They marry the girl their parents have found for them after weighing all the pros and cons.'

'After weighing all the gold and silver, you mean!' cut in the girl. 'This dowry of yours is supposed to be a "gift of affection"? I say it is sheer hypocrisy to say so. When a boy and a girl have a "love marriage,"[4] where are these "gifts of affection" then? If they have an intercaste marriage, or a Hindu girl marries a Christian or a Muslim boy, will the girl get the furniture, house, 'fridge and TV her loving parents would have given her if it had been arranged and these things expected by society? Of course not! The neighbours don't expect them to give it. Her parents are allowed to show they don't "love" their daughter enough to give her all these things as she has gone against tradition. She has chosen her own life herself! What a farce! "Affection" indeed!'[5]

'Is no one going to stand up for husbands?' We looked around. It was a man in his mid-thirties with lines of worry criss-crossing his forehead. "I mean to say,' he went on, 'you people don't seem to realise that a man has problems also!'

Half amused, half interested, we turned to him.

'In many families the father is a very real head. Now I wanted to be a doctor, but I was forced to go into my father's business as there is no other son. I have been selling cloth for six years, but I am still depednent on him for money. I am married and my parents taunt my wife all the time for not bringing enough dowry with her at our marriage. She bears it all quietly as I have told her that whenever I can get enough money together we shall move out of the joint family.' He coughed nervously looking around him as he lowered his voice; 'But she knows and I know that this will never happen. Still we go on living in our dreams.'

'Wouldn't it be better if you stood up for your wife and for her family? After all they must have given your parents as much as they could afford?'

'What?' He almost jumped out of his skin. 'Speak to my father? You don't know what you are saying! He is a heart patient and may, God forbid, have an attack! But more than that, he would throw me out of the house. Then where do we go to? We have two school-going children. You don't know our traditions. How can you even make such a suggestion?'

'Why don't you tell these ladies that you are comfortable where you are, and who the devil cares what they say to your wife?' a deep voice called over his shoulder as its owner came into the compartment. 'Look here, young man. 'I have employed and sacked many young men who have come up suddenly in life because of their father's money, but have little spine to go with it! So I know what I'm talking about, even if these ladies are blissfully ignorant! I know for instance, that the green revolution and the white revolution have plunged many a young man into a pool of comforts and he floats among the good things of life. A man of this sort is not interested in a dowry; but he will slip as easily behind the steering wheel of a car squeezed out of his bride's family as a well powdered hand into a fitting glove!'

'I can see sir, that city life has twisted your views,' said a bespectacled man, clad in hand spun material. 'In my native village, there was one BA Pass young man who was a teacher in the government school. He had an arranged marriage and very much liked his wife. However, the gods wished differently. From the moment of her putting foot inside his father's house, his mother and father began to scold her bitterly since table fan and sewing machine were not in item list of her dowry. He was entirely dependent on his father's money. Therefore he could not raise his voice. He suffered too much, but in silence. One night he could not tolerate any further, and since the irrigation water from the canal was due to enter their fields, he asked his father for permission to do the work of diverting the water channels for the night. The next morning they found his body hanging from the rope in the well. You cannot appreciate such situations unless and until you are yourself living in these conditions.'

'Well, young man, I don't hate my own sex, and your poor friend had a very sorry end. I feel bad for him. However the class of fellows I see every day are different. I know how they lived before and how they plan to live now. Take it from me, the moment a man has managed to better his position in life, trouble steps into his home hand in hand with greed.'

'What kind of situations do you find these young couples living in?' I asked him.

'Well, ma'am, this young man who has married a girl his parents chose for him, comes into my company with some education, speaking bad English because he thinks it beneath his dignity to speak decent Hindi, as he wants desperately to be the great guy. He's a middle class youngster. His wife has brought in a whacking big dowry. He's a bright young fellow, so he goes up the ladder fast. He brings his little wife to parties with half her dowry slung round her neck so that he can impress everyone. She is an attractive kid, but is not used to treating men as anything other than as fathers or brothers. She finds the heavy drinking and flirting very upsetting. Also she can't talk much English and withdraws into herself. She is confused in this mixed-up world and so is he.'

'Now our young fellow sees his wife being admired, it boosts his pride. Then she starts to smile back at a young man or two; but that won't do at all! Oh no! So home they go and have a big fight. He beats her up because he is frustrated and is basically just as unhappy with the unfamiliarity of the set up as she is, but will die rather than confess this. She tells him her parents have poured their lives down the drain to give him the dowry his people demanded. He says he never wanted any b....y dowry. He had signed an anti-dowry pledge. It was his parents who wanted the dowry, he shouts working himself up. Is he not expected to honour their wishes? He is by now even more confused than ever. She has no one to share her troubles with. The company wives are beings from another planet. They broke off from the joint family and she is all alone caught between the new and the old.'

'But don't you see the man is also caught. He too cannot afford to challenge his parents!'

'Can't afford?' The young girl's voice knifed through us all. 'He hasn't the guts! I have never seen such a bunch of jelly-spined men as ours. I remember a social worker coming to our college one day. She asked the boys whether they would go against their parents' wishes if the girl they loved was from a poor family or from another caste and could not give the dowry expected. I never forget the long shameful silence. Finally one boy said, "Why should I not take a dowry when my parents have spent so much on my education? Why should they be the sufferers?" Humph! Sufferers indeed! Are they educating him for marriage or because he is their son? They just want to collect good things and get rich quick—TVs, cars, foreign trips, all at the expense of their wives' families, but they don't want to stand up for them against their darling parents! They'll torture her while saying, "this is hurting me so much more than it hurts you!" The bonus keeps on flowing in from her people so long as you don't actually kill her!'

'The saddest part of it is that a man grows up to expect the prop of dowry,' said a quiet, handsome woman. 'It works both ways. He does not make an effort to stand on his own feet because he knows his wife will bring him a good dowry and he will not have to try. He also loses confidence in his own ability to fend for himself because he knows he will be fed by the dowry all through his life.' She quietly wiped a tear as she turned to the window. No one spoke for a while.

'One thing I must speak,' said the social worker who had been trying to put in a word for some time. 'Why they are burning the girl's body so quickly? Isn't it very suspicious? Then why can't gormint[6] pass a law to stop this? How can doctor say, "murdered woman is dead with natural causes" when he is examining a burnt body?'

'Because, dear lady, his palm has been greased,' rumbled the cultured voice of the company director. 'It's as simple as that. Why should a doctor be any less human than anyone else? He can smell black money like all the rest of us!'

The social worker glared at him.

'Yes, yes,' said the middle-aged man looking around him nervously and lowering his voice to an inaudible mumble, 'You are right. It's this black money that has been circulating for thirty-forty years that is solely responsible for dowry. They want to get rid of it, and so they say they will give these things because she is their daughter. Also the in-laws demand it because black is there to give.'

'Black is certainly there to give, and Black is always beautiful. The law is no impediment. It's easy to get around it as we all know,' said the company director lighting his pipe. 'The interesting point about the Dowry Prohibition Act is that while it bans the giving and taking of dowry, it does not ban the giving and taking of "gifts." It says quite clearly that gifts of any kind given at a wedding will not be considered dowry, unless they are given in order to hook a bridegroom.[7] Now where is the court of law which can prove anything when a Hindu marriage has no written contract, and no one will admit to taking as dowry what he can get anyway as presents?'[8]

The middle aged man coughed nervously, nodded and buried his face in his newspaper.

'Ever since this anti-dowry business became stepping stone to the high position in politics, it has been very bad for the genuine young man,' said the *khadi* clad man, 'If he has taken anti-dowry pledge like many thousands were taking in 1976, and if he is from small minority really wanting to stop this evil, then the girl's side are asking him that what is the wrong with him that his parents are so anxious to marry him off without demanding any dowry! Another thing: Also girl's side is now taking advantage of anti-dowry hue and cry. So the girl is saying she will tell to the police and the courts that she is being tortured for extraction of dowry, and her parents are enabled to extract anything from the boy. So this threatening and blackmail is not always only for the girl!'

'Aha!' laughed the young girl fiercely, 'you are getting a taste of your own medicine!'

'There is another thing.' It was the sad woman who still continued to look out of the window as she spoke in a strained voice. 'We must not forget that it is not always only the in-laws who are to blame. Sometimes the girl's own parents exploit her. They postpone her marriage, sometimes forever, to suit themselves. She is made to take up a job, and all her earnings go to her father even when he has his own income, and she can never marry as she grows old so soon.'

There was yet another silence, and a long engine whistle.

'Yes,' laughed the young girl, trying to put us all at ease. "I have a friend whose *fiancée* was dead set against dowry, but the girl whose parents were this sort, forced him to demand it from them. She said this was the only way she could get even a bit of her six years' earnings back, and that this was her due! It serves them right, I say," she concluded, throwing the tragic profile by the window a sympathetic glance.

'The trouble is,' said the enlightened lady who had recovered from her earlier outburst, 'that our society sets a double standard for boys and girls. Just look at this newspaper! Here is a nationalised bank's advertisement: It advises parents to save for their childrens' "happy future." Can you see the "happy future" the picture shows? Education for the boy and a happy marriage for the daughter! You spend all your money to give your boys a Western education, and strain every nerve, cut every possible corner to send them abroad. They are not mature enough when they go! They know little about the abiding values of their own country. They pick up superficialities and cherish them as "progress." They return wanting the best of both worlds, all mixed up. Your aim in sending them abroad is now becoming confused with a desire to tip the marriage scales better in your favour. Your daughter stays at home and minds the house and children.'

'Whose daughter are you talking about?' sniffed the old woman. 'Not the daughters we see nowadays! They are all busy minding themselves!'

'*Mataji*, I am talking of the poorer girl. The lower middle class girl who knows she will get education but not too much. Enough for marriage. She does not take her schooling or her college seriously as she knows she will be the first casualty in case of illness at home, lack of funds or her own impending marriage! Her brother has to be educated. For her education is a side line which can easily be given up. This is the plague in our thinking.'

I closed my eyes. Through the branches that swished past, I could almost see our early ancestors' double standard glaring balefully at me. I shivered.

'If we had some kind of education that was related to our lives and could help us become real people and enable us to become independent, thinking men and women, there wouldn't be any need for dowries and expensive weddings,' said the young girl. 'As it is, we live with Shakespeare and Milton, dream our way through school and college, and live our real lives at home. I can't blame village and town people for not sending their girls to school. Pass by any nursery school and you will hear them chanting. "Jack and Jill wentuppa-hill" and "Goosey, goosey-gandal!" They don't know what it means. It doesn't fit in, and it certainly doesn't make any sense in India today!'

'I don't understand all this high language,' mumbled the old woman. 'All I know is that the old values are gone. The pride of an Indian woman used to be in suffering, being unselfish, listening to her elders and making her husband and children comfortable before herself. Modern girl's tolerance is over. They don't try to make a peaceful settlement as they used to. Nobody tries to adjust. First thing they want to do is blame everybody and cry and fight, and now they don't mind even going to get a divorce in the courts, *hai hai hai*! What I say is, was there no peace in our homes? Whatever happened, did we not swallow it? Whatever our *maliks*[9] said, did we not put their words on our head and our eyes? We did not interfere. This was their work. They did not interfere with the work of the household. We ruled there and we followed our lords. We brought up good children...'

'*Mataji*, excuse me, but the children you brought up are our fathers and mothers.' It was a burly young Sikh in army uniform. 'Our mothers are full of greed and our fathers want money and land from the girls we make our wives! Simple religious ceremonies which cost next to nothing in all religions are embroidered to cover money giving in many different ways!'

'Son', said the elderly gentleman gently, 'think before you speak like that to your elders.'

'I mean no disrespect, sir,' said the young Sikh amiably, 'I merely want to point out that your old ideas don't fit into our modern world.

They may have been all right in your days, but now tractors are ploughing the fields. The farmer is a changed man and even the businessman has different ideas. The Western countries have put men on the moon and you want us to step backwards.'

'Our fathers make use of their position as heads of their families,' he went on calmly. 'They make demands. Our mothers also rule the home and want to continue ruling over their daughters-in-law, so that their sons may not run away from them and leave them uncared for in their old age. How selfish are these things! Their demands are becoming more difficult to fulfill as when everyone's standard of living gets higher, more costly items come into their list. You get my point?'

'*Beta*, why are you talking needlessly about things you do not know?' quavered the old lady rubbing her hands in her lap.

'*Mataji*, I am an earning man. A normal man wants to live well, eat well and get on well in life. But I want to earn my money myself with the sweat of my brow. I don't want to feel that my house, my 'fridge, my car are all gifts from my father-in-law. Gifts that he had to give because his nose would get cut off in society! Certainly not! I would rather die! But you see what your old ideas are doing in new bottles?' he said addressing the old people directly. 'I am on my way to see a girl my parents have selected for me to see. She must be rich, She must come from a "good" family, but I may not like her. Do you understand?'

'So what are you planning to do, *sardar sahib*?[10] I asked. 'Planning to do, *behnji*?' He turned sharply to me, all full of youth, vigour and devil-may-care. 'I have already made up my mind not to accept my parents' choice and look for some girl I want to marry myself!'

'But wouldn't that upset your parents?'

His eyes twinkled. 'Oh they would have to listen! After all it is my life and my wife! I don't want dowry and all that sort of trading! I want a girl with a beautiful face and a good figure. I want a robust wife. If she has some education that's all right, but that's no problem!'

'And what about her—I mean the girl you are going to see? Won't she be embarrassed by your refusal?'

A hearty laugh was my answer. 'Embarrassed? Why? She can refuse me also. I won't be embarrassed!'

The train stopped at a little station. He laughed again, folded his hands in an all embracing *namaste*, and got off — very male, and very much lord of the earth he trod...

Across from us by the far window sat an obviously pregnant young woman who, I had noticed, had been listening intently to our entire conversation. Occasionally she would grimace sourly, at other times a flash something like life would pass over her deadened young face. As the train moved on she called out, her young voice harsh and rasping unnaturally;

'Yes, yes. It is all quite right for you great people to speak all the time about no dowry and father who has got money to give you good brain and no dowry and so-on-so-on.' She laughed a little wildly. Suddenly she tapped her swollen abdomen. 'See, here is my five month child that will be born with no father for protection! I am also fifth class pass, but I could not continue studies because my brothers had to pass their class, and my father is not too much rich like you. We are poor people,' she said, aggressively proud. 'Not like you all!'

I studied her hardened face and the pride of poverty that would not allow the smallest crack in the carefully jointed armour.

'Where is your *malik, behnji*?' I asked gently.

'Who? My...my *malik*? He...he—is—' All of a sudden she broke down. The brave mask cracked through and through and fell away exposing the naked face of a terrified child. A dam-burst flood of words followed:

'On my wedding night, those parents of his—they started the trouble about dowry. They are just throwing all suits and *saris* of my dowry and saying, "What is this? So poor, so torn and bad stuff?" ' Her pinched face flushed with anger as she went on, 'My father is a poor man. On occasion of *Karvachauth, Baisakhi, Ekadashi*, he was giving not less than Rs. 1,000[11]—in sweets and clothes to them.' She stopped to take a quivering breath, pressing her abdomen with her pathetic little hand. We dared not interrupt this real life torrent.

'They are demanding, demanding...always demanding! Then when I was alone in the house with my *sasur*[12]...he wanted me, he forced me to...' She stopped, her face taut with the horror of that memory.

The clanking wheels took over in the long strained silence that followed.

'Where are you going now, *beta*? asked the *gramsevika* tenderly.

The young woman turned on her like a tiger cat, and just as suddenly the fire left her face. Her voice died down to a low drone:

'He wanted me to earn money after he, after he forced me—He wanted me to earn money by any illicit method for him—you understand? But even though he forced me, I am still an Indian lady, and I shall never take this such extreme step of selling my body carrying my child in my stomach. So I ran away! I ran away,' she continued agitatedly. "It is my child and I did not tell to "him." I ran away, to my mother, and he—he threatened me for my life that I have run away from him carrying his child. My father, he told to me that I have cut his nose in village because I am running away. So I am going now to anywhere.' Her voice was paper thin, at cracking point. 'I am going to go to work and protect my this child, or I will beg. It is easy; or I will jump into the well if there is nothing for me.'

We could not trust our voices. We were ashamed to look any more on her life, spread-eagled and palpitating before us on a dissection table...

The train slowed down. She picked up her small bundle of belongings.

'Where will you go?' repeated the *gramsevika*.

'Come with me,' said the educated woman. 'I will help you to live a better life. I'll help you into a hospital and we will take care of you.'

'Please,' I said, 'don't go out alone!'

She gave us all a long long look, and as the train stumbled to a stop, smiled contemptuously at us, got up awkwardly, heaved the bundle on to her shoulder and left.

NOTES AND REFERENCES

1. A village level social worker.
2. Sister.
3. Mother.
4. "Love" marriage as distinct from an arranged marriage.
5. It is interesting to note here what the *Manusmriti* has to say on this subject: '*A maiden who chooses for herself, shall not take with her any*

ornaments, given by her father or her mother, or her brothers; if she carries them away, it will be theft.' *Manusmriti:* IX: 92, Max Mueller: XXV: p. 343 (1964).

6. Government.
7. The Dowry Prohibition Act, 1961: 2. *Explanation 1: 'For the removal of doubts, it is hereby declared that any presents made at the time of a marriage to either party to the marriage in the form of cash, ornaments, clothes or other articles, shall not be deemed to be dowry within the meaning of this section, unless they are made as consideration for the marriage of the said parties.'*
8. Adapted from Amarendra Nath Mukerjee's article: 'Gaps in Dowry Prohibition Law,' *Amrita Bazar Patrika*, 14 November 1975.
9. Masters.
10. A term of respect, often used for Sikh gentlemen.
11. Hindu festivals:
    (*a*) *Ekadashi*: A religious fast which is observed twice in every lunar fortnight.
    (*b*) *Baisakhi*: falls in the month of Baisakh/Vaisakh (Approximately April/May). A time of great celebration in Punjab, when the Sikhs celebrate the inauguration of the Khalsa (the army of the pure) by the tenth of their religious leaders, Guru Gobind Singh, in 1699.
    This day is also observed by the Buddhists as the day on which the Buddha attained enlightenment.
    (*c*) *Karva Chauth*: The *karva* is an earthen pot with a spout which is filled with water and decorated. This fast is kept exclusively by married women. The god Shiva and his consort Parvati are worshipped, and their blessings solicited for the welfare of husbands.
    Married daughters are traditionally given presents of jewellery, clothes and sweets.
12. Father-in-law.

12

It is High Time

It is 22 December, 1976

The court room is grim and silent as the judgment is delivered: 'Dowry has been a social evil in this country for several centuries. Human tears have failed to satisfy this devil and now it has started demanding human blood. Even the lives of numberless young girls have failed to quench the thirst of this monster. It is high time that this evil was fought on a social plane as well as by the State...Instances are not wanting where parents had to load themselves with an unbearable burden of debt to pay dowry and themselves died in poverty. Instances are also not wanting where girls committed suicide only because they did not want their parents to die under the burden of debt to pay dowry. The present case is one where this evil did not cease to act even after the performance of marriage...'[1]

The sentence: Life imprisonment for torturing and murdering a young woman to extract money and valuables from her parents. An old man of seventy, his twenty-six-year-old son and thirty-five-year-old daughter are led away to pay for a crime which should rest squarely on society's shoulders—A crime to which it has too often shut an eye or turned a deaf ear while its mouth smiles encouragement at the criminal. Its only expression of involvement has been a horrified whispering of the dreadful details of the crime relived with ghoulish relish—and then—a long long silence—until the next time....

It is 21 July, 1978

Mrs. Ranjana Verma, two and a half months pregnant, commits suicide. Before sprinkling herself with kerosene oil and setting herself on fire, she writes to the man who 'weighs all his talk with money':[2]

'My Lord,

I am going away. Please forgive me..I just wanted to say that when your new bride comes, try and listen to her point of view...I am taking with me the only thing I have left of yours, and for this also I ask your forgiveness...'

To her parents:

'Respected *Pitaji*[3] and *Mataji*....

I want your forgiveness for the fact that only two and a half months ago you had to spend so much money on my wedding and now you will have to spend once more on my funeral....'

To her sister-in-law:

'...When my marriage was first arranged your family said that we do not want anything, but we know that those who say this want something. But my parents did not give that much as your parents gave you at your wedding. The reason for that is that you were the only daughter whereas I am the youngest and the fourth daughter of my family. On May 16 when we were in Dalhousie he[4] told me that my people had not given fine clothes. Then when my clothes came he did not like even those. All the time he kept on insulting my parents and my brothers and sisters. Which girl wants that she should quarrel with her husband? I also wanted that we should live together lovingly but God was not willing...You must get him married again. But tell him not to nag her by saying...that her such and such relation, why did he give only Rs. 10...

After my death let only him light the pyre..'

Where is the action?

It was on the 20th of May 1961 that the Dowry Prohibition Act became part of the law of our land. Sufferers of the system are still looking for action. On 8 May 1978 it was announced that 'Government are considering amendment of The Dowry Prohibition Act, 1961, to make it more effective. The question of making the offences under the Act cognizable is also under consideration...the proposals related *inter alia* also to ceiling on presents, restriction on extravagance at marriages and prohibition of display of presents and enhancement of punishments. *As this is an important social legislation, some time is likely to be taken to arrive at decisions on the issues involved.*'[5] (emphasis mine.)

There continue to be many discrepancies in the laws concerning women's rights in India. Woman legislators and social workers, like their counterparts all over the world,[6] are continuing their impassioned pleas for a change in attitude towards the whole concept of the role of woman. Change is coming slowly to our sub-continent, but the little sapling needs to be protected and carefully nurtured. Pakistan has already decreed that dowry should not exceed five thousand rupees.[7] The rigidity of the orthodox mind is under attack.

Women firmly ensconced in their citadels of power are just as responsible for the subjugation of others of their sex as men who value property and fame above human dignity.

'Most women,' said Mahatma Gandhi, 'are co-sharers, in spite of the law being against them, in their husbands' power and privileges...Though, therefore, they may vote for radical reform in academic discussions over inequalities, when it comes to acting up to their vote, they will be found to be unwilling to part with their privileges..'[8]

No amount of legislation can take the place of a frontal attack on a tradition imprisoned mind which will not take its ostrich head out of the sand. Legislation which does not have popular support is doomed. It will only succeed in creating a barrier between law-makers and those they are trying to help. A basic change of attitudes which can only be achieved by constant and tireless striving must go hand in hand with legislation. The Emergency which drew a curtain of fear over India during 1975 and '76, prodded the wheels of government, and fear motivated organisations and dowry seekers and individuals to violent motion and superhuman effort. It frightened dowry seekers and givers into clinching under-the-counter deals while the outward fanfare of anti-dowry protestations blared. But because it did not address itself to the rock-bottom problem of re-education of minds long enslaved by accepted patterns of behaviour, the evils of the system have re-emerged hydra-headed and revitalised for fresh encounters.

Although it was fear psychosis that released the adrenalin for the implementation of programmes in that period, and dowry became a dirty word in public; the exercise showed that there is no reason at all why such programmes need an atmosphere of fear to prosper. Minds liberated from dread can combine to gun down long entrenched problems from every angle—problems which the government alone cannot tackle. A dove-tailing of programmes implemented by sympathetic, trained social workers aided ably by voluntary organisations would be mutually beneficial. A second look at the Indian woman as a person of worth in her own right is essential. This kind of woman can then be projected and unobtrusively find her way into school and college text books, comics and other reading matter of general interest. Extra-curricular activities on the college and school campus could continue the process of re-evaluation of the Indian woman, helping broaden the country's mental horizons.

It only needs men and women of good will who will pick up the gauntlet and accept the challenge:

> 'As for you young girls,' said Mahatma Gandhi, 'to you I will only say that if I had a girl under my charge I would rather keep her a maiden all my life than give her away to one who expected a single pice for taking her for his wife...Swaraj[9] is not meant for cowards. Promise that you will wipe off the stain of dethi lethi,[10] that you will die to restore your sisters and wives to their dignity and freedom.'[11]

While the government discusses changes and amendments in legislation, it could publicise names and addresses of those organisations to whom distressed women and families could turn, by advertising regularly in the national and local papers in every language. The ubiquitous transistor together with film and television could carry programmes devised by sensitive media persons on subjects which closely affect women.

The programmes that enthused young people and channelised their energies helping create conditions where they could solemnly pledge themselves to fight the bribe of dowry, where colleges adopted villages and tried to disseminate education against such an evil—good programmes—should not be discarded. Every little gain counts in this kind of warfare. Where a thousand false antidowry pledges were taken, a hundred couples may have been helped to take sincere vows. Mass weddings with a one rupee token dowry that were reported by the media throughout 1975 and '76, may have boosted the public image of the odd organiser, but they must also have encouraged many men and women to regain their dignity and self-respect. The Sikh community has tried to do this. The total expenditure for a Namdhari Sikh couple walking four times around the sacred fire along with hundreds of other couples in a mass marriage, is only a few rupees.

Although lavish weddings continue to blare their extravagance over the country, many South Indian communities are becoming increasingly aware of the necessity for simple weddings, and even though expensive hotels and marriage halls still continue to rake in their profits, there is at least the occasional item extolling a simple wedding that manages to squeeze its way into a newspaper.

In October 1974, fifty thousand *Jat* villagers comprising nearly 70 per cent of the population between Delhi and Mathura assembled at a conference of village panchayats, and solemnly vowed that they would give their daughters a maximum of eleven utensils, eleven sets of clothes, jewellery not exceeding ten grammes of gold and fifty grammes of silver at their weddings. Tea and cool drinks were to take the place of wasteful menus. Bands, dancing and fireworks would not be permitted, and a token gift of one rupee would be given at the *Kanya daan* ceremony. This mini revolution has set the pace in this area[12] and the villagers keep a sharp watch for defaulters.

'Tilak, dahez chhor do—
Jaati paati tor do!'

'Down with Dowry! Down with Caste!' In Bihar the Chhatra Yuvak Sangharsh Vahini, an active student organisation has mobilised three hundred women to agitate from village to village in the Madhubani district to fight against womens' subordination. Dowry and casteism is on their list as is agitation against the annual market where women are bought and sold.[13]

There were no illuminations in little Chhatera village in Haryana when young Pramila was married in 1976. She offered her groom a coconut, and one rupee exchanged hands. 'I did not take any dowry when my son got married,' smiled the bride's mother, 'and I don't like to give any for my daughter.'

'After all,' said her father, 'all the villagers know I can afford the lights and fanfare, but I am not going to do it...It is the educated who have to lead the way.'[14]

These are the people who need to be helped out of the all-engulfing mouth of the 'Gimmee.' Loving fathers and mothers who are anxious to do their best for their children could so easily combine to help the young couple set up their new home with the financial burden equally shared by both sets of parents. Intercaste marriages with a token payment towards the expenses of a simple wedding ceremony—all these and many other ways of fighting greed should be welcome additions to our arsenal.

While the wheels of government turn frustratingly slowly, things are happening among the people—isolated sparks perhaps, but enthusiastic enough to merit the widest support:

When a lawyer in Gorakhpur in tradition bound Uttar Pradesh broke off his son's engagement with a local girl[15] after the *tilak* ceremony[16], he did not know he was walking into something that would engulf him and his family honour.

'Dog of Dowry!' 'Worm of Dowry!' screamed the banners. His effigy hung from an electric post, and a loudspeaker installed near the placards informed passersby of his despicable behaviour. The jilted girl's father, seriously affected by the shock was rushed to hospital. Under the banner of The Samaritans, the city shook off its centuries old apathy to fight for the girl who had been turned down for a higher offer of dowry. One can only hope that the spineless son who followed with such alacrity where his father led, and discarded an honourable commitment for greater gain, will also feel the edge of community censure. It will need constant prodding to keep a roused society's conscience at pricking point.

Rita's death, allegedly by burning on 29 March 1979 in Amritsar sparked off processions and threats of a fast unto death if the government did not take any active steps against the dowry evil. According to the papers[17] Rita was admitted to hospital in the middle of March and died about two weeks later. Her statement led to the arrest of her husband, her father-in-law, her mother-in-law and two sisters-in-law who had been pressing her to get her family to give them more dowry. Her parents had already given fourteen thousand rupees, but this did not satisfy her in-laws and she was forced to go home. She was brought back in February through the intervention of a social worker, only to die soon after leaving a one year old daughter living with her husband's family.

It does not happen very often, but occasionally the neighbours react sharply. On 12 January 1979 an angry crowd of fifteen thousand people set fire to a house in Srinagar in fierce protest against the suspected murder of young Mehbooba who had been married to her cousin barely three months before.[18]

The deaths in Delhi of twenty-four year old Tarvinder Kaur (The Times of India, 2 June 1979) and of Kanchan Chopra young mother of a four month old infant, which followed each other in quick succession have brought an awareness of the problem into every newspaper reading home in the capital. A spate of public demonstrations by local organisations notably the Stree Sangharsh Samiti and the Nari Raksha Samiti, and other concerned citizens have been held. More massive demonstrations are planned to press for stringent measures against perpetrators of such crimes.[19]

But the see-saw of public response is notoriously unreliable. Kitchen deaths are so convenient and they recur with such gruesome regularity, the sequence so horrifyingly predictable, that it lays layer on layer of insensitivity on minds already gorged on tales of violent death.

A young wife whose parents cannot give any more to her husband and his family is a dead weight and to be gotten rid of. So one fine day, kerosene oil does its job and another 'accident' occurs. Social welfare organisations collect to make fiery speeches outside the house. The victim succumbs to her injuries and there the matter ends. The families next door heave a sigh of relief. The 'dowry death' is reported in the papers.

'Poor girl,' say the neighbours, 'she was driven to suicide! Such is the terrible fate of our daughters!'

Who is guilty?

Not the husband and his family. After all, poor girl, she couldn't bear him a son, and what is a man without a son? The husband and his family mix freely with their smiling neighbours. He marries again. '*Ghee*[20] and sugar in your mouth dear,'[21] say the neighbours to the new bride, 'Your-in-laws are wonderful people!'

Apathy is after all, so much more comfortable...

It is neighbourhood and community boycott alone that can form a circle of strength around a wife threatened with torture or death. This alone can condemn the family that would exploit her body for gain to social oblivion and keep the contaminated money from becoming an effective bribe.

The cry for help is so poignant that if the layers of apathy wrapping it around were to crack and fall, the scream would be unbearably piercing.

A note inserted in the newspapers asking for information concerning persons who help families solve their dowry difficulties inundated me with a flood of letters. Few who read my note saw anything beyond the word 'dowry.' Clutching at a straw, they all sat down to open their hearts to an unknown woman who seemed concerned with their personal problems. Each one had a greater misery to recount. I have in the last three years, received over three hundred letters.

Among these heart-rending letters, I found at least fifty from people who were troubled enough about the subject of exploitation of a woman's person for money, to try and do something about it. These are people of every religious persuasion—their ages ranging from twenty to seventy years and above—atheists, priests, *yogis*, students, lawyers, businessmen, writers, government employees, school teachers, politicians, bridegrooms, fathers, mothers—everyone seems ready for the spark that will co-ordinate, unite and sustain effort.

A young college girl tries to organise a No-Dowry Society. A cabman offers a five per cent discount on cabs hired from his stand for marriages without dowry. A village girl offers a coconut to her bridegroom as an auspicious symbol in lieu of dowry. Another belle turns back a wedding party because the groom has demanded a scooter from her impoverished parents. A college student refuses 'charity' from his bride's parents. Another young man plans to institute a scholarship for poor students with the money his parents-in-law insist on giving with their daughter. A young lawyer places his services at the community's disposal. A scientist wants a dowryless wedding. A husband and wife belonging to different religions form a teacher team to promote weddings without dowry. A religious organisation looks beyond its confines to help anyone in need. Another 'ardent social reformer' is starting an organisation for intercaste marriages, widow remarriage and a home for the old and sick. A college principal sends her students from house to house spreading awareness of the evils of dowry giving.

Then—a doctor asks a very pertinent question: 'In over thirty years of freedom we have not been able to get an answer to this dowry question. What can you do?'

Very little, I am forced to answer; but that very little we shall try to do.

A mouse sees his best friend the lion caught in a huge net. There are three alternatives before him:

He can suppress his conscience, look the other way, and scamper off.

He can sit by his trapped friend and lament that the task is too big for him to tackle since he is after all just one little mouse.

He can put his mind to the job and start nibbling at the netting.

Fruit orchards are springing up miraculously on public land in and around Poona—land which had so far seemed useless where scruffy little children rolled and tumbled. A city doctor decided one day that he had a use for all the pips of the fruit eaten at his table. He collects them and plants them wherever they have the slightest chance of taking root. He may not live to see the scruffy children pluck and eat the fruits of his labours. He has not waited for agencies to work on complicated projects. His one man effort is producing trees of hope...Nibbling at the net is something everyone can do, even with caste, community, father or mother ranged against one. With enough nibblers, there will be enough holes in the net to free the lion. There will be no need to sit and wait for 'someone to organise something.' Once the lion is out, important things like 'nose' and 'face' will suddenly become of no consequence as everyone will have been too busy nibbling to have concerned themselves with these things. The most important matter in hand will be the freeing of the mind from the snare of fear and insecurity. Men and women suddenly freed will realise that society and tradition are made to serve humanity: that these are paper tigers blown up beyond all reason by their own minds to suit the convenience of greed.

Nibblers have to work against time to save exploited men and women around the world, so that Neena, Meera and others like them may not have to die.

But to be a dedicated nibbler, today's realities have not only to be faced, they have to be engraved on our consciousness. These realities come in various shapes and sizes, but the final mould is always the same: the exploitation of humans by humans....

'With despair and sorrow I am writing this to you. I am from middle class family. I am 26 and my sister is 24 and one more is 23. I hate marriage because of dowry. We people cannot dream of marriage...How long this difficulty will be there? I feel it is better to take poison together...'

'My heart is burdened with sorrow. Pray for me. I have two daughters, 28 and 29 years old. I cannot afford to marry them off. I have taken a loan. What shall I do?'

'If I do not take money in my son's marriage, how will I get dowry for my daughter? Who will marry her then? The only way left for me is to become corrupt and to make the money by underhand means instead of asking dowry since it is against my conscience.'

'We are ten daughters and we are all over marriageable age...Our father is destitute...In our parts unmarried girls cannot go into homes to find the work. The society will say they are bad girls, and even if anyone wants, they will not marry them. We are therefore all in the home although we have passed SSLC.[22] What is our future? Can you tell me?'

'Our family is very very poor...12 members: 6 girls, three boys. One died. Father is old. Mother is ill. We have to get medicines. I am first daughter. I am 27 years old. No possibility of money. How can I have marriage?'

'Her husband demanded Rs. 5,000 dowry from me. I have given some before, and some I would give after marriage. I was unable to pay...She is with child and they are sending her. Now she is with me. He will not take her back.'

'My daughter has done her B.A. Hons. We have no money for dowry. Boy is good and demands only wedding expenses and reception expenses. Even that we cannot give. How can I see my daughter unmarried because only for lack of this dowry?'

'I am a retired man. I cannot see my daughter suffer in this society. She is a very good girl and even to get a job as a teacher in a village they are asking for Rs 10,000 as donation. She is beautiful even though I am saying it. Many boys are brought to see her. They are impressed but all want either fifteen thousand as dowry or they want her to have a job. We are caught in this grip of circumstances.'

'I am thirty-one years old—Perhaps too old to get married. In our parts they want dowry in gold sovereigns—at least four. I have been working very hard, managed to collect one sovereign worth. My mother is frail and I have four younger brothers and sisters. Can I use that sovereign and see them starve before my eyes?'

'Here even a peon is demanding at least Rs. 8,000 in dowry.'

'I have done shorthand typing. There is no job for me. If I run away to become a nun, I may do that, but if I go to a convent—good one, I shall have no money and then who will pay for my aged parents and the family's food every day?'

'I would like to share with you a shattering experience in my neighbourhood. I was a guest at my friend's marriage. Her father was dead and brothers had put their money altogether to have her married off. They had agreed that there was to be no dowry. But just before the seven steps,[23] the bridegroom's party demanded Rs 10,000 or the marriage would not take place. My friend fainted with the shock. She is a B.A; B.T. We were all very stunned that how such a strange happening could be possible in these days. Suddenly a kind gentleman whom we do not know wrote a cheque for the full amount and gave to them. They were not ashamed. The marriage ceremony was completed by the grace of God. Is that not a shocking fate for a girl!'

The answer is an expectant silence....

NOTES AND REFERENCES

1. *The Indian Express*, 23 December 1976.
2. *The Sunday Statesman*, 6 August 1978: 'Letters written At Death's Door.'
3. Respected father.
4. Her husband.
5. (*i*) Starred question no. 296; Rajya Sabha: answered by the Minister of Law, Justice and Company Affairs on 8 May 1978. (Courtesy: The Ministry of Law and The Department of Social Welfare).
   (*ii*) 'Dowry Act:
   The Minister of State for Home Mr. Dhanik Lal Mandal said the Government was considering amending The Dowry Prohibition Act

1961 to make it more effective. The question of making offences under the Act was also under consideration.' *The Statesman,* 4 May 1979.

6. The Government of Greece has appointed a special committee composed of professors of law and jurists to go into matters concerning women and the law. They have recommended that dowry be abolished.
   Note: Dowry has since been abolished in Greece. 'Each spouse retains the assets he or she had before marriage independently, but the institution of common ownership is established by the reform of The Family Code (Law 1329/83)':
   The Status of Women in Greece, and extract from 'A Fresh Look at Greece: The Country and the People', Athens, 1988: Sicily's House of Representatives also made a unanimous decision to 'abolish the time-honoured, church blest custom of dowry.' The Times of India, 1 February, 1955.
7. *The Statesman*, 26 July 1976.
8. D.G. Tendulkar, Mahatma. Delhi, The Publications Division, Ministry of Information and Broadcasting, Government of India, revised edition, 1961, Vol. 2, p. 367, Mahatma Gandhi writing in 'Young India,' 17 October, 1929.
9. Independence.
10. Giving and taking.
11. From Mahatma Gandhi's address to Karachi students, February 1929 as quoted by D.G. Tendulkar in *Mahatma*, Delhi, revised edition, 1961, Vol. 2, p. 346.
12. *The Sunday Statesman,* 6 August 1978: 'The *Jat* Revolt Against Dowry'—by Tavleen Singh.
    Here it is interesting to note that as far back as 1852, the problem of dowry was tackled in Mainpuri by a group of illiterate Rajputs who agreed on fixing a ceiling on dowry payments:
    (*i*) Ceiling for Rajahs and noblemen ... Rs 500.
    (*ii*) Ceiling for Zamindars ... Rs. 250.
    (*iii*) Ceiling for common people ... Rs 100.
    (*iv*) Ceiling for poor peasants ... Re 1.
    This decision was given material sanction. Critics of the measure argued that the dowry law had been instituted by God, but the progressives had the last word. It was man made, they said, and therefore not inviolable. Although this enlightened decision remained localised, it proved that determination can accomplish the impossible. (Surrinder Khullar, quoting The Urdu Akhbar, Delhi, 8 February 1852, in *The Weekly Round Table*, 26 August 1973).
13. Radha Kumar, 'Rural Womens' Rights,' in *Voluntary Action*, May 1979.
14. *The Hindustan Times*, 'Our Village Chhatera,' a report in the issue of 1 March 1976.

15. 'Dog of Dowry,' editorial, *The Sunday Standard*, 5 March 1978.
16. A ceremony corresponding to an official engagement.
17. *The Statesman,* 31 March 1979.
18. *The Indian Express*, 13 January 1979.
19. Following growing agitation over increasing 'dowry' deaths in Delhi towards the late seventies, a police anti-dowry cell was started. This later developed into a full police unit under a Deputy Commissioner of Police called the Crimes Against Women Cell. This unit has the power to take cognisance of any case involving the victimisation of women in Delhi. A few states have also made a beginning on these lines.
20. Clarified butter.
21. Signifying an auspicious beginning.
22. Secondary School Leaving Certificate.
23. The seven steps taken by the bridegroom and the bride around the sacred fire. These complete a Hindu marriage ceremony.

13

Genesis

How far back can we go to right an ancient wrong? Attitudinal sin against woman begins in the womb. With tradition requiring the young bride—barely in her teens—to produce sons and yet more sons, female foetal deaths have soared in the past sixteen years.

The nations of the South Asian Association for Regional Cooperation (SAARC) declared 1990 The Year of the Girl Child, and 1990 to 2000 The Decade of the Girl Child. The Government of India on its part, developed a National Plan of Action for The Girl Child to focus on her survival and development. The year of writing was to have marked the culmination of efforts to be made to prevent female foeticide. With all the good will in the world, this has not happened.

The Amniocentesis test meant specifically to identify mental abnormalities in the foetus also reveals its sex. This is still being widely misused for sex determination and subsequent abortion of the female foetus. The old cry, 'Doctor, kill it if it's a girl!' still rings through hospitals and private sex clinics around the country. Sex tests of the late 1970s had already become dirty words by 1982 with a newspaper exposé of an Amritsar clinic advertising its gruesome wares, aborting the female foetus in the name of family planning. The uproar that followed forced it to close shop. Advertisements resurfaced in 1986 as it moved to Delhi. A veritable harvest of such 'clinics' followed, but little action was taken. The Medical Council of India moaned, 'Neither has the Medical Council of India the time nor the man power to initiate action against such errant doctors.' The Union Minister for Health confessed, 'the government is helpless in dealing with quacks.'[1] However by 1996, when the Medical Council of India was asked by The National Human Rights Commission to examine the ethics of these tests which were using sex determination as 'an alibi for female foeticide', it admitted that this practice would henceforth be considered 'infamous conduct'. Amendments to the regulations in The Code of Medical Ethics were also made to enable disciplinary action in such cases.[2]

'Easy, safe, dependable,' crooned the sinister advertisements. In 1991 the pernicious original advertisement by the Amritsar team resurfaced. 'Pay Rs. 500/- now' (for Amniocentesis) 'save Rs. 50,000/- later' (for the daughter's dowry). The message went straight to the heart of despairing parents overburdened with the fear of another daughter, of guarding her virginity and facing a lifetime of indebtedness after the expensive marriage and dowry giving were over.

Now they have hope. Their yearning for a world full of sons can be realised. Time honoured patriarchal tradition has at last discovered the possibility of co-existing with hi-tech pre-natal diagnostic techniques. Conveniently at hand is The Medical Termination of Pregnancy Act 1971.[3] Put all these ingredients together, and hey presto, the decision is made! The unscrupulous medical practitioner glows with patriotic zeal as the abortion he has just conducted will serve the cause of bringing the country's soaring population down.[4] A doctor, in a BBC film in 1994 on this subject remarks, 'This test will help in limiting the population of the country,' even as he admits to collecting one thousand pounds a week for wiping out over a million female foetuses.

Doctors involved in these murders argue that such tests are 'humane' and necessary for 'the injured psyche of victimised women.'[5] Another lady doctor in the BBC film adds, 'In India we feel a family is incomplete without a son'. By 1994 big business names like Blue Star, Philips and Hitachi while personally regretting the use their ultrasound equipment is being put to, admit that gynaecologists are their biggest customers. There has been a resounding silence on the part of The Association of Obstetricians and Gynaecologists, The Indian Medical Association and other responsible bodies on this prickly subject.[6]

Media exposés and agitations by activists have been keeping up the pressure for the stoppage of this blatant dehumanisation. Heated debates and sustained lobbying finally forced the states of Maharashtra and Rajasthan in 1988 and 1994 respectively to enact laws banning the use of these tests for sex identification. Ultimately the Central Government with its back to the wall introduced The Prenatal Diagnostic Techniques (Regulation and Prevention of Misuse) Bill 1991 in The Lok Sabha in September 1991, banning the use of such tests for unethical purposes. The Act was finally enacted in 1994.[7]

However, this legislation has been deemed inadequate and demands have already been made for a review, to enlarge its scope by bringing within its ambit all future technologies in this field. The Act needs to clearly specify that identification tests for foetal abnormalities may only be conducted at apex institutions.[8] Existing loopholes must also be plugged before it becomes yet another ineffective piece of legislation

While government drags its feet attending to more pressing problems, the country's sex ratio drops steadily down from 972 females to 1,000 males in 1901 to 927 in 1991.[9] State governments look the other way as their recently made laws are openly flouted. Women from Yemen, Dubai and from around India abort their female foetuses for medical charges ranging from Rs. 500/- to Rs. 5,000/- Even families from the slums have joined the queue.[10] 'What kind of a life will she have if she is born?' agonises a young mother of two daughters. 'My neighbour's girl was stolen and sold. *Bhagwan* knows whether she is killed or worse!'

The desperate longing for a son led hopeful couples to take part in a *Putrakameshti Yagna*[11] held at Kochi in Kerala towards the end of 1992. The lowest castes were not invited. One thousand one hundred and thirty couples were chosen from five thousand applicants. Each participant paid two thousand rupees. Of the three hundred couples who allowed a follow-up study, only 42 pregnancies were confirmed. One presumes that only mothers with enough faith would have borne the promised sons.

It is interesting to note that in China, the obsession with sons often results in the abandonment of baby girls.[12] There have even been cases of husbands forcing their wives to sleep with men who are known to have fathered sons.[13]

In India, hesitantly but surely, the winds of change are beginning to blow. According to a recent study, Goa has shown the way. With 73 per cent of its girls literate, with access to health care facilities, marrying on an average at twentyfive years, the status of women in this state has vastly improved. The result is that they are able to bring a more informed attitude to bear on family planning without the usual frenetic pressures. Even women, rural and urban, with just two daughters and no son, are not keen to try for another child. Seventy per cent of the women with two living children, whatever their sex, do not want any more, and either plan to, or have already had themselves sterilised. The infant mortality rate in Goa is one of the lowest in India, at 32 per 1,000 live births. The fertility rate has fallen to 1.9 children per woman, with a high percentage of fully immunised children.[14]

However, there are sizeable interstate differences: Goa, Kerala and Tamil Nadu have already achieved a low rate of fertility. At the other end of the spectrum are: Uttar Pradesh, Madhya Pradesh, Bihar, Assam, Haryana, Rajasthan, Dadra and Nagar Haveli where birth rates are higher than the national average.[15]

'Our bodies belong to us, 'they are not to be used for experimenting and for statistics,' says Fatima Dourado in Brazil. Brazilian women 'are mostly malnourished with low access to health services. We feel that more research should be done on contraception for men. Why should women shoulder the main burden of contraception?'[16] This cry echoes half way down the world in the Indian woman's heart.

There is now an effort in India to research need assessment to probe methods of contraception that are culturally acceptable and able to provide as broad a spectrum of options as possible for women to choose from. Each method must come with complete information on the risks and benefits involved, so that the choice may be made with a full awareness of what it entails. Unfortunately it is not always that the risks are mentioned. A vital ingredient of this 'cafeteria' approach to family planning entailing informed choice, is counselling, which concerned doctors feel should form an important part of medical studies. Sadly, this is the first casualty in busy hospitals and other places which have a large patient intake. Implementation should also be extremely carefully monitored With half the Indian population under 24 years of age, the problem of providing easy access to correct information has become most urgent. How daunting a challenge it is, has been shown by a recent survey in Uttar Pradesh, one of the most populous states in India. Here it was found that 40-44 per cent of the population are anxious to space their children or to stop having any more, but have no information on how to do this.[17]

All products, whether government sponsored or otherwise, oral, injectibles or intra-uterine devices must be mandatorily passed by The Toxicology Review Panel and by The Ethics Committee composed of physicians, lawyers and other experts, a number of whom are women. The final approval is given by The Drug Controller of India. Male and female vaccines are still in the process of being researched. The process of testing is laborious and time consuming. Tests on sub-human primates is the last stage of pre-human trials. The process of bringing the product to the human trial stage can take up to twenty years or more with numerous checks.

Indonesia's heavy investment in education and health, and enlisting the aid of religious leaders has done wonders for its women. Education means marrying later. With more women in the labour force, a small family norm is easier realised. With accessible health services, less children die and the need for more does not arise. Sri Ratmei, a devout Muslim has a baby girl and plans on just one more child. She says she will be happy whether it is a boy or a girl, 'but I won't have any more children.'[18]

The International Conference on Population and Development, 1994 had stressed that 'the improvement of women's political, social, economic and health status' was the key word to population control. In his Independence Day speech on 15 August, 1995, The Prime Minister announced a welcome raise in allocation for education to 6 per cent of the Gross Domestic Product. Women feel that The Department of Family Welfare has been emphasising the fertility control aspect so far at the expense of basic community socio-economic improvement. Since 1994, there is a visible change in the approach to family welfare. Target setting in sterilisations for women is being phased out. There is a shift in emphasis to focussing on improvement in the quality of life. The progress of this new approach will be watched with interest.

In this connection, the recommendation by The National Commission for Women in 1995, for six months maternity leave twice in a woman's working career, and a separate call for a three month period of paternity leave has been tabled in Parliament. It is to be hoped that it will be actively considered by government. It would be of immense benefit to the family and to the community as a whole; however, for this to be successful, innovative programmes for the sensitisation of men to women's needs would be essential if they are to share in the domestic workload. Some states have already put the scheme into practice. Breast feeding for six months would help space children the natural way. This, together with the Commission's recommendations on flexibility in working schedules and positive steps for promotions would lessen the pressures on women, in the organised sector, even though a large number of women in the unorganised sector may not be benefitted. Meanwhile, on February 1, 1996, the Maternity Benefit (Amendent) Act 1996 providing for six weeks leave with pay for working mothers wishing to terminate their pregnancy, came into force. It remains to be seen what long term effect this legislation will have on the family planning scene.

As for men's role in fertility regulation, The 1994 Cairo conference had called on governments to 'increase the participation and sharing responsibility of men in the actual practice of family planning methods,' and to 'ensure that women and men have information and access to the widest possible range of safe and effective family planning methods.' Noting that 97 per cent sterilisation operations are performed on women and only 3 per cent are male vasectomies, government has asked the states to step up the men's performance to at least 10 per cent, and where this has already been reached, to 15 per cent.[19]

Of late, researchers in some technically developed countries have been concerned at the possibility of potential links between vasectomy and prostate cancer. Reports of studies vary considerably. A US research team[20] that had previously reported an association between vasectomy and cancer, found no such linkage in a subsequent study. A new Danish study of seventy four thousand men vasectomised between 1977 and 1989 also showed no association between the two.[21]

Research under this programme, launched by The World Health Organisation in 1972, is continuing in China, Nepal, Korea, and in India where The Indian Council of Medical Research is working on studies on men vasectomised at least 10 years earlier. The findings, which are expected in about a year or so, should 'ensure a balanced assessment of long term consequences. The marginal risks have to be assessed against the immediate safety and possible long term protection against cardio-vascular diseases' in which the prevalence is high in India, '...in an over-all balance of risks and benefits.'[22]

After the forcible sterilisation programme during the Emergency 1975-77, there was a distinct downward trend in the vasectomy graph, with a corresponding rise in laparoscopic sterilisation performed on women: an operation which should ideally only be performed by an experienced gynaecologist with hospitalisation. Towards the end of the 1980's this tapered off, and mini-laparotomy, a small incision enabling the tying up of the fallopian tubes has becomes popular in the '90s. This is an uncomplicated method which can be used by any qualified doctor. It is therefore deemed appropriate for field conditions.[23]

One of the reasons why a large number of women opt for sterilisation is that vasectomy, like all other contraceptive methods for men or women, is not always foolproof.[24] Barrier methods like the diaphragm for women also have a 14 per cent failure rate. Lack of privacy at home and women's incomplete knowledge of their own physiology also sometimes add to their problems. This has often resulted in pregnancies for which many women have had to suffer character assassination and community censure. Barrier methods for women together with some injectibles are in the trial phase at the ten Human Reproductive Research Centres attached to medical colleges in the country where research is carried on by the Indian Council for Medical Research. Bearing the brunt, among many other things, of most contraceptive programmes, exposing themselves to discomfort or worse, women are expected to accept all this as part of their lot. The slightest suspicion of anything likley to go wrong with the men's contraceptive programme immediately becomes a cause for global concern. It is necessary to make balanced and thorough assessments of all programmes.

Following the call for greater transparency in procedures and planning in family welfare, local committees have been set up in some of the centres of the Indian Council for Medical Research. These centres have been inviting the participation of persons concerned with women's welfare to interact with them. The Family

Welfare programme is also involving non-governmental organisations in a number of welfare schemes. Women's organisations and other concerned persons, as much as the government realise the urgent need for extensive monitoring of drug administration and other methods of contraception to ensure satisfactory procedures and to prevent malpractices. Consequently, it is important to respond favourably to these overtures. A great deal more might be achieved were dedicated persons to work together, realising each other's limitations, rather than at cross purposes. A greater flow of easily accessible information would also be to everyone's advantage.

A Constitution (79th Amendment) Bill, 1992 was introduced in Parliament to incorporate population control and the small family norm within the framework of Article 47 of the Directive Principles of State Policy, which enjoins the State, among other things, to 'raise the standard of living and to improve public health.' The Bill also seeks to incorporate the same in Article 51 A of The Fundamental Duties of the Citizens of India.[25] The proposed amendment seeks to disqualify persons from holding office in Parliament or legislatures if they have more than two children. It would not, however, apply to anyone who had more than two children at the commencement of this amendment, or within a period of a year after its coming into force.

This concept has already come into force at the *panchayat* and municipality level in Maharashtra, Rajasthan and Haryana and in a number of other States. There are fears that this may go against the spirit of *Panchayati Raj* which provides for reservation of seats for women in *panchayats* and municipalities. Women are not always in control of the number of children they bear, and this might in fact reinforce male decision-making power.

Much more thought must be given to making men understand the importance of their role as responsible partners in determining the size of the family. This should be made to appear a matter of pride as in Indonesia, where for a man, to be a family planning volunteer is to be part and parcel of his country's development.[26] He also needs to be enthused with the idea that his macho image will be enhanced if he takes some of the burden off his wife's overloaded body. Early in 1996 the Ministry for Health and Family Welfare introduced a programme making the primary health centre, in close consultation with the village community, entirely responsible for assessing family welfare and health care needs in the community. This programme is aimed at reducing dependence on government, which should now be seen as a supportive partner that supplies funds, services and technical assistance. 'Think locally, act locally and support nationally,' is the new slogan. Addressing their own needs could be an exhilerating experience for the village. Accountability at all levels should be an essential ingredient of such an ambitious programme.

Men and women must be approached as intelligent human beings. Accurate information on risks and safeguards—present and future—is essential for open-minded and practical discussion. Before making a choice of contraceptive, they should be quite clearly told that no contraceptive is infallible, and that each has some side effect. The great importance of keeping in touch for regular monitoring must be impressed upon them. It is only after this kind of plain speaking and clear thinking that truly informed choices can be made, and the guinea pig syndrome be finally laid to rest. Family planning programmes will continue to be grounded unless they go hand in hand with countrywide programmes focussing on the basic needs of the community as a whole, better living conditions, accessibility to education and work prospects.

As we move into the twenty-first century, the world takes on a science fiction character...On 9 August, 1995, The New Delhi Legislative Assembly passed The Artificial Insemination (Human) Bill 1995 which it is hoped, will give childless couples access to a safe, duly regulated supply and sale of human semen or ova for artificial insemination. This will not only legalise the whole process, but also enjoin a close check on semen banks to prevent the spread of HIV 1 and 2. It has made it obligatory for medical practitioners not to separate the XX and the XY chromosomes which are responsible for the birth of female and male infants respectively. They will also be expected to keep complete records on donors and receivers so as to obviate any dispute concerning succession.[27]

'The womb is my oyster,' exclaims the hi-tech scientist as he places yet another experiment among the dream merchants' wares. The next target could be the already much talked about designer baby boy. The newly crowned surrogate mother has not yet made it big in India, but thoughtful medical practitioners are already beginning to seek ethical guide-lines on all such matters still in the twilight zone.

With the first ever Indian test tube baby already over twelve years old, and the first test tube baby boy to be born to a fifty one year old tribal mother, delivered on 7 July, 1995,[28] could our very own genetically manipulated, made to order 'fair, blue-eyed baby boy' be far behind?

NOTES AND REFERENCES

1. The Hindustan Times, August 3, 1982.
2. Human Rights Newsletter, Volume 3 No. I, January 1996.
3. While The Medical Termination of Pregnancy Act 1971 specifically states that only a doctor may conduct an abortion, The Indian Penal Code 1860 in Articles 312 and 315 states: 'whoever...' terminates a pregnancy, can do so, if it is done to 'save the life of the mother.'
4. In the BBC documentary film 'Let Her Die' by Emily Buchanan, Assignment, 1994.
5. The Times of India, Bangalore, 12 July, 1993.
6. Sex Tests give Filip to Ultrasound Business, by A. Srinivas, The Pioneer, 26 September, 1994.
7. The Prenatal Diagnostic Techniques (Regulation and Prevention of Misuse) Act 1994.
8. Women Take on Sex Clinics, Alpana Varma; The Times of India, 2 December 1994.
9.

Sex Ratio: Year	*Females per 1000 Males*:	*Sex Ratio*: Year	*Females per 1000 Males*:
1901	972	1951	946
1911	964	1961	941
1921	955	1971	930
1931	950	1981	934
1941	945	1991	927

(Sex Ratio: India: 1901-1991/Census of India 1991. Final Population Totals: Brief Analysis of Primary Census Abstract, Series-1, Paper 2 of 1992: as quoted in UNESCO papers: Glimpses of Girlhood in India 2: Girls: A Dwindling Minority.)

Statewise figures show Haryana in 1991 had only 865 women to 1000 men, Uttar Pradesh: 879, Punjab: 882, and Rajasthan: 910 women to 1,000 men.

10. Female Foeticide Rampant as Government Looks the Other Way, Sharmila Chandra: The Pioneer, June 30, 1993.
11. *Putrakameshti Yagna*: A religious prayer ceremony held for the fulfillment of the desire for a son.

International Putrakameshti Yagna, by Dr. Anil Kumar Mishra, Woman's Era, November 1, 1992.

12. Jian Wandi: Development of Women's Rights in China, News From China, January 12, 1994.
13. Associated Press quoting a Chinese paper from Beijing, The Pioneer, 23 January, 1995.
14. The National Family Survey: a collaborative project of The Ministry of Health and Family Welfare and a number of research bodies around India covering 24 states. in: Sons or Daughters, Goans Don't Discriminate, by Anita Katyal, The Times of India, 2 July, 1995.
15. Annual General Report: Ministry of Health and Family Welfare, 1994-95, I.I. 3.
16. Family Planning Success Stories (Asia Latin America) by Rahul Singh, U.B.S. 1994, p. 170.
17. Birth Control — a Dismal Picture in U.P., Usha Rai, The Indian Express, 17 July, 1995.
18. Rahul Singh, *op.cit.* Chapter 2, p. 68.
19. Centre sets Targets for Vasectomies, by Anita Katyal, The Times of India, 6 July, 1995.
20. Safety: Vasectomy and Cancer: Research Continues, Outlook, Volume 13, No. 1., p. 8, May 1995.
21. Progress, a UNDP/UNFPA/WHO/World Bank Special Programme of Research, Development and Research Training in Human Reproduction, No. 32.
22. Health Consequence of Vasectomy in India, S.P. Tripathy; C.R. Ramachandran and P.Ramachandra: reprint no. 5529, Bulletin of the World Health Organisation, 1994, 72 (5): 779-782.
23. The Indian Council for Medical Research.
24. Failure of the vasectomy method may be attributed to a number of causes, among them: recanalisation, an unsuccessful operation for any reason, insufficient stress being laid on after care instructions concerning the necessity for the use of a condom or any other reversible method of contraception for up to 6 weeks after the operation. It could also be due to the instructions having been inadequately understood and therefore not followed. Voluntary Sterilisation, An International Fact Book, John A. Ross, Sawan Hong, Douglas Huber: The Association for Voluntary Sterilisation 1985, Chapter 8.
25. Annual Report, Ministry of Health and Family Welfare, New Delhi, 1994: 3.2.4.
26. Rahul Singh, *op.cit.* p. 62.
27. Artificial Insemination Bill Passed: Express News Service, The Indian Express, 10 August, 1995.
28. Motherhood at 51, Bodo Woman in Guwahati Claims the Honour: Seema Hussain, The Week, 6 August, 1995.

14

My Little Queen

When six month old Harpreet Kaur's father and paternal grandmother made her suck Sulphuric Acid on 27 February, 1994, they did not realise that 1994 was part of The SAARC Decade of The Girl Child. The entire village community of Jurhadi in Kharar, Punjab stood by Harpreet's mother, while the village elders jointly fought for justice[1]. At a time when three baby girls are estimated killed every month and tossed into garbage dumps in Delhi[2], this positive demonstration of community solidarity stands out like a beacon light.

Women conditioned down the ages still continue to perpetuate the ritual murder of their newborn girls. The infants are smothered even today with sand bags or with their mothers' placentas. Sleeping pills are thrust between their lips and poison smeared upon the breasts that should nurture them. If they still manage to stay alive, it is a simple matter to snap the wispy little necks between a thumb and forefinger. Usilampatti in Tamil Nadu has gained considerable notoreity in this respect. The Kallar community has a tradition of violence. The snuffing out of a baby girl's life is considered essential because her very presence is a blot on the family name; that is, if she happens to be the second or the third daughter— The first is needed to help in the household chores. She is also a potential liability for the community, as elsewhere in the country, to be fed and taken care of until her marriage. On that dreaded occasion, even a casual labourer of the area demands nothing less than a dowry of ten thousand rupees with video coverage of a 'grand' wedding.[3]

The baby killers of Salem in Tamil Nadu and in Rajasthan were featured in a BBC programme in 1994.[4] When the killings first came to light, the state government sat up and began to take notice. An Indian Council for Child Welfare cradle baby scheme was started together with conscientising work in an effort to put a stop to the practice. The killings, however, continue, with just a few babies managing to reach the cradles put up for them in 1993.[5] Loving parents in the BBC film told the film team, 'We would rather give seven bodies to *Yama*' — the god of death 'than one to a stranger.' In fact when Poovathy gave her one week old baby poisoned milk, she was shocked to find herself arrested for such a common practice.[6] Although the Tamil Nadu government sponsored monetary schemes have benefitted around twently thousand girls, and The Community Services Guild is enthusiastically working to improve the women's situation while physically stopping female infanticide in their areas, female foeticide is in fact gaining ground. Ultrasound tests have become much cheaper, and towns where the social workers are less watchful oblige with an operation table. Thick jungles and quiet streams have many a sordid tale to tell.[7]

A gynaecologist from a hospital in the area told me what a shattering experience it was for her to bring baby girls into the world only to have them literally snatched away by their fathers despite the pleading of nurses wanting to adopt them. 'She must die, or it will be a disgrace for us.'

In April, 1995 the midwives of Bihar hit the headlines. Over 1,200 baby girls are killed every year in the Katihar District of Bihar. The *dais*[8] who put salt or urea into their mouths at the instance of their fathers, wrap up the dead bundle and consign it to the river, or strangle the baby and dispose of it in the jungle. For this act of kindness they receive Rs. 25/- per death, that is, Rs. 25/- to Rs. 100/- a month. The practice originated with the Rajputs, but now seems to cut right across caste lines.[9]

The little girl as she grows is vulnerable to abuse. Sexual abuse of children within the four walls of the house has always been with us, but it is only recently that it is being exposed. Mothers are gradually plucking up enough courage to mention the dread secret outside the four walls of the house. In most cases however, family conditioning does not equip them to take positive action, as the battle would be against the men of the house who are also their mainstay. However, the groundswell is growing and there will be no stopping the tidal waves that must follow. Among the most recent and the most sordid of such cases is that of an Under Secretary in The Ministry of Home

Affairs who has been accused of exposing his eight year old daughter to group sex and other unpardonable indignities. A case was lodged with The Crime Against Women Cell in Delhi on 25 April, 1995.[10] The furore that reached Parliament House was so great that he and all the others involved in this nefarious business were arrested. On 31 January, 1996 the Additional Sessions Judge H.R. Malhotra declared that the crime did not fall within the ambit of Section 375 of The Indian Penal Code - rape, but that the accused would be charged with 'outraging the modesty of a woman' - Section 354 IPC and 'Carnal intercourse against the order of nature' - Section 377 IPC.[11]

This trivialisation of the mental and physical trauma of the victimised child was further highlighted by the grant of bail soon after this judgement, to one of the accused for the purpose of attending a marriage. The case is being handled by The Central Bureau of Investigation.

Most of the crimes against children occur because the child knows and trusts the criminal. It is only when the 'game' becomes strange or painful that she cries for help. On 29 April, 1992, The Supreme Court set aside a High Court judgement convicting young Dr Naval Dubey of an 'attempt' to rape an eight year old girl on 2 September, 1982.[12] Dubey was convicted of rape, even though, he had used his medical knowledge to keep the child's hymen intact.[13] He is presently serving a term of seven years rigorous imprisonment with a fine of twentyfive thousand rupees. The child's parents had persevered through social ostracism and injustice, finally getting justice after ten long years.

The Supreme Court made the following statement, 'Though sexual assaults on female children are not reported..there is an alarming and shocking increase of sexual offences committed on children...they become easy prey...Therefore such offenders who are a menace to society should be mercilessly and inexorably punished...judges who bear the Sword of Justice should not hesitate to use that sword with the utmost severity, to the full and to the end if the gravity of the offence so demand.'

Recorded cases of rape of children below 10 years of age fell from an alarming 1099 in 1991 to 532 in 1992 and rose again to 634 in 1993. (table appended at end of chapter) Since such cases are under reported, each one is the articulated cry of a thousand more who could not speak. The vicious sex racket reported in July 1994 in Jalgaon, Maharashtra where five hundred school girls were silenced and sexually abused for 13 years by two municipal councillors and the son of an ex-municipal councillor is a case in point. The children were petrified because compromising videos had been made of them during these sessions.[14] It is important to realise that little boys are equally at risk. The sordid case of seventy year old Freddy Peats who enticed homeless boys to his 'orphanage' in Goa earned him world wide notoriety. After abusing the children himself, they were hired out for tourist sex over a number of years. The law finally caught up with him. On 15 March, 1996 The Sessions Court Marmagao found Peats guilty of child abuse and also of several allied charges brought against him.[15]

Making the little ones aware of the dangers that surround them is essential, living as they do with the threat of AIDS fast assuming monstrous proportions. The pernicious myth that all sexually transmitted diseases including AIDS are cured by sex with a virgin, the younger the better, is still in circulation. This is believed not only by highway truck drivers, but by thousands of men around the country, posing a lethal risk for the already vulnerable girl child. In view of the alarming increase in child abuse and rapes of minors, the National Commission for Women has passed an ordinance declaring that a minor's testimony should be of supreme importance regardless of the child's origins. This would obviate the necessity for a traumatising medical examination. The testimony should also be recorded by a woman police officer in supportive and familiar surroundings. The age of the offender should have no relevance to the nature of the crime. This ordinance was submitted to government in early 1996.[16] In spite of demand for separate legislation on the sexual abuse of children, nothing has happened so far. The National Commission for Women has called for amendments in The Indian Penal Code, The Criminal Procedure Code and in The Indian Evidence Act to make it an all-inclusive legislation incorporating sexual abuse of the child. It has demanded that anti-rape legislation be made more stringent. Women's voices have been raised demanding a separate law to deal with child rape. The age of consent is also sought to be raised from the present sixteen years to eighteen years to protect the young bride from sexual congress until she is ready for it.

Growing up without any feeling of self worth, the child often finds herself used and disposed of as goods. Eight year old Guddi of Agithi Village in Ratlam found herself mortgaged by her father on 1 February 1982 to Gulab Nath. After slaving and begging for him, he sold her to Bhuvan Nath for whom she worked for eight months, before she was finally married off to his ten year old son. Both Guddi's mortgage and sale deeds were duly entered on stamp papers of Rs. 5/- each.[17] A number of little girls are lured or sold into prostitution, while yet others find themselves working long hours in factories. Proposals for urgently needed reforms in child labour laws are being made, and the 1986 law is expected to undergo much needed changes in the near future.

Literacy among women and girls in India is still abysmally low. The 1991 census puts the male literacy rate at 64.20 per cent, and female literacy at 39.9 per cent.[18] India allocated 3.5 per cent of its Gross Domestic Product to education (1990), and over 1.6 per cent to health. The education allocation is to be increased to 6 per cent of the GDP in the next Five Year Plan (1997-2002) This together with the added incentive of free midday meals for eleven crore primary school going children over a period of three years to start with, will help lessen the little girls' drop-out rate after the primary level. This continues so far to be very high, especially in the Northern states of Rajasthan, Uttar Pradesh, Bihar and Madhya Pradesh. Sulabh International, a voluntary social organisation providing on-site low cost sanitation, is planning a massive programme for providing suitable lavatories in rural areas. This would be a boon for women and girls who have to work or attend ill-equipped rural schools far from home, with no privacy for their special needs. Their parents' ever present worry about the girls losing their virginity, and the heavy work load awaiting them at home, gives the little ones no option but to drop out. Their knowledge of the world is nil. It is essential for the state to provide them with creche facilities in rural and urban areas to relieve them from the burden of caring for their smaller siblings, and to enable them to avail themselves of educational facilities.

The marriage festival of Akha Teej and others like it in Rajasthan and elsewhere come with the predictability of clockwork during the harvest season. The ouster in the late 1980s of Nanalal, Scheduled

Caste member of the Jaggannath Pahadia Ministry in Rajasthan at the instance of Mrs. Indira Gandhi for getting his two minor daughters married,[19] has had little impact on the marriage scene. Children are being married amidst joyous celebrations as always. It is only in the villages near larger towns that the functions are in lower key, and the parents a little wary of press photo-graphers.[20] According to The International Planned Parenthood Foundation's latest report, out of four million marriages which take place in India, three million are those of girls under eighteen.[21] So much for The Child Marriage Restraint Act.

Social workers and women development workers in Rajasthan feel such marriages are a direct result of extreme poverty. It is economical to marry a number of children at one sitting. Even the jewellery made for a child bride requires less silver, and the little girl makes a most 'adjustable' bride. Often for the same reason the wedding feast doubles as a funeral celebration for any elderly relative of the families to be connected by the marriage. The venerable member would have lived a long and full life and the young ones are about to embark on theirs. So both occasions call for joy. Child marriages being so intertwined in local cultural patterns are normally only interfered with by women's groups if the children getting married are below fourteen or fifteen years old.[22]

In this context, it was most exhilerating to read a news item from Hissar in 1993[23] about a courageous grandfather in a remote village in the district who obtained a court order to stop the marriage of his ten year old grand daughter Shiela to thirty five year old Dharambir. One can only hope that this far-sighted gentleman would have found some others like himself to form a support group to which other little girls like his grand daughter Shiela can turn for future guidance.

NOTES AND REFERENCES

1. Gilvester Assary in Chandigarh Newsline, 10 May, 1994.
2. Malvika Kaul in The Pioneer, 9 September, 1993.
3. The Killing Field, Gita Aravamudam, The Week, 3 April, 1994.
4. BBC film: Assignment: Let Her Die, documentary by Emily Buchanan, 1994.
5. The Killing Field, *op.cit.*

6. Drive Against Tamil Nadu Infanticide, The Times of India, 4 December, 1992.
7. Salem Revisited, Usha Rai, The Indian Express, 12 December, 1995 and 28 December, 1995.
8. Midwives
9. A survey of 35 midwives by Bal Mahila Kalyan, a Bihar non-governmental organisation, quoted in Midwives Forced to Kill Girl Child, Pranava K. Chaudhary, The Times of India, 22 April, 1995.
10. Karam Chand Jakhu: with the help of Sakshi, a violence intervention centre that has been closely following the case.
11. Women's Body will Challenge Jakhu Court Order, The Times of India, 4 March, 1996.
    India is likely to be drawn into the dragnet of the child sex trade. This is already showing signs of spreading in the Konkan coast with small girls and boys being lured into this perverted form of tourism.
12. S. Ratnavel Pandian and Fathima Beevi jj (1992) 3. Supreme Court Cases 204:58.
13. Never Say Die, Madhu Kishwar, Manushi, July - August 1992.
14. Shocking Revelation, editorial, The Pioneer, 1 July, 1994.
    Allegedly blackmailed by the leader of a gang of young men from well-to-do families in Pandharkarwada, District Yavatmal, a fifteen year old girl burnt herself to death on 4 January, 1996 in a macabre replay of the sex scandals of Jalgaon and Malegaon. The girl's father and activists are demanding action against the police believed to be involved.
    Teenage Girl Commits Suicide in Malegaon-like Scandal, The Indian Express, 24 January, 1996.
15. The Silent Scream: Commercial Sex Abuse of the Child, Hutokshi Rustomfram, The Lawyers Collective, Vol. 10, October - November 1995.
    Also: Peats Convicted of Child Abuse in Marmagao Case, The Indian Express, 16 March, 1996. See Addenda p. 245.
16. The National Commission for Women. There has been a public outcry in the past few months against the sexual abuse of children. Conferences and workshops have been held on the subject. Newspapers and magazine are publishing legal options available to victims and offering advice on how to address the problem. Meanwhile, a nineteen year old victim of the Malegaon sex scandal who had been threatened for reporting it by friends of the accused, was gang raped by five persons. The police took two days to register her complaint. The Indian Express, 12 March, 1996.
17. Girl Mortgaged and then Sold in Ratlam, Madhya Pradesh, The Times of India, 4 June, 1983.

18. Census of India Part II B (i) Series I, India. Primary Census Extract for General Population: Vol. I, Office of The Registrar General of India, Ministry of Home Affairs, New Delhi.
19. Rajasthan in the Throes of Social Upheaval, Rajinder Sawhney, The Times of India, 9 October, 1988.
20. Bid to Stall Marriages Foiled. The Hindustan Times, 27 April, 1993.
21. The Times of India, 30 May, 1994.
22. In Defence of Child Marriages, Usha Rai, The Indian Express, 13 May, 1992.
23. The Times of India, 26 November, 1993.

Addenda

Victims of Rape By Age-Groups 1989-1994				
Year	*Below 10 Years*	*10-16 Years*	*16-30 Years*	*30 Years & above*
1989	369	1965	5646	1772
1990	394	2105	6028	1541
1991	1099	2630	5377	1319
1992	532	2581	7000	1621
1993	634	2759	7038	1792
1994	734	3244	7442	1798

Crime in India 1993, p. 266, and 1994: p. 216 National Crime Records Bureau Publications, Ministry of Home Affairs, New Delhi.

AIDS Cases in India:

As on December 31, 1995:

Total Number Reported:		**2109**
Male:	-	1580
Female:	-	529
Statewise Incidence:		
Maharashtra	-	1041
Tamil Nadu	-	372
Punjab Chandigarh (U.T.)	}	100
Manipur	-	99
Delhi	-	89
Kerala	-	76
Madhya Pradesh	-	60
Karnataka	-	51
West Bengal	-	39
Gujarat	-	24
Goa (U.T.)	-	12
Uttar Pradesh	-	8

As on March 31, 1996.

Total Number Reported:		**2528**
Male:	-	1849
Female:	-	634
Statewise Incidence:		
Maharashtra	-	1242
Tamil Nadu	-	492
Manipur	-	104
Punjab Chandigarh (U.T.)	}	100
Pondicherry	-	100
Delhi	-	99
Kerala	-	96
Madhya Pradesh	-	65
Uttar Pradesh	-	56
Karnataka	-	51
West Bengal	-	43
Gujarat	-	25
Goa (U.T.)	-	12

(U.T: Union Territory)

Other States have a much lower incidence. These tables are based on monthly reports received at The National AIDS Control Organisation, Ministry of Health and Family Welfare, New Dehli.

JUST
MARRIED

15

Marry Her Off !

To marry a daughter 'off' is still a heavy responsibility. I read again the letter sent to me by young Mariamma from Kerala, 'They are demanding Rs 5,000/- and 2 gold sovereigns for dowry. Better we all take poison.' The shock had driven me to the telephone, and a doctor friend had acted swiftly to avert the calamity. In 1988 tragedy struck two families for the same reason. Three lovely sisters in Kanpur, Uttar Pradesh, and four sisters in Alappulli, Palghat, Kerala were found only a few months apart, hanging from ceiling fans in their homes. They understood only too well that they were liabilities...

Mariamma's five thousand rupees and 2 gold sovereigns pale into insignificance before the impossible escalation for dowry demands these days. 'Dowries spiral heavenwards,' wrote Mary Roy, Principal of a girls' School in Kottayam, Kerala, in 1993. 'One of my ex-students got married for a dowry of one and a half crore rupees cash.' — ten million rupees. With Gulf money still pouring into the state, and fields and greenery giving way to incongruous palatial buildings and luxurious life styles, the steep increase in dowry demands is sending a continuous stream of educated girls into convents and the nursing profession in other states. The latter profession is often used as a stepping stone to work abroad, and is now fast gaining respectability.

There is little difference in the dowry and lavish wedding scene elsewhere in the country. From the highest political figure to the lowly subsistence worker, wedding expenditure continues to be completely unrelated to real life. For those who can divert the machinery of state for a good cause like a daughter's wedding, the sky is the limit. The 'honour of the family' remains uppermost in all calculations. A Parliament House replica or a Rajasthani palace complete with elephant can be set up by the wedding genie overnight to accommodate hundreds of guests. The latest extravaganza was a marriage in an aeroplane in flight.[1] Cash gifts can total lakhs nowdays. Of the several containers filled with gift envelopes at a wedding, one container alone took five hours to count.[2]

This seems chicken feed compared to recent reports of the expenditure over the wedding of the Tamil Nadu Chief Minister's foster son in September 1995, which reportedly had three lakh invitees, and an estimated expenditure of three crore rupees on the decoration of the marriage *pandal* — pavilion alone which stood on fifty acres of land in Madras.[3] Entire trains have been booked for government ministers at weddings, and dowry is creating a need in cultures where it never existed in this form before. Muslims in Uttar Pradesh reportedly give the bride and her groom all they will ever need in their lives together. The dowry can range anywhere from twentyfive thousand to twentyfive lakh rupees.[4] Even in Muslim dominated Malaysia, status has begun to dominate marriage plans. With the bridegroom bearing the brunt of wedding costs as in other Muslim countries like Kuwait and Saudi Arabia where grooms are looking for less demanding foreign brides, exorbitant demands are being made in Malaysia also, two thousand dollars (5,000 *ringgit*) is the norm these days.[5]

For the power and the glory accruing to the family that has managed to hook a son-in-law from The Indian Administrative Services, the rates offered in the 1970s would seem laughable compared to those listed in a 1987 report.[6] While an Assistant Commissioner of Income Tax would bring twenty lakh rupees in assets, an Indian Administrative probationer belonging to the prestigious Bihar cadre, would come for about forty lakh rupees. Latest reports (1995) place the Bihar cadre in the most sought after slot. Uttar Pardesh, Rajasthan, Madhya Pradesh and Andhra come close seconds with amounts ranging from sixty lakhs to one crore rupees.

Computers double for match makers now. All that needs to be done is to fill in personal data: religion, caste, sub-caste, preferences etc., and hey presto!— the perfect match is yours!

In among the marriage advertisements, neatly classified—religion, caste and sub-castewise, — is tucked away an occasional surprise. I discovered a portable genset sketched, prettily tied with a bow, carrying this succint message: 'Marriages are made in heaven and sustained by Shriram portable gensets: Uninterrupted power for life long bliss.[7] Make a marriage vow with Godrej Storwell' is another. Anything to take care of the Joneses! Bring this down to the level of the local washerman, and you will find him giving his daughter a dowry in 1996 that you yourself could ill afford : A sewing machine, a 'fridge, a cooler, all her ornaments and clothes, all the normal furniture they might use, fifty thousand rupees or more, a scooter perhaps, and naturally, clothes for her groom, his mother and his sisters as well. He will spend a lifetime of labour to repay this debt at heavy interest, but no one can fault him for not having done his duty by his daughter. The 'Gimmee' of the 1970s still holds sway.

Meera and Shashibala, two sisters, were the brides-to-be at Muradnagar Uttar Pradesh. Seventy thousand rupees, a sum their watchman father could ill afford, had been given to their future in-laws as settled. Further demands were made, but when even more was demanded at the ceremony itself, and fake jewellery for the brides was sought to be passed off as real, the brides' family called the wedding off.

A happy ending was supplied by two brothers from a family known to the girls' parents. 'They may not be rich, but at least they will not trouble our girls, and the boys are good,' beamed an ailing Rajwati.[8]

It is strange indeed that at a time when the government has gone through the painful process of amending the anti-dowry legislation twice over, and has stiffened the penalties for crimes related to dowry, the Unit Trust of India, that carries the government's special blessings, should float a sure fire scheme ingeniously entitled, 'Dowry Trust'[9]. This scheme purports to relieve the rural father of all his financial worries concerning his daughter's marriage. This of course is not explicitly stated. He is promised a handsome amount twenty-one times his original investment which will release him from the clutches of the dowry system. Within six months of this scheme being launched, seven lakh rural fathers had already invested in it, hypnotised by the picture conjured up by the UTI of a paradise peopled with smiling in-laws warmly embracing the new brides whose fathers proudly present their new relations with a huge one-time-payment dowry. No more time-to-time demands, and no more dowry deaths!

There is no getting away from such deaths in real life as bride burning and worse continue to plague the country. Dowry deaths rose steadily from 4,215 in 1989 to 5,157 in 1991. The figures declined to 4,962 in 1992, rising to 5,817 in 1993, coming down again in 1994 to 4,935, with Uttar Pradesh leading each year, and Delhi topping the Union Territories.[10]

The continuing upward swing of this macabre graph caused the setting up of The Lok Sabha Joint Parliamentary Committee in December 1980 with a mandate 'to examine the question of the working of The Dowry Prohibition Act 1961.'[11]

It made several useful recommendations in a very comprehensive report on 11 August, 1982, which elicited only desultory interest from the government. This negative attitude of the government together with the law enforcing machinery's lack of commitment finally led to the founding of The Dahej Virodhi Chetna Manch in 1982. This was a forum for awareness and a full-fledged war against the evils of the dowry system.[12]

It was formed by the bonding of twenty-five women's organisations together with students, youth groups, teachers, trade unions and other voluntary agencies.

On the night of 1 December 1980 Sudha Goel was set on fire in Delhi with an almost full term son in her womb. Her neighbours rushed to rescue her from the flames. A false declaration claiming accidental death was set aside by S.M. Aggarwal, Additional Sessions Judge on 27 May, 1983. Sudha's husband Laxman Kumar, his mother Shakuntala and his brother Subhash were sentenced to death. This judgement was hailed as historic, and was received with great enthusiasm. Widely publicised by the media, it brought about a much needed awareness. The High Court, however, acquitted the three accused on 3 November, 1983 causing great public indignation. On 23 September, 1985 The Supreme Court upheld the trial court's views, and sentenced Laxman Kumar and his mother to life imprisonment, setting Subhash free for lack of evidence.[13]

The Sudha Goel case brought the fiery debate on dowry killings to a head. Members of the newly formed Dahej Virodhi Chetna Manch organised protest meetings, marches, street corner plays and debates. The media joined forces and the pressure was kept up until The Dowry Prohibition (Amendment) Act 1984 was passed.[14] Few of The Joint Parliamentary Committee's recommendations were incorporated in this flawed amendment.

Section 2 of the original Act defined dowry as 'any property or valuable security given or agreed to be given before or after marriage *in consideration of marriage*.' In spite of The Joint Parliamentary Committee's recommendation that the ambiguous phrase 'in consideration of marriage' be deleted, the amendment merely replaced it with another: '*in connexion with*', which continues to cause confusion.

This amendment virtually legalised the giving of presents '*of a customary nature*'. This nebulous phrase leaves itself wide open to any number of interpretations. A number of other grey areas continued. Among some of its good points were that it made the cognisance of an offence simpler. It included Central and State Government recognised welfare institutions or organisations among those who could make a complaint on behalf of the victim.

The renewed clamour by women's organisations and a continuing blitzkrieg by the media immediately following the passing of this amendment finally climaxed in the enactment of The Dowry Prohibition (Amendment) Act 1986, passed on 8 September, 1986.[15] *This amendment has made the period during which a demand for dowry will be punishable much more realistic* by replacing the words '*or after the marriage*' with 'or *any time* after the marriage.' This covers the many instances where continuous demands are made for goods even several years after the marriage. Fines and punishments have been made severe. Advertising inducements for marriage in the form of money, property, share in business is also culpable. Section 6 provides that when a woman dies within seven years of marriage in unnatural circumstances, her property must be transferred to her parents, or be held in trust for her children. These have been specifically mentioned as her heirs, to safeguard her property from misappropriation.

Section 304-B clarifying the nature of a dowry death for the purpose of the law, has been inserted in The Indian Penal Code. This draws a connection between cruelty and harassment of the woman for dowry just before her death. It puts the onus of proof of innocence on the husband and his relatives, and provides for severe punishment which may extend for life. This Section has also been inserted in The Code of Criminal Procedure 1973.

An amendment has also been made to The Indian Evidence Act of 1872 by the insertion of Section 113-B which reiterates that the court shall presume that the accused caused a dowry death, *if it is proved that the woman had been subjected to cruelty or harassment by the accused just before her death.*

Both the amendments provide for the appointment of Dowry Prohibition Officers by state governments who are expected to see that the anti-dowry legislation is complied with. They are also expected to collect evidence for the prosecution in the 'taking and abetting of' dowry, and are to assist the state governments in related matters. These officers are to be assisted by a committee of five social workers which must include at least two women. A number of states have already implemented this clause.

Although it is useful that all gifts at weddings should be listed, this has not been made mandatory which makes this clause ineffective. Its existence is also not widely known.[16]

Another clause-4-A of this amendment attempts a ban on advertisements offering inducements by way of publishing property, business shares or any other bait '*as consideration of marriage*'. One glance at the matrimonial columns of any Indian newspaper will prove how well meaning but ineffective such legislation can be:

'Match for extremely beautiful, high status family girl...multicrore turnover...affluent family having own properties...lucrative business, well placed in society...multinational industrialist match..'[17] need anything more be said?

Speaking in 1988 when the debate on dowry legislation was at its height, Professor N.R. Madhavan had made a valid point when he had said, 'the enforcement thrust of social legislation ought to be preventive and educative, whereas The Dowry Prohibition Act is more reactive and punitive.'[18]

All in all however, the amendments to dowry legislation have done some good. They have provided for a great deal of welcome interaction between social groups and government agencies. The introduction of section 304-B in The Indian Penal Code which defines a dowry death, of Section 304 in The Code of Criminal Procedure 1973 in the First Schedule, and again in The Indian Evidence Act 1872 (presumption as to dowry death), have all been useful in helping victims of this crime.

On the first anniversary of the death of Shalini Malhotra who was doused in whisky and set alight on 18 April, 1989, concerned organisations held a meeting in Delhi where Kamleshwar's television film *Jalta Sawaal* — A Burning Question, was shown. In the film, the dying Shalini said her death was not an accident, and that she had given the statement under threat. Her husband Pravin married again, and later allegedly committed suicide.

Twenty six year old Arveen Rana née Arora was allegedly strangulated in 1988. Her father was at this meeting anxiously demanding a time limit for such cases. Arveen's case has taken seven troubled years to reach the stage where the Sessions Judge Prithvi Raj has said that sufficient material was available for framing dowry death charges against her in-laws.[19]

Old cases are rarely followed up. Often parents or relatives of the dead woman are under threat or do not have the means or the will to follow through expensive cases that drag on for years. Sometimes 'compensation' money changes hands and seals mouths. In Anita's case registered by herself on 25 December, 1985, two years after she was thrown out of her marital home after torture and continuing dowry demands, her husband had married again. The case was finally heard by a *Mahila* Court in Delhi. Here the Metroplitan Magistrate Sunita Gupta sentenced Anita's husband Hari Ram to three years rigorous imprisonment and a fine of five thousand rupees.[20]

Some cases like that of Shashi Bala done to death in 1979 are still being followed up by committed lawyers and dedicated parents. Tripta Sharma, an employee of The Central Ordnance Bureau, Delhi, who married Jitendra Pal Sharma on 22 November, 1983, died in May 1986. The police took two years to finalise the charge sheet. Many delays later the trial began in 1993. On 20 October, 1993 The Sessions Judge III R.K. Sharma acquitted all the accused saying Tripta had committed suicide probably due to a 'mental problem'. The judge was unmoved by the prosecution's evidence which included a medical report which indicated post mortem burning.[21]

The case was sent up in appeal to the High Court, Allahabad in 1994/95 and is being followed up.[22]

In 1983 The Additional Judge S.M. Aggarwal had stated that the husband of a woman dying in suspicious circumstances should be debarred from marrying for five years, and that a woman's dying declaration, the most important document in these cases, should not be taken at face value by the police, as there are many pressures on the dying woman, especially the fact that anything she might say would affect the treatment of her children. Again, if she gets well after telling the truth, her own condition could be worse than before.

Sentencing a fifty year old mother-in-law to death for burning her twenty year old daughter-in-law Krishna in Delhi, November, 1988, The Sessions Judge Dinesh Dayal had said in his forty seven page judgement on 28 July, 1994, 'The person who perpetrates a barbaric crime without any human consideration must be given the extreme penalty... to give lesser punishment to the accused would render the judiciary... suspect, and the common man will lose faith in the courts of law.'[23]

A number of states have made their own amendments to the 1961 dowry legislation. Among these is The Karnataka Marriages (Registration and Miscellaneous) Act 1976[24]. This finally received the President's assent and was published in The Karnataka Gazette Extraordinary on 24 February, 1984. The Act offers Rs. 1,000/- to couples for an intercaste/inter-community marriage. Wedding presents are permitted from specific persons. A marriage tax is to be levied on 'luxury' weddings whose expenses exceed Rs.5,000/-. The dowry is to be transferred to the bride or to her heirs. Marriage returns are to be filed, a tax paid and a memorandum of marriage is also expected to be prepared and signed. The social boycott hoped for in the 1976 Bill has been considerably watered down. Section 21 allows for the disqualification of any person imprisoned under The Karnataka Marriages (Registration and Miscellaneous. Provisions) Act 1976 from election or appointment as a Councillor during incarceration, and for five years thereafter.

Understandably the debate on these provisions will, in time, change its form and shape further.

Meanwhile, Orissa has had an alarming spurt in dowry crimes. In a bid to stem the rot, the Government of Orissa initiated a move to handcuff and publicly parade the main culprits who were seen as instigators of the crime. These were identified mainly as mothers-in-law and sisters-in-law. The programme was generally welcomed. The state government warned grasping in-laws and printed booklets on the subject. The police were departmentally advised to use this method only in cases where guilt had been established *prima facie*. The High Court however decided otherwise and struck down the handcuffing and parading as violative of Article 19 of The Constitution, leaving the state government and the police in a quandary.[25]

Many questions arise on the subject of dowry and dowry crimes. Opinion is gradually veering around to a realisation that although greed and consumerism are often the main objective, greed and the desire to exercise power are two of the basic motivating factors for the continuance of this evil. The main stress points caused by daily expectation and incompatibility can erupt at any time, and dowry is the most convenient peg to hang it all on.

In a series of thought provoking articles in *Manushi* in the late 1980's,[26] Madhu Kishwar had tried to analyse the reasons why the highly motivated anti-dowry campaign of the early 1980's had not achieved the desired effect. A continuing contact with the cultural and societal situations in which victimised women found themselves was essential for the total commitment demanded in activism. At the base of it all lay an insecure young woman without any rights in her natal home, always being readied for another unknown home of which she was not yet a member, and so had not yet earned her right to any share in it. Everything in her natal home would belong to her brothers. In such a situation, would it be right to ask her to also forego her dowry? Madhu Kishwar strongly advocated equal inheritance rights for a daughter in her paternal home. She would then be appreciated as a person in her own right, functioning from a position of strength, not as a liability that needed a dowry to make her acceptable. This has begun to happen. A number of states have passed laws making daughters equal partners with sons in the Hindu undivided family. Some other religious communities are also changing their personal laws to conform to the need for gender equality.

Legislation however, can only be at best an enabling agent. It cannot transform itself into a fairy wand. Fierce debates continue on the state of anti-dowry laws, their feeble implementation, calls for further amending of existing amendments, and for the creation of umbrella legislation to simplify procedures. The drama continues against a back drop of tradition sanctioned custom that is alive and very well indeed. Our laws are unrelated to ground realities, and are far and away ahead of societal norms. They will be forced to bow before unwritten codes of customary procedure until we achieve, as we must, the miracle of attitudinal change at ground level.[27]

NOTES AND REFERENCES

1. Air India, 1994.
2. Megabuck Marriages, The Week, 29 August, 1993.
3. Three Lakh People will Attend Wedding of the Century, V.R. Mani, The Times of India, 7 September, 1995.
4. Ibid.
5. High Cost of Dowries in Malaysia, Agence France Presse, Kuala Lumpur, 14 June, 1995.
6. The Indian Dowry Service, Charulata Joshi, The Spectrum, The Times of India, 22 March, 1992.
7. The Times of India, 22 January, 1995.
8. Sisters find their Match after Making Greedy Grooms March, Sonal Manchanda, The Indian Express, 19 June, 1996.
9. Editorial, The Weekend Observer, 3 July, 1993.
10. Crime in India 1993: National Crime Records Bureau, Ministry of Home Affairs, Government of India: Chapter 7: Crimes Against Women, Incidence of Crimes Against Women 1989-93, 7.3.1, and 7.4.3: Analysis of crime rate for various States and Union Territories, and Crime in India 1994.
11. This Committee had the approval of The Rajya Sabha.
12. The five convenors of The DVCM were: All India Women's Conference, The Young Women's Christian Association of India, The National Federation of Indian Women, The Mahila Dakshata Samiti, and The All India Women's Democratic Association.
13. Amarendra Nath Sen and Ranganath Mishra jj. AIR 1986 Supreme Court 250. Volume 73.
14. The Dowry Prohibition (Amendment) Act 1984—incorporated at the end of this edition.
15. The Dowry Prohibition (Amendment) Act 1986—at the end of this edition.
16. In the Pratibha Rani case, The Supreme Court has demanded that provision be made for the preparation of exhaustive lists of gifts given

at weddings, so that there would be no doubt as to ownership in case matters should come to a head. See chapter 5 'His Share, Or Mine?'

17. The newspapers of 23 July, 1995.
18. Dowry Prohibition Act: Does the law provide the solution, or itself constitute the problem? (Social Audit of Dowry Legislation, University of Delhi. 1988)
19. Dowry Trial will proceed after 7 years, New Delhi, The Times of India, 16 May, 1995.
20. R.I. to Husband in Dowry Case, The Times of India, 6 July, 1995.
21. Judge acquits all in Tripta case, The Times of India, 25 October, 1993.
22. A Mahila Dakshata case being followed up with the help of WARLAW-Women's Action Research and Legal Action.
23. Mother-in-law sentenced to death, The Times of India, 30 July, 1994.
24. Discussed at length in Chapter 8 of this book: How Filthy is Lucre? p. 135.
25. Anti-dowry scheme violative of law, Rajaram Satapathy, The Times of India, 22 May, 1995. In the neighbouring state of Bihar, a National Family Health Survey conducted under the aegis of the Union Ministry of Health and Family Welfare shows that in over 31% cases more than Rs. 25,000/- together with gifts and cash are given by 89% of all marriages in Bihar.
    Dowry Practice Rampant in Bihar, says Family Survey, The Indian Express, 13 January,1996.
26. Madhu Kishwar in Manushi No. 48, 1988. No. 53: July-August 1989. No. 78: Sept-Oct. 1993.
27. See Addenda, Dowry deaths and female suicides.

Addenda

Incidence of Dowry Deaths in India: 1990-1994					
State	1990*	1991*	1992*	1993**	1994***
Andhra Pradesh	344	411	424	575	396
Arunachal Pradesh	0	0	1	0	0
Assam	24	14	11	19	13
Bihar	243	263	170	338	296
Goa	0	0	1	2	0
Gujarat	125	103	123	114	105
Haryana	126	144	209	166	191
Himachal Pradesh	21	30	18	18	4
Jammu & Kashmir	8	9	30	20	1
Karnataka	216	227	209	266	170
Kerala	11	13	18	10	9
Madhya Pradesh	397	423	353	370	354
Maharashtra	858	828	727	746	519
Manipur	1	0	0	0	0
Meghalya	0	0	2	0	0
Mizoram	0	0	0	0	0
Nagaland	0	0	0	0	2
Orissa	64	63	152	254	169
Punjab	103	99	101	147	117
Rajasthan	166	152	250	369	298
Sikkim	0	0	0	0	0
Tamil Nadu	86	97	75	79	83
Tripura	5	7	3	5	6
Uttar Pradesh	1516	1597	1783	1952	1977
West Bengal	420	538	174	256	85
Total States:	**4734**	**5018**	**4834**	**5706**	**4795**
UNION TERRITORIES					
Andaman & Nicobar Islands	0	0	0	0	1
Chandigarh	0	2	1	3	3
Dadra & Nagar Haveli	0	0	0	1	0
Daman & Diu	0	0	0	0	0
Delhi	102	133	121	107	132
Lakshadweep	0	0	0	0	0
Pondicherry	0	4	6	0	4
Total Union Territories	**102**	**139**	**128**	**111**	**140**
Total All India:	**4836**	**5157**	**4962**	**5817**	**4935**

Compiled from: *Crime in India 1992, pp. 238-239. National Crime Records Bureau, Ministry of Home Affairs, New Delhi. Chapter 6, pages 238-240.
**Ibid, 1993, p. 262.
***Ibid, 1994, p. 226.

Incidence of Female Suicides by Causes During 1989-1994
(*Selected*)

Causes of Suicides	1989	1900	1991	1992	1993	1994
Quarrel with Parents-in-law	2117	2353	2690	2423	2628	2495
Quarrel with Spouse	1913	2545	2401	2748	2750	2799
Dowry Dispute	964	1298	1310	1370	1486	1613

Accidental Deaths and Suicides in India 1993-1994, National Crime Records Bureau, Ministry of Home Affairs, New Delhi.

16

Holy Matrimony

'What therefore God hath joined together, let not man put asunder,'[1] says Holy Writ, but in the the past few years the sacred adhesive has been wearing rather thin. 'There is less tolerance and adjustment among these over-educated women,' say the elders, shaking their heads sadly. They themselves are worn out after years of toleration and adjustment. Certainly the day to day tensions of modern living bring the tolerance level down until the day one thoughtless word can bring a couple to breaking point. Too many of these wives have watched their mothers wearing themselves out trying to keep an impossible marriage alive. Women are beginning to realise they do not need to live silently in hell any more, nor do they have to force their children to watch off-screen horror shows in their homes every night. Pushpa, a university teacher's teenaged children gave her an ultimatum. They were leaving, they said. She could stay on and get beaten if she wanted. Pushpa got herself a divorce.[2]

In 1995, Delhi alone has registered 25 divorces a day, while Kerala's divorce rate has shot up to 350 per cent in the last few years[3]. Wife bashing is common to every community and religion. Even though nowadays the occasional divorce is manipulated by a wife to get herself and her relatives a tidy sum if her husband is pliant enough, the vast number of women are in situations that have gone well beyond control. The controversial triple *talaq* at one sitting as a valid form of divorce continues to be challenged and debated within the Muslim community itself.

Although Hindu law advocates strict monogamy, bigamy has been found to be widespread in the community. Monogamy is supposedly practiced by most of the religious communities in India. Islam allows a man to marry up to four wives, but with a stringent moral proviso:

'But if you fear that you cannot do justice, marry only one'.[4] Conversion to Islam for the sole purpose of marrying again, however, continues in spite of all these injunctions.

In a Supreme Court judgement on a writ petition[5] before Justice Kuldip Singh and Justice R.M. Sahai, Justice Kuldip Singh categorically stated that for a man to marry again, a legal divorce from his first wife was a necessity.

'We hold that the second marriage of a Hindu husband after conversion to Islam, without having his first marriage dissolved under law[6] would be invalid...violative of justice, equity and good conscience... It is not the object of Islam nor is it the intention of the enlightened Muslim community that the Hindu husbands should be encouraged to become Muslims merely for the purpose of evading their own personal laws by marrying again. We therefore hold that the second marriage of a Hindu husband after his conversion to Islam is a void marriage in terms of Section 494 IPC.' Concurring with the judgement, Justice R.M. Sahai said, 'no religion permits deliberate distortions. To check misuse, many Islamic countries have codified the personal law, wherein the practice of polygamy has been either totally prohibited, or severely restricted.[7]

Few women in such a situation realise that to avail themselves of the provisions of Section 494 of The Indian Penal Code mentioned in this judgement, they need only go directly to a first class magistrate in their area, and not necessarily to the police. Andhra Pradesh is the only state so far, to have amended Section 494 of The Indian Penal Code to make it more effective.[8]

The revival of the *Maitri-Karars*[9] in Gujarat after their being banned in 1982, and the resultant exploitation of gullible women is causing concern. These pacts, usually between influential men, and women chosen by them to live in an extra-marital relationship with them, were earlier registered by The Registrar of Marriages. The document though not valid in a court of law, imparted an air of respectability to the connection. Although this phenomenon has resurfaced, the numbers involved are steadily decreasing. Children born of these unions are entitled to maintenance during their minority under Section 125(I) (b) of The Code of Criminal Procedure which provides for legitimate as well as for illegitimate children. Cases of exploitation are proceeded against.[10]

The interesting thing about any law is its aura of permanence. Any attempt at change is taken as a challenge to authority. More particularly is this the case where the law has been of advantage to the powerful. When these laws happen to be as hoary as Christian marriage laws, any talk of change in the established system of woman's servitude starts alarm bells ringing. What is worse, in a multi-religious tradition, allowing change in one minority's personal laws could send political signals to other groups as well. The Indian Christian Marriage Act is a vintage Act dating back to 1872. The Indian Divorce Act which applies to Indian Christians is even more ancient, going back to 1869. Framed along the lines of The English Matrimonial Law, these laws were passed by the British Parliament in London, and have had no relevance in the Indian context at all. Although the English law has been updated from time to time, its Indian counterpart has stood eternally unmoved like the Rock of Ages.

The personal laws of most of the religious communities have been amended over the years, some for the better: others with little to commend the change. The Parsis have reviewed their 1936 marriage laws and now have The Parsi Marriage and Divorce (Amendment) Act 1988 (Act 5 of 1988). The Muslim marriage laws have undergone some controversial changes, and the Hindu marriage laws have also been amended.

Even laws applicable to foreigners residing in India have been amended. The Christians alone find themselves forced to cling to inequitable laws which are over a century old. On 29 July, 1985 the then Law Minister A.K. Sen had told the Rajya Sabha that government's policy was not to amend personal laws of minority communities unless the initiative came from the. communities themselves.[11] Thus it was imperative that the initiative come from the Christians, and it did.

Over the years there has been countrywide discussion of Christian law reform. Looking closely at their laws, the Christians discovered that the only law governing adoption was The Hindu Adoptions and Maintenance Act 1956. This, like all Hindu laws, applies only to Hindus, Sikhs, Jains and Buddhists. Other religious communities may not adopt a child, as each is governed by its own personal laws. They can at best be foster parents under The Guardianship and

Wards Act of 1890, until the child is 18 years old. A National Adoption Bill has ben defeated twice in Parliament over the past eighteen years. It is however heartening to note that there has been an upward trend of late among those allowed by law to adopt children, in adoption of baby girls by prospective parents belonging to the middle and higher income group.[12]

After a great deal of heart searching and accommodation of diverse points of view, The Christian Marriage Bill 1994, The Indian Succession (Amendment) Bill 1994 and The Indian Christian Adoption Bill 1994, piloted by The Joint Women's Programme with the complete involvement and concurrence of churches, organisations and all shades of opinion within the Christian fold, were submitted to the government in February 1994. There, for the moment, despite continuing demands for attention, the matter rests.

Meanwhile things have been happening in Kerala. On 20 July, 1994 a Special Bench of the Kerala High Court decreed that 'Ecclesiastical tribunals have no jurisdiction to annul marriages involving the civil rights of parties .. a Christian marriage can be declared null and void only by a decree of Court as provided for in Sections 18 and 19 of The Divorce Act.'[13] Finally the Kerala High Court decided that those whom God had joined together could have an option.

Sonia Mary Zachariah was married to P.C. Zachariah in 1972. She and her little daughter were deserted a few years later. After a separation of ten years, Sonia Mary moved the High Court for a divorce. E.J. Amni was married in 1980 and deserted by her husband a year later. Both women challenged Section 10 of The Indian Divorce Act 1869 as violative of their fundamental rights. According to this section in the Act, a Christian husband can divorce his wife on grounds of adultery alone. She, on the other hand, would have to prove 'incestuous' adultery on the part of her husband, or adultery coupled with a number of other unpalatable enlisted grounds for divorce.

24 February, 1995 brought good news for Christian women in Kerala. The High Court of Kerala pronounced Section 10 of The Indian Divorce Act 1869 'violative of the fundamental rights guaranteed to them and other similarly situated Christian women under Articles 14, 15 and 21 of The Constitution of India.'[14]

'Under the Indian social set up, the judges stated, 'it is well nigh impossible for a woman to prove adultery of her husband.' The judges went on to modify Section 10 of the Act to make adultery, desertion and cruelty independent grounds for divorce. They also castigated The Central Government for not taking a 'final decision on the recommendations of The Law Commission in its ninetieth report for making amendments to Section 10 of the Act. The direction issued,' noted the judges, 'was to take a decision within six months from the date of receipt of a copy of the order dated 13-12-1990. In spite of such a peremptory decision, The Central Government has not even cared about the decision if any taken in the matter.' In spite of cases filed in court and voices raised in protest against the discriminatory nature of this antiquated Act, it remains firmly in the statute books.

Quoting Justice V.R. Krishna Iyer, the judges said, 'The sex equality clauses of our Constitution will remain frozen and be a perpetuation of ancient injustices unless activist judges share the new concerns and values.'[15]

NOTES AND REFERENCES

1. Mathew 19 : 6, The Bible.
2. Cactus Lives, The Week, 14 May, 1995: Vijaya Pushkarna, V.K. Santhosh Kumar, Lalita Iyer and Aditi Nair.
3. *Ibid.*
4. The Quran checked and revised by Mahmud Y. Zahid-Dar-Al-Choura —1980.
5. Writ petition (civil) no. 1078 of 1989: Smt. Sarla Mudgal, President, Kalyani and Others: D/10. 5. 1995.
6. Section 13 of The Hindu Marriage Act 1955.
7. 'Syria, Tunisia, Morocco, Pakistan, Iran, The Islamic Republics of The (former) Soviet Union are some of the Muslim countries to be remembered in this context.' R.M. Sahai j.
8. The offence has been made cognisable, non-bailable and non-compoundable.
9. Friendship pacts.
10. Maitri-Karars Common in Gujarat, Anand Kumar, The Asian Age, 16 June, 1995.
11. The Hindustan Times, 30 July, 1985.
12. The Tiny Angel is the Rage of Adopting Couples, Soma Wadhwa, The Pioneer, 22 August, 1994.

Bringing Home a Baby, The Week, 15 May, 1994, Vijaya Pushkarna, with Shaukat H. Mohammad and Tanya Kamdar.

The Government of Maharashtra passed The Maharashtra Adoption Act on 9 August, 1995. This will be applicable to all regardless of religion, caste or sex, and supersedes all legislation or customs relating to adoption. This Act awaits the President's assent. It has been widely acclaimed as progressive and secular and could lay the foundation for a uniform civil code in the State. It is to be hoped that other states will follow this lead.

Anju Jain, The Lawyers Collectives, Vol. 10 - No. 9, September 1995.

13. AIR 1995, Kerala 16: Special Bench. K.T. Thomas, V.V. Kamat and K. Narayana Kurup, jj. (O.P. No. 4319 of 1991 L).
14. The High Court of Kerala at Ernakulam—M.M. Pareed C.J, T.V. Ramakrishnan and P. Shanmugan (O.P. No. 4319 of 1991 L).
15. Justice V.R. Krishna Iyer, in Human Rights and The Law.

17

His Share, or Mine?

Pratibha Rani and Suraj Kumar were married in 1972 at Ludhiana. Pratibha Rani was harassed and tortured, and the jewellery, ornaments and clothes amounting to Rs. 60,000/- entrusted to Suraj Kumar and his father misappropriated. On 12 March, 1985, a three judge bench of the Supreme Court declared unequivocally in a majority judgement, that the Hindu woman 'is the absolute owner of' her *stridhan*.[1] Justice S. Murtaza Fazal Ali speaking for himself and Justice Sabyasachi Mukerji said, 'The position of *stridhan* of a Hindu married woman's property during coverture[2] is absolutely clear and unambiguous; she is the absolute owner of such property, and can deal with it in any manner she likes...without any reference to her husband.' If used in times of family financial constraint, her husband 'is morally bound to restore it or its value when he is able to do so... The concept that dowry becomes the joint property of both spouses as soon as she enters the matrimonial home ... even if there is a break in the matrimonial alliance, *is in direct contravention of Hindu Law of Saudayika which has been administered since more than a century by High Courts, Privy Council as also this Court,'* emphasis mine. 'It is a criminal breach of trust.' Justice A. Varadarajan while dissenting, said, 'Even if the *stridhan* property of a married woman is placed in custody of her husband or in-laws, they would be deemed to be trustees and bound to return the same if and when demanded by her.'[3]

By this judgement *stridhan* was defined as 'gifts made to the bride before her marriage by her parents, as well as those made by her in-laws after her marriage.' The judges were insistent that an exhaustive list of gifts be prepared in triplicate : one each for the parents of both parties, and one for the magistrate.

The judgement was received with delirious acclaim by women, and has since been most useful in the restitution of property on the breakdown of a Hindu marriage.

Later in 1985, seventy-five year old Shah Bano stood in the same court, the highest in the land, to hear an appeal made by her ex-husband against the monthly payment to her of Rs. 179.20 as maintenance dismissed. This amount had been fixed by The High Court.

Shah Bano married Mohammad Ahmad Khan, a prominent advocate of Indore in 1932. He had an annual income of approximately sixty thousand rupees a year. Their three sons, a technical assistant in a textile mill, a manager of a transport company, and a branch manager of a bank, were all well settled. Forty three years of married life went up in smoke when in 1975 Shah Bano was thrown out of her home. It was only after three years that she filed for a subsistence maintenance on November 6, 1978. It was after this that her husband divorced her in the form of an irrevocable *talaq*. This exempted him from any obligation for any maintenance after the *talaq*.[4]

In August 1979, the magistrate at Indore ordered a monthly payment of maintenance to Shah Bano of Rs. 25/- She appealed to The High Court for an increase in the amount. The High Court raised the maintenance to Rs. 179.20 per month. This was the exorbitant sum Shah Bano's well-heeled ex-husband could not spare his wife of forty-three years standing. He appealed to The Supreme Court against the order.[5] Mohammad Ahmad Khan claimed he had paid two hundred rupees a month to Shah Bano for two years, and that he had deposited three thousand rupees as dower in court for the three month period of *Iddat* after divorce.[6] However, the court was considering a reference under Section 127 of The Code of Criminal Procedure, where an order has been made under Section 125, that payment shall continue until the ex-husband has satisfied the court that he has paid all the amount due to his ex-wife under personal or any other law, that he is bound to pay her *as the law then stood*.[7] Since the court was not convinced that this had in fact happened, it confirmed the judgement of The High Court, also awarding Shah Bano ten thousand rupees in costs, noting that an application for an increase in the amount due to her would be considered by the court.[8]

In December 1985, a cyclostyled statement '*Zameer ki Awaz*'. which purported to have Shah Bano's thumb impression appeared together with a statement from her which implied she was returning the money as a 'sacrifice to Allah'.[9]

Standing her ground with dignity, travelling from court to court in her quest for a pittance for subsistence living, Shah Bano found herself embroiled in a major debate that had little to do with her own life. She died after the sound and fury was over, but not before her case had sparked off a turbulent debate over the jurisdiction of the secular law of the land and the personal laws of religious communities, in this case, The Muslim Personal Law. This brought about the hurried passing of the controversial Muslim Women's Protection of Rights of Divorce Act 1986. This Act states that 'a reasonable and fair provision and maintenance be made and paid to' the divorced wife within the *iddat* period by her former husband. It enumerates her dues : her own for the *iddat* period, her children's maintenance for 2 years, her *Mehr* or Dower and properties given her before and after marriage. If any or all of these are not paid, the ex-husband may be proceeded against under The Code of Criminal Procedure. As for the divorcée, if the 'Magistrate is satisfied that' she 'has not re-married, and is not able to maintain herself after the *iddat* period,' he may direct the relatives that would have inherited her property to pay her 'fit and proper' maintenance, failing them, her children if any, her parents and other relatives, in that order, finally leaving the spent woman at the door of the Waqf Board.

Commenting on this Act, Justice V. D. Tulzapurkar, former Justice of The Supreme Court said, 'A glaring instance of an abject surrender to pressures exerted by fundamentalists, obscurantists and religious fanatics of the largest minority community in the country with electoral considerations in mind would be difficult to find.'[10]

On 3 April, 1987, The Supreme Court awarded Rs. 300/- a month to Begum Sabanu *alias* Saira, and Rs. 200/- to her minor daughter as maintenance to be paid by her ex-husband Abdul Gafoor, with arrears. These payments were to be made to Begum Sabanu his first wife, and their daughter, with effect from the date of his second marriage. The Shah Bano judgement was quoted among others by the court, which categorically stated 'the right to maintenance conferred by Section 125 of The Code of Criminal Procedure can be exercised irrespective of the personal law of the parties.... The explanation to Section 125 (3)' fortified the court's view.[11]

A number of progressive Muslim women and other liberal Muslims are beginning to come together to form opinion groups around the country to try to incorporate safeguards for women in more comprehensive *nikah namahs* — marriage contracts — in matters of divorce terms, dower and allied matters.[12] In its issue of May 1996, Communalism Combat published a copy of a Bill drafted by the Muslim Intellectual Forum, Bihar, which attempts to codify certain aspects of Muslim law in these matters and also deals with inheritance.

Barely had the commotion over the Shah Bano case died down, than a landmark judgement was delivered by the Supreme Court in the celebrated Mary Roy case, whereby The Travancore Christian Succession Act of 1916 and The Cochin Christian Succession Act of 1921 stood repealed as of April 1951 with retrospective effect from 1 April, 1951, the date on which the princely states in the country were integrated with the Union of India. The Indian Succession Act 1925 (Chapter II of Part V) was extended, and made applicable to the Indian Christians residing in Travancore and Cochin (which were designated as Part-B States). By this judgement, the state laws (discussed at length in Chapter 8) were declared invalid. This means that after this positive judgement delivered by Chief Justice Bhagvati and Justice R.S. Pathak, when the head of a household dies without leaving a will, instead of the miserable pittance she would have received earlier, '*a wife shall inherit a one-third share. The remaining two-thirds shall be divided among heirs both male and female.*'[13]

This was made possible because Mary Roy, an intrepid crusader for women's rights, had presented a writ petition in The Supreme Court challenging the consitutionality of the Travancore Christian Succession Act of 1916. The judgement stated that the Travancore and Cochin States had merged in 1949 to form the Part-B State of Travancore-Cochin.

All Part-B States, inclusive of Travancore-Cochin were governed by The Indian Succession Act ever since its enactment in 1925. '*As such, any law there was in force in the Part-B-State of Travancore-Cochin immediately prior to 1st April, 1951 would stand wholly repealed, and intestate succession to the property of Indian Christians in the territories of the former state of Travancore-Cochin is governed by the provisions contained in Chapter II of Part V of the Indian Succession Act of 1925.*'[14] emphasis mine.

Christian women whose husbands had died without leaving a will could not believe their ears. Predictably the storm clouds followed with the backlash coming almost immediately from the establishment. The judgement had been interpreted as a frontal attack on 'Christian' laws. The fact that it applied solely to those families where the head had died intestate was all but forgotten. However, understandably, there was a hue and cry as Kerala was convulsed with fear that all titles to property derived from intestate succession would be invalidated. The fact remains that between the date of judgement 1986 and 1994, only 25 cases demanding equal rights in property from 1951 were registered.[15]

Emboldened by Mary Roy's stand a few women ousted from their homes after the head of the family's death began to emerge from the twilight to think about getting their due.

Among these cases is that of Aleykutty Chacko, over seventy years old, a retired teacher, eldest daughter of Aley Chacko ailing and over ninety. They were disinherited on the death of their father, together with four other sisters by the brother they doted on and made sacrifices for. The will said to have been written by the father whose right hand was paralysed long before his death, was produced in court by the brother. It was declared false by both the District and High Courts. The brother has gone in appeal against the judgement. Aleykutty however, who was responsible for her brother's entire education, is determined to stay on in the little mud hut she has made in her father's property and fight for their rights, as after the will has been declared a forgery, the property should be divided according to the Indian Succession Law 1925. Dr M.M. Thomas, former Governor of Nagaland and noted Christian opinion leader from Kerala declared, 'Any dilution of the law of equality is unjustifiable.' A number of opinion makers and liberal church leaders supported this unequivocal stand.[16] A Private Member's Bill submitted by P.J. Kurien in October 1986 sought to 'validate all... imovable property transactions from I.4.1951 to 23.2.1986'. This has been referred to a select committee.

The rush for making wills was so overwhelming that some of the established churches were allegedly instructing their congregations in the art of drafting them. It is quite understandable that there would be a number of problems in re-allocating property or goods, especially when vultures would be on the look out how best to feather their own nests at the expense of the old and the uninformed. However, in the interests of justice, some personal adjustments must be made in a spirit of reasonableness and understanding.

Does a girl have a right to an equal share with her brother in her father's property? Should she go empty-handed to her new home when she marries, or should she do so supported by her family, secure in the knowledge of her own inheritance? What rights does she have in her marital home of which she will now be an integral part, presumably until she dies? Women's organisations have been trying to get her an honourable share in her husband's property for many years, but the government's reply has always been that demand for this kind of major adjustment must come from the community concerned. This in turn, would require a change in personal laws. The merry go round whirls on as dusty shelves make room for more and more files...

At an unusual conference in Bangalore in March 1994, where forty widows, young and old, from all religious communities interacted with representatives of concerned organisations, academics and legal experts, this was precisely the subject that was emphasized. These courageous but marginalised women from around the country, made it abundantly clear that all land and property in the marginalised home must be in the joint names of both spouses, and be automatically transferred to the widow in the event of her husband's death. The distressing condition of abandoned widows who spend the remainder of their meaningless lives chanting *bhajjans*[17] by the hour in Varanasi for a morsel of food and a roof over their heads, exploited and abused by all, is a direct result of insecurity. They have nowhere to go to for life and dignity. The widows were one and all against the custom of forcible re-marriage to their dead husbands' kin to ensure that the property stays within the family. They demanded this practice be declared illegal. They also wanted any land given to their husbands by the government to be in the joint names of the spouses. In spite of their tragic lives, these women from cloistered traditional backgrounds laughed as they related how they had shocked orthodox men with the new confidence they had gained after working with various concerned organisations. There was only one pithy question with which they silenced societal censure, 'When you die, what do you want your wives and sisters to be, women like us, or the walking ghosts you would like us to be?'[18]

The Maharashtra Government made a welcome gesture when it gifted thirty-three plots of land as joint holdings to couples on Independence Day 1992.[19] Maharashtra also seeks to give women decision making roles in the political and economic sphere, taking into account the increasing number of woman headed households. These, like the market mammies of Africa are becoming more numerous around the country with the steady migration to the cities and the rising rate of divorce. Hopefully this policy will survive any political changes that may take place[20] 'A woman and an old fence can be discarded any time.' This old Mizo adage holds true even today in Mizoram. A Customary Law Committee was set up as far back as 1980 to review and to codify customary laws with only two women in a body of twenty.

Things continue as before. The State Commission for Women is not yet functioning. The mere pronouncement of the words, 'I divorce you' will throw a woman out of her home forever. She gets no maintenance. Her children are expected to go with her ex-husband who may, if he so wishes, leave them with her at any time with no talk of maintenance. Women even lag behind men in higher studies due to the gender bias.[21] However, they are slowly becoming more self possessed, and realising their own worth.

A daughter's rights in her natal home, an equal voice in family and property deliberations as well as equal inheritance, are being discussed in several families. A number of states have enacted amendments to The Hindu Succession Act of 1956, and have given full rights to daughters in the undivided Hindu joint family property. Andhra Pradesh in 1983 and Tamil Nadu in 1989 are among the states that have taken this decision, even though certain clauses in the amendments may need some revision. According to these amendments, if the daughter dies, her share will automatically go to her children, and if she has none, to her father, brothers and sisters. Kerala had earlier solved this by enacting The Kerala Hindu Joint Family

System (Abolition) Act of 1975.[22] Both the Tamil Nadu and Andhra Pradesh Acts conclude that the fact that the woman was not a member of a coparcenary was responsible for the evil of dowry demand. It remains to be seen whether this wrong can be righted by this measure. On 28 July, 1994 the much debated Karnataka Act No. 23 of 1994 joined the others in amending The Hindu Succession Act 1956 to grant the Hindu daughter membership with equal rights in the undivided Hindu joint family property. This Bill had been debated for two years.

On 22 June, 1994, the Chief Minister of Maharashtra stated that The Maharashtra Government 'would statutorily rest in *women of all communities* the right to joint ownership of properties and assets on solemnisation of marriage', and among other things, 'place one-fifth of all government and *panchayat* land and income under the control of women's committees.'[23]

Just a year after these grandiloquent gestures, The Maharashtra Government decided to disqualify members of *panchayats* who may have more than two children. This is the same concept as a Constitution Amendment Bill introduced in Parliament in 1992.[24] This is being carried out in *panchayats* and muncipalities in a number of other states as well.

According to Bina Agarwal,[25] in the North and North Western states of India resistance to daughters inheriting agricultural land is the highest. *Gram*[26] *panchayats* continue to feel strongly that land should be inherited by sons alone. Haryana has tried time and again to cut daughters off from agricultural property in their natal home. The state even went so far as to seek the Centre's permission to amend The Hindu Succession Act 1956 to make this possible.[27] The Rajya Sabha however, was assured in 1989, by the then Human Resources Development Minister Mr. P. Shivshankar, that 'The Centre would not allow any state to pass "abominable laws" denying property to women.'[28] These attempts are certain to recur from time to time, and must be treated with the contempt they deserve.

Debate and speculation on the possibility of a uniform civil code surfaces every once in a while. In the Shah Bano case Chief Justice Y.V. Chandrachud had said that a beginning in this direction has to be made 'if The Constitution is to have any meaning.'[29] Justice Kuldip Singh, in the Sarla Mudgal case[30] requested the Government of India through The Prime Minister of the country to have a fresh look at Article 44 of The Constitution of India and "endeavour to secure for the citizens a uniform civil code throughout the territory of India." Justice R.M. Sahai[31] said, "The desirability of a Uniform Code can hardly be doubted: but it can concretise only when the social climate is properly built by the elite...statesmen...who should 'instead of gaining personal mileage rise above and awaken the masses to accept the challenge.'

Any talk of a Uniform Civil Code is likely to raise many hackles. Some communities feel it is being used as a ploy for the imposition of laws governing the majority community on the rest of the country. A number of informed Hindus are equally unhappy with their own laws which they think need reviewing. This is especially the case in the area of women's inheritance and the registration of marriages. They regret the nullifying of the traditional right to inheritance by women in some Southern and North Eastern communities by the Hindu Succession Act of 1956, and the non-registration of marriages that leads to bigamy which is hard to prove in a court of law. Village women seem inclined to think their *panchayat* will understand their situation better than an impersonal court. Recently, a Hindu woman whose husband was fined for bigamy by the *panchayat* received the amount of the fine as compensation.[32] A Uniform Civil Code conceived as an option would be acceptable to all. The Special Marriage Act 1954 and the Indian Succession Act 1925 are already in use by all communities. Goa's common civil code is functioning since the Portuguese introduced it in 1867.

The first big step in the right direction would be to urge *all* communities to re-evaluate their personal laws along broad principles of human justice and equality. The commonalities that would gradually emerge from this exercise could form a solid base. At a later stage, an equitable Uniform Civil Code could be built on this to dispense even-handed justice and human dignity to all. The Parsis already have The Indian Succession (Amendment) Act no. 51 of 1991 which will now give their women equal succession rights to property with the men. The Christians submitted The Indian Succession (Amendment) Bill 1994 also an equitable amendment with equal shares for sons and daughters, which is still awaiting official approval. It is extremely desirable that government set aside all fears of political repercussions and expedite legislation on all pending Bills on these important issues. Wrapping them in cobwebs will only aggravate the problem.

While the succession debate goes on, the problem for daughters desiring a share in the responsibility of looking after and maintaining their old parents remains the same. Section 125 (i) (d) of The Code of Criminal Procedure still implies that the maintenance of parents is the sole responsibility of the son. Since the masculine possessive '*his*' is used, 'his father or mother, unable to maintain himself or herself,' the inference is clear. Since the son will be the parents' mainstay in their old age they will continue to differentiate between him and his sisters, whether the sisters may be willing and able to help look after their parents or not.

Even though this undesirable pronoun remains in the statute books, some judges have set precedents by giving it an enlightened interpretation. Dr. Mrs. Vijaya Manohar Arbat, a physician, appealed against the High Court order asking her to pay the maintenance stipulated under Section 125 (i) (d) of the Code of Criminal Procedure, to her father unable to maintain himself. Justices G.L. Oza and Murari Mohan Dutt upheld the High Court decree stating conclusively that 'the use of the word ' "his" does not exclude the parents claiming maintenance from their daughter,' as ' "his" not only denotes a male but also a female...Apart from the law,' noted the Court, 'Indian society casts a duty on the children...to maintain their parents' if they are unable to do so themselves, and 'to look after' them 'when they become old and infirm...otherwise they would be destitute'.[33]

So as we move into another century, the daughter still continues to be some one else's property and valued only as such. A glass of water offered to her parents as they visit her in her matrimonial home, will still have a few rupees discreetly slipped under it. The girl's family cannot be beholden to their daughter's in-laws even for a glass of water.

NOTES AND REFERENCES

1. Woman's wealth. Air 1985. S.C. 628 from Punjab and Haryana.
2. Period of marriage.
3. Air 1985. S.C. 628 from Punjab and Haryana.

4. Shah Bano, by Janak Raj Jai, Advocate, Supreme Court, Rajiv Publications, New Delhi, 1986.
5. The Bench was composed of V.V. Chandrachud C.J., D.A. Desai, O. Chinappa Reddy, E.S. Venkataramiah and Ranganath Mishra jj.
6. During *Iddat* it is compulsory for a Muslim husband to maintain a wife.
7. Dues in the case of payment to a Muslim wife are:
   1. *Mehr* at marriage.
   2. The mandatory *Iddat* maintenance.
   3. *Mataa* - payable under Chapter 2, verse 241 of the Quran which states: ' "And for divorcees reasonable provision is due from the righteous." ' and because of this *ayat* verse 'a group of scholars hold *Mataa obligatory in all cases* whether of divorce by delegation, or of *Mehr* paid, or of those divorced before consummation or of those after consummation, so held Imam Al Shafei, God bless him and his.' (Imam Shafei's Ruling on Al Quran 11.24.1: Commentary on The Holy Quran by Ibn Katheer (d. 1373 A.C. Damascus). Source: Danial Latifi, senior counsel, Supreme Court of India.
8. AIR 1985 SC, Vol. 72: Chandrachud C.J. 1985 Cr. L.J. 875 from M.P.
9. The Sunday Correspondent, quoted by Janak Raj Jai in Shah Bano, *op. cit.*
10. For a Common Civil Code, V.D. Tulzapurkar, The Times of India, October 19, 1986, Sunday Review.
11. Editor's note: AIR 1987 Supreme Court II03 (from Kerala) A.P. Sen and S. Natarajan jj. D/3-4-1987.
12. Muslim women come up with novel ideas on *talaq*, Jyoti Punwani, The Pioneer May 9, 1994.
13. Emphasis mine, AIR 1986, SC 1011 Vol. 73:D/24-2-1986 Justice Bhagwati, C.J. Justice R.S. Pathak: Mary Roy vs. State of Kerala and Others.
14. *Ibid.*
15. Back to square one? Leela Menon, The Indian Express, 24 July, 1994.
16. The Forum of Christian Women for Women's Rights, The Kerala Council of Churches, constitution experts, some members of The Legislative Assembly and human rights activists.
17. Hymns.
18. Conference on Widows in India, Bangalore, 22-25 March 1994: convened as a result of a project spanning 47 villages in seven Indian states by Marty Chen of The Harvard Institute for International Development.
19. The Pioneer, 16 August, 1992.
20. The Times of India editorial Blueprint for women, 24 June, 1994.
21. Mizo Customary Laws Shackle women to a Primitive Past, Press Trust of India, the Assam Tribune, June 11, 1996.

22. Property rights for women: Geeta Ramaseshan, The Indian Express, Madras, 10 June, 1989.
23. New Job Schemes for Women Likely, Paranjoy Guha Thakurta, The Pioneer, 31 July, 1994.
24. Woman's place, The Times of India, 23 June, 1995.
25. A Field of One's Own — Gender and Land Rights in South Asia, by Bina Agarwal, Cambridge University Press, 1994.
26. Village.
27. The Hindustan Times, 9 August, 1989: Haryana Bid to Cutt off Daughter's Share.
28. The Times of India, 10 August, 1989.
29. AIR 1985 SC 945.
30. Writ petition (civil) No. 1079 of 1989 on 10 May, 1995.
31. *Ibid.*
32. Women Veto a Common Civil Code, Jyoti Punwani, The Times of India, Sunday Review, 23 July, 1995.
33. AIR 1987 - Supreme Court 1100, from 1986 Cri L.J. 1399 (Bom).

USED MODEL
FOR SALE

18

This Woman is Mine!

One of the commonest threads that runs through all global societies, behind closed doors or out in the open is violence against women. It is the one issue that talk shows, international print and electronic media, studies of rural and urban societies and world conferences on women's issues have in common.

A glance at world news coverage in recent years confirms this. A confidential US Army survey mentions 'spousal abuse' as 'occurring in one of every three army families each year'. It also mentions that child abuse is on the rise.[1] Nineteen year old Libby Saum gave a hair raising account of her exposure to the unnecessarily brutal and humiliating procedures in the SERE [2] course meant to alert women serving in the force, of the possibility of sexual attack during operations. Beaten, with severe injuries and videotaped without clothes, she was one of several traumatised young women cadets subjected to this treatment at the prestigious US air force academy in Colorado.[3]

In China 60 per cent of the women interviewed on the International Women's Day 1993 said domestic violence, job discrimination and continuing Confucian notions of female inferiority made them wish they were men.[4] A survey of 12,300 Canadian women in 1993 by a government agency 'Statistics' showed that they 'face the greatest risk of violence from men known to them, and South Asian residents face 'an epidemic of wife abuse'.[5]

The then United Nations Secretary-General Boutrous Boutros-Ghali stated in his speech at the Fourth World Conference on women at Beijing 1995, that 'National studies in ten countries estimate that between seventeen per cent and thirty eight per cent of women have been physically assaulted by a partner. An estimated hundred million girls suffer genital mutilation.'[6]

'At least two million girls are at risk of genital mutilation—approximately 6,000 per day' around the world.[7]

Nowadays those who can afford it are operated on in hospitals. This mutilation is performed in the Arab world, Sub-Saharan Africa, Malaysia, Indonesia, Egypt and wherever immigrants have settled elsewhere in the world.[8] The battle against this form of woman control is being fought in many international fora. A proposal to discontinue this practice even reached the stage of being debated in the French National Assembly. Although not passed, the fact that it had reached this stage at all sent out strong signals to residents in the country who carry out this reprehensible tradition.[9]

After fourteen girls died of this operation which is performed any time between one week and puberty, President Daniel Arap Moi of Kenya banned the practice in the country in 1985, but implementation of the law here as elsewhere, leaves a great deal to be desired. It is interesting to note that this operation, clitorodectomy, used to be performed in Western countries as late as the beginning of the twentieth century to cure masturbation and 'hysteria'.[10]

In our own subcontinent, extreme forms of fundamentalism and feudalism combined with brutal anti-woman tribal laws continue to create hell on earth for women in societies governed by these laws. Saner secular laws are by and large disregarded or lack implementation... While the die-hard Taliban clamps down on Afghan women's rights, keeping girls away from schools, and threatening women with severe retribution for working outside the home or going out unaccompanied and unveiled,[11] their sisters in Turkey have won a major victory over the enforcement of virginity tests on their daughters. Failure to pass these resulted in expulsion from educational institutions.

The Turkish Women's Association declared, 'the bodies of our children belong to them only. No one else can be authorised to control our daughters' bodies.'[12]

The then United States Government has passed an enactment to control increasing crime against women in a bid to make women safe within their homes and outside. The Biden Violence Against Women law was passed in September, 1994.[13] Bangla Desh has also responded to the increasing violence against women by enacting The Women and Children Repression (Special Provision) Act, which provides for capital punishment for rape, murdering for dowry and trafficking in women and children.[14] After numerous reports of sex attacks, incest and abuse exposés since August 1995, Italian women members of Parliament have forced through a Bill re-defining sexual violence providing guarantees for victims and raising the minimum sentence for rape to five years.[15]

In India, violence and crime are part of every day living. Raped by her factory boss in 1982 in Khandwa town, Pushpa ran to her husband for protection. He rewarded her by pouring kerosene over her and burning her to death.[16] His name had been sullied. His property had lost its worth, and he had no more use for it.

Kamla who made national headlines in 1981, was believed to belong to the Bedia community. Prostitution for them has been a way of life for as far back as anyone can remember. The same is true for many others like the Banchhras settled between Ratlam and Mandsaur in Madhya Pradesh, and the Bachada tribe along the Madhya Pradesh-Rajasthan border. The women support their families through prostitution. A recent study conducted with the aid of The Red Cross reveals that Sexually Transmitted Diseases are common among this group. Out of 465 women tested, 50 per cent were infected. This has been traced to truck drivers and cleaners carrying STD and HIV. 1.93% of the Banchhra women tested were found to be HIV Positive.[17] Their menfolk indulge in petty thievery, deal in drugs, or solicit for their bread earning sisters. The Bedias, totalled about sixteen thousand six hundred and eighty two persons a few years ago. They normally cater to rich landlords, politicians, administrators and businessmen. Bedia girls are initiated into the business by their own parents. Some like Kamla are sold. In 1981 Ashwini Sarin, an enterprising journalist, decided to go to Morena in Madhya Pradesh, buy a woman there and bring her to Delhi to expose the stark truth behind the flesh trade. So Kamla came to Delhi. The media lapped this up. The situation of women like her was brought home to the country. A film and plays were made on her. As suddenly as she came, Kamla vanished. Even though Ashwini Sarin returned to Morena in 1984 and wrote a series of articles on the flesh trade continuing to flourish as before, Kamla could not be traced.

Two reports were submitted on the trade in women in the Morena and Rajasthan areas; one by Virendra Gopal Nigam, Commissioner, Chambal Division, Morena, and the other by Meena, Deputy Inspector General, Criminal Intelligence Department, Rajasthan Police. The Nigam Report submitted on 12 June, 1981, called for a Special Police Force for the bettering of social conditions in the Bedia community and for a protective home for these women in Gwalior. The Meena Report recommended, among other things, a Special Police Squad to check the kidnapping and sale of women in the area, asking for priority attention to be given to this crime.

A writ petition was presented to The Supreme Court by three media persons in this matter.[18] The order given by The Supreme Court was delivered on 23 November, 1993. Justice Jayachandra Reddy and Justice G.N. Ray stated that 'the concerned state would do well by taking all necessary steps suggested in the two reports for eradicating this evil.'[19] A newspaper report of 1987[20] indicated that the Madhya Pradesh government had given assurances to The Supreme Court that the flesh trade would be curbed, but that it continued unabated.

By 1995 eleven Bedia women were assured employment by the District Collector in Sukha Village, Madhya Pradesh, if they renounced prostitution. This was made possible by a Netherlands funded scheme for the empowerment of women and the Mahila Samakhya, a government sponsored programme with successes in a number of states.

On February 1, 1982, eight year old Guddi was mortgaged by her father in the Ratlam area to Gulab Nath. After slaving and begging for her master, she was sold to Bhuvan Nath for whom also she continued to perform the same tasks. After eight months of this treatment, she was married to Bhuvan Nath's ten year old son. The three men involved in the buying and selling, including Guddi's father, were arrested. It is interesting to note that both Guddi's mortgage and sale deeds were duly entered on Rs. 5/- stamp paper at Agithi Village under the Piploda police station's jurisdiction.[22]

In 1987, a fond mother Ram Bai, decided to present her son with a present. So she bought a girl for him from a flesh trader for four thousand rupees. Three weeks later, the trader wanted the girl back. Ram Bai wanted her money back as the deal was over. The matter was upheld by two courts which were applying Pre-Independence case law in such cases, and almost gave official recognition to the contract of sale. It was only when the trader appealed to The Madhya Pradesh High Court against the order, that Justice T.N. Singh of the High Court drew attention in his strongly worded judgement to Articles 21 and 23 of The Fundamental rights enshrined in The Constitution, by which a citizen's liberty is ensured and traffic in human beings prohibited. He also drew attention to Article 51-A (e) of The Fundamental Duties of a citizen which prohibits 'practices derogatory to the dignity of women.' In view of these directions of The Constitution which had supremacy over any other practice, the deal was declared illegal and void. Hence no money could be returned.[23]

Little is known of the present situation of trafficking in women and children in these and other areas. Hopefully some positive facts will come to light. There is need for revisiting these places and for authentic information, not necessarily sensational, to be publicised.

Meanwhile marriage in the 1990s continues to be a commercial transaction. A poor woman in Arunachal Pradesh is worth 2 *mithuns*.[24] A richer bride may fetch 6 or 7 of the animals. Women here are so conditioned, that a school teacher trying to inculcate self worth in her girl students told them not to despair, as the day was not far when a woman would be worth a thousand *mithuns*.[25]

As late as October 1993, fourteen year old Usha was handed over by her father to thirty-two year old Veer Sain in settlement of a debt of twenty thousand rupees.[26]

Meanwile similar conditions continue in the hilly regions of Uttar Pradesh, particularly in the Jaunsar Bawar area. Here the price of a woman, *chhoot* has now shot up to a minimum of ten thousand rupees which can go up to eighteen thousand rupees or above. Around the Lakhamandal area there are now *Ashram Padhiti* — boarding schools for young lower caste Kolta girls who get free board and lodging as well as clothes. They also learn knitting, sewing and other crafts. Fewer husbands and relatives send their women to the brothels of Delhi, Meerut and elsewhere. Those who do, face societal censure and the practice is no longer common.

The lower castes are still more or less bonded economically to the higher caste Rajputs and Pundits, but they are now beginning to experience a new feeling of community as Scheduled Castes and

Scheduled Tribes. With the reservation of seats for women in the quota reserved for Scheduled Castes and Tribes in the local government, their status has begun to improve. The women are beginning to savour the sweet sense of power as Lakhamandal brings in the first Kolta woman *Pradhan* for the block, to be in power for five years. However, there is much to be done. A health survey is a necessity. The population has never heard of AIDS, and oppression overt or covert has to be tackled firmly.[27]

The buying and selling of women's bodies is a practice as old as time. One would have thought that the nineteen eighties and nineties would have brought a change in attitudes. A countrywide survey of girls sold into prostitution with poverty as the main reason conducted in 1987 is revealing.[28] The study cites the case of a girl who was sold into prostitution for ten thousand rupees, to pay for her sister's wedding. She worked all night as a prostitute, and all day as a house maid to repay the loan taken from a pimp, so that she could earn her freedom. The report has shocking evidence of some Nari Niketans,[29] and village level workers as well as government servants[30] who have sold girls into prostitution themselves.[31]

Used, cast off, bought or sold, *Devadasis* fall in the same category under many different names. Coming from poverty stricken areas, little girls become women overnight. They are dedicated to Goddess Yellamma as maids, catering to the desires of men in her name. Parents sell daughters, husbands sell wives. They have been led to believe that the goddess will give them her favours in direct proportion to the number of girls they dedicate, so there is a steady supply of minor girls to the temples. They simply flow through the portals of the temples into the glitter and misery of commercial prostitution in Bombay and other major cities. From their parents and village elders upwards, everyone gets a cut in the deal.

Even though the governments of Karnataka and Andhra have enacted laws against the system, the dedications still continue, but with less fanfare, on full moon nights in smaller and less well known temples than the Saundatti temple District Belgaum, Karnataka.

The Karnataka Devadasi (Prohibition of Dedication) Act 1982, amended in 1984 now offers five thousand rupees to anyone marrying a *Devadasi*. Penalties for performing or abetting in dedication ceremonies are severe and the State Government has been empowered to make rules for the implementation of this Act. Unfortunately although a great deal of rehabilitation work is in progress, the Act is not being implemented as it should be. Maharashtra is reviewing legislation in this matter. The Karnataka Government Social Welfare Department together with non-governmental organisations are working with the *Devadasis*, training them to make marketable goods like soap, chalk, toys, rope, and teaching them other skills. Homes are being made for them with government loans. Workshops to understand and alleviate their problems, introducing them to a better way of life have been held, and dedications are becoming less frequent.[32]

However, the measures taken by the government in the past decade are yet to make a definite impact on the *Devadasi* system. Programmes of rehabilitation apart, 'longer term benefits for *Devadasis* arising out of these are not discernable.'[33] 'Licence this profession,' Rewabai had said in March 1983. 'We are not here by choice. No one can stop this profession...therefore let it be licensed:.. with medical check ups.'[34] Ten years later, in 1993 doctors discovered that out of two thousand one hundred and six *Devadasis* examined at a health camp, one hundred and sixty-eight had AIDS and one hundred and ninety-one had other sexually transmitted diseases.[35]

The woman's fate hangs on the attitudes of the interpreters of the law, whether it be the Suppression of Immoral Trafficking in Women and Girls Act, 1956, or its amended incarnation : the Prevention of Immoral Traffic Act, 1986. The latter certainly is more realistic. Punishments are more severe, particularly in case of molestation of minors and small children, which can get the accused life imprisonment. This needless to say, has not happened in the many cases of such abuse. The substitution of the word 'person' for 'female' wherever it appears in the old Act is welcome as it now includes the prostitute as well as her client. However, it is interesting to note that Section 6 of the original Act provides for a penalty of *six months imprisonment and or a fine of five hundred rupees for 'wilful exposure of 'her' person.* The amended Act adds the following in Section 11 to the above Section 8 of the original Act: 'Provided that where an offence under this section is *committed by a man*, he shall be punishable with *imprisonment for a period of not less than 7 days, but which may extend to 3 months.*' The woman meanwhile, if caught 'soliciting..again,' will serve *one complete year in jail as well as pay a fine of five hundred rupees.*

The booking of a client is extremely rare. In spite of the strict ruling against sex with minors, pimps continue to offer clients 'clean, young girls, Sir, very beautiful' for a fee. The police continue to receive their protection money. The many loopholes in the Prevention of Immoral Traffic Act 1986 have finally moved the government to have this Act and the Indecent Representation of Women (Prohibition) Act 1986 studied by The National Law School for possible changes.[36]

As a result of terrorism and militancy in the Punjab, Kashmir and the North East in the past several years, a number of threatened families have taken refuge in Delhi and in some other towns. The government grant for each family has been most inadequate for the running of a household and feeding and educating children.

Jobs are hard to come by. As a result, decent families are being drawn into the dragnet of discreet prostitution.

Good looking girls from highly educated upper and middle class families are being increasingly lured by the promise of easy riches offered by the call girl racket, particularly in Bombay and Delhi where they cater to rich clients from West Asia and elsewhere. It is interesting that while Punjabi girls do not even form 1 per cent of the impoverished exploited prostitutes of India, 80 per cent of the call girls are from that state alone. It is a startling fact that no medical examination facilities are offered to brothels anywhere in the country except in Bombay, and that only for the record. Horrifying indeed considering the spread of AIDS in the country.[37] Of late another phenomenon is emerging. Young married women are being forced into prostitution to add to their matrimonial families' wealth. These cases are on the increase in large cities.

A negative emphasis on trying to uproot this profession has not worked down the ages, and is not likely to do so. It is more important that stress be laid on positive alternatives for women in this position. The government has to face up to its responsibility for the health of mind and body of the country's citizens. A positive approach to health care and a sensitivity to their problems would be a good starting point. Education, job training and employment will keep them from being pulled back into the profession. Schooling for their children, registration and medicare together with a supportive caring attitude with some security for old age would go a long way to help these women explore other avenues of work.[38]

On 25 March, 1988 The Supreme Court issued notice to the Union of India and to the Delhi Administration as well as to the principal of the primary school where children from these localities studied that the father's name would not be necessary in application forms for entry to the school. The mother's name would suffice. The children could also stay as residents in the school.[39]

At 7 a.m. on 15 March, 1990, 112 persons were forcibly removed from their mothers' rooms in Delhi's red light area. The police detained them under The Juvenile Justice Act 1986 for being 'neglected children'. Photographs published in blatant contravention of the law caused the prostitutes thus identified great social harassment. Some so-called social welfare organisations went so far as to acclaim the heartless raid. The Chairman of The Juvenile Welfare Board decried the raid, adding that the so called 'juveniles' had babies with them, and the 'boys' had beards. However, it took another 5 years (until 24 February, 1995) for the court to declare that the action of the Board was correct and that the 'children' were not neglected. Media attention and protests by the mothers concerned, together with the judgment of the sessions court has stopped further raids by the police.[40] The point made was that a mother does not necessarily become less caring if she works as a prostitute.

Meanwhile caste and family honour continue to dog our steps. Fifteen year old Roshni, a high caste girl had eloped with Brijayandra, a low caste man in his early twenties. As punishment for an inter-caste marriage which had dishonoured Mehrana Village, the village *panchayat* decreed they were to be killed. They were axed on the border of Uttar Pradesh and Rajasthan and burnt before the police reached the spot.[41]

When in 1993 Shivpati's twenty year old son Rajesh picked a few peas from his higher caste neighbour's field, he was forced to watch his mother paraded naked through the entire village just to 'smash' his 'pride.'[42] Many such inter-caste crimes are reported, but the stony acceptance of these gory deeds should be a matter of grave concern. Villagers and relatives of yet another young couple from Khandrawali Village in Muzaffarnagar District watched dry eyed and even approved as the girl's uncle chopped off their heads as a harsh but necessary lesson for the transgression of societal norms.[43]

Fire has always wielded a strong symbolic influence on minds the world over. India is no exception. The custom of *sati* is one of its most powerful manipulative instruments. The well known Roop Kanwar *sati* was by no means the only *sati* that took place during the period under review.

Seventeen year old Javitri whose husband—an engineering student—was killed by miscreants, rushed to his home town in grief, only to find herself blamed for his death. Cut to the quick, she decided to commit *sati* in Jari Village, Uttar Pradesh in July 1979. She was followed by sixteen year old Om Kanwar of the Shekhawat clan who burnt herself on her husband's funeral pyre in August 1980, apparently without coercion, in the presence of an admiring crowd of two lakh persons in Jhadli Village 70 kilometres from Jaipur. The village *sarpanch* managed to bring the police by sunset to the spot, only to find it was all over.[44]

Fifty-five year old Dasiya of Kusuma Village, Uttar Pradesh, ministered to her paralysed husband for forty years, committing *sati* when he died in 1981. This was photographed in detail despite threats, by a courageous journalist Charan Pal Gupta. Between 1981 and 1983 there were at least six *satis* in Bilaspur District of Madhya Pradesh alone. Twenty-four year old Gayatri of Pangara Village fifteen kilometres from Kusuma, became a *sati* on 26 August, 1983. This was witnessed and condoned by the local administration, senior police officials and local politicians. In the same month Police Superintendent Prakash Nayudu managed to persuade an elderly astrologer to convince the inhabitants of a village in Panna District, Madhya Pradesh that dusk was an inauspicious time for the performing of *sati*. This done, the police moved in and quietly took the middle-aged Midiabai who was being forced into the act, safely away. Twenty-five year old Baijanti Bai of Umaria Dhirha Village in Madhya Pradesh was not so fortunate and became a *sati* on 26 September, 1986. One hundred and seventy persons were arrested at the site, jailed and later set free on bail. The scare of the possible arrest of her own sons following her contemplated *sati* stopped Dasiya Bai in Village Budra twenty kilometres from Baijanti Bai's village a year later, on 12 October, 1987.[45]

The most publicised *sati* in the sixteen years, since 1980, was that of young Roop Kanwar, an educated girl whose father was a teacher and father-in-law an educated government servant. She was burnt on her husband's funeral pyre on 4 September, 1987. Among those who came to pay their respects at the *sati* site which became something of a shrine, were a sitting judge of the Supreme Court, the Speaker of the Lok Sabha and a former Chief Justice of the Rajasthan High Court.[46] The entire country was electrified. Liberal minded citizens, media persons, activists, students and a few enlightened clerics like Swami Agnivesh mounted a sustained campaign against this gruesome form of oppressive fundamentalism. A group of young media persons created a powerful documentary film in very difficult circumstances, on the *sati* with on the spot filming and debate, entitled 'From The Burning Embers'.[47] It will never be quite clear whether Roop Kanwar was a willing *sati* or not, but voluntary or not, the impact of her action made an imense impact on the country, sparking off debate and agonised questioning among many young persons.

The Rajasthani girl brought up in traditional schools, has always had little doubt that this is the best way to achieve ultimate deification. Throughout her schooling she has sung songs in praise of *Ma Sati*[48] heard the tales of glorious *satis* and of the powerful *sat* that emanates from them. She knows that this energy can consume all who would dare to obstruct its progress to a triumphant finale.

Local tradition, reinforced by superstitious awe combine with the fear of social ostracism and the wrath of caste groups. At such moments even the police are often found to be incapable of interfering in the proceedings. Everyone stands to gain from the *sati*. Honour and glory accrue to the two families, power to the religious authorities and wealth and prosperity to the village as a future pilgrimage centre. As for the *sati* she goes in a blaze of glory and does not have to endure the accursed life of an unwanted widow.

Many years ago, Narayani Devi, daughter of a princely family of Rajasthan is said to have burnt herself to death to save her honour from the murderers of her husband. This act of courage is acclaimed by thousands in India and in South East Asia who revere her as a goddess: Rani Sati. Her blessings are invoked on family occasions, and newborn babies are brought to her temples to receive her blessing. As for the *sati pratha*[49] itself, it is believed to be gradually dying out.[50]

The Commission of Sati (Prevention) Act 1987 was rushed through by the Centre as a knee jerk reaction to the public uproar over the *sati* of Roop Kanwar, even though the original Act could have served the purpose if used in conjunction with existing legislation on criminal procedure.

The woman who is not interested in becoming a glorious *sati* needs a viable alternative and a powerful support structure that will guard her from the fierce opposition and social ostracism that would inevitably follow her refusal to immolate herself. This can only be done by a sustained and determined effort to demystify these and other traditionally sanctioned murders. It would entail an entire process of re-education. Without this continuing effort, this Act too will join its predecessors in a comfortable sleep on dusty shelves.

Conflicting views in ministries concerned with dowry and *sati* legislation have stalled a review of present laws in these subjects. The argument is whether the provisions of both the Acts can be incorporated in The Indian Penal Code, or whether special courts and prosecutors should be appointed to look into the possibility of further amending existing legislation in these matters.[51]

Sporadic cases of *sati* continue to be reported.[52] Had it not been for an alert watchman who rushed to inform the police of an impending *sati*, in the little village of Sopada about 60 kilometres from Jodhpur in March 1994, the Banda area of Uttar Pradesh would have had a *Sati Mata* of its very own. As it happened eighteen year old Rukmini was saved from a fiery death. The District Administration took her and her late husband's relatives under their care for questioning.[53] On 26 September, 1994, Banda was all agog. The normally sleepy little village of Pareri was enthusiastically collecting wood and incense sticks for a pyre to be built for teenaged Pawan and her dead husband in the fourth incident of its kind here. Brijlal the village watchman alerted the District Administration which swung into action and arrested Pawan. She was given a stern warning against committing suicide and released with two women guards who were deputed to stay in her house with her. Speculation that the desire for property was behind this aborted *sati* is rife.[54]

Witches are still branded, tortured or burnt with the complete approval of local society. An occasional gruesome case captures the headlines once in a while.

Random attacks on lone, helpless women have a cathartic effect on the community. Their death is supposed to remove famine, sickness or any other curse from the area. '*Jeb Katri*'[55] were the two words branded on the foreheads of four women from Sangrur in Punjab, arrested on mere suspicion. The branding was meant to serve as a warning to small time thieves. The public furore that resulted made the police atone for their sins by getting expensive plastic surgery performed on the women free of charge.[56]

By 1995, a number of unsuccessful operations later, the marks still remain. Whether the cruelty or violence is physical or mental, the aim is identical. The powerless must be kept in their appointed place. Swami Nischilananda of Puri, who, according to reports, was responsible for stopping a recitation of The Vedas by an erudite lady at a public function in Calcutta in January 1994, as he felt this was not permitted for a woman,[57] would, by this act, have violated her mind just as much as any physical assault would have done.[58]

Caste, revenge, power assertion in all its ramifications and political clout have expressed themselves in the period under review in religious rioting, continuing militancy and terrorism: The carnage in Delhi-1984, the Ahmedabad riots-1985, Fundamentalism in Ayodhya-1992, the reported mass rape of Muslim women in Surat-1992, the blasts and vicious rioting in Bombay-1993, the atrocities on Uttarakhand demonstrators-1994, the mass rape of brick kiln bonded labourers near Rohtak - December 1995, bomb blasts in Delhi - 1995 and 1996, and the continuing insurgency in Kashmir and in the North East — the list is endless. All these and many more have brought violence into sharp focus. In the ultimate analysis it is the poorest and most disadvantaged that suffer the most. From among these, it is the women who face the greatest hardship and have, perforce, to show the greatest strength, as they are the corner stone of every little demolished home which must be rebuilt after each calamity.

NOTES AND REFERENCES

1. The Living Room War by Mark, Thompson: 23 May, 1994.
2. Survival Evasion, Resistance and Escape.
3. Cadet's Sex Ordeal 'Worse Than War' by Christopher Goodwin, Los Angeles, The Sunday Times: The Times of India, 13 June, 1995.
4. The Pioneer April 16, 1993 quoting the Associated Press, Beijing.
5. World Update, The Pioneer, 15 December, 1993.
6. U.N. Newsletter, 9 September, 1995, vol. 50, no. 36.
7. *Ibid.*
8. Genital Mutilation is a Cruel Reality, by Kusum, The Pioneer, 9 November, 1994.
9. Female circumcision, The Pioneer, 12 December, 1994.
10. Kenyan men prefer 'circumcised' women, KISII, Kenya, 18 March, 1993: The Times of India, 19 March, 1993.
11. Women Anxious About Their Role in a Taliban Led Afghanistan: The Associated Press in The Stateman, 5 March, 1996.
12. Inter-Press Service, Istanbul: The Pioneer, 14 February, 1995.
13. The Lawyers, Volume 10, no. 5, May, 1995.
14. The Pioneer, 12 July, 1995.
15. Italian Feminists welcome new Bill on Rape and Sexual Crimes, Richard Owen in Rome, The Times, London, quoted in the Statesman, 10 February, 1996.
16. The Indian Express, 16 May, 1982.
17. AIDS study Trails Truckers, Kalpana Jain, The Times of India, 24 August, 1995.
18. Coomi Kapoor, Arun Shourie and Ashwini Sarin.
19. Order dated 23-11-1993, and Others—petitioners vs State of Madhya Pradesh and other respondents.
20. Six years after Kamla Trade is Almost Legal, M.J. Anthony, The Indian Express, 2 March, 1987.
21. Defying their Destiny, Bharat Desai, India Today, 15 October, 1995.
22. Girl Mortgaged and Then Sold in Ratlam, The Times of India, 4 June, 1983.
23. Six Years After Kamla, Trade is Almost Legal, M.J. Anthony, The Indian Express, 2 March, 1987: Also, Where Women Carry a Price Tag, Sanjay Suri, The Indian Express, 8 March, 1987.
24. Bisons.
25. Women in Arunachal: Sold at Birth, Bartered for Bisons, Sudamahi Regunathan, The Pioneer, 2 December, 1992.
26. Harijan Hands Over Daughter to Creditor, by D.S. Kumar, The Times of India, 8 October, 1993.
27. Avdash Kaushal, Chairman, Rural Litigation and Entitlement Kendra, Dehra Dun.

28. Trafficking in Women and Children for Sexual Exploitation by Sister Rita Rozario of The Joint Women's Programme 1987.
29. Protective homes for women run by government.
30. Additional material from The Times of India, 4 May, 1987: Distress Sale of Girls by Families, by Usha Rai.
31. Although cases registered under the Immoral Traffic (Prevention) Act 1986 have shown a steady decline since 1990 when 16,426 cases were recorded, to 12,496 in 1993, and 10,132 in 1994, the stories behind the many that were not registered will never be known.

Cases Registered Under The Immoral Traffic (Prevention) Act 1986		
Year	...	Number of Cases:
1990	...	16,426
1991	...	14,639
1992	...	12,580
1993	...	12,496
1994	...	10,132
Crime in India, 1994; p. 220. National Crime Records Bureau, Ministry of Home Affairs, New Delhi.		

32. The Dalit Sangharsh Samiti is working in this field.
33. Impact of Legislative Prohibition of the *Devadasi* Practice in Karnataka: A Study, by Asha Ramesh, May 1993.
34. Yellamma's Daughters of the Night, by Imran Qureshi, The Indian Express, 6 March, 1983.
35. *Devadasi* system prevalent in many states. The Pioneer, 8 June, 1994.
36. Ministries Tangle Stalls Dowry, '*sati*' Laws Review, Anita Katyal, The Times of India, 22 June, 1995.
37. See AIDS table Chapter 2.
38. *Aaj ki Amrapali* (Hindi), Sarla Mudgal, National Book Publishers, Delhi 1993.
39. Kalyani and several other organisations had been asking for such a provision for some time. Source: Sarla Mudgal, President, Kalyani, a social work organisation.
40. To be a Mother (or Child) on G.B. Road, a report by The AIDS Bhedbhav Virodhi Andolan, The Lawyers Vol. 10, No. 6, 1995.
41. Caste Put a Noose Around Them, Tabish Khair, The Times of India, 30 March, 1991.
42. Kurmis Perpetuate Feudalism in U.P. Villages, N.K. Singh, The Pioneer, 25 January, 1994.
43. Villagers Unmoved by Hacking of Couple, Gurmukh Singh, The Times of India, 12 August, 1993, also The Pioneer, 11 August, 1993: Dalits Beheaded for Falling in Love, Meena Baghel.

44. Sati in Modern India, a report by K. Sangeri and S. Vaid, presented in summary form in April 1981 at The National Conference on Women's Studies, Bombay.
45. The Burning Issue, The Indian Express (Magazine) 10 January, 1988, reported by Vidya Subramaniam, Chandrakant Naidu, Pushp Saraf and Charu Shahane.
46. Judges Among *Sati* Devotees, The Indian Express, 31 August, 1988: also SC to Take up Sati Mela Case: The Times of India, 31 August, 1988.
47. Mediastorm, now Mediastorm Cooperative.
48. Mother *Sati*.
49. Custom of *sati*.
50. Shri Shiv Shankar Babna, Trustee, Rani Sati Charitable Trust, Delhi.
51. Ministers' Tangle Stalls Dowry, '*Sati*' laws review, Anita Katyal, The Times of India, 22 June, 1995.
52. Sati Cases Registered under The Commission of Sati (Prevention) Act 1988.

1989: total cases registered:	36:	Uttar Pradesh and Maharashtra together reported 29 cases. Rajasthan-I.
1990: total cases registered:	52:	
1991: total cases registered:	17:	Haryana-9, West Bengal-6, Bihar-I, Pondicherry I case.
1992: total cases registered:	1:	Andhra Pradesh.
1993: total cases registered:	5:	Gujarat-2, Haryana-2, Rajasthan-I.

All persons accused in the 1987 Roop Kanwar, *sati* case were honourably acquitted in October 1996 for lack of sufficient evidence. This controversial judgement which re-affirms the stranglehold feudal values have over Rajasthan society is like to be appealed against.

53. The Times of India, 19 March, 1994.
54. Teenaged Widow Attempts *Sati*, The Pioneer, 8 October, 1994, by K. Rajit Ram.
55. Pick pocket.
56. Women are Not for Branding, The Pioneer, 13 January, 1994.
57. Women Unfit to Recite Vedas: Seer: Special Correspondent, The Pioneer, 19 January, 1994.
58. Wronging Rights, Frontline, 25 February, 1994.

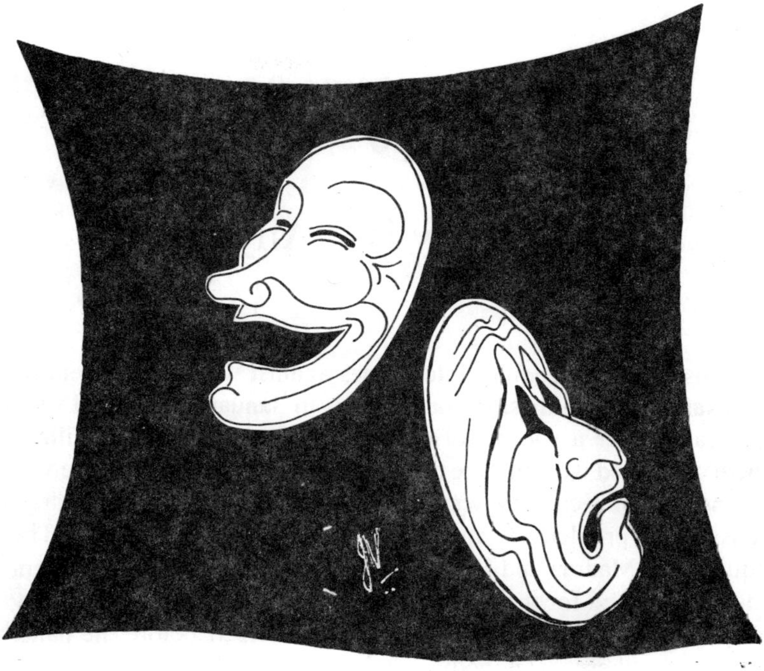

Because my mouth
Is wide with laughter
And my throat
Is deep with song,
You do not think
I suffer after
I have held my pain
So long?

Because my mouth
Is wide with laughter
You do not hear
My inner cry?
Because my feet
Are gay with dancing
You do not know
I die?

Langston Hughes, 'Minstrel Man' in *The Crisis*, December, 1925.

19

Whose Body is it Anyway?

An unusual public enquiry into crimes against women was held by The National Commission for Women in January 1995 in Delhi. This came after a successful experiment in a Pondicherry village where victimised women were dispensed justice by women themselves. The next public enquiry was held in December 1994 in Madras, focussing on problems women faced in the unorganised sector. The enquiries in Madras and Delhi were held before a jury of eminent judges renowned for their sensitivity and concern. Raped by twenty policemen, a Rajasthani woman prostrated herself before the panel screaming, 'there is nobody who can help me, not even the government or the Supreme Court!' She was one of fifty women and girls from five to fifty years old at the Delhi enquiry, who related horrific personal experiences ranging from child rape and bigamy to custodial rape.[1]

The shocking silence of the 1970s is still around us. Countrywide statistics of registered rape cases in 1993 totalled 12,242. 1994 totalled 13,208.[2] In both years the highest rape figures were obtained from Madhya Pradesh, Uttar Pradesh, Maharashtra and Bihar and Rajasthan in that order, with Delhi recording the highest number of cases from among the Union Territories.[3]

Statistics available with the National Crime Records Bureau show that rape among children below ten years increased from 233 in 1988 to 1,099 in 1991. Figures dipped to 532 in 1992, but rose again to 634 in 1993, and to 727 in 1994.

There has been a steady upward trend in acquittals in these cases over the last few years. Eighty per cent of rape cases were still pending trial at the time of writing.

When Santobai, a starving tribal woman was gang raped by ten drunken men including forest guards and a school master in September 1982, she did not know that an anti-rape law would be passed a year later that might have protected her. 'Santobai was not raped, only murdered' remarked the officer-in-charge of the police station at Kesla, Madhya Pradesh. He made a very cogent statement which has stood the test of time. 'The law', he said, 'will remain loyal to the culprits, and we will remain loyal to the law.'[4] The strict accountability of the police is a very necessary ingredient in the legislative process. Without keen vigilance in this matter, courts will continue to let perpetrators of crimes off the hook.

On the night of 26 March, 1972, fifteen year old Mathura, a tribal labourer was assaulted and raped by a Head Constable and a police constable. This had taken place inside the Desai Gunj police station in Maharashtra. The case would never have been registered if it had not been for a vociferous crowd that gathered outside and forced the authorities to file a first information report. Dazed by the attack, Mathura could never have imagined her rape case would have far reaching implications.

As it happened, The Mathura case became a rallying point for all thoughtful citizens, with legal experts calling for a fresh look at existing legislation on rape. On 1 June, 1974, the sessions judge at Chandrapur, Maharashtra called young Mathura 'a shocking liar whose testimony is riddled with falsehoods and improbabilities.' A slur was cast on her character, and no rape proven. However, the Nagpur Bench of the Bombay High Court reversed the order, sentencing the two constables to rigorous imprisonment, stating that Mathura's silence because of intimidation could not be taken to mean that she had consented to the act of rape. The dismissed constables filed an appeal before the Supreme Court, where the judgement was completely reversed and the accused constables acquitted. On 15 September, 1978, a bewildered Mathura heard the honourable judges[5] state that since she had no marks of struggle on her body, and had not raised an alarm, nor offered any resistance, it followed that she had 'consented to the act' and that 'the alleged intercourse was a peaceful affair. The onus is always on the prosecution to prove afirmatively each ingredient of the offence it seeks to establish,' the judgement continued, 'such onus never shifts.'[6]

This judgement from The Supreme Court sent shock waves throughout the country. There was a storm of protest and a demonstration before The Supreme Court calling for a rehearing of the case. Four eminent university legal experts, Lotika Sarkar, Upendra Baxi, Vasudha Dhagamvar and Raghunath Kelkar wrote an open letter to The Chief Justice of India denouncing the judgement which 'snuffs out all aspirations for the protection of human rights of millions of Mathuras.' Several demands were made for the re-opening of the case including one by the Government of Maharashtra[7] but they were all brushed aside on technical grounds. The Mathura Case had become a *cause celébre.*

If Mathura had been in The Supreme Court on 24 May and on 2 June, 1983, she whould have felt somewhat vindicated. Both cases were in appeal. The first case was from Gujarat where two girls aged 12 and 13 had been sexually assaulted on 7 September, 1975 by a government servant, father of one of their friends. The case was heard by Justices A.P. Sen and M.P. Thakkar. Justice M.P. Thakkar, delivering the judgement said, 'human goodness has limits—human depravity has none. In the Indian setting, refusal to act on the testimony of a victim of sexual assault in the absence of corroboration as a rule, is adding insult to injury. Why should the evidence of the girl or the woman who complains of rape or sexual molestation be viewed with the aid of spectacles fitted with lenses tinged with doubt, disbelief or suspicion? To do so is to justify the charge of male chauvinism in a male dominated society.' The Court upheld the substantive sentence imposed by The High Court retaining the fine, but unfortunately reduced the sentence of rigorous imprisonment from 2 1/2 years to 15 months since the accused had lost his job because of The High Court judgement and endured seven years of humiliation.[8]

In the second case there was a more positive judgement. Sheikh Zakir, an influential person of Purnea, Bihar, raped Barki a twenty-five year old Santhal woman on 7 August, 1968. He was convicted by both the trial court and the High Court and sentenced to 5 years rigorous imprisonment. His appeal was heard in the Supreme Court by Justices E.S. Venkataramiah and V. Balakrishna Eradi. The judgement delivered on 2 June, 1983 stated, 'The prosecuritx and her husband were from a backward community living in a remote area..they could not be expected to rush to a doctor after the occurrence of the incident, and the absence of any injuries on the person of...the helpless victim of rape might not by itself discredit the statement of the prosecutrix.' The five year rigorous imprisonment sentence was upheld and the appeal dismissed.[9]

Meanwhile the national debate on the weakness and the ineffectiveness of anti-rape legislation continued. It was strongly felt that although the judges were, by and large, sensitive to the traumatic predicament of the rape victim, the rapist invariably received a light sentence. The Law Commission was asked to study these laws. Finally, The Criminal Law (Amendment) 1983 was passed on 26 December, 1983. This measure clearly stated that a woman's personal conduct before the crime would not have any bearing on the proceedings of a rape case, and that the onus of proving innocence for custodial rapes only, as it would have been in Mathura's case, where the accused were custodians of the law, would be shifted to the accused instead of the victim as had so far been the case. Also since custodial rape is more heinous than rape by persons who are not called on by the law to protect the victim, *reliance would be placed solely on the evidence of the victim*. In the case of a pregnant woman being raped, or gang raped, it would be presumed that the victim did not give her consent, as would be the case in other custodial rape cases.

The minimum punishment for custodial rape was now fixed at a mandatory 10 years of rigorous imprisonment. This was an important step taken for the rights of women though it was only custodial rape that was singled out for such severe punishment.

It is a sad commentary on the importance attached by parliamentarians to this legislation, that on the day the Bill was passed, only fifteen members of Parliament and one minister deemed it necessary to be present on the occasion in Parliament House.[10]

By 31 January, 1989 Suman Rani, a young girl who had been repeatedly raped in the premises of the Bhiwani police station on 21 March, 1984, found the amended law did not seem to apply in her case. In spite of both the trial court and the High Court having awarded the two guilty policemen the new Act's mandatory punishment of 10 years rigorous imprisonment, and having condemned the crime in no uncertain terms, the Supreme Court willed otherwise.

While quoting the senior counsel's conclusion that Suman Rani 'was a woman of questionable character and easy virtue with lewd and lascivious behaviour,' the Court reduced the sentence of the two accused from 10 to 5 years each. This judgement from the apex court was blatantly discriminatory as against that of the trial court that had so admirably stated that 'even a girl of easy virtue is entitled to all the protection of the law and cannot be compelled to sexual intercourse against her will.'[11]

Another landmark of the last sixteen years is the sordid case of Maya, Tyagi. On 18 June, 1980, Maya together with her husband and some friends was on her way to a wedding when their car stalled at Baghpat in the vicinity of Meerut. After an altercation with the police, her husband and friends were shot dead in cold blood. Four month pregnant Maya Tyagi was stripped naked and dragged to the police station before a crowd of some two thousand five hundred people. Here, she said she was gang raped and brought out bleeding. It took three years for the case to be filed. Maya had alleged rape and brutal torture. Although the prosecution had cited 120 witnesses, several adjournments and the posting of the case in far off courts over the years made Maya give up any hope she might have entertained of justice. Miraculously her baby Deepak was saved. 'For us', she said darkly, 'the government is blind.'[12] On 24 January, 1988, Mr. Vishnu Dutt Dubay, Additional and District Judge, sentenced six of the policemen involved in the shooting of Maya Tyagi's husband to death. Others were awarded life imprisonment, but the main culprit got off as he was absent from court.[13]

On July 1990 two nuns of St. Mary's Convent, Gajraula, Uttar Pradesh, were raped and five sisters assaulted in the convent. The convent's money was also stolen. After five years,[14] a positive judgement was delivered at the Supreme Court by Justice Venkatachala, indicting and suspending three officers including the sub-inspector and the doctor who had made serious charges against the character of the nuns, as well as the officer-in-charge of the police station. The state government had to pay compensation to the tune of 2.50 lakhs to each of the two nuns and one lakh each to the sisters assaulted.[15] The Gajraula incident had also created a furore as a prominent weekly had named the victims in direct contravention of Section 228 A of The Indian Penal Code which expressly forbids publication of a rape victim's identity without her permission. On 13 April, 1995 five more nuns who were planning to start a nursery school in Surya Nagar on the Delhi Uttar Pradesh border were seriously injured by unknown assailants.[16]

The toll mounts up. The *sathins*[17] who have been working to implement the Women's Development Programmes of awareness, literacy and development in Rajasthan found one of their number in trouble. On 22 September, 1992 Bhanwari Devi was gang raped by five men from the powerful Gujjar cast for having tried to stop a child marriage in Bhateri Village in the Bassi Assembly constituency in 1992 at the instance of the state government. She was completely ostracised by her husband's family and the village for making the fact of her rape public. She received The Neerja Bhanot Award for her courage and dedicated work, but found all her support systems crumbling before an all powerful caste structure. In 1995, The Women's Development Programme invited the *sarpanches* (heads) of the area on February 23, to seek their support for their awareness programmes against child marriage. At the meeting, 39 *sarpanches*, 13 of whom were women, humiliated Bhanwari Devi and tried to pressurise her to withdraw the case against her molestors who had ben arrested, as this was a blot on the honour of their caste and society. They implied her award and compensation money had been manipulated. A Gujjar even offered the Women's Development Programme Rs. 21,000/- to get his fellow caste members freed. This blatant coercion shook 30 of the male *sarpanches* who along with the 13 women later admitted to have been pressurised to speak with one voice at the meeting. One of the women went as far as to say, 'the government might as well wrap up its reservation policy for women on panchayats if the men insist on shouting and do not allow us to function![18]

Power and caste emerged triumphant at the District and Sessions Court, Jaipur on 15 November, 1996, where Bhanwari Devi and her supportive husband Mohan awaited an elusive justice. All five of the men accused of the gang rape were acquitted as clean upstanding 'upper caste men', even including 'a *Brahmin*'. 'The rape,' stated the judge categorically, 'could not have taken place, because Bhanwari was from a lower caste.' Moreover, the accused were middle-aged men and therefore 'respectable citizens.' 'Rape,' the judgement continued, is 'usually committed by teenagers.' Mohan's credibility as a witness was summarily dismissed as unlike a 'traditional husband', he stood by and did not protect his wife. This, whilst the same judgement convicted two of the five men who had assaulted Mohan as he tried to save Bhanwari, for simple assault. Bhanwari Devi was branded 'a liar' and her testimony discounted as worthless.

This grossly discriminatory judgement has shocked all right minded citizens. A writ has been filed in the Supreme Court seeking to 'enforce women's right to an environment free from sexual violence in the workplace', especially when they are employed as agents of change in traditional minded and hostile surroundings. Several national organisations, lawyers and the National Commission for Women are signatories to this cause, and a forum has been formed by Bhanwari Devi's co-workers and several others to support her. The Central Bureau of Investigation has filed a case in this behalf.[19]

However, there is a glimmer at the end of the tunnel. When Bodhisattwa Gautam, a lecturer in Kohima inveigled a trusting girl student into a liaison in 1989, he did not know he would be responsible for that glimmer. On the young woman's insistence, he secretly married her. Two forced abortions later, he deserted his gullible victim. Forced to face the truth, she filed a case against him. Gautam's efforts to deflect the course of justice failed, and the Supreme Court dismissed his petition. In a historic judgement, the court ordered him to pay Subhra Chakraborty Rs. 1000/- as interim compensation while the case was being heard in Kohima, plus 'arrears of compensation at the same rate from the date on which the complaint was filed until this day.' The judges held that 'rape is less a sexual offence than an act of aggression aimed at degrading and humiliating women.'[20]

With this positive judgement which should go a long way towards rehabilitating the rape victim, the wronged woman's right to interim relief has been established, it is hoped that lengthy bureaucratic procedures and other delays do not come in the way of prompt payment.

Picking up courage to report a rape at a police station is a shattering experience for women all over the world. For a village woman whose life is hemmed in by taboos it is even more so. Thirty year old Neetaben Goswami was raped on 6 July, 1991 by three of the most influential men in Dadva Village, District Bhavnagar, Gujarat. She and her husband approached The District Superintendent of Police. Many travails later, including the burning down of their home and shop, they reached The High Court. Neetaben was given police protection and the culprits were jailed. Braving social ostracism and continuing threats from her attackers out on bail, this gutsy woman stood for and won the village elections. Now as *Sarpanch* of Dadva Village promising a radical health reform programme, she is a symbol of hope for the 5,000 villagers who live under an ever-present threat from anti-social elements.[21]

Rural women seem to prefer going to their *panchayats* or municipalities with their cases even though they may not always get justice, but they feel the members of these bodies can empathise with their situations better than impersonal courts who speak incomprehensible legalese and function in an alien atmosphere, also because the decisions are made faster. This has become more so since the reservation of seats for women by The *Panchayati Raj*. A 1994 study, 'Atrocities Against Women in the Punjab' seems to confirm this. The researchers found that while dowry killings and eve teasing was an urban phenomenon, wife beating, molestation and rape were preponderantly rural based. Even though the lowliest and least influential were normally judged unfavourably, a large number of cases were brought to *panchayats*, municipalities, *mahila mandals*[22] and voluntary agencies, and were not registered with the police. Five thousand six hundred and seventy-eight cases of rape went unreported as against 83 registered with the police and eleven thousand, one hundred and ninety-eight molestations were not reported as against 30 reported. The unreported cases went to the groups mentioned above.[23]

The need for a special kind of court sensitive to women's issues had been mooted since the late 1960s: a court which could ensure confidentiality, where women judges were preferred and an informal atmosphere prevailed without the presence of expensive lawyers. It was felt that stressful adversarial litigation vitiated domestic disputes, and that a family court with flexible procedures would better serve the purpose of discussion and settlement. A number of legal luminaries have been prominently connected with this idea. The Law

Commission in its 54th report in 1973 and in its 59th. report in 1974, repeatedly called for the establishment of family courts. On 14 September, 1984, the Family Courts Act was finally enacted. These are civil courts in which judges with at least seven years judicial experience are appointed. Preference is given to women judges. Reconciliation and the preservation of the institution of marriage is of primary importance. The court's jurisdiction is that of a district court and appeals can be made to the high court. Counsellors, social welfare agencies and medical experts are represented on the bench.

The court can lay down its own procedures. Family courts are already functioning in a number of states with varying degrees of success. Some women's organisations and authorities on the subject feel that a restructuring is needed. These courts need to be set up in each district of a state so as to provide easy access to families in trouble. A review must be made every six months. Others feel that the heavy handed emphasis in family courts on reconciliation at all costs, has sent many women weeping back to their original stressful situations. Others feel it is difficult to deal with insensitive judges and juridical problems between family courts and high courts. Hopefully a regular review of the progress of these courts by state governments will gradually ease their growing pains, and the family courts set forth on their task in the spirit of service as was originally intended.

Mahila courts, women's courts, were started in 1994. They have the same procedure as criminal courts. A woman judge and a woman public prosecutor deal with matrimonial disputes, property and guardianship. They have the same jurisdiction as a district court. Men who originally objected to appearing before a woman judge are now glad to receive even-handed justice. Unfortuntely a heavy back log of cases plagues these courts.

It would be unrealistic to leave out of this update a minor but unfortunate trend in the nature of crime which is beginning to surface in the last year or so. The Delhi Police's Crime Against Women Cell states that nearly 15 per cent of the nine thousand cases registered with them until July 1994 were genuine cases of husbands falsely implicated by their wives under Section 498 A of The Indian Penal Code and under other legislation which has ironically so far been a boon for the majority of women brutalised in their marital homes.

These legal provisions are being misused by some women and their families to extract money and goods, or merely for vendetta. Occasionally muscle men are also brought into the act.[24] Some cases have occurred of decent parents-in-law who, in the present climate of concern for the young wife, become easy targets for constant criticism and are not allowed to lead a dignified life. These cases are however minuscule compared with the overwhelming numbers where wives are at the receiving end.

However, this process must be nipped in the bud, and stern action taken to prevent the misuse of laws which are the result of so much concern and dedicated work. There is a great need for studies on this and other perversions of the legal system. Awareness and support systems must be built up in neighbourhoods so that exploitation of anyone who is innocent and dependent ceases.

NOTES AND REFERENCES

1. Women losing faith in courts, police: Press Trust of India, The Times of India, 17 January, 1995.
2. National Crime Records Bureau.
3. See table on Incidence of Rape in India, p. 304.
4. A Women Against Ten Men in a Rest House, Sudip Mazumdar, The Indian Express, 4 November, 1982.
5. Jaswant Singh, P.S. Kailasam and A.D. Koshal jj.
6. Tukaram and another vs State of Maharashtra: 1979 AIR SC 185.
7. The Indian Express: 3 February, 1982.
8. 1983 3 Supreme Court Cases 217.Cr. Appeal No. 68 of 1977 A.P. Sen, M.P. Thakkar jj.
9. AIR 1983 Supreme Court 911: Cri. LJ 1285: E.S. Venkataramiah and V. Balakrishna Eradi JJ.
10. The Statesman: 2 December, 1983.
11. 1989 Supp(1) Supreme Court Cases 286, before B.C. Ray and S. Ratnavel Pandian, jj. Decided on January 31, 1989.
12. The Statesman, 18 June, 1985: Neerja Choudhury.
13. The Sunday Observer, 1 January to 6 Febuary, 1988: Justice Delayed is Small Compensation by Jyoti Malhotra.
14. The All India Women's Democratic Association and others were active in the nuns' cause.
15. Compensation Ordered for Rape Victims: The Times of India, 2 February, 1995.
16. The Times of India, 3 April, 1995.
17. Grass root workers of Rajasthan.

18. Raped Activist's Struggle for Justice, Divya Arora, The Pioneer, 8 September, 1993: The Irrelevant Women of Feudal Rajasthan by Bhavdeep Kang, The Pioneer, 22 October, 1993: Sarpanches elect to Humiliate Bhanwari, Usha Rai, The Indian Express, 22 March, 1995.
19. Crime and Acquittal, Editorial, The Indian Express, 28 November, 1995:
    Also: press release 22 November, 1995, signed by several women's organisations and The National Commission for Women, The writ has been filed in the Supreme Court by Vishaka a Rajasthani organisation.
20. 1995 (7) Scale: page 228: Shri Boddhisattva Gautam vs Miss Subhra Chakraborthy, Kuldip Singh, S. Saghir Ahmad, jj.
21. A Rape Victim Strikes Back Through The Ballot, Suresh Samani and Aparana Borker, The Indian Express, 17 August, 1995.
22. Women's organisations.
23. A study for the Chandigarh based Institute for Development Studies by Dr. Pramod Kumar and Ms. Rainuka Dagar, Sponsored by The State Department of Social Welfare. Most Crimes Against Women go Unreported, Surinder Awasthi, The Times of India, 31 May, 1995.

24. Delhi Registers Abnormal Rise in Husband-bashing, Poornima Joshi, The Pioneer, 8 July, 1994. See attached table on suicides.

Table 1. 1993 Age-wise Distribution of Suicides by Causes (Selected) All India — Male and Female

Age in Years	*Below 18*		*18-30*		*30-50*		*Above 50*		*Total Women*	*Total Men*	*Combined Total*
	M	*F*	*M*	*F*	*M*	*F*	*M*	*F*			
Causes											
Quarrel with Parents-in -law	256	306	927	1644	620	586	122	92	2628	1925	4553
Quarrel with Spouse	106	171	928	1762	938	731	229	86	2750	2201	4951
Dowry Dispute	2	106	38	1155	19	218	6	7	1486	65	1551
Age-Wise Totals	364	583	1893	4561	1577	1535	357	185			

Table 2. 1994 Age-wise Distribution of Suicides by Causes (Selected) All India — Male and Female

Age in Years	*Below 18*		*18-30*		*30-50*		*Above 50*		*Total Women*	*Total Men*	*Combined Total*
	M	*F*	*M*	*F*	*M*	*F*	*M*	*F*			
Causes											
Quarrel with Parents-in -law	257	343	993	1608	503	487	107	57	2495	1860	4355
Quarrel with Spouse	136	193	1035	1727	979	797	265	82	2799	2415	5214
Dowry Dispute	10	149	47	1267	11	194	6	3	1613	74	1687
Age-Wise Totals	403	685	2073	4602	1493	1478	378	142			

Tables 1 and 2 are compiled by the author from 'Age-wise Distribution of Suicides by Causes' from Accidental Deaths and Suicides in India 1993 and 1994 respectively, National Crime Records Bureau, Ministry of Home Affairs, New Delhi.

Addenda

Incidence of Rape in India

State	1990	1991	1992	1993	1994
Andhra Pradesh	599	688	763	827	873
Arunachal Pradesh	18	32	25	29	28
Assam	423	427	442	508	530
Bihar	731	633	1019	775	1130
Goa	10	18	12	13	8
Gujarat	232	253	285	266	356
Haryana	131	134	215	189	258
Himachal Pradesh	54	91	83	87	110
Jammu & Kashmir	118	124	123	136	109
Karnataka	159	177	150	220	281
Kerala	174	203	212	168	197
Madhya Pradesh	2302	2532	2658	2486	2929
Maharashtra	859	885	961	1107	1304
Manipur	14	13	17	5	5
Meghalaya	29	27	25	21	34
Mizoram	63	44	34	32	44
Nagaland	1	1	1	0	2
Orissa	239	285	302	372	436
Punjab	57	59	61	87	108
Rajasthan	740	803	818	890	1002
Sikkim	3	9	11	4	9
Tamil Nadu	243	250	232	186	237
Tripura	74	57	73	69	61
Uttar Pradesh	1524	1400	1735	1754	2078
West Bengal	543	461	615	740	743
Total (States)	9340	9606	10872	10971	12882
UNION TERRITORIES					
Andaman & Nicobar Islands	3	3	5	3	4
Chandigarh	11	7	15	4	6
Dadra & Nagar Haveli	3	4	1	0	2
Daman & Diu	1	1	1	1	1
Delhi	150	161	215	255	309
Lakshadweep	0	0	0	0	0
Pondicherry	10	11	3	8	4
Total (Union Territories)	178	187	240	271	326
Total (All India)	9518	9793	11112	11242	13208

Crime in India 1990 to 1994 publications: Crime Against Women, National Crime Records Bureau, Ministry of Home Affairs, New Delhi.

20

Where do we go from here?

The mental churning of the late 1970s and early 80s with daily exposés of the vicious torture and killing of young married women, an increasing number of rapes, female foeticide, religious fundamentalism and subsequent riots, brought about an intense desire in a number of educated and privileged women to make a positive contribution. Those were heady days when several admirable beginnings were made and a feeling of *camaraderie* among workers grew. Women with special skills : artists, lecturers, dramatists, poets, lawyers, writers, business persons, film makers and others from all walks of life formed a number of organisations, many of which continue to this day. Others acted as catalysts. A number of thoughtful men with progressive ideas joined in. Women and media cells began to monitor the portrayal of women in the media with follow-ups on relevant themes. Plays, debates and writings attacked the growing cancer of inter-religious suspicion and violence. Women began to discover they were not alone. Women's oppression and dowry deaths formed part of the repertoir of a number of street plays by groups who focussed on the plight and empowerment of the powerless and marginalised. On 1 January 1989, While The Jan Natya Manch[1] was performing a street play upholding workers in their struggle for a dignified life, they were attacked by an anti-worker group incensed by the players' identification with the workers' cause. Safdar Hashmi, the moving spirit and leading light of the group was killed.

Naming all the persons and action groups around the country working for the awakening and empowerment of women would be a herculean task. I only mention a few by way of illustration while saluting the many others to whose dedicated work we owe the immense spread of awareness, the positive judgements and humane laws, even with their many limitations, that have created the more open climate that exists today. Manushi, the magazine that has championed women and given them a forum, brought out its first issue on 1 January, 1979. Baiji, a Marathi magazine for women appeared about the same time, while Kali for Women, a publishing house for books for women was established in 1984.

Meera Dewan's film 'Gift of Love' on torture and rape for dowry was screened the same year. Add to these, the later contributions made by numerous dedicated film makers, thinkers, planners, professionals and women in decision making positions...

Nevertheless, the question that springs to the mind is where do we go from here? How do we deal with continuing die-hard attitudes? Participants in a tribunal on rape and dowry crimes find an Indian magistrates's statement printed on the brochure: 'When a woman walks alone, she asks to be raped.'[2] Young Shanti from Madras is told by her father that her husband has a right to beat her. A women's organisation in Bangalore[3] is unable to stop a twentytwo year old woman's marriage to a man whose first wife died after suffering fourteen years of violent harassment for not getting him three lakh rupees from her father. An investigation against him was still on. When the dead woman's parents join their pleas to those of the women's organisation, the father of the bride-to-be states he has already paid fifteen thousand rupees to the groom. His honour is at stake. Whatever is written in his daughter's fate cannot be changed.

When Shanta spurned a most eligible bachelor from a dowry hungry family in the 1970s, she shattered the town's image of a sacrificing bride and her abject family, earning laurels for her school master father and her family. For the same reason Minoo Duggal, a twenty-five year old school teacher refused to marry an army captain in October 1994. Her father, a Colonel, posted a notice on the marriage hall announcing, 'Today's marriage cancelled due to heavy dowry demands. Inconvenience regretted.' Minoo, planning to return to teaching, was lionised, and the newspaper office which had carried the report was flooded with callers seeking the 'courageous' girl's whereabouts.[4] Barely six months later the papers reported she was being blamed for having disgraced her family and jeopardised her marital prospects. Hopefully Ms. Duggal treats this with the contempt it deserves.[5]

Meera and Shashibala, two sisters, were brides-to-be at Muradnagar in Uttar Pradesh. Seventy thousand rupees—a sum their watchman father could ill afford, had been given to their prospective in-laws as settled. When even more impossible demands were made at the ceremony itself and fake jewellery for the brides was sought to be passed off as real, the brides' family called off the wedding.

There was a happy ending with two brothers from a family known to the girls' parents, offering themselves as grooms. 'They may not be rich,' beamed an ailing Rajwati, 'but the boys are good and will not trouble our girls.'[6]

Eighteen year old Dimple from Muzaffarnagar, Uttar Pradesh, stopped her wedding when she found her almost-would-have-been husband surprising her parents during the ceremony with a demand for a scooter, a 'fridge and a colour television set over and above what had already been given him. The groom was kept hostage for three days until his mother arrived to settle the wedding bills. An exultant Dimple exhorted girls in similar situations to 'act boldly' to end 'the dowry menace'. She has no regrets and plans to continue her studies.[7]

Ingrained attitudes hound us even when Indians settle abroad as was the case with Priya Bhat, chosen Miss University in Delhi. She fell in love and secretly married Feisal Khan. Changing her religion and her name, she flew to live with his family in Canada. A baby girl was born to them. Priya now Naazish, was found murdered in the family car. Her father-in-law was charged with the murder. The shocking fact is that this was not the only case of a woman being murdered in the sixty thousand strong Indo-Canadian community.[8]

What is a daughter worth today? Madhubala Mittal, a bright sixteen year old pre-medical student from the Punjab died in a road accident in 1983. Her parents' plea for a one lakh rupee compensation including four to five thousand rupees for medical expenses was rejected outright by the presiding officer of The Motor Accident Claims Tribunal. His argument was that quite apart from not earning anything, 'she must rather be a liability for the applicants.' Since the unproductive young girl was a 'burden' on her parents, 'they could not have suffered any pecuniary loss.' Later, the High Court awarded the parents forty thousand rupees. The harried parents went in appeal to the Supreme Court which awarded them one lakh rupees as compensation deeming the amount asked 'very reasonable', together with an interest of '12 per cent per annum from the date of the claim until the payment from the respondents.' The Court castigated the Tribunal for its 'utter insensitivity' and dubbed its order 'perverse'. The High Court also came in for censure for having whittled down the 'meagre' amount of one lakh rupees to forty thousand.[9]

Everyone remembers the appealing little face of eleven year old Ameena who was prevented from following her sixty year old husband Yahya H.M. Al-Sagish to Saudi Arabia in 1991. She made headlines every day. Now she lives forgotten in Hyderabad[10] Fatima, Asiya Begum, Shahnaz and Kaneez Begum, all between fourteen and fifteen years of age, and a host of others have since been married or sold off to elderly foreigners. Occasionally, uninformed handling of the situation has led to avoidable disaster. Be that as it may, crimes against women and children have become so routine that they have become part of cursory breakfast reading. A spurt of interest, a sigh or two, and we forget it all. These are all far too divorced from our own lives to alter the taste of the tea.

But somewhere, almost imperceptibly, a quiet current is flowing. A moving tribute to a daughter, the first of its kind that I noticed, appeared in the papers in 1983[11] when dowry deaths were very much in the news. A wedding photograph of a beautiful bride caught my eye. It was accompanied by an excerpt from a Supreme Court judgement: 'Gurinder Kaur was a girl of good family, of refined character and well educated. Brought up in a house where the dowry system was regarded as an evil to be opposed, it can be presumed that she rebelled strongly against the attempts at extortion directed against her father. The greed for dowry and indeed the dowry system as an institution calls for the severest condemnation.' This was a tribute not only to Gurinder Kaur, but also to her parents who dared to go public in their condemnation of evil at a time when it took courage to stand up and be counted. It is most ironic that this heartfelt cry of the 1980s pleading for the empowerment of women *before* they are killed is still a subject for seminars today. Another positive gesture came from Jyoti Vinod Chagedia, a twenty-one year old mother of two who was hospitalised in a critical condition after she was allegedly hurled out of the window of her marital home by her mother-in-law. Even her children were not allowed to meet her. She donated her eyes to the eye bank, so that 'my eyes could see my children.' Subsequently the children were brought to her by order of the court.[12]

Sporadic cases are beginning to be reported of neighbours who are taking supportive action in these matters. Unfortunately the emphasis continues to be more on action after things have gone well beyond control, and the victim is either dying or is already dead.

When Kiran Bala was done to death in Chandigarh on 27 June, 1986, Ashvini Kumar was sentenced to ten years rigorous imprisonment by the sessions court with a fine of thirty thousand rupees for her murder. This was entirely due to the dedicated struggle of her neighbours and some local organisations to bring the murderer to justice.[13] The men of The Punjab Provident Employees Union stood firmly with their women neighbours and organisations in denouncing one of their own sex who had transgressed the law of nature.[14]

In the case of the death of twenty five year old Shashikala on 7 November, 1987 in the small town of Tiptur in the Tumkur District of Karnataka, it was not just a neighbour or two, but the entire population of the little town of around forty thousand inhabitants that turned out to condemn a death they were certain was a murder. They forced the police to handcuff Shashikala's doctor husband. A procession of thousands escorted the body to the cremation ground with coolies shouting that even they knew how to treat their wives although they were poor. A small tea shop worker screamed, 'they gave him three lakhs, but he wanted more!' No local lawyer would touch his brief.The boycot against the family was enforced spontaneously in adjacent towns as well. When Shashikala's in-laws left Tiptur to stay with their other son in neighbouring Ammasandra, the local residents and the police forced them to leave. Dowry had become a vile word indeed![15] This torch of neighbour power was picked up by the neighbours of twenty-six year old Daljit who was burnt to death on 27 April, 1992.[16] A neighbour who braved the billowing smoke said, 'I saw her burning. I am willing to do anything to see that justice is done.' In spite of adverse circumstances and threats, a number of Daljit's neighbours are also determined to help. In Tripta Sharma's case,[17] her colleagues from The Central Ordnance Depot had been most forthcoming in their help, and one particularly, has been extremely useful in establishing the prosecution case, maintaining records and evidence which were left out by the police. This kind of sensitivity needs to be applauded and encouraged if the arduous battle against crime against helpless victims is to be won.

Lawyers and social workers agree that a time frame must be set for every trial with day-to-day hearings by the judge,[18] and that investigations must be carried out by special investigating teams which should include women's organisations.[19] For lack of this kind of organisation, and with the collusion between some lawyers and the powers that be, it has taken seven years for the process of Arveen's trial to be set in motion at all. Forty dates had been set for this trial over this period.[20]

After so much time witnesses cannot be expected to remember crucial details. Others can be bought over. Even the murdered woman's relatives have been known to succumb to the lure of money.

Slowly but surely our age old one-to-one relationship with the Creator is beginning in sporadic cases, to take the form of a triangle of concern which includes the neighbour. Women are also beginning to see themselves as persons of worth. They are entering politics, the police, the armed forces, the media, banking, business, the airlines, and the field of self-employment. Ila Bhat's Self Employed Women's Association (SEWA) that has helped thousands of women in the unorganised sector: vegetable sellers, the landless, fisherwomen, weavers and the lowest caste *Dalit*[21] women, can now use their resources to market their products and manage their own money. With the help of Friends of Women's World banking, it has become possible for these marginalised women numbering about forty-five thousand, to run their own enterprises in just a few years. Landless and *Dalit* women are also being involved in this scheme in Kerala, Karnataka, Maharashtra, Gujarat, and along the Madhya Pradesh-Uttar Pradesh border. With training in management skills, accounting and linkages with insurance companies and development corporations, these women are beginning to walk the road of achievement. The ultimate objective is to set up an Investment Indian Women's Fund.[22]

In spite of opposition from their men, women from the North East where there are strong Mothers' Union groups in Nagaland, Mizoram and Manipur, fight against liquor, drugs and vice. Violence has been used against women in Himachal who have been fighting for the same cause. In Orissa and Andhra Pradesh and elsewhere, women have managed to a great extent to win this battle. In some states these liquor wars have resulted in a ban on the sale of liquor.

Women and the police have had a continuing uneasy relationship, generally antagonistic and mutually suspicious. Speak to any poor woman in the country, and a picture of a brutal, baton wielding cop will immediately emerge. In spite of gang rape, atrocities, inexcusable roles during riot and other explosive situations, the 1980s and '90s are seeing some slow but discernable hints of a change in this relationship. The age-old trend still continues, but there has been an opening up with enlightened leadership in the police force itself taking the lead. Unfortunately, this does not often peter down to the lower *echelon* and the beat constable. However, there is a questioning and introspection among the police themselves looking for a change in attitudes towards women and interrogation and investigative techniques. The possibility of womens' crisis control service centres run by sensitised women is being mooted.

Experienced counsellors are beginning to receive invitations to conduct counselling courses for the police from the level of Assistant Commissioner of Police downwards. Counselling is focussed on gender sensitisation, the learning of inter-personal skills and on communication techniques. Some of these courses have been carried out in Delhi, Bombay, Calcutta, Hyderabad and other cities. Karnataka's *Mahila Samakhya*, a government sponsored project, conducts workshops for the police from district level down to the lowest cadre. The root of the trouble however, lies at the level of the local police station. It is here that the traumatised victim needs to be reassured, and made to remember each detail of the incident necessary for a comprehensive first information report. The victim's entire future depends on the commitment of the staff of the police station. They can make or break her. This is also where a good policeman should be willing and able to explain to her what her rights are according to the law. A very great deal more needs to be done to bridge the gap of fear between women and the police.

Women have now entered the police and are here to stay.[23] Unfortunately far too often they feel they are expected to conform to the usual callous image. It is of the utmost importance that an overhaul of police attitudes to the public be undertaken and intensive re-education and sensitisation programmes be taken up around the country for them. Some states are experimenting with starting all woman police stations, notably Tamil Nadu, Karnataka, Madhya Pradesh, Gujarat, Kerala and Uttar Pradesh.[24]

Delhi's Anti-Dowry Cell run by the Police has been upgraded and enlarged to form a full-fledged Sanctioned Unit—The Crime Against Women Cell. Seminars and workshops by concerned organisations are also inviting police personnel as participants or observers. With alert media persons, a burgeoning of interested human rights and other groups, together with enlightened members of the judiciary, a climate is sought to be created which should lend support to positive elements in the police force. This reciprocity is already showing some positive results. There are many miles to travel before long entrenched power systems can be persuaded to change, but the road must be taken and no diversion sought.

HAPPENINGS:

Six hundred women gathered in Delhi from around the country in January 1994. Although brought together for political purposes, the only subjects they spoke of were the ones closest to their hearts. They talked of sky rocketing prices, unequal wages, of the feudal structure in their villages, of daily rapes by the police, of being tortured in custody and being paraded naked in the market place; of baby girls molested by their fathers, of wife beating and fears of another woman being brought into their homes. They spoke of illiteracy being at the base of their lack of confidence and self worth. They turned to each other as to new found sisters, resolving to work together to fight exploitation.[25]

Dalit women were the next to meet at a unique gathering in the capital, finding kindred spirits in each other creating a supportive atmosphere. Although a great deal of work is done at governmental and non-governmental levels, the gap between the educated and the rural and urban poor is still immense.

They called for much greater severity in dealing with crimes against them, as then alone would they get the confidence they desperately need.[26]

In 1995 *Dalit* women were in the news again joining hands with *Devadasis* to combine forces against common oppression : in particular to fight against the dedication of women and girls to serve in temples as 'brides' of the gods.[27] Even as delegates to the Fourth United Nations Conference on Women at Beijing, September 1995 called vociferously for the empowerment of women worldwide, an eight hundred year old tradition of women's enslavement was sought to be revived. Five aspirants, all educated and already employed elsewhere, turned up at the famous temple of Sri Jagan-nath in Puri, Orissa for an 'interview' amid public protest and threats of agitation against this regressive move. Two old *Devadasis*, relics of a vanishing tribe who were expected to help in their induction by adopting them, refused to subject other women to the life of penury and indignity they themselves were still suffering. Interestingly, the applicants were looking for 'part time' work.[28]

With the spread of awarness, women are beginning to gain confidence and make their voices heard. They are upset by the Centre's proposal to limit government health schemes to families that have less than three children, and to restrict maternity benefits to women who have two children or less. Keeping Indian social norms in mind they ask, 'can they really say that we women are the sole decision makers in our families and have the final word as to the number of children we wish to have? The debate is on.

It would be better to increase positive inputs instead of using threats of discontinuing benefits. The literacy campaign in Kanyakumari at the Southernmost tip of India includes health, self learning, small family norms, legal issues and self-employment opportunities. This comprehensive programme aimed at the general well bring of the individual has paid dividends. It has brought the birth rate down to 14.8 per thousand, and the improvement in general health is remarkable.[29]

Video has been successfully used as a development tool in Ahmedabad based SEWA Self Employed Women's Association, for twenty-two thousand women in the informal sector. Women no longer need the lady-do-good approach as a blessing from the gods. They need people who are willing to live in their midst, interact with them with an understanding reciprocity, teach them what they know, and learn from them what they will never understand from books or newspapers. They want to deal with people who will move on to another area only when they are quite satisfied that the women have been sufficiently equipped with the knowledge of how to hold their own as competant citizens who cannot be browbeaten any longer.[30]

The miniscule presence of women in politics can be partly attributed to the increasing criminalisation of politics. With the rampant corruption and the oppressive presence of religious fundamentalism in party politics, women are retreating into the shadows from where they had emerged so triumphantly almost half a century ago. The call for ridding the political system of criminals and of breaking the nexus between criminals and industrialists is gaining urgency. The brutal murder and incineration in a Delhi hotel's open air oven of twenty-nine year old Naina Sahni, a prominent member of a powerful political party on the night of 2 July, 1995 allegedly by her husband Sushil Sharma, a former president of the same party, has brought this nexus into sharp focus. The case is proceeding. Political power is often used to exploit women sexually or to subdue them. Women these days, are sometimes elected for reasons other than their profiency in politics. Often they themselves give into a system of political functioning based on religious fundamentalism. Social action for the wider community cannot be separated from political participation.[31] Women's groups are realising that this is a growing imperative. The reported involvement of leading politicians in major scams and cover-ups led women activists and concerned citizens to insist that all political parties field candidates with a clean image, and commit themselves to ensuring a sizeable representation of women in all legislatures. It is a tribute to their persistence that this was reflected in the manifestos of all major parties in the 1996 elections. The United Front's common minimum programme has pledged reservation of one-third membership in the Lok Sabha and State Assemblies for women. Further, it will consider reserving one-third of all government posts for women, if necessary by amending the Constitution. All laws are also to be reviewed to remove gender discrimination.

Government has announced sizeable social welfare schemes. Others are expected to follow. A subsistence pension for the old and a one time assistance on the death of the family bread winner, a rural group life insurance scheme for poor households with easy premiums, and monetary assistance to mothers below the poverty line during maternity for the first two live births are other schemes officially announced on Independence Day, 1995.[32]

Future development schemes for women's needs at the lowest level are also to form the basis of district level schemes which hold promise of women's participation in decision making processes.[33] It is to be hoped that these schemes will weather political storms.

Meanwhile, women singly or in groups, are working on several quiet revolutions: Madras had never heard of women masons before 1994. They had always been seen as assistants supplying mindless labour while the skilled men did the main job. Now, trained by a voluntary construction group[34] the women are working as competent masons earning thirty rupees for a day's work. Local societal attitudes however do not always allow them to work on construction sites. Anjali's husband is a rickshaw puller who was won around to seeing his wife in a different role, as a full-fledged mason. He now chips in with the household chores. These women some of whom are illiterate but good masons, plan on educating their daughters for a secure future.[35]

In March 1994, N.N. Indira the first woman Inspector of Police in Karnataka presented the Chief Minister a Guard of Honour composed of the staff of the first all woman police station in Karnataka. These police stations are mushrooming all over the state, promising to deal effectively with crimes against women.[36]

Thirty-five year old Hazra Begum who plied her cycle rickshaw in 1992 on the streets of Delhi, found the going rough in a male dominated profession, until her tenacity proved her as good as a man. Her presence and her smile are in the air, even though she is no longer seen plying the roads.[37]

A congenital heart disease did not stop Girija of Kerala from completing her Bachelor's degree in Economics and her Master's degree in Hindi. Compelled to face the reality that a degree does not ensure a job, in January 1987 Girija decided a part time job as a roadside sweeper with two hundred and sixty rupees a month was honest work not to be sneezed at.[38]

Nirmala Devi Pande, a poor illiterate *Brahmin*, wife of a small time *Pujari*[39] is a news vendor since 1972. Ostracised by her family and high caste community for carrying on 'demeaning work', she is loved by her clients and colleagues and enjoys her trade. She has built a small house with her savings, and plans on a permanent news stand for herself.[40]

'I have made up my mind, and I will do it,' declares seventy year old Shefali Chatterjee, as she enters the boys' class in The National Open School Delhi, with a walking stick to ease her arthritic progress. She sits with her grandson in the Sunday class, and plans to study for the class ten examination, oblivious of the occasional snicker. Shefali's education was interrupted by the death of her parents when she was a student in class six. An early marriage, children and grandchildren later, this plucky lady adjusts her bifocals and says brightly, 'I have a tremendous desire for knowledge.'[41]

Women in the Rajasthani village of Sui decided to get together to beat the drought. While humans managed to subsist on dole, the cattle were starving. There was no fodder, so the women decided that 1987 was to be the year of the Women in Sui. Without asking anyone's permission in this most traditional of rural societies, they approached a voluntary organisation[42], hired lorries and went and bought fodder directly from Bikaner, a city they had never seen before. They returned to a storm of male anger and the village headman's displeasure. Despite the latter's machinations, they managed to get an eighty thousand rupee subsidy, and against threats of stoning, wired in a deserted field to grow fodder for their animals. Strangely enough not a stone was thrown. The shamefaced villagers began to pay for the privilege of grazing their cattle in the field. Sui today is a flourishing village with stacks of fodder, a women's co-operative and a provision store run by the women themselves. Their husbands and the village are proud of them.[43]

All is not bliss and sunshine however; although *Panchayati Raj* has given many women confidence, the desire to gather all the sheaves into one barn at the expense of others is a basic malady. Several *panchayat* leaders have been taking advantage of government schemes to feather their own nests, collecting funds for non-existant buildings, payments for persons who are either dead or employed elsewhere, and even money for training youth for self employment has been going into training children for illegal carpet weaving. The children's pay was not received by them even three or four years after the special project was completed. The good news is that the *Mazdoor Kisan Shakti Sanghathan* has been holding public hearings and booking *sarpanches* and others found guilty. Money extorted is being repaid. The battle continues.[44]

For the women of Banda in Uttar Pradesh *Panchayati Raj* is making waves. In the last five years these illiterate women have been trained to work as hand pump mechanics, tractor drivers and masons like their sisters in Madras. The *Mahila Dakiya* is a women's newspaper written and published by neoliterates and half literates that circulates between the villages of the area,[45] airing common grievances and finding ways to sort them out. Graphic illustrations help make a point. The possibility of becoming a *pradhan* of the village through the 33 per cent reservation of Scheduled Caste and Scheduled Tribes for women has electrified them. With the villages dependent on their skill and understanding of mechanics, caste is the first casualty as these women enter every house where there is a job to be done. The Mahila Dakiya was awarded The Media Foundation's Chameli Devi Award in March 1996 for its courageous and enterprising work as an outstanding women's media collective.[46]

There is excitement in the air for Kultikori Village in West Bengal's Midnapore District. All the male members of the *Panchayat* stepped down and elected women candidates for all the seats in the *panchayat*. They are extremely proud of their '*didis*' — sisters. These young women, after a government orientation course, are handling budgets and beginning to show their worth as administrators. Boys and girls are cycling to school and intercaste marriages are frequent.[47] Certainly women *panches* are suppressed by men who cannot abide the thought of giving up their power and prosperity, but by and large the 72nd Constitutional Amendment has created a watershed from where there is no turning back.

In 1980 the government had invited a Delhi based research organisation[48] to a small village in the Bankura District of West Bengal. A *Samiti*[49] with collective ownership was created. 'Help us,' they pleaded. The expert shook his head. The *samiti* members took a calculated risk. Thick forests of *Arjun* and *Asan* trees have replaced the arid land. The tribals have been repaid a hundredfold. Income generating programmes based on the revitalised land: fodder, animal husbandry, silk worm rearing and *tussar* silk spinning and weaving and a host of others are organised and carried out by the twenty *samitis* with over two thousand members. They have formed a federation of their own members to oversee their affairs themselves. They are now moving out into the neigh-bouring areas.[50]

Bihar's face is changing as women like Nirmala from a typically conservative family in a remote village in Muzaffarpur move out from the confines of their homes. Nirmala moved out for the first time after her husband had deserted her. She joined a voluntary organisation and started her own handicraft centre in the village. She is now going to Delhi and Madras for the sale of her products.[51]

Centuries old tradition can change overnight. This was amply demonstrated in the case of Sheila and Dammam, two sisters of the Kanjar community in Sansi, Rajasthan. Kanjar maidens are completely stripped and turmeric is applied to their bodies in full view of an invited audience of women who are plied with drink during the ceremony. The sisters refused to part with their underwear. The shocked elders and *sarpanch* decided to modify the custom only when workers and officials of the Women's Welfare Department and a social institution made an ingenious suggestion that complete stripping might be offensive to God who sees everything. This clinched the matter, and Sheila and Dammam went happily through the ceremony in their undergarments, drinking a bottle each of Thums Up instead of the customary alcohol.[52]

These are not examples of miserable women pleading for pity and help with begging bowls in their hands. These are women who, once equipped with knowledge, are able to come together to overturn centuries old waggon loads of dehumanisation and exploitation overnight. They are not thinking of themselves alone. They know they are integral parts of their community, so they address themselves to the larger need.

As city dwellers battle their way through the overcrowded lanes of their lives, the household scene is changing. Most families now have both parents working full time. The load falls heavily on the woman who is expected to be a combination of Supermom and *Sati Savitri* who must sacrifice everything in the service of her husband and his relatives. After performing all these tasks, she changes hats in a flash and becomes the modern decision making executive, secretary, glamorous receptionist, telephone operator, scientist, teacher or nurse. Advertisements in the media that have so far underlined old stereotypes of women as helpless sex objects or elegant housewives are gradually undergoing a change. While mother is still the magician at the washing machine, papa and sons are at last realising they also have a hand in household responsibilities. Sometimes papa cooks the food on the latest model of stove, while mama returning from office, smiles happily to see father and son bending over scrumptious food. Even though traditional advertisements still boost the perfect washing soap that saves the wife from a scolding and salvages the family honour from impending ruin, the new papa ads are winning out. It is dad who carries his baby lovingly in a soap advertisement and models the latest suitings while carefully seeing to the baby's needs. What's more, he is the adopted daughter's hero. House husbands were featured in a popular magazine, organising the home, enjoying cooking, baby sitting and all the chores traditionally asigned to wives. Incidentally, the perfect husband is also the perfect boss in his office.[53]

Just when it seems as if all is going well with the ad world, a newspaper flicks open on a sketch of a traditionally demure bride with her head modestly covered. 'Before she becomes a bride,' it says, 'prepare her to be a wife.'[54] It would be interesting to note the reaction of the advertising agency to the unthinkable suggestion of asking parents to prepare their son to be an ideal husband before *he* becomes a bridegroom! Turn over another page and you come across a couple in a close embrace, the woman, for a change, heavily covered in a floppy shirt. This, believe it or not, is an advertisement for casual wear in a pose that is expected to win over satellite TV viewers.[55]

Television communication is in double-speak where women are concerned. The 'golden oldies while projecting the self-abnegating wife and mother also portray her antithesis, a glitzy incarnation who leaves no holds barred in torrid, vulgarly suggestive mindless song and dance sequences. Savage violence and terror are strongly re-inforcing the image of the new hero as a macho brute, burying his sensitive, principled predecessor in the rubbish heap. His beloved is now allowed to be as brutal as she wants in retaliation. Serials project passion and promiscuity freely in family relationships, with a more than generous sprinkling of money power and political clout, in a frantic effort to win audiences away from satellite TV. Saner elements were glad to hear of the inclusion of women in the membership to The Censor Board for Film Certification and its advisory committees, but what difference the fifty per cent membership has made still remains to be seen.[56] Meanwhile it's blood, guts and sex all the way...

Parallel cinema and the theatre are occasionally seen to be trying to project an independent thinking woman often in conflict with social norms. By and large, women although often brought up traditionally, seem to respond to change much more favourably than men, perhaps because they have little to lose and a whole new world to explore.

The rising graph of crimes against women is raising the conscience of thinking men around the globe. They are gradually beginning to realise at long last how vulnerable a woman's mind and body are, and how much she has been exploited by family and society.

A young man in a BBC television programme[57] said, 'There should be a rethinking by men of their own sexuality. They must realise that dehumanising women is not part of their rights.' In 1983, Professor Vikram Nanda and Indu Prakash Singh had tried to do just that in Delhi. They formed a small group of five friends who worked separately as well as in conjunction with women's organisations on following up reported cases of violence against women under the name of 'Men Against Violence on Women.'

In 1993 in the heart of Bombay, a group of young men got together to work against domestic abuse, the hidden crime no one dares to speak about. Starting with the slogan 'Women are not for battering', these youths have formed a support group for those who suffer from home battering and other crimes committed behind closed doors. Harish Sadani's Men Against Violence and Abuse—MAVA produces street plays that establish instant identification among receptive crowds. They work together with like-minded groups to try and eradicate this evil.[58]

As more and more groups form, trying to make the world a saner place, networking is becoming more and more important. The electronic and print media have an important role to play in picking up the scent of some of these quiet, unobtrusive workers. They need to be put in touch with each other, with the country and the world.

On 4 May, 1978 the lovely graduate Shashi Bala[59] was married. There was no talk of dowry, although a number of gifts were given to the groom's family. After the marriage a demand was made for a scooter which the bride's parents promised they would give as soon as they were in a position to do so. By 15 March, 1979 things came to a head and on the 17th of March, six months pregnant Shashi Bala was burnt to death in her marital home. The death of Shashi Bala is one of the earliest bride burning cases that shook the conscience of the country. Seventeen years later, the case still drags on. 'Kill your daughters when they are born,' cried her distracted mother Satyarani Chaddha beating her breast, 'for when they grow up, they will not be allowed to live with dignity'!

Today, after years of anguished running from the lowest to the highest in the land, Satyarani is a woman with a mission. Involved in the founding of an organisation that opens its arms to hopeless women and supports them through tortuous legal processes, she finds comfort in sheltering them in loving and caring surroundings.[60] 'Aunty's' stentorian voice adds strength to any demonstration against violence or injustice perpetrated on women in the capital or elsewhere, and puts the fear of God into those who would exploit a trusting young bride and her anxious parents.

A continuing and persistent struggle against torment at home and at work has brought beautiful Chandra back to the soil. A fighter *par excellence*, she is an indomitable woman for whom every set back is a challenge. Establishing a farming community of twentyeight villages in a little known area of Andhra Pradesh,[61] Chandra's infectious exuberance and personal commitment are instilling confidence and a sense of purpose in scores of women. They receive training in health, literacy, local self-governance, management of finance and social forestry in a secure and understanding ambience. Chandra's never-say-die attitude inspires her large rural family with an awareness of themselves as responsible, caring human beings.

One small step, say the carpers, placing on record irrefutable evidence of ever more terrifying wrongs and repressions. A moment's silence and an ear to the ground will bring the throb of unpublicised work being quietly done by hundreds of invisible individuals and groups scattered around the country. The many positive anonymous happenings that are too noiseless to make sensational headlines.

NOTES AND REFERENCES

1. A pioneering theatre group working with street theatre since 1978.
2. Women's Political Watch, February 1995, New Delhi.
3. Vimochana: 'A share of Infamy by Shakuntala Narasimhan, The Hindustan Times, 28 November, 1993.
4. The Hindustan Times, 11 and 12 October 1994.
5. Materialsm & Greed spurring Dowry Deaths, Molly Moore, International Herald Tribune, 21 March, 1995.
6. Sisters Find Their Match After Making Greedy Grooms March, Sonal Manchanda, The Indian Express, 19 June, 1996.
7. And the Bride Put Her Foot Down, The Indian Express, 15 July, 1995.
8. Victims of Attitude, Salim Jiva, Vancouver, India Today, 28 February, 1994.
9. Supreme Court order: Civil appeal 1995 . Civil Appellate Jurisdiction, 29 August, 1995 arising out of SLP(C) No. 15815 of 1988) J.S. Verma, N.P. Singh, Venkataswami jj.
10. Ameena Was Just Another Story, O.M. Farooq, The Pioneer, 28 November, 1993.
11. The Hindustan Times, 9 August, 1983.
12. Dowry Victim Donates Eyes to Bank. The Times of India, 29 July, 1984.
13. Punjab Istri Sangh and The Young Women's Christian Association.
14. Neighbour Power, Jamila Verghese, The Indian Express, 2 June, 1988.
15. Why Tiptur Rose up in Anger, Nupur Basu, The Indian Express, 13 December, 1987.
16. The Sunday Observer, 21-27 June, 1992. This case is being followed up by The National Federation of Indian Women.
17. See Chapter 15.
18. See Lectures on Criminal Procedure, R.V. Kelkar, Eastern Book Company, 1980, p. 152, Expeditious trial [S. 309 (1)].
19. The Long Wait for Justice, The Hindustan Times, 16 June, 1993.
20. Dowry Trial Will Proceed After 7 Years, The Times of India, 16 May, 1995.
21. Oppressed.
22. Development, a Creditable Scheme to Empower Women, Usha Rai, The Indian Express, 5 May, 1995.

23.

Police Women in India				
Police Strength		*1992*	*1993*	*1994*
Civil Police (Actuals)	Total men and women: (including District armed Police)	919670	937339	950382
Civil Police (Actuals)	Total Women: (including District Armed Police)	13845	14443	14954
Armed Police (Actuals)	Total men and women:	262245	260599	279916
Armed Police (Actuals)	Total women:	647	655	655
Crime in India 1992, 1993 and 1994 publications: Police Strength, National Crime Records Bureau, Ministry of Home Affairs, New Delhi.				

24. Police Women Battle Prejudice in the Forces, Sujata Gotaskar, The Pioneer, 26 January, 1994.
25. Indian Women's Common Denominator of Oppression, Soma Wadhwa, The Pioneer, 16 January, 1994.
26. Dalit women join Hands to Fight Oppression: The Times of India, 8 March, 1994.
27. Devadasis Yearn for Freedom, United News of India, The Hindustan Times, 21 August, 1995.
    Five Turn up for Devadasi 'Interview', Press Trust of India, The Indian Express, 12 September, 1995.
28. Devadasis Reject Successors, The Times of India News Service, 13 September, 1995. Women's groups continue to protest against this continuing degradation of women and girls.
29. Literacy Campaign has Kanyakumari Enthralled, Sabina Inderjeet from Kanyakumari, The Times of India, 10 November, 1994.
30. Alternative Media Role Discussed, The Times of India, 10 February, 1994.
31. Towards Beijing, A Perspective from the Indian Women's Movement, prepared by seven organisations.
    All India Democratic Women's Assciation,
    All India Women's Conference,
    Centre for Women's Development Studies,
    Joint Women's Programme,
    Mahila Dakshata Samiti,
    National Federation of Indian Women,
    The Young Women's Christian Association of India.

32. Rao Schemes to Woo Poor, Backwards, Express News Service, The Indian Express, 30 July, 1995.
33. Indira Mahila Yojana launched, The Hindustan Times, 21 August, 1995.
34. The Madras Municipal Corporation, trained by Nirman Mazdoor Panchayat Sangam.
35. Another Male Bastion Falls, Aruna Srinivasan, The Hindustan Times, 13 August, 1994.
36. The Times of India, 20 March, 1994.
37. Queen of the Streets, Dibang, The Illustrated Weekly of India, Against All Odds, 4-10 January, 1987.
38. *Ibid.* Serene Dignity, Venu Menon.
39. A priest.
40. Defiantly Delivering the Daily News, Abdul Qadir, The Times of India, 8 February, 1994.
41. Thirsting for '*Gyan*', Grandma Goes to School, Parul Chandra, The Times of India, 23 June, 1995.
42. *Urmul.*
43. Fodder for Thought, Sonora Jha Nambiar, The Times of India, 6 March, 1994.
44. *Panchayat* Leaders Cashing in on Government Schemes, V. Radhika, The Pioneer, April 6, 1995.
45. Made possible by the government sponsored Mahila Samakhya programme. *Nirantar*, a Delhi based non-governmental organisation provides the needed technical inputs. Local village editions are connecting and transforming lives in these rural areas.
46. Mahila Dakiya Makes News, Rita Manchanda, The Pioneer, 24 April, 1995.
47. Grassroot Women, Udayan Namboodiri from Kultikori Village and others, The Indian Express, 5 March, 1995.
48. Centre for Women's Development Studies.
49. Organisation.
50. The Bankura Story: Rural Women Organise For Change: text by Nalini Singh, produced by The International Labour Office, New Delhi: Technical Co-operation Report, 1988.
51. Bihar Women Stepping out of the Shadows, Deepak Mishra, The Pioneer, 9 June, 1993.
52. Gutsy Tribal Girls Roll Back Naked Custom, Sumita Paul, The Times of India, 3 September, 1995.
53. Daring to Care, The Week, 6 February, 1994: Jayashree Ramamohan, with Sejal Shah, Maria Abraham and A. Majumdar.
54. The Foundation for Marriage Agency, Delhi: The Times of India, 7 November, 1994.
55. The Indian Express, 6 August, 1995.

56. The Pioneer, 17 December, 1994.
57. Everyman: 26 March, 1995.
58. Men take up Challenge for Abused Women: Namita Devidayal, The Times of India, 1 August, 1993; also India Plus TV's The First Edition: Despatch, aired on 31 May, 1995.
59. Also known as Kanchan Rani. This case, originally with Mahila Dakshata, is still being followed up: WARLAW, *Shakti Shalini.*
60. *Shakti Shalini.*
61. *Stree Sangshema* Trust in Penukonda and Kotacheruvu Mandals.

Appendix

The Dowry Prohibition Act, 1961

(MAY 20, 1961)

(1) This Act may be called the Dowry Prohibition Act, 1961.

(2) It extends to the whole of India except the State of Jammu and Kashmir.

(3) It shall come into force on such date as the Central Government may, by notification in the Official Gazette, appoint.

2. *Definition of "dowry"*: In this Act, "dowry" means any property or valuable security given or agreed to be given either directly or indirectly—

(a) by one party to a marriage to the other party to the marriage; or

(b) by the parents of either party to a marriage or by any other person to either party to the marriage or to any other person;

at or before or after the marriage as consideration for the marriage of the said parties, but does not include dower or *mahr* in the case of persons to whom the Muslim Personal Law (*Shariat*) applies.

Explanation I. —For the removal of doubts, it is hereby declared that any presents made at the time of a marriage to either party to the marriage in the form of cash, ornaments, clothes or other articles, shall not be deemed to be dowry within the meaning of this section, unless they are made as consideration for the marriage of the said parties.

Explanation II. —45 of 1860. The expression "valuable security" has the same meaning as in section 30 of the Indian Penal Code.

3. *Penalty for giving or taking dowry*: If any person, after the commencement of this Act, gives or takes or abets the giving or taking of dowry, he shall be punishable with imprisonment which may extend to six months, or with fine which may extend to five thousand rupees, or with both.

4. *Penalty for demanding dowry*: If any person, after the commencement of this Act, demands, directly or indirectly, from the parents or guardian of a bride or bridegroom, as the case be, any dowry, he shall be punishable with imprisonment which may extend to six months, or with fine which may extend to five thousand rupees, or with both:

Provided that no court shall take cognizance of any offence under this section except with previous sanction of the State Government or of such officer as the State Government may, by general or special order, specify in this behalf.

5. *Agreement for giving or taking dowry to be void*: Any agreement for the giving or taking of dowry shall be void.

6. *Dowry to be for the benefit of the wife or her heirs*:

(1) Where any dowry is received by any person other than the woman in connection with whose marriage it is given, that person shall transfer it to the woman—

(a) if the dowry was received before marriage, within one year after the date of marriage; or

(b) if the dowry was received at the time of or after the marriage, within one year after the date of its receipt; or

(c) if the dowry was received when the woman was a minor, within one year after she has attained the age of eighteen years; and pending such transfer, shall hold it in trust for the benefit of the woman.

(2) If any person fails to transfer any property as required by sub-section (1) and within the time limited therefore, he shall be punishable with imprisonment which may extend to six months, or with fine which may extend to five thousand rupees, or with both; but such punishment shall not absolve the person from his obligation to transfter the property as required by sub-section (1).

(3) Where the woman entitled to any property under sub-section (1) dies before receiving it, the heirs of the woman shall be entitled to claim it from the person holding it for the time being.

(4) Nothing contained in this section shall affect the provisions of section 3 or section 4.

7. *5 of 1898. Cognizance of Offences*. Notwithstanding anything contained in the Code of Criminal Procedure, 1898,—

(a) no court inferior to that of a presidency magistrate or a magistrate of the first class shall try any offence under this Act;

(b) no court shall take cognizance of any such offence except on a complaint made within one year from the date of the offence;

(c) it shall be lawful for a presidency magistrate or a magistrate of the first class to pass any sentence authorised by this Act on any person convicted of an offence under this Act.

8. *Offences to be non-cognizable, bailable and non-compoundable*: Every offence under this Act shall be non-cognizable, bailable and non-compoundable.

9. *Power to make rules*:

1. The Central Government may, by notification in the Official Gazette, make rules for carrying out the purposes of this Act.

2. Every rule made under this section shall be laid as soon as may be after it is made before each House of Parliament while it is in session for a total period of thirty days which may be comprised in one session or in two successive sessions, and if before the expiry of the session in which it is so laid or the session immediately following, both Houses agree in making any modification in the rule or both Houses agree that the rule should not be made, the rule shall thereafter have effect only in such modified form or be of no effect, as the case may be, so however that any such modification or annulment shall be without prejudice to the validity of anything previously done under that rule.

10. *Andhra Pradesh Act 1 of 1958. Bihar Act 25 of 1950*: Repeals: The Andhra Pradesh Dowry Prohibition Act, 1958, and the Bihar Dowry Restraint Act, 1950, are hereby repealed.

Various States have enacted Amendments to this Act, widening the definition of dowry, stipulating a higher level for judicial hearings and enhanced penalties for offences. These Amendments were passed by West Bengal 1975, Bihar 1976, Punjab 1976, Haryana 1976 and Himachal Pradesh 1976 and 1978.

In the case of Punjab, Haryana, Orissa and West Bengal, a clause not included in the Central Act : Penalties for Depriving Any Party of the Rights and Privileges of Marriage, has been introduced.

Himachal Pradesh has made provision for an under-aged or mentally deficient person, or an aggrieved wife to be represented by another person with the leave of the court, to make a complaint on their behalf.

Previous to the enactment of Central dowry legislation, a few regional laws had been passed and some attempts made by various communities to control the giving and taking of dowry. Some of these have been overtaken by events. Among them were: The Sindhi Lethi Deti Act 1939, The Bihar Dowry Restraint Act 1950, The Andhra Pradesh Dowry Prohibition Act 1958 and The Jammu and Kashmir Dowry Restraint Act 1960.

The first and second Amendments to The Dowry Prohibition Act 1961, passed in 1984 and 1985 respectively, have been discussed in chapter 15, Marry Her Off!

The Criminal Law (Amendment) Act, 1983 (condensed)
(No. 43 of 1983) December 25, 1983

Insertion of new Section in the Indian Penal Code, 1860.

New Section 228A : *prohibits disclosure of the identity of victims of sexual offences*, including rape under Section 376 and Sections 376 A to D of the IPC, without the consent of the victim, or if authorised in writing by the authorities or next of kin if the victim be a minor or of unsound mind. Violation is punishable with up to two years imprisonment and fine.

Replacement of Sections 375 and 376 IPC with new Sections defining sexual offences and punishment:

Section 375. Rape: Rape entails sexual intercourse with a woman, with penetration, if against her will, without her consent or forced consent, consent under mistaken belief that the partner is her lawful husband; if consent is obtained from a woman of unsound mind, or under the influence of drugs or intoxicants administered to her; if she is under 16 years of age, or if a wife be under 15 years of age. Sexual intercourse with a wife over 15 years of age is not deemed rape.

Section 376. Punishment for rape: shall be for not less than 7 years, and shall extend to a life term or to 10 years with a fine. In case of the rape of a wife not under 12 years of age, the punishment shall extend up to 2 years or a fine, or both.

In all cases, imprisonment shall be of either description (i.e. simple or rigorous). *The Court may, however, for sufficient reasons to be recorded, impose a punishment of less than 7 years' imprisonment.*

In case of rape by a police or prison officer, a public servant or a member of the management or staff of a hospital, a supertintendent or manager of a jail or remand home, or a women's or children's institution, or anyone who holds authourity within a police station, prison or hospital: the rape of a pregnant woman or of a girl under 12 years of age, shall be punished with a term not less than 10 years R.I. or extending up to life imprisonment and a fine.

Gang rape: Rape by more than one person is gang rape, in which each offender shall be held liable.

Section 367A to C : Sexual intercourse with a separated wife, without her consent shall be rape, and shall be punished with imprisonment up to 2 years with a fine.

Section 376B : A public servant taking advantage of his official position : intercourse with a woman in his custody, inducement or seduction *even if not amounting to rape*, shall be punishable with imprisonment up to 5 years with a fine. The same applies to *Section 376 C a superintendent of a jail, remand home, or other place of custody* established by law, or of a women's or children's home. *Section 376 D: The same applies to any member of the management or staff in a hospital.*

Amendment of Section 327 (Code of Criminal Procedure 1974) This Amendment provides that *the above-mentioned sexual offences* under the Indian Penal Code shall be tried *in camera*. The Court may, however grant limited access to a particular person but here too, shall *not permit publication of the proceedings*, except with its further permission.

The First Schedule to the Code of Criminal Procedure is amended to make the above-mentioned offences cognisable and bailable except *in case of rape where the offence is non-bailable. Action in rape related cases shall be heard by sessions courts*

New Section II4 A in the Indian Evidence Act inserted: In cases of rape under Section 376 IPC, *the presumption of rape and of lack of consent shall favour the woman.*

The Criminal Law (Second Amendment) Act, 1983
December 25, 1983

This Amendment adds a new chapter to the Indian Penal Code, 1860:

Chapter XX A: Of Cruelty by Husband or Relatives of Husband: Section 498-A:

The husband, or any relative of his who subjects a woman to cruelty likely to drive her to commit suicide, cause grave injury, or endanger life, limb or health (physical or mental), or harass her in order to coerce her or her relatives to accede to any demand for any property or valuable security, or for their failing to comply with these demands, shall be punished with up to 3 years imprison-ment and shall be liable to a fine.

Amendment of Section 174 in The Code of Criminal Procedure:

In case of *suicide or death of a woman within 7 years of her marriage* in circumstances that raise reasonable suspicion; or if in such an event, the relatives of the woman request a police officer, or if he considers it expedient to do so, he shall immediately give intimation to the nearest executive magistrate empowered to hold an inquest, and shall proceed to the site of the crime, and *hold an investigation in the presence of two or more respected persons.*

Amendment of Section 176 in The Code of Criminal Procedure:

This Section has been consequentially amended in conformity with the Amendment of Section 174.

Insertion of new Section 198-A in The Code of Criminal Procedure:

This provides that no Court shall take cognisance of an offence under Section 198-A except on a police complaint, or complaint by the aggrieved person, or an immediate relative, or with the leave of the Court, by certain other relatives by blood, marriage or adoption.

Amendment of the First Schedule: in The Code of Criminal Procedure:

The punishment for cruelty to a woman shall be imprisonment for 3 years and fine. The offence shall be cognisable if reported to an officer in charge of a police station by the aggrieved woman, her relatives by blood, marriage or adoption or by notified public servants, in case she has no relatives. The offence shall be non-bailable and triable by a first class Magistrate.

Amendment of the Indian Evidence Act, 1872, the following insertion shall be made after Section 113:

Section 113-A: Presumption as to abetment of suicide by a married woman:

This provides that in Section 498-A cases (i.e. suicide within 7 years of marriage on grounds of cruelty), *the Court may presume abetment* of suicide by the husband or by any of his relatives.

Some Central Acts Affecting Women

Indian Penal Code	...	1860
Converts' Marriage Dissolution Act	...	1866
Divorce Act	...	1869
Christian Marriage Act	...	1872
Evidence Act	...	1872
Married Women's Property Act	...	1874
Guardians and Wards Act	...	1890
Marriage Validation Act	...	1892
Births, Deaths and Marriages Registration Act	...	1886
Code of Civil Procedure	...	1908
Maintenance Orders Enforcement Act	...	1921
Legal Practitioners (women) Act	...	1923
Child Marriage Restraint Act	...	1929
Hindu Inheritance (Removal of Disabilities) Act	...	1928
Parsi Marriage Age and Divorce Act	...	1936 (amended 1939)
Arya Marriage Validation Act	...	1937
Dissolution of Muslim Marriages Act	...	1939
Matrimonial Causes (War Marriages) Act	...	1948
Part B States Marriages Validation Act	...	1952
Special Marriage Act	...	1954
Hindu Marriage Act	...	1955
Hindu Minority and Guardianship Act	...	1956
Hindu Succession Act	...	1955
Women's and Children's Institutions Licensing Act	...	1955
Young Persons' Harmful Publications Act	...	1956
Supression of Immoral Traffic in Women Act		1956
Married Women's Property (Extension) Act		1959
Orphanages and Other Charitable Homes (Supervision and Control) Act	...	1960
Hindu Marriage (Validation of Proceedings) Act	...	1960

Dowry Prohibition Act	...	1961
(printed in text with amendments)		
Maternity Benefit Act	...	1961
Hindu Adoptions and Maintenance Act	...	1956
Beedi and Cigaratte workers (Regulation of Employment) Act	...	1966
Registration of Births and Deaths Act	...	1969
Foreign Marriage Act	...	1969
Medical Termination of Pregnancy Act	...	1971
Code of Criminal Procedure, 1973	...	1974
Equal Remuneration Act	...	1976
Regulation of Employment Act	...	1981
Plantation Labour (Amendment) Act	...	1981
(The employer shall provide and maintain suitable rooms for children of women workers)		
Cine-workers and Cinema Theatre Workers (Regulation of Employment) Act	...	1981
Criminal Law (Amendment) Act (on rape)	...	1983

(New sections: 228A, 376A, B, C, D, also amendments in Penal Code 357 and 376. Section 327 of The Criminal Procedure Code amended to provide in camera inquiry.)

New Section II4A added to The Indian Evidence Act:
(Presumption of absence of consent.)
Criminal Law (Second Amendent) Act 1983
(Necessitated by increase in dowry deaths)
New Section 498 A added in The Indian Penal Code, and 198 A added in The Code of Criminal Procedure. Sections 174 and 176 dealing with cruelty amended.

Hindu Widows' Remarriage (Repeal) Act	...	1983.
Family Courts Act	...	1984
Dowry Prohibition (Amendment) Act	...	1984
Dowry Prohibition (Amendment) Act	...	1986
Muslim Women (Protection of Rights on Divorce) Act	...	1986
Suppression of Immoral Traffic in Women and Girls (Amendment) Act	...	1986

(Name changed to : The Immoral Traffic (Prevention) Act 1956)
Indecent representation of Women (Prohibition) Act 1986
(Prohibits indecent representation of women in the media.)
Juvenile Justice Act ... 1986
Child Labour Act ... 1986
Mental Health Act ... 1987
Equal Remuneration (Amendment) Act ... 1987
(to provide gender justice.)
Commission of Sati (Prevention) Act ... 1987
(Necessitated by Roop Kanwar's sati in Deorala, Rajasthan)
Maternity Benefit (Amendment) Act ... 1988
(Shops and establishments employing 10 or more workers to be covered by Section 2. Section 5 to be extended to cover leave etc...)
Parsi Marriage and Divorce Act ... 1988
(Brought in line with The Hindu Marriage Act, 1955)

Scheduled Castes and Scheduled Tribes
(Prevention of Atrocities) Act ... 1989
Constitution (Sixty First) Amendment Act ... 1989
(to reduce the voting age from 21 to 18 years.)
National Commission for Women Act ... 1990
(To achieve gender equality in all spheres of life and equal participation in the development of the nation.)
Indian Succession (Amendment) Act ... 1991
(To erase the discrimination between Parsi sons and daughters in male intestate property.)
Family Courts (Amendment) Act ... 1991
(Provides for 'revision' in place of 'appeal' in Section 125 of The Criminal Procedure Code.)
Constitution (73rd Amendment) Act ... 1992
(*Panchayats.*)
Constitution (74th Amendment) Act ... 1992
(Municipalities.)
Prenatal Diagnostic Techniques (Regulation and Prevention of Misuse) Act ... 1994
Maternity Benefit (Amendment) Act ... 1996

Index